WITHDRAWN

EAST MEETS WEST

東西交流

耶穌會士在中國

西紀 一五六二年——一七七三年

EAST MEETS WEST

The Jesuits in China, 1582–1773

EDITED BY

Charles E. Ronan, S.J.

AND

Bonnie B. C. Oh

A Campion Book

LOYOLA UNIVERSITY PRESS

CHICAGO

©1988 Loyola University Press
All rights reserved
Printed in the United States of America

Loyola University Press
3441 North Ashland Avenue
Chicago, Illinois 60657

Library of Congress Cataloging in Publication Data

East meets West.

    Papers read at a symposium sponsored by Loyola Univer-
sity, Chicago, October 1982.
    Includes bibliographies and index.
    1. Jesuits—Missions—China—Congresses.   2. China—
Church history—Congresses. I. Ronan, Charles E. II. Oh, Bon-
nie B. C. III. Loyola University of Chicago.
BV3417.E27   1988   266'.251   87–2704
ISBN 0–8294–0572–0

*To the Jesuit missionaries of China,
especially the missionary scholars
Joseph Dehergne and the late Francis A. Rouleau*

SHENSI

SHANSI

PEICHIHLI

• Peking

• Tientsin   Gulf of Chihli

Tsinan

SHANTUNG

YELLOW
SEA

• Sian-fu

HONAN

NANCHIHLI

Yangtze River

Yangtze River

• Nanking

Soochow • Shanghai

Sung-king

Hangchow
Ningpo

• Lan-ch'i

Ching-te chen

CHEKIANG

KIANGSI

• Nanchang

• Chiench'ang

• Nanfeng

FUKIEN

• Foochow
• Fu-ch'ing

EAST CHINA SEA

Taiwan island

KUANGSI

• Shao-chou

KUANGTUNG

Chao-ch'ing • Canton

• Macao

Shang-ch'uan island

SOUTH CHINA SEA

0   50 100   200   300

MILES

FOW

Contents

Illustrations

The Jesuits' China, *map*, vi

Acknowledgments

WRITING THESE ACKNOWLEDGMENTS has been a pleasant, fulfilling task for the editors, for it gives us the opportunity to express our gratitude in a permanent form not only to those whose generous benefactions made the China Jesuit Symposium (Loyola University of Chicago, 7–9 October 1982) the success that it was but also to those whose constant support has made possible the publication of the papers delivered at the symposium.

Topping the list of benefactors is the Fred B. Snite Foundation of Chicago, Illinois; we owe special thanks to its directors, Mr. and Mrs. Terrence J. Dillon. The foundation's funding of the symposium played a major role in its happy outcome, and we are deeply grateful. We also wish to extend our heartfelt thanks for financial assistance to the administrators of the Loyola University Mellon Fund, Alice Hayes, Thomas Bennett, and Lawrence Biondi, S.J.; to the Chicago Province of the Society of Jesus and its former provincial, Father J. Leo Klein; to the Jesuit Community of Loyola University and its former rector, Father Gerald Grosh; and, finally, to Robert Monks, former director of Loyola's School of Continuing Education. To all of them we are heavily indebted for their unflagging interest and support.

Our gratitude goes also to the members of the China-Jesuit Symposium Committee who gave so freely of their time and advice; to Mary Lawton, chairperson of Loyola's Fine Arts Department; to Hanns Gross and Robert Bireley, S.J., both members of Loyola's History Department. We are also indebted to John Murphy, S.J. of Loyola's Classical Languages Department for his assistance with various problems of Latin translation; to Donald Rowe, S.J., curator of Loyola's Martin D'Arcy Gallery of Art, for use of the gallery for receptions at the time of the symposium; to three Jesuit colleagues, the late Frederick Manion of the Jesuit Historical Institute in Rome, Peter Bernardi, student of theology, and Michael Woods, Campion Hall, Oxford, England, and to Sinologist Antonio Sisto Rosso, O.F.M. of Rome, for their patient searching out of bibliographical details; finally, to Bennett Bronson, associate curator of Asian Archeology and Ethnology at Chicago's Field Museum of Natural History, for the loan of rubbings of Jesuit monuments in China which were on display in Loyola's Cudahy Library at the time of the symposium, and to Michael Tang, S.J. for his impressive art work at the time of the symposium: his portrait of Matteo Ricci in water colors and his attractive symposium program.

We would also like to acknowledge with gratitude the sympathetic interest of our colleagues in the History Department, especially Dr. Walter Gray, former department chairperson; and the enthusiastic support of Mr. Alvo Albini, the former director of Loyola's Department of Public Relations, who brought the symposium to public attention through newspapers, radio, and television. Our gratitude also to Annette Nigro, Sylvia Rdzak, and Ruth Kirsinas, departmental secretaries, for their generous cooperation; to Robert Rehn, former director of Loyola's Media Services, Wayne Kupferer, manager of Loyola's Media Support Systems, and to Wayne Magdziarz, general manager of Loyola's WLUW radio station for their expert technical assistance at the time of the symposium; and, lastly, to the group of student "gophers," whose care and attention to numerous physical details so contributed to the smooth running of the symposium: John Poynton, Joel Mendes, Kari McBride, Charles Kaffka, Daniel Keefe, Paul Chemello, Michael Durkin, Peter Lane, Daniel Maksimovich, William Dahlborn III, Gary Green and his fraternity brothers, and three Jesuit seminarians: Russell Conboy, Timothy Jennings, and Richard Soo.

Special thanks are also extended to those responsible for the excellent Book Exhibit held at Loyola's Cudahy Library at the time of the symposium: to Theodore Foss, associate director of the Institute for Chinese-Western Cultural History at the University of San Francisco; to Yvonne Damien, Roy Fry, and Sister Bonaventure Price, S.S.S.F., all staff members at that time of Cudahy Library; to Brother Michael Grace, S.J., university archivist, Sister Mary Fogarty, B.V.M., formerly of the university's Martin D'Arcy Gallery of Art, Lorna Newman, interlibrary loan librarian, Paul Murphy, S.J., theological student at Weston College, Weston, Massachusetts, and again to Robert Bireley, S.J.

for coordinating the exhibit and for his preliminary "spade work" in preparing the symposium.

Our acknowledgment and thanks also to all those who have had a share in the production of this book: to Kathleen Sim of Loyola's Computer Center, to our research assistants, Frederick Schmidt and John Zemler, to our indexer, Sandi Schroeder, and to our long-suffering typists: Michael Bjornson, Erin McCarthy, Timothy Sarbaugh, Margaret Ryman, Ronald Gregory, Robert Becker, Patricia Robertson, Adeline Finnegan, Sharon Marquez, and Lori Witt. Finally, our gratitude to Frank Williams and Durrett Wagner of The Bookworks Inc. of Chicago, Illinois, and to Lois Fusek for their expert guidance and assistance, and a special word of thanks to Daniel Flaherty, S.J., director of Loyola University Press, to George Lane, S.J., editorial director, and to the staff of the Press for the handsome book they have brought out.

In conclusion, we wish to apologize for our tardiness in publishing, but the vicissitudes of academe, full teaching loads, and other inevitable delays were the principal culprits. Efforts have been made, however, to update the volume by the addition of a supplementary bibliography of select publications, largely post-1982, pertinent to the Jesuits in China and by the inclusion in the endnotes of several post-1982 studies. A number of these publications are the contributions of several participants in the Loyola China Jesuit Symposium: David E. Mungello, Jonathan D. Spence, Bernard Hung-kay Luk, Theodore N. Foss, Edwin Van Kley, Harrie Vanderstappen, John W. Witek, Piero Corradini, Joseph Sebes, Albert Chan, and Joseph Dehergne.

Charles E. Ronan, S.J.
Bonnie B. C. Oh
Co-editors

Abbreviations

NCE	*New Catholic Encyclopedia*
AHSJ	*Archivum Historicum Societatis Iesu*
ARSJ	Archivum Romanum Societatis Iesu
DMB	*Dictionary of Ming Biography*
Jap.-Sin.	Japonica et Sinica section of the Jesuit archives in Rome (Archivum Romanum Societatis Iesu).

Explanatory Notes

Since these essays have been edited not only for Sinologists but also for non-Sinologists and students of Jesuit history, the following items might prove helpful:

bonze
: A bonze is a Mahayana Buddhist monk, especially of China, Japan, and adjacent countries.

chin-shih
: The meaning of this term is "presented scholar." Charles O. Hucker, in his *Dictionary,* defines it as "a degree or status often compared to the academic doctorate in the modern West, conferred on successful candidates in the highest-level regular civil service recruitment examinations, qualifying them for appointment to government office" (p. 167).

chuan
: chapter.

daimyo
: Daimyo, which translates "great name," designates a hereditary lord in Japan, head of a feudal domain.

college
: To facilitate matters, the English term "college" is used to translate *colegio* (Spanish), *colégio* (Portuguese), and *collège* (French), but it is not an accurate translation. In the presuppression Jesuit Order (pre-1773), the use of the term by the Jesuits laboring in the Far East by no means always corresponded to the Jesuit institutions of Europe. The term was also employed to designate a residence with no school attached. In his *Repertoire,* Joseph Dehergne defines *collège* in these terms: "the principal residence to which is attached, at least for financial reasons, several dependent residences" (p. 408).

li
: principle.

li
: a Chinese measure equal to approximately one mile.

romanization	Both the Wade-Giles romanization system and the place-name spellings of the *Postal Atlas of China* have been used throughout the book.
Shang-ti	Owing to a divergence of opinions among authors, two different translations of *Shang-ti* are used: "Lord on High" and "Divinity on High." Dr. Peterson argues that his English translation (Divinity on High) maintains the distinction implied by the two Chinese terms, *Shang-ti* and *T'ien-chu*.
titles of books and articles	For the benefit of non-Sinologists, the following style is used in the text, endnotes, and bibliography:

text: The English translation is given first, followed by the romanized Chinese title in parentheses. If the work is cited again in the text, only the English translation is given.

endnotes: The romanized Chinese title is given first, followed by the English translation in parentheses. If the work is cited again in the notes, only the romanized title, usually shortened, is given.

bibliography: The romanized Chinese title is given first, then the Chinese characters, followed by the English translation in parentheses. Shortened-title references in the bibliography are in English.

translations	Unless otherwise specified in the endnotes, any translation in the text or the notes was made by the author of that chapter.
ts'e	volume.

Introduction

DURING THE YEARS 1982–83, a number of scholarly conferences were held in several countries to commemorate the 400th anniversary of the arrival in China of the Italian Jesuit Matteo Ricci. His arrival and his method of cultural accommodation opened one of the most fascinating chapters in the history of Christian evangelization. Symposia and conferences were sponsored in Italy, France, Taiwan, Hong Kong, the Philippines, Japan, and the United States. Even the government of the People's Republic of China undertook to restore the tombstone of Ricci and refurbish the area around his tomb, an area which also included the tombs of two of his Jesuit colleagues, the German Johann Adam Schall von Bell and the Belgian Ferdinand Verbiest.

This revival of interest in Ricci and the Jesuits in China represents a renewed awareness and recognition that Ricci and the Jesuits of the sixteenth, seventeenth, and eighteenth centuries had done far better than their twentieth-century counterparts in understanding China and fostering amiable relationships between the East and West. The Jesuit method of propagating Christianity through cultural accommodation was the brain child of Francis Xavier, the celebrated Jesuit missionary to the Far East, and was applied to China by Alessandro Valignano, the Jesuit Visitor to the Far East. These Jesuits were the direct inspiration for Ricci, who firmly implemented the method in China and set the pattern of Jesuit work in the country for years to come. The method of cultural accommodation represented, in the words of Wolfgang Reinhard, the German historian, "one of the few serious alternatives to the otherwise brutal ethno-centrism of the European expansion over the earth."[1] Pope John Paul II said that Ricci "succeeded in acquiring, through determined, humble, and respectful commitment such a vast and profound knowledge of the classic Chinese culture as to make him a true 'bridge' between the European and Chinese civilizations."[2]

It is generally agreed that the Jesuits had come at a most propitious time to promote the mutually respectful relationship between East and West for which they are so famous. Both sides were about equally matched in cultural attainment. After many centuries of backwardness, Europe had finally caught up and perhaps even surpassed China by the end of the sixteenth century, especially in scientific discovery and technical advances. But the fruits of the new European advances were not yet widely evident, while the myth of a highly civilized China and fabled riches of the East persisted in the minds of European adventurers.

The reality in the China of the sixteenth century, however, did not quite fit the European image of that empire. By the time Matteo Ricci arrived in Macao in 1582, the two-hundred-year-old Ming dynasty, which had been in decline for some time, had been temporarily rejuvenated owing to the solid reform program of the notable statesman and grand secretary, Chang Chü-cheng. At the time of Chang's death in 1582, the empire, ruled by the nineteen-year-old Wan-li emperor (r. 1573–1620), was prosperous: its granaries full and its economy sound. Unfortunately, however, this situation was not of long duration. Due to serious weaknesses in government and the flagrant misbehavior of the emperor during his remaining forty years on the throne (his forty-eight-year reign was the longest since the second century B.C.), all gains were wasted away. In the absence of strong rulers, the decline of the Ming dynasty began to manifest itself in disruptive ways: protracted factional strife among scholars, a pernicious dominance of eunuchs, and a damaging power struggle between the scholars and eunuchs. The Ming intellectuals were alienated not only from politics but also from Confucianism, that is, from the established orthodoxy of the Neo-Confucian school and of the inherited tradition of earlier times. This alienation occasioned a marked intellectual diversity and curiosity among the Chinese that led them to inquire into other teachings, such as the Christianity brought to China by the Jesuits.

Far away, Europe was experiencing similar unsettling conditions, characterized by growing diversity in religion, in the intellectual atmosphere, and in political entities. The Protestant Reformation of the early sixteenth century had put an end to the Catholic Church's dominance in spiritual leadership, just as Renaissance humanism had put an end to its position as the foundation of knowledge and wisdom. The rise of modern states and the incessant disputes among them played their part in the disintegration of the medieval unity of Christendom. Since the beginning of the sixteenth century, Europe had been engulfed in constant warfare which culminated in the Thirty Years' War. In this atmosphere, the Society of Jesus was canonically established in 1540, and gifted individuals joined the Order to defend and spread the Catholic faith throughout the rest of the world, according to the mind of the founder, Ignatius Loyola. Coming from this unsettled and yet creatively diverse atmosphere, the Jesuit missionaries were more receptive and more willing to accommodate to different ideas and cultures. The model among them in the matter of cultural accommodation was Matteo Ricci.

Ricci was born 6 October 1552 in Macerata, Italy, a town within the papal states and close to the Adriatic Sea. Like many places that remained loyal to the Church, Macerata was swept by the fervor of the Catholic Counter Reformation, promoted especially by the members of the newly established Society of Jesus. It is interesting to note that Ricci was born two months before the death of Francis Xavier on the island of Shang-ch'uan off the southern coast of China. The first and greatest Jesuit missionary to the Far East, Xavier had left Japan after approximately two years of successful work, convinced that China held the key to the conversion of the whole of Asia. Xavier's dream was passed on to many who came after him.

Ricci entered mainland China in 1583. From 1552 to 1583, twenty-five Jesuits had gone to China but were permitted to stay only a short period of time. In addition to the Jesuits, there were twenty-two Franciscans, one Dominican, and one Augustinian whose fate was the same. During the 1570s, when Ricci entered the Society of Jesus as a novice, volunteered for the Eastern mission, and was sent to Portugal for eventual departure to Asia, Alessandro Valignano became the head of the Eastern mission. In 1577, he came to Macao as the Jesuit Visitor and initiated a new policy of evangelization, the policy of cultural accommodation.

This new policy, which Ricci executed so ably, took into

consideration the high level of civilization in the Asian countries, recognized the futility of trying to make Westerners out
of Asians, and demonstrated a willingness to accommodate
to the native culture. By the time young Ricci completed his
theological studies in Goa and arrived in 1580 at Cochin on
the Malabar Coast, where he was ordained, the Jesuits had
built a Chinese parish at Macao. Valignano then sent for Ricci
and Michele Ruggieri, both of whom had a reputation for
religious piety, zealous energy, and talent in language. Ruggieri followed Portuguese merchants to Canton on several
occasions, but Ricci, at Valignano's orders, continued to concentrate on studying the Chinese language. Ricci arrived at
Macao in 1582 but did not set foot on mainland China until
the summer of 1583, although many curios, including his
watch, preceded him to Canton and aroused considerable
curiosity about the Jesuits. Unexpectedly, Ricci and Ruggieri
were granted permission to come to the seat of the prefecture
in Chao-ch'ing, and on 10 September 1583, they went well
stocked with European novelties donated by a Portuguese
merchant. Little did Ricci realize that this was to be the first
leg of his long journey to Peking and that he was never to
leave China again.

For the first several years, Ricci and his fellow Jesuits
preached to the common people, much like the Buddhist
monks. They dressed like them, shaved their heads, and cut
off their beards. At the same time, they attracted the attention
of the learned sector of the population with maps, clocks,
prisms, and other items from Europe as well as by exhibiting
their knowledge of the Chinese Classics. By 1597, when Ricci
became head of the China mission, he had established a reputation among Chinese intellectuals as a scholar of considerable depth. Also by this time he and his Jesuit colleagues, advised by one of the earliest Chinese converts, had changed
their attire and taken on the dress and appearance of Confucian scholars and begun their work primarily among the
literati.

Recognizing that there was a theistic tradition in ancient Confucianism, Ricci used existing Chinese terms, *t'ien* (heaven)
and *Shang-ti* (Lord on High), to introduce the God of Christianity. The word he eventually adopted for God was *T'ien-chu*

(Lord of Heaven); this term, finally agreed upon after long, protracted dispute, has remained the word for God in China and the rest of East Asia. By 1591, Ricci's language skill and knowledge of the Classics were sufficient to translate the Confucian *Four Books (Ssu-shu)* into Latin with the assistance of Chinese scholars. Once the literati became the main target of Jesuit conversion, the *Four Books* were chosen for translation and remained the object of the continuous translation project of the Jesuits into the beginning of the eighteenth century. The reason is obvious: In the eyes of the literati class, they were Confucian canons, and a deep mastery of them was essential for an aspiring scholar-official. In addition, they provided the newly arrived Jesuits with an excellent text for learning the language because they were relatively brief and written in a simple style.

For similar reasons, the Jesuits chose a commentary on the *Four Books* by Chang Chü-cheng, the aforementioned grand secretary and imperial tutor of the Wan-li emperor during the first ten years of his reign. Chang had written the commentary in colloquial style to instruct the young emperor, and the Jesuits selected it not only because of its simple style but also because of the political and intellectual prestige it contributed to their Confucian-Christian synthesis.

This emphasis on the *Four Books* was to change in the late seventeenth century, as the Jesuits shifted their mission tactics from the literati to the emperor. However, Ricci's primary attention remained focused on the literati class, and he wrote with them in mind. Noting the special value Chinese placed upon interpersonal relationships, Ricci wrote in Chinese his *Treatise on Friendship (Chiao-yu lun)*, but he never lost sight of his real aim in China and continued to work on a catechism as a useful means to introduce Christianity to the Chinese. This work was entitled *True Meaning of the Lord of Heaven (T'ien-chu shih-i)* and was published in 1603. Even after taking up residence in Peking, Ricci never saw the emperor, but he continued to cultivate friendships with the literati (who were fascinated by his scientific knowledge) and to spread the gospel among them with sincerity and religious zeal.

How much did Ricci and his colleagues really understand

China and its culture? What obstacles did they face and how did they deal with them? To the extent they were successful, what were the reasons for their success? What effect did they have on China? In the following pages, several distinguished scholars take up these questions about Jesuit activities before and after Ricci.

In October 1982, Loyola University of Chicago hosted one of the symposia held during 1982–83 to observe the 400th anniversary of the beginning of Ricci's mission in China. The papers read at that symposium constitute the nine chapters of this book. (The papers have been adapted for publication.)

Chapter 1. Jonathan Spence, in his symposium keynote address, "Matteo Ricci and the Ascent to Peking," deals with Ricci from his early life in Italy to his death in Peking. Spence intends his phrase "the ascent to Peking" to encapsulate his own views of the long journey that made up such a large portion of Ricci's life; there were at least four aspects of the "ascent": geography, linguistic ability, growth in sensitivity, roots in Western classics.

Ricci, after having journeyed from Goa to Malacca and on to Macao, slowly moved out from south China and turned northward to Peking. Ricci also developed excellent linguistic skills, advancing to preaching with an interpreter's assistance and to hearing confessions in 1584, to speaking without an interpreter and reading and writing moderately well by 1585, to first translation attempts into Latin in 1593, and to first efforts on his own at original composition by 1594. A less obvious but quite significant ascent was Ricci's growth in sensitivity, whereby "he learned to take Chinese values ever more seriously." He also studied Confucianism so meticulously that he could borrow arguments from Chinese philosophy to counter the claims of the Buddhists. As his sensitivity rose, Spence notes, Ricci abandoned his initial dream of converting thousands of Asians en masse and became reconciled with "slow, patient work among an intelligent, skeptical, and often hostile group of scholars". Spence describes Ricci's intellectual activities at this time in these words: "This is the period that saw him move from the first simple catechism drawn up with

Ruggieri, through its increasingly complex revisions, to the final linguistic and intellectual tour de force of his later works of theological argumentation like the *True Meaning of the Lord of Heaven*... and the *Ten Essays on the Extraordinary Man*."

Spence's fourth aspect of Ricci's ascent is "hard to indicate precisely," but it has to do with the fact that Ricci, as Spence reminds us, "had his roots in the intellectual soil of classical Rome and the reinterpreting of those roots that was central to Renaissance humanism." Thus, the Italian Jesuit in China maintained a close intellectual tie with the Roman classics and continued to think and express his thoughts in light of these masterpieces. For example, Spence takes Vergil "to stand for the solace and wisdom of the classical Roman tradition which was always present at Ricci's side." In his writings, Ricci drew continually from this tradition; "he deliberately," Spence points out, "uses Roman and Latin models to get ideas across to the Chinese." Ricci's teaching of the faith could not be separated from these pagan and humanistic roots.

But it was not all "ascent" for Ricci, for there was much personal and mental anguish that went with his work in China. Spence points out that this can be most clearly seen in a careful reading of Ricci's letters in the 1580s and 1590s. Some of the Scripture passages cited in his letters are somber in mood and allusion. He even quoted lines from Vergil's Aeneid about the "descent" to the underworld.

Spence concludes his paper with a description of another ascent — Petrarch's ascent of Mount Ventoux, which he wrote about in 1336 during his exile in France. According to Spence, a certain bond can be traced between Petrarch and Ricci. Ricci was ecstatic when he reached Peking and composed songs that could be sung by Emperor Wan-li's court and played on the harpsichord he had presented to the emperor. One song tells of a shepherd boy, who, "disconsolate with life on his own mountain," had become "entranced by the vision of a better life on a distant peak that looks far more beautiful. Arriving there after much toil, he finds the new mountain no better than the old one." Thus, as Petrarch had progressed on Mount Ventoux and realized the folly of rejoicing in the mountain and turned his inner eye toward himself, so did Ricci realize in 1601 that he had reached his own "Mount Ventoux" and that he might never see Europe again.

Chapter 2. Joseph Sebes in his "The Precursors of Ricci" examines the experiences of Ricci's forerunners and Ricci's mission policy. Sebes points out that there were many who entered China before Ricci, but he is important because he ushered in a new era in Asian mission history with his accommodation method.

Sebes emphasizes the fact that in all of Ricci's various and seemingly nonreligious activities, he never lost sight of his primary goal to preach to gospel and convert the Chinese at all levels simultaneously. Ricci early realized, however, that in the upper echelons, "things other than religious teachings would be the attraction." Later, the Italian Jesuit acknowledged that among the reasons for his renown, his religious teachings were the last, outranked by the fact that, to cite one example, as a foreigner he had learned to speak, read, and write Chinese.

Sebes also reminds the reader that the Chinese were impressed by Ricci's personality, sincerity, and piety. The Chinese literati, with their Neo-Confucian tradition of emphasis upon personal cultivation, appreciated his moral conduct. Therefore, Sebes continues, "in the end it was the unethical behavior of the later missionaries that hurt the mission more than anything else." Without the Jesuit method, the missionaries in opposition to Ricci and his method of accommodation would never have been able to set foot on Chinese soil. Thus, Sebes says, "one may say that the Jesuit thesis was a balanced halfway dialectic based upon reasonable premises that were admissible by Catholic moral principles and made imperative in order to win a hearing for the Gospel."

Chapter 3. John Witek's "Understanding the Chinese: A Comparison of Matteo Ricci and the French Jesuit Mathematicians Sent by Louis XIV" compares the activities of Ricci and other early Jesuits with the French Jesuits who came nearly a century after Ricci's first arrival in China. Witek observes that, although both the earlier and later Jesuits continued the effort to understand Chinese, the nature of the mission changed in the course of a century. The French Jesuits were functionaries in the imperial court. Gerbillion and Bouvet, for instance, were thrust into the role of imperial tutors and had little time to cultivate friendship among literati as had Ricci and other earlier Jesuits.

Witek concurs with other contributors in this volume that the reasons for Jesuit success stemmed from their exemplary conduct and their knowledge of the Chinese language and Classics as well as Western sciences. But he further notes that "Christianity became tolerated in China in 1692 not because all the government officials accepted it or because a significant number of scholars became converts. Rather, it was considered to be a promoter of general harmony in Chinese society. . . . The Edict of Toleration became at least in part the Chinese and Manchu response to [the] Jesuit effort of understanding the Chinese."

Chapter 4. Harrie Vanderstappen in his slide lecture, "Chinese Art and the Jesuits in Peking," focused upon "the basic dichotomy between the spiritual message the missionaries were intent on bringing and the framework in which it was presented." The framework, he writes, included the "gifts, the technical skill, and, certainly in the eyes of the Chinese, the strange, exotic, and, in many ways, admirable mental and practical ability of the missionaries." They used their art, Vanderstappen points out, "to illustrate Christian doctrine," and whatever artistic worth these illustrations had, he goes on to say, was superseded in Chinese eyes "by the strange and new technical qualities they saw." Vanderstappen agrees with Sebes that the Jesuits employed the arts as a means to bring home their spiritual message.

Despite the efforts of Jesuit artists, however, "the impact of Western artistic tradition was mainly limited to technical matters," such as topography, perspective, and lifelikeness. But the novelty did not wear well, and the Western artistic tradition seems to have all but disappeared with the lack of imperial patrons after the death of the Ch'ien-lung emperor (r. 1736–1796). Vanderstappen concludes that the traditional artistic heritage in Chinese art seems to have been barely touched by Western traditions.

Chapter 5. Willard Peterson in his "Why Did They Become

Christians?" looks at the whole phenomenon of Jesuit mission activities through the eyes of three prominent Chinese who in the early seventeenth century were converted to Christianity; Peterson tries to make some sense out of the conduct of the three men: Yang T'ing-yün, Li Chih-tsao, and Hsü Kuang-ch'i. He explains their conversion mainly on intellectual, cultural, and sociological grounds.

In Yang's case, Peterson points out, Neo-Confucianism and Buddhism both failed, so he resolved his search "for an externally determined source of moral values" by accepting heaven and the Lord of Heaven. Li was attracted to Christianity through the science brought by the missionaries and by the strengths of Ricci's moral discipline. What struck him at first was Ricci's map of the world; but more than geography, Li became interested in the "learning from heaven." Thus, according to Peterson, Li and Yang "found in the ambiguous 'heaven' a source of knowing and a source of discipline that was external and universal."

Of the three, Hsü seemed to be the only one who went through something of an internal change before coming to accept Christianity. Peterson notes that Hsü was drawn to Ricci as much as Li was but that the Italian Jesuit seems to have played a lesser role in Hsü's baptism, which took place in Nanking in 1604. Moreover, Peterson continues, Hsü "was persuading himself more than he was being persuaded" and in his search for truth, he discovered it not in science or Ricci's character but in "the Learning from Heaven, which as exemplified by the missionaries, added an earnest quality and a discipline to the moral values he inherited from his tradition."

Peterson concludes that each "approached Christianity in different ways, with different needs and questions, but they each found in it a moral discipline based upon an external, universal source." They had been looking "for new intellectual bases to fortify traditional values which were widely perceived to have been eroded." Yang, Li, and Hsü came in touch with the Learning from Heaven and "found its answers persuasive," but there was "nothing inevitable about their choice."

Chapter 6. Albert Chan puts the period of Jesuit activities

in China in historical perspective in his essay "Late Ming Society and the Jesuit Missionaries." He depicts the sad state of government and society of China at the end of the Ming dynasty. He observes that just about the time Ricci arrived, the steady decline of the dynasty had been temporarily halted because of the decade-long reform effort of Grand Secretary Chang Chü-cheng, one of the most talented statesmen of the dynasty.

Chang was a man of resolute will. As government head, Chan writes, he rigorously pushed through government reforms; and as the imperial tutor, he drew up a course of studies which the emperor "had to follow regularly and diligently." On Chang's death in 1582, the empire was financially sound and much stronger. However, the years of prosperity did not perdure. The decline of the dynasty, Chan continues, became evident "in the behavior of the emperor," who did nothing to halt the rapid decline of imperial finances, continued his luxurious living, became involved in foreign wars, turned increasingly to avaricious eunuchs for advice at the expense of the scholar-officials, and became so completely involved in his private affairs that he neglected the duties of his office, never presiding at the important New Year courts after 1588, seldom holding audiences with his ministers, and not even acting on the memorials sent to the palace.

It was in this situation that Matteo Ricci and other Jesuits entered China. The scholar-officials were concerned about the erosion of traditional moral values, about the conduct of government, and about the visible decline of the empire. They were, therefore, attracted to the new teaching the Jesuits brought because they were led to think that the belief in the new teaching would produce moral men like Ricci, whom they greatly admired. They were also interested in the scientific knowledge the missionaries had brought and were impressed with their knowledge of the Chinese language and Classics. Chan explains Jesuit success in terms of the converging of such external factors as timing, Jesuit character, and Jesuit knowledge of science and of Chinese studies.

Chapter 7. In "A Serious Matter of Life and Death: Learned Conversations at Foochow in 1627," Bernard Luk treats the fundamental problem of how much people of different cultures can really understand each other. To illustrate his point, Luk chose an interesting series of philosophical dialogues that took place at Foochow in 1627 between Jesuit Giulio Aleni, Intendant Ts'ao, and Yeh Hsiang-kao, a retired grand secretary under three emperors from Wan-li to T'ien-chi. Aleni was one of the most learned of the second generation of China Jesuits but never served in the capital. Yeh was a bitterly disillusioned old man with no will to live. His life's work, he felt, was in vain as a result of court corruption and factional politics.

Luk points out:

> In the intellectual sphere, the Jesuits took the position that there was nothing incongruous between Catholic doctrine and what they held to be the "pristine" Confucianism of the Classical texts. Anything in contemporaneous Confucianism that conflicted with their teachings, the missionaries attributed to a corrupted transmission of the doctrines of the Chinese sage. They equated the Heaven of the Classics with the Christian God, and rejected Taoism, Buddhism, and the Neo-Confucian metaphysics that grew out of the Sung synthesis of these schools with older forms of Confucianism. . . . The Jesuits contended that they were attempting to restore the original Confucianism and to bring it to its fruition. In this way, they hoped to ease the acceptance of Christianity by the Chinese literati.

Yeh was obviously impressed with the sincerity of the Jesuit and with the moral aspects of Christianity. But he "considered the rewards of heaven," Luk writes, "as a product of the mind of the virtuous." He also considered Confucius and the sage kings of ancient China — "all incarnations of the Lord on High" — equal to Jesus. Aleni did not understand the Neo-Confucian concept of impersonal ultimate, and Yeh and Ts'ao did not understand the personal God.

Luk concludes with a rhetorical question: "Did the twain meet under the Jesuits' policy of accommodation with Confucianism?" And he responds: "If the learned conversations at Foochow in 1627 were any indication, then most of the time the minds did not overcome the very high conceptual barriers, . . . but the hearts did meet in mutual appreciation." The dialogue between the East and West did not get to the core of the matter.

Chapter 8. Theodore Foss's "A Western Interpretation of China: Jesuit Cartography" emphasizes the more practical and, in many ways, more enduring contributions of the Jesuits: their cartographic activities in China. The Jesuits produced maps in the service of the Chinese imperial court but also for the use and furthering of the Catholic mission and to meet the demands of the European scholarly community so curious about China.

The Jesuits' map making, according to Foss, began as early as 1584, only a year after Ricci's arrival in China, when he "produced a Chinese version of a European map of the world which he had brought with him." Ricci soon found that the map was an important device to attract the interest of the Chinese in his work. By 1602, he was able to produce a world map with Chinese terms and place names and with China positioned in the center. It became "one of the most celebrated maps in the history of cartography."

The Jesuit cartographic work resumed late in the seventeenth century under the sponsorship of the K'ang-hsi emperor (r. 1661–1722), who felt the keen need for an accurate map because of the rapid expansion of the empire. The high point of the Jesuit mapping in China, Foss goes on to say, was an actual survey of the Chinese empire. The result was the Jesuit atlas of 1708–18 and its various editions, which remained a basis for the maps of China, Tartary, and Tibet until the late nineteenth century. But Jesuits did not do it alone. They were significantly aided by Chinese knowledge and Chinese co-workers. Foss reminds us that the cartographic tradition in China dates back to 150 B.C. and that the Chinese had amazingly accurate maps in their possession. In fact, for Tibet, Korea, Japan, and the extremities of Manchuria, the Jesuits used the information provided by Chinese and Manchu authorities. Thus, without this native assistance and knowledge, the Jesuits could not have finished the atlas of the Ch'ing empire. Foss concludes: "the result was a work that won the Jesuits the favor of the emperor of China, gave them a better view of their mission territory, and allowed them to travel to remote places in the empire."

Chapter 9. David Mungello in his "The Seventeenth-Century Jesuit Translation Project of the Confucian *Four Books*" discusses the early interest of the Jesuits in the *Four Books* and their later shifting to other Chinese Classics. This shift, he points out, led to a protracted postponement of the *Four Books*' translation, making the complete translation appear only in the early eighteenth century, over a hundred years after the publication of the first three books in the beginning of the seventeenth century. Even in Europe the earlier interest in the translation of the *Four Books* had waned, and when the translation was published, it was little noticed by the scholarly community in Europe. Mungello traces the cause of declining interest in the *Four Books* to the change of the imperial dynasty in China which also affected Jesuit mission strategy.

The Jesuits first became interested in the *Four Books*, according to Mungello, because of Ricci's accommodating mission strategy and because of the practical need of finding a simple text as a language primer for newly arriving missionaries. To supplement their language instruction and to aid in understanding the *Four Books*, the Jesuits needed a commentary on the *Four Books*, one "appropriate for the Confucian-Christian synthesis" they hoped for. The Jesuits chose the commentary by Chang Chü-cheng — for its simplicity of style, for its excellent blending of philosophy and practical affairs, and for the authority given the commentary by the reputation of its author, the former grand secretary. The Jesuit interest in the *Four Books* naturally led to mutual respect and cordial relations between the Chinese literati and the Jesuits, because for the literati class, the *Four Books* were, as Mungello states, "of pervasive pedagogical, moral, ideological, and social significance; and a deep involvement with them was prerequisite for an aspiring scholar-official."

He goes on to point out that in the late seventeenth century the situation had changed. The new Ch'ing dynasty was firmly established, and the K'ang-hsi emperor began his long vigorous reign of sixty years during which the empire rapidly grew in size, wealth, and population and attained a cultural brilliance that defied comparison. The new generation of Jesuits, many of them from France — also ruled by a similarly energetic, absolute ruler, Louis XIV — increasingly became oriented toward the emperor and imperial court and away from provincial literati. Since the *Four Books* were far less important for the emperors than for the literati, Mungello concludes, the Jesuits studied and translated other Classics, such as the *Book of Changes (I Ching),* and other works praising the person of the emperor and the Chinese imperial government. These, in turn, became prominent motifs among the admirers of China in Europe's eighteenth-century Enlightenment.

A theme that ran throughout the papers read at the symposium was that the Jesuits' success, such as it was, could be attributed to their timing, their accommodation policies, their exemplary conduct, their scientific learning, and their knowledge of Chinese language and philosophy. But there was some disagreement among the commentators and panel discussants regarding these reasons for their success and, indeed, the degree to which they were successful at all.

Commentator Wm. Theodore de Bary found the secret of Ricci's success in his profound understanding of Neo-Confucianism and Neo-Confucianists. According to de Bary, Ricci understood the Chinese and their philosophy so well that he even found likenesses between the Neo-Confucian imitation of Confucius in the *Analects* and the Christian imitation of Jesus in the Bible. Such intellectual prowess of the Jesuit sharply contrasted with that of the nineteenth-century missionaries. Commentator Yu-ming Shaw agreed with de Bary that the nineteenth- and twentieth-century Western church, whether Protestant or Catholic, was not as careful in choosing missionaries to Asia.

According to commentator Edwin Van Kley, however, the Jesuits failed because Ricci and his associates in fact misled the Chinese into believing that faith in the Lord of Heaven would produce virtuous people. Such misrepresentation was to have immediate and dire consequences; for when other missionaries came and engaged in not-so-virtuous squabbles over doctrine and the methodology of evangelization, the Chinese became disillusioned. Ricci had also vastly idealized the Christianity of Europe, Van Kley pointed out, and the discovery by the Chinese later on of the true state of affairs might well "explain why Christianity lost its attraction." Van Kley also disagreed with Albert Chan that Ricci's method was slow but sure; neither Ricci's goal of Christian China, he continued, nor the goals of the protagonists of the Self-Strengthening Movement (a nineteenth-century reform movement) were realized. The nineteenth-century Chinese reformers as well as the Christian missionaries had to begin from scratch. The reason for this, as commentator Yu-ming Shaw argued, was because Catholic missionaries and their activities were terminated prematurely.

Panel discussant Donald Lach urged that Ricci alone not be held responsible for the eventual failure of his earlier success. During a hiatus of about fifty years between the death of Ricci and the coming of Martino Martini, many things happened in both China and Europe to undermine Ricci's work. One of these was the internal division among Jesuits after Ricci's death and following the closing of the Japan mission; over seventy conferences were convened and the rationale and the details of Ricci's method were vigorously disputed. Other undermining factors were the change in the total mission program of the Church and the continuing rivalries among Catholic nations, which were so severe that Rome itself could not assert authority.

Peter Hu, S.J. of Taipei took issue with Willard Peterson, arguing that the Chinese conversions could not be explained by external factors alone. Hu felt that the Chinese converts had no difficulty understanding personal love of God because they were accustomed to personal relationships; so it is much more than appreciation for a moral discipline based on an external universal source that explains the conversions. The Chinese converts, according to Hu, had an experience of "inculcation," the experience of faith. Therefore, there was something inevitable in the conversion of persons like Yang and others once they allowed themselves to be drawn through the inspiration of the Holy Spirit by the Father to the person of Christ.

Hu made a distinction between accommodation and inculturation. Accommodation or adaptation consists in external modifications being given to the expression of Christian doctrine without a corresponding interior change. Inculturation, however, is the faith experience lived; and, according to Hu, to regard the Jesuit and Chinese experience of the sixteenth and seventeenth centuries only as accommodation is missing the central point. It is precisely because of this internal change, he went on, that the Chinese converts came to understand the basic religious concepts of Christianity with the result that the Jesuit impact was much greater than the two previous attempts to introduce Christianity to China.

The concrete results of the Jesuit activities in China, however, seem small compared with their superhuman efforts over a period of two hundred years: only 300,000 converts out of a population of over 100 million Chinese. Nor was their experience durable enough to become a model for later Sino-Western contact. But the Jesuit experience was a success in the sense that it stands out as a memorable episode in world efforts at cultural accommodation; further, to quote Reinhard again, it has been "one of the few serious alternatives to the otherwise brutal ethno-centrism of the European expansion over the earth." As for the Chinese, panel discussant Lach affirmed that, although Christianity foundered in China, the effect upon the kingdom and upon Chinese thought of an expansion of geographical understanding permanently changed the Chinese world view.

Bonnie B. C. Oh

NOTES

1. Wolfgang Reinhard, "Gegenreformation als Modernisierung? Prologomena Zu einer Theorie des Konfessionellen Zeitalters, " *Archiv für Reformationgeschichte* 68 (1977):241.

2. *Address of Pope John Paul II at the Gregorian University session on October 25, 1982 of the Macerata Conference commemorating the 400th anniversary of the arrival in China of Matteo Ricci, S.J.* (Rome, 1982), 4.

PART ONE

Jesuit Activities in China

Matteo Ricci and the Ascent to Peking

JONATHAN D. SPENCE

IT TOOK MATTEO RICCI (1552–1610) forty-nine years to get to Peking. We cannot tell at exactly which point in his life the desire to get there was sown, but of course the Counter Reformation world into which he was born was full of dreams for the containment of Protestantism at home and the spread of the Catholic faith abroad. Ricci's home town, Macerata, presently being restored physically and administratively, was in the papal domain, and we can see three nearby geographical loci that may have given wing to his thoughts. One was Loreto, with its powerfully patronized shrine to the Virgin Mary, and its evocation of miracles in her name. A second was Ancona, a port that looked east across the Adriatic and was famous as a center for trade with the Middle East and as a haven for Jews, many of whom had been converted to Christianity. A third was Rome itself, restored to Christian power (if not yet total purity) after the reforms of the Council of Trent and from the time of Pope Pius V onward embarked on ambitious yet phased expansion overseas.

Ricci had initially been meant for a career in law, but he entered the Jesuit Order in 1571 and studied for six years in Rome, Florence, and Coimbra before traveling to India in the spring of 1578. While he was a student in Rome, the acting master of novices was Alessandro Valignano (1539–1606), that brilliant and formidable Jesuit churchman from Chieti, who as Visitor to the East was to have such a profound effect on mission work in India, Japan, and China. Valignano's own visions of a

purified, expansive, yet loving Church may have been passed
on to the young Ricci's mind. From Ricci's own pen the only
remark we have about early motives is to be found in a letter
he wrote to his school friend Giulio Fuligatti, recalling how
in Macerata and Rome they had dreamt of missions in the
Indies, yet had realized how service could be also as broad
at home, for "one needs no thrust of the steel to be a martyr,
nor need one embark on a long journey in order to be a
pilgrim."[1]

Ricci reached Goa, on the western coast of India, in September 1578. He was to be either there or slightly to the south
in Cochin until the spring of 1582, and this period marks his
true apprenticeship for the later labors in China. In entering
this strange new Indian world, he entered also into a world of
doctrinal and strategic problems of quite exceptional complexity.
These included tensions between different religious Orders
within the Church, arguments over the role of the Inquisition,
differences between Spain and Portugal (until their union in
1580) and thereafter between both those countries and the
papacy, and clashes between strong-willed individuals such as
Valignano and Francisco Cabral, S. J. (1528–1609).

Valignano was to prove a central figure in Ricci's Peking journey. Born in 1539, Valignano entered the Jesuit Order in 1566.
In the Roman college, he studied theology, philosophy, and
physics, and mathematics under Clavius (Christoph Clau, S.J.,
1538–1612), and by 1571 was appointed acting master of
novices. In this role, during the autumn of that same year, he
administered the first-year examinations to the young Matteo
Ricci. Valignano then served for a year as rector of the college
in Macerata before the General of the Jesuit Order, Everard
Mercurian, summoned him in 1573 to be Visitor to the missions
in India. This order, by the nature of the Church's organization
at the time, gave the thirty-four-year-old Valignano at one swoop
powers equivalent to those of the General himself over all the
Jesuit missions from the Cape of Good Hope to Japan.[2] Valignano's
assignment was to reinfuse the Asian missions with spiritual
ardor, to bring extra manpower to make possible some respite
from field work and refreshing of spiritual resources for the
missionaries, and to handle the thorny problem of whether to

establish separate mission bases in India beyond the Ganges, in the Moluccas, in Malacca, and in Japan.

Valignano had high hopes for success in India, and these were shared by the General, even if it meant upsetting the Portuguese. It is an intriguing index of Mercurian's independence of spirit, as well as of the pressing need for new recruits of high intellectual caliber, that among the thirty-two men the General assigned to Valignano and the additional eight Valignano selected, with his General's agreement for service in the East, were numerous *confessi*, that is, "New Christians" formerly of the Jewish faith. The incumbent Portuguese clerical power holders warned that King Sebastian (r. 1557–1578) and his uncle, the Cardinal Infante Dom Henrique, would be sure to object and that the Portuguese clerics and *fidalgos* in India who despised the converted Jews would protest vigorously. Valignano doubtless thought that these same senior Portuguese fathers were overharsh in their demands for rigor, discipline, and corporal punishment throughout the Order, improperly claiming this was the true intention of their founder, Ignatius Loyola (1491–1556). Valignano, disagreeing, insisted on the need to follow a road based more on trust and love. The Portuguese, he wrote in a letter of early 1574, "bear on their very features the marks of their inner bitterness. Moroseness and melancholy are everywhere in evidence."[3]

Valignano did surprisingly well with King Sebastian at an audience in January 1574, and this increased his natural optimism. He requested of the king one hundred *scudi* (and more if necessary) in travel fares for each of the thirty Jesuits, cabins near the stern of every ship with fresh air and storerooms, a special ration of flour so they could make their own bread rather than subsist on ship's biscuit, and additional funds to pay for those in Lisbon awaiting passage to the East. All this Sebastian granted, with an additional allowance for wine. At last, forty-one missionaries, all filled with zeal by two months of final training, sailed with Valignano in March 1574, reaching Goa in September.[4]

Despite this most auspicious beginning, after only a year's residence in Portuguese India, mostly in Goa, Valignano wrote a careful letter painting its future in the darkest hues; he describes a government system so bad that the Jesuits hesitated to hear the confessions of the civil and military officials and depicted a society of badly paid soldiers, poorly armed forts, shabby fleets, and a vilely unfair system of justice.[5]

Two years later, en route to Malacca in 1577, a year before Ricci arrived in Goa, Valignano wrote a new and careful assessment of Indian realities that was as harsh as anything written by the Portuguese. His experience of Indian heat, disease, vice, and lethargy led him to lump the peoples of India with those of Africa as little better than the "brute beasts." He added, "A trait common to all these people (I am not speaking now of the so-called white races of China or Japan) is a lack of distinction and talent. As Aristotle would say, they are born to serve rather than to command."[6] He showed no awareness of or interest in the achievements of Indian culture and philosophy, or the shaping of their millenia-old religions.

Ricci followed a rather similar path. At first, on arriving in Goa, he showed euphoria about the prospects of success in India, stimulated almost certainly by the fact that the great Mughal ruler, Akbar (1542–1605), had invited three Jesuits to his court just after Ricci's arrival and had also sent a magnificent embassy by sea to visit Goa. Ricci also felt moved by the need to instruct Indians fully in Christian theology and not to treat them as intellectually second-class citizens, as did many of his colleagues.

But within a year or so, Ricci, ravaged by a sickness that forced him to Cochin for recuperation, depressed by the deaths of several friends, chagrined by the low educational level of many of his fellow Catholic religious in India, and baffled and perturbed by what little he could understand of Indian literature and culture, was beginning to sound just like the Visitor. By December 1581, his letters show that he was convinced there was no real hope of converting Akbar and that indeed the only reason that he had invited the Jesuits to his palace was that he had "a certain natural curiosity to learn about new schools of thought" and also wanted to keep in with the Portuguese on account of the civil war he was fighting with his own brother.[7] One of the most dejected passages Ricci ever wrote, expressing his boredom and frustration, can be found in a letter dated 1 December 1581 to his Jesuit colleague, the historian Gian Pietro Maffei (1533–1610):

> All those here known to your reverence are in good health and well occupied: only I am here accomplishing nothing, and have been ill twice this year; I am put to making a formal study of theology because there is nothing else for me to do except to hear an occasional confession.... I would gladly bear all the travails that accompany the voyage, and ten times over, just to spend one day with you and my other old friends.[8]

Such nostalgia was not helpful, Ricci knew, and was ungenerous to those in Goa who tried to cheer him up with their love and encouragement; but, he continued to Maffei in shock of realization, he had "taken on that characteristic of old men who spend all their time praising time past."

As Ricci grew despondent with India, he became excited by Japan, and once again we can see how Valignano anticipated and influenced his views. In a letter from Cochin, dated 18 January 1580, to his former theology teacher in Coimbra, Ricci wrote excitedly that the rector of the college in Malacca, along with the military commander Mathias d'Albuquerque, had just arrived in Cochin, bringing copies of the "Annual Letter" of Valignano. In it, Valignano announced the dramatic news of the conversion of the "King of Bungo," lord of "five kingdoms" in Japan. By the thirtieth of the same month, Ricci had elaborated this early enthusiasm into a full-fledged hope that the conversion of this king and his son would be followed not only "by all the kingdoms this man controls, which number five or six, but by the whole of Japan." Ricci had another, more personal reason for praising these successes: One of the missionaries credited with the conversion of twelve thousand souls in Meaco was a Jesuit father from his home town of Macerata, Giulio Piani (1538–1605), a man from a well-born family, fourteen years Ricci's senior.[9]

And yet, so great are the paradoxes and dissonances of this period, and so complex the forces working on Ricci himself, that just as he began to rejoice at Valignano's Japanese message, Valignano was changing his tune. In 1579, when Ricci from his vantage point in India was reacting with such enthusiasm to

the news of the Society's triumphs in Japan, Valignano was writing to the General, Everard Mercurian, that there was no way
the fifty-five Jesuits in Japan (of whom only twenty-three were
priests) could handle the spiritual needs of a group of converts
now numbering a hundred thousand. The Church "was asking
too much of her sons"; further, the news of Japanese successes
that had been reaching India was quite different from reality.
Valignano now realized that the Japanese, whom he had praised
in advance as "white" and as "simple pious folk" were in fact
"the most dissembling and insincere people to be found anywhere." He felt himself to be "in a state of anxious uncertainty
and at his wits' end, at a loss for an answer." He agreed on
strictly logical grounds that seminaries for native Japanese
youths must be opened and better language schools developed
for the Europeans. But "when will we be in a position to ordain
native candidates and draw on them for help? I cannot say, nor
indeed do I see how this scheme would work."[10]

Japanese cruelty, dignity, depravity, and hypocrisy were so
complex that he despaired of analyzing the situation accurately.
And even after conversion, the Japanese seemed "tepid" in the
faith. Perhaps it were "better to have no Christians than Christians of that type!" A little Christian learning might be a dangerous thing, as Valignano saw in his role as a leader in the Counter
Reformation. Since many Japanese believed that "by invoking
the name of Amida (Buddha)" they would be saved, one had
to confront the melancholy fact that "their views of justification
resembled those of the Lutherans." Thus, tepid congregations
led by poorly trained priests might allow Protestantism to
flourish.[11]

As Valignano began to grow disillusioned about the Japanese
nature and character, he reflected back to the ten months he
had spent in Macao during 1577 and 1578. It now seemed to
him that it was the Chinese, not the Japanese, who were "the
most capable, well-bred people in the entire East."[12] In a long
draft section to an essay on the Far East, written in Japan in
October 1579, he spelled out the contrasts between Japan and
China. Though this whole passage was cut from the essay by
Valignano in 1580 and could not have been seen by Ricci, it
may serve to illustrate vividly how a sequence was being repeated:

In the mid-1570s, euphoria for Japan had succeeded the disappointment with India; by the end of the decade, China, unsullied by personal knowledge, was becoming the focus for euphoria as dejection about Japanese realities deepened. Here are Valignano's words as transcribed by Schütte:

> In China no one can carry weapons; here they invariably go about heavily armed. The Chinese love to see blood flow, and blows are the order of the day; the Japanese never beat their children or servants or blame them or utter a harsh word; they simply use the sword right away and kill without hesitation. The Chinese noblemen and better class citizens live in walled towns, whereas the better class in Japan live in the country. The Chinese wear their hair long like women; here they not only cut theirs short but actually pull it out so that they remain bald-headed. The Chinese go about in long clothes; here they wear short ones and of such a cut that it really seems they do the reverse on purpose. The Chinese are serious in the pursuit of letters and prize learning highly, showing little interest in arms; the Japanese, on the contrary, pay no regard to learning.

At this point Valignano paused briefly on the topic of diet, noting that the Chinese love of meat and standard fare made them "like Europeans," whereas "one can scarcely describe or imagine" the Japanese meals. He then attempted to draw some deeper characterological dissonances between the two peoples:

> The Chinese women are very retiring and modest and are seen in public rarely or never; the Japanese enjoy more freedom and are looser in their conduct than women anywhere else. The Chinese set little store by their priests, the so-called bonzes, and pay them no respect, whereas the Japanese have the greatest regard and esteem for theirs. The Chinese are very enterprising, lively and alert in their actions and decisions, while the people here are the slowest, most indecisive and prolix in the world; they can never bring a business affair to a conclusion, nor can one hope to treat them with any success. The Chinese will have no friendly relations nor converse with outsiders, while the Japanese are very fond of strangers. The Chinese have the best government imaginable and are sticklers for ordered ways, while here no order or government prevails. In short, they behave in a way quite the reverse of the Chinese and indeed of any other nation.[13]

When Valignano reached Macao, almost a decade had gone

by since the scandal-ridden period when Cabral and Organtino Gnecchi-Soldo (1532–1609) had battled over their claims to lead the Jesuit Order, and Manuel Travassos, captain-major of the Great Ships to Nagasaki in 1569 and 1570, had outraged the community by his brutal ways and rough and ready business dealings. In the now-tranquil city, Valignano learnt enough about China to realize that intensive language preparation would be essential before any progress could be made. So despite his greater current interest in Japan, he had the foresight to order some able Jesuits to apply themselves at once to Chinese language study. In answer to this summons, Michele Ruggieri, S.J. (1543–1607) arrived in Macao from Cochin in 1579. He, in turn, asked that Ricci (with whom he had originally traveled to India and been stationed in Cochin) be ordered to join him. Ricci left Goa in the spring of 1582 and arrived in Macao on 7 August.[14]

A perplexing problem that arises here is why Ricci, sick and exhausted and depressed in India, desperately ill on the rough sea voyage from Goa to Macao, underwent such a change of heart and mind that he could reembark on his ascent with renewed love, tenacity, and skill. His excitement can be seen in a letter to a friend written from Macao at this time, in which he termed the move from India not just a journey but a "leap" (*salto*).[15] It seems that it was the Chinese language that caused his change of heart, but even that is too simple; it was the Chinese language by virtue of its contrast to Greek. This contention, it would seem, can be proved from Ricci's own letters. Writing to Maffei, 30 November 1580, he mentioned that he had been ordered by his superiors to teach an intensive course of Greek and that he felt he would "never free" himself from this grammar. Although his teaching was interrupted by a serious illness, he was ordered back to Goa to continue his studies after his convalescence in Cochin, and Ricci worried aloud that he did not know if this order would lead him to "end [his] study of this grammar or end [his] life."[16]

If any readers have suffered through schoolboy compulsory Greek as long and unsuccessfully as the present writer did and been as tormented and dejected by the complexity of its grammar as compared to Latin or Romance languages, then they

might understand the passion that appeared in Ricci's letter
from Macao, dated 13 February 1583, to his old Roman rhetoric
teacher Martin Fornari:

> I have recently given myself to the study of the Chinese language
> and I promise you that it is something quite different from either
> Greek or German. In speaking it, there is so much ambiguity
> that there are many words that can signify more than a thousand
> things, and at times the only difference between one word and
> another is the way you pitch them high or low in four different
> tones. Thus when the Chinese are speaking to each other they
> can be sure to understand — for all the written letters are dif-
> ferent from each other. As for these written letters you would
> not be able to believe them had you not both seen and used
> them, as I have done. They have as many letters as there are
> words and things, so that there are more than seventy thousand
> of them, every one quite different and complex. If you would
> like to see examples I can send you one of their books with
> an explanation appended.
>
> Each word is one syllable, and the fastest way to write them
> is to paint them, so they use a brush just like our artists. The
> greatest advantage of this is all the countries that use these letters
> can understand each other's correspondence and books, even
> though the languages are different. That is not so with our letters.

Ricci then gave the example of the word for "sky" as it might
be rendered with a pictogram able to be commonly understood
by all cultures, even though one would find totally different
pronunciations for that same word in Japan, Siam, and China,
or in Latin, Greek, and Portuguese. One might not have thought
this was very encouraging for the exhausted traveler, but then
he delivered his punch line, which emphasizes with admirable
concision the contrasts to Greek:

> What is of help in all this is that their words have no articles,
> no cases, no number, no gender, no tense, no mood; they just
> solve their problems with certain adverbial forms which can
> be explained very easily.[17]

Ricci's optimism that had so shortly before led him to hope
for the conversion of all India through Akbar, and then all of
Japan through Nobunaga, was now centered on the Chinese
people. Writing Fornari, he stated that "we hope for the greatest
service to God, since as the Chinese put little trust in their

idols it will be an easy thing to persuade them of our Truth if
we can deal with them directly."[18] His first view of Chinese
bureaucrats in Macao was summed up in a series of images
that could be grasped by his readers as relating directly to their
own upbringing and experience in Rome, Macerata, or Coimbra:
The officials were like gods, their halls large as churches, their
benches of office like altars, their hats like cardinals; they beat
their subjects as commonly as European teachers beat their
pupils; their officials were carried on men's shoulders in a palan-
quin like the pope; the guards had emblems like the Roman
fasces. The one disadvantage of this was an extraordinary severity in their laws which ensured, as Ricci expressed it in
1583, that "they hold their whole territory so subjugated that
no one can raise his head."[19]

Ricci does not seem to have worried about the application
of this severity to his own person; indeed, he thirsted for the
chance to join his Jesuit colleagues, Ruggieri and Francesco
Pasio (1554–1612), who had entered China in December 1582.
Though these two suffered early setbacks, Ricci was able to
enter China in 1583 and to settle at Chao-ch'ing with Ruggieri
in the autumn. It is from this time that one can begin to count
Ricci's true apostolate in China.[20]

The phrase "the ascent to Peking" has been used to encapsulate the present writer's views of the long journey that consti-
tuted so much of Ricci's life. In one obvious sense this was a
cartographic ascent, a movement from south to north, as Ricci
moved from city to city toward his goal. He had already journeyed from Goa to Malacca and Macao. Now he was to be in
Chao-ch'ing near Canton from 1583 to 1589; then in northern
Kuangtung at Shao-chou from late 1589 to 1595; in Kiangsi province at the city of Nanchang from 1595 to 1598; in Nanking, on the Yangtze River (after a brief but ineffective foray
to the edges of Peking), from 1599 to 1600; and finally in full
residence in Peking by 1601.[21]

In another sense, the ascent was one into growing linguistic
skills as Ricci, a first-year language student at Macao, moved
to initial preaching with interpreters' aid and to hearing confessions in 1584; to speaking without an interpreter and reading
and writing moderately well (*mediocremente* as he put it) by

1585; to an initial attempt to translate the *Four Books* (*Ssu-shu*) of the Confucian Classics into Latin in 1593; and finally, in 1594, to the first stabs at original composition without the help of other Chinese scholars.[22]

This is a story that has fascinated generations of scholars, and Ricci's activities in each of these Chinese cities, besides being charted in his own journals (edited by Nicolas Trigault, S.J. [1577–1628] and translated by Louis Gallagher, S.J.), have been analyzed by Otto Franke, John Young, Wolfgang Franke, George Harris, and the four Jesuits Pietro Tacchi Venturi, Pasquale D'Elia, George Dunne, and Henri Bernard-Maitre, to name only a few.[23] They have carefully listed the Chinese friends he made, his slow but steady progress in gaining converts despite great difficulties, and his skillful use of scientific and mathematical knowledge to woo members of the Confucian elites to study the beliefs and embrace the faith that lay behind these surface techniques. It is his tact and skill in this missionary work that have won him high and deserved praise.

That saga is not repeated here. Instead, other aspects of the final stages of the ascent are suggested that have perhaps received less attention. In the first place, it might not be too presumptuous to see in Ricci's eighteen years in China, before he finally settled in Peking, a type of ascent in sensitivity in which he learned to take Chinese values ever more seriously; studied Confucianism so carefully that he could borrow arguments from Confucian texts to counter the theological claims of the Buddhists; gave up the dream of thousands of converts that had enthused him with reference to India, Japan, and China seen from without; and reconciled himself to slow, patient work among an intelligent, skeptical, and often hostile group of scholars. This is the period that saw him move from the first simple catechism drawn up with Ruggieri, through its increasingly complex revisions, to the final linguistic and intellectual tour de force of his later works of theological argumentation like the *True Meaning of the Lord of Heaven* (*T'ien-chu shih-i*) and the *Ten Essays on the Extraordinary Man* (*Chi-jen shih p'ien*).

Despite the bold front that Ricci put on all his endeavors, a detailed reading of his letters through the 1580s and 1590s shows some of the personal and mental anguish that went with the outward successes and apparently deepening devotion. "This sterile land" (*questa sterilità*) he called China in his letter to Fuligatti; to other friends, China was *questa roca* or *un deserto si lontano*, and the Chinese *questa remotissima gente*, among whom he felt "abandoned" or "cast off" (*bottato*). The Chinese marveled, he told his brother Orazio, that he was white-haired and while "not yet advanced in age should already look so old." "They do not know," he added, "that it is they who are the cause of these white hairs [*cani capelli*]."[24]

The passages of Scripture that Ricci cites at intervals in his letters are also reflective, even somber, in their mood and allusions: Genesis 29:15–30, on Jacob being tricked by Laban and having to work seven more years for Rachel; Genesis 47:1–31, on service to Pharaoh in Egypt; Psalm 126:5–6 on a "time to sow in tears, not bring in the sheaves rejoicing"; 2 Corinthians 11:25–27, on stones and shipwrecks, water and robbers, and betrayal; and Matthew 10:16, on the sheep among wolves.[25]

Intriguing also is one other side of Ricci's ascent, hard to indicate precisely yet reminding us that we must not narrow our historical visions of these men of the Counter Reformation. Ricci, like so many of the fine scholar-missionaries of his time, had his roots in the intellectual soil of classical Rome and the reinterpreting of those roots that was central to Renaissance humanism. Images from Dante are not inappropriate here, and perhaps it is not stretching things too far to suggest that in Ricci's Indian years there are elements of the self-knowledge and sorrow that came to Dante in the *Inferno*, while in Ricci's China years one can see elements of the growing wisdom and wonder that came to Dante in the *Purgatorio*. But it is preferable to take the analogy in a different direction and say that is it Dante's wise and constant companion Vergil who also accompanied Ricci through the first two stages of his pilgrimage (as he did Dante, too, before the Latin poet regretfully turned aside from the final climb to Paradise, since being pagan he could venture no further).

Vergil is taken here to stand for the solace and wisdom of the classical Roman tradition which was always present at Ricci's side as he made his own slow and difficult ascent. In the *Aeneid*, Vergil describes how Aeneas gets permission to go down to the underworld to see his dead father Anchises and is warned by the Cumaean Sybil that "the descent to Avernus is not hard. Throughout every night and every day black Pluto's door stands wide open. But to retrace the steps and escape back to upper airs, that is the task and that is the toil." (6.124–211) It was touching to find that Ricci quoted these lines in a letter of 12 October 1596, written in Nanchang.[26]

Besides the melancholy force of such allusions, Ricci's classical learning shows itself in two ways. First, he attempts to summarize the meaning of China's ethical and philosophical stances in a language that will be intellectually precise to his friends back home in Portugal and Italy. Thus, he talks of the role of rhetoric in the Chinese educational structure, of the *Four Books* as being "in the moral vein of Seneca" or of their moral sentiments forming a pattern of argument comparable to Cicero's *Family Epistles*.[27] Expanding out from these Latin examples, he draws too on Greek analogies, comparing elements of Chinese governance to Plato's "speculative Republic" and calling the Mandarins "Epicurean."[28]

Second, he deliberately uses Roman and Latin models to get ideas across to the Chinese, surely because he felt such models would have a greater initial impact than images drawn from the Old or New Testament. At all costs, he had to avoid the blurring in the Chinese mind of Christian principles with those of Buddhism, and so at times he used Latin examples that spoke directly to Neo-Confucian concerns. This can be seen strongly in two of Ricci's works: *Treatise on Friendship* (*Chiao-yu lun*) and *Western Memory Techniques* (*Hsi-kuo chi-fa*). These he wrote in Chinese during 1595 and 1596, as he grew confident of his growing linguistic powers. In the friendship treatise, as D'Elia has so elegantly shown, Cicero, Seneca, Ovid, Plutarch, and Quintilian bear far more of the burden than Augustine, Ambrose, or Chrysostom.[29] And in Ricci's book *Western Memory Techniques*, on which he set much store for eventual influence over the Chinese which would lead to their conversion, he drew almost the whole work from Cicero, Quintilian, Seneca, and above all Pliny's *Natural History*, though of course the attempt to render all this into classical Chinese was Ricci's alone.[30]

In conclusion, let us take leave by considering the ascent

that would have lain third in the Counter Reformation con-
sciousness, immediately after those of Christ Himself and of
Dante. This is Petrarch's account of his ascent of Mount Ventoux, written in 1336 during his exile in France. A bond between Ricci and Petrarch can be traced owing to the delightful
fact that almost as soon as Ricci reached Peking in 1601, he
burst into song. Not with his own voice, indeed, but with his
pen; for the Wan-li emperor (r. 1573–1620) was so delighted
by the small harpsichord presented to him by Ricci that he
ordered the missionary to compose some songs that could be
sung by court performers along with the instrument. Ricci obliged, and eight of the songs that he wrote at that imperial
summons in 1601 have come down to us. Most of them hark
back to Horaces's *Odes*, but the third song is different. It tells
of a shepherd boy, disconsolate with life on his own mountain,
entranced by the vision of a better life on a distant peak that
looks far more beautiful. Arriving there after much toil, he finds
the new mountain no better than the old one.[31]

"Oh shepherd boy, shepherd boy!" goes Ricci's song, "isn't
it better to change yourself than to change your dwelling place?
Wherever you go, how can you ever free yourself from your
self?" So too had Petrarch progressed, according to his own
account, on Mount Ventoux, initially "almost benumbed, over-
whelmed by a gale such as he had never felt before and by
the unusually wide and open view" until he saw the folly of
rejoicing in the mountain and its view "and turned his inner
eye toward himself."[32] But Petrarch had not reached this insight
unaided. As he tells us in the same essay, his spiritual guide
was St. Augustine, whose *Confessions*, consulted for guidance
on the mountain top, fell open to the passage where the bishop
writes of men who "go to admire the high mountains" and in
doing so "desert themselves." Nor was Augustine alone in Petrarch's thoughts but warred rather with the Roman historian
Livy, whose account of Philip of Macedon's mountain climbing
had triggered Petrarch's own ascent.

Thus, as Ricci attained his goal in 1601 and settled in Peking,
past and present Christianity, China and ancient Rome rolled
briefly into one harmonious hymn. He had nine years left until
his death in which to draw his Chinese plans to fruition, and

he knew with absolute certainty he would never see Europe again. Did he, for a moment, recall another lovely passage from Petrarch's same essay?

> I had better look around and see what I had intended to see in coming here. The time to leave was approaching, they said. The sun was already setting, and the shadow of the mountain was growing longer and longer. Like a man aroused from sleep, I turned back and looked toward the West.[33]

NOTES

1. For the full background on Ricci's life and education and for the entire meticulously annotated text of Ricci's manuscript of the *Historia*, see Pasquale M. D'Elia, S.J., ed., *Fonti Ricciane: documenti originali concernenti Matteo Ricci e la storia delle prime relazioni tra l'Europa e la Cina 1579–1615*, 3 vols. (Rome, 1942–1949); Wolfgang Franke's fine essay in L. Carrington Goodrich and Chaoying Fang, eds., *Dictionary of Ming Biography 1368–1644*, 2 vols. (New York, 1976), 2:1137–44; Jonathan D. Spence, *The Memory Palace of Matteo Ricci* (New York, 1984). Valignano is well analyzed in Josef Franz Schütte, S.J., *Valignano's Mission Principles for Japan*. Vol. 1. *From His Appointment as Visitor Until His Departure from Japan (1573–1582)*. Part 1. *The Problem (1573–1580)*, trans. John J. Coyne, S.J. (St. Louis, 1980). The quotation from Ricci's letter to Fuligatti is in Pietro Tacchi Venturi, S.J., ed., *Opere storiche del P. Matteo Ricci, S.J.*, 2 vols. (Macerata, 1911–1913), 2:214.
2. Schütte, *Valignano's Mission Principles*, 1 (Part 1):30–35, and esp. 44 n. 106, 52 n. 122.
3. Ibid., 60, 67, 71.
4. Ibid., 76–78.
5. Ibid., 104–8.
6. Ibid., 131.
7. Tacchi Venturi, *Opere storiche*, 2:25.
8. Ibid., 26.
9. Ibid., 7–8, 10, 10 n. 2.
10. Schütte, *Valignano's Mission Principles*, 1 (Part 1):269, 272–73, 279–80.
11. Ibid., 269–97, 308.
12. Ibid., 282.
13. Ibid., 286–87.
14. Ibid., 186.
15. Tacchi Venturi, *Opere storiche*, 2:27.

16. Ibid., 17.
17. Ibid., 27–28.
18. Ibid., 28.
19. Ibid., 29.
20. Ibid., 32–33.
21. *Supra*, note 1.
22. Tacchi Venturi, *Opere storiche*, 2:49, 60, 65, 117, 122.
23. For bibliography, see Wolfgang Franke, *DMB*, 2:1144. See also John D. Young, *East-West Synthesis: Matteo Ricci and Confucianism* (Hong Kong, 1980).
24. Tacchi Venturi, *Opere storiche*, 2:67–70, 90, 234, 279.
25. Ibid., 75, 94, 106–7, 163. The identification of biblical quotations is from Tacchi Venturi.
26. Vergil, *Aeneid*, trans. William Francis Jackson Knight (New York, 1970), 151.
27. Tacchi Venturi, *Opere storiche*, 2:69, 117–18, 237.
28. Ibid., 45, 57.
29. Pasquale M. D'Elia, S.J., "*Il Trattato sull'Amicizia*. Primo Libro scritto in Cinese da Matteo Ricci, S.J. (1595). Testo Cinese. Traduzione antica (Ricci) e moderna (D'Elia). Fonti, Introduzione e Note," *Studia Missionalia* 7 (1952):425–515.
30. See Ricci's *Hsi-kuo chi-fa* (Western memory techniques) and Pliny's *Natural History*, 7.24.88–91. Ricci also drew his *Erh-shih-wu yen* (Twenty-five discourses) almost totally from Epictetus's *Encheiridion*, as has been graphically shown by Christopher Spalatin, S.J., "Matteo Ricci's Use of Epictetus' *Encheiridion*," *Gregorianum* 56/3 (1975):551–57. The present writer is grateful to Father Spalatin for giving him a copy of this valuable essay at the Loyola University of Chicago conference in October 1982.
31. Pasquale M. D'Elia, S.J., "Musica e canti Italiani a Pechino (marzo–aprile 1601)," *Rivista degli studi orientali* 30 (1955): 131–45. The present writer is grateful to Thomas M. Greene for following up in correspondence the leads he first presented in his remarks on Petrarch in *The Light in Troy: Imitation and Discovery in Renaissance Poetry* (New Haven, 1982).
32. Ernst Cassirer, Paul Oskar Kristeller, and John Herman Randall, Jr., eds., *The Renaissance Philosophy of Man* (Chicago, 1948), 41–45.
33. Ibid., 43. Regarding St. Augustine, see his *Confessions*, trans. with Introduction by R. S. Pine-Coffin (Baltimore, 1961), 216.

2

The Precursors of Ricci

JOSEPH SEBES, S.J.

H OW WOULD WORLD OPINION REACT today if the Pioneer satellites should prove as realities the fantasies of UFOs, of Star Trek, of "Close Encounters of the Third Kind"? Or that there really are extraterrestrials on other yet unknown planets in this galaxy of ours or in galaxies yet to be discovered? How would we categorize these E.T.s? Would they be welcome? Would they be considered equal to us earth dwellers? Would they be participants in our dispensation? The situation was not dissimilar when in the fifteenth and sixteenth centuries the Portuguese and the Spaniards, having expelled the Muslims from the Iberian peninsula which they had ruled since the eighth century, discovered a "new world" during the ensuing Age of Discovery.

Beginning in about 1418, the Portuguese, under the direction of Prince Henry the Navigator (1390–1460), King John II (r. 1461–1495), and their successors, discovered for Europe the African continent south of the Sahara and sailed around Africa's southern tip, called by them the Cape of Torments (Cape of Good Hope being a later euphemism), reaching India in 1498, the same year Christopher Columbus embarked upon his third voyage to the Spanish New World, which he had discovered for the Crown of Castile in 1492 in his westward quest for a sea route to India.[1]

The popes supported these voyages because in their origins they had been crusading ventures; further, they declared all the territories hitherto unoccupied by Christian princes as the inviolable crown property of Portugal and Spain respectively and granted both trade monopoly in their areas.

During the early stages of these discoveries, both Christian nations coveted the Indies. Therefore, to avoid conflicts, papal intervention was sought to establish lines of demarcation, which would clearly and officially designate spheres of influence — thus the papal Bulls of 3 and 4 May 1493. However, the Treaty of Tordesillas of 1494, with new lines approved by the pope, superseded the arrangements of 1493, and each country pledged to propagate Christianity in its newly discovered territories. From these rights and privileges sprang the Spanish *Patronato Real* and the Portuguese *Padroado*.[2]

Thus, Portugal could make a fresh effort to establish firm rule in the territories adjudged to her. When, on 1 March 1498, Vasco da Gama encountered in Mozambique the first Arab ship laden with Indian freight, further Portuguese exploration and expansion had a new motive: profit from the spice trade. Profits, however, did not replace the crusading spirit; they only diluted it. While the African obstacle had been overcome and India was in sight, it was still necessary to safeguard this achievement against Islam at the zenith of its power.[3] The events which occurred in the Near East and the Mediterranean basin are witness to this. The victories of the Ottoman Turks over Venice at the dawn of the sixteenth century sealed the decline of Venice as the commercial capital of a Europe dependent upon the traditional trade with the Islamic world of the East and opened the road for the Ottoman Turks into Central Europe.

To reach India from Africa, the Portuguese relied upon Muslim Arabs. Sailing from Malindo (in Kenya) to Calicut, on the Malabar coast, in 1498, Vasco da Gama's ship was guided by the Arab pilot Ahmad ibn Majin. Thus, the Portuguese had reached India, and the East Asian seas lay open to them.[4] However, control of the traditional trade routes with the East still remained in the hands of the Mamelukes of Egypt. It was in 1507 that the two main channels of this trade route with the East, the Red Sea and the Persian Gulf, were closed when two key fortresses, Socotra and Hormuz, were taken from the Muslims by the Portuguese. The backbone of Islam's resistance was broken in 1509 at Diu, when the Muslim fleet was defeated. In 1510, Goa was taken. In 1511, Malacca fell to the Portuguese, who shortly afterward erected a fortress on the Spice Island of Ternate. The trade routes were redirected around Africa, and Lisbon became the commercial capital of Europe for the sixteenth century. The new motto of Portugal was "Spices and Souls."[5]

But the Portuguese did not stop here. By 1513, Jorge Álvares had reached China., and a trade mission followed in 1514; in 1515, Raphael Perestello traveled in a Chinese junk to South China. Simão Peres d'Andrade, in 1517, sailed up the Pearl River to Canton. Tomé Pires, the first Portuguese ambassador to China, reached Peking in 1520. In 1542, António da Mota, with two companions, first reached Japan, driven there by a storm. In a few decades, Islam's front had been turned by an out-flanking movement and its communications severed in the rear. The East was once more in direct contact with the West. Europe had discovered, or rather rediscovered, Africa and Asia, a new world.[6]

The Portuguese discovery of a sea route to India and points east had come at a time when the Turks had squatted down on the medieval land routes to the East, making them difficult and unprofitable to merchants. The Jesuit lay brother, Bento de Góis (1563–1607), traveled overland from Agra to China in 1602 at the request of Matteo Ricci (1552–1610) to rediscover the land route and to test Ricci's hypothesis that the Cathay of Marco Polo and of the medieval friars was China. On his death bed, de Góis remembered how "this journey had been very long, very wearisome, and beset with dangers. Therefore should no member of the Jesuit brotherhood attempt to follow his example." In spite of this warning, a few attempts were later made to find an alternative route to the equally lengthy, wearisome, and dangerous sea route. They were, for the most part, planned through Russian territories after the overland contact with China had been established.[7]

As great as the Portuguese accomplishment was, China had long before discovered what today we refer to as Southeast Asia, South Asia, and Africa. From 1405 on, under the Yung-lo emperor (r. 1403–1424), seven great expeditions under the leadership of Cheng Ho (1371–1433) had gone as far west as Africa.[8]

With the reaching of Japan, the age of discovery ended and

the colonial period began. Portugal then as today was a small country and could not hope to conquer the vast Asian and African territories. But being a sea power, she aimed at ruling the trade routes by maintaining a strong grip on important harbors and trade centers by establishing trading factories and fortresses to protect her interests.[9]

As the Portuguese in Southeast Asia and the Spaniards in the Philippines discovered this new world with its strange cultures, they soon realized that the Christian faith was the property of the Europeans only. All non-Christian cultures were, at first, looked upon by many as the work of the devil. This realization gave the Europeans a sense of destiny, a will to conquer and proselytize unknown to medieval Europe, a belief in their own superiority as "a chosen race, a royal priesthood, a holy nation, a people set apart."[10]

However, to the peoples of the East, these newcomers from the West were considered barbarians. The Chinese called them Franks (Fo-lang-chi); they later referred to the Dutch as barbarians with red hair (Hung-mao-i). The Russians, who approached China from the northwest, were counted among the northern barbarians and called Lo-cha and O-lo-ssu.[11]

The early missionaries who left Europe to convert this new world also tried to westernize it in the process. In the territories belonging to Portugal, converts were, at the time of their baptism, not only given a Christian name but also urged to take Portuguese surnames, wear European clothes, and observe European rites. The Spaniards did the same in their sphere. Any adaptation of European culture, not to mention Christian doctrine, was considered to be against God. The spirit and example of Paul of Tarsus, who accommodated Christianity, hitherto a small Jewish sect, to Greco-Roman culture, was overlooked and ignored. The main object of the founding of the Jesuit Order by Ignatius of Loyola (1491–1556) in 1534 was the defense and propagation of the faith. His sons, inspired by his spirit expressed in the Order's Institute, Constitutions, and Spiritual Exercises, imitated St. Paul and tried to follow his example. Few such attempts have ever been made.[12]

The first missionaries to come to this new world under the

Padroado were Franciscan and Dominican friars, who took up the arduous task of evangelization where their medieval predecessors had left off. Also, some secular priests served as chaplains at Portuguese fortresses. Then, with the coming of the Jesuits in 1542, the first phase of the history of the Portuguese missions in the Orient ends. Profound changes began to take place.[13]

Among the first Jesuits to arrive was Francis Xavier. The Society of Jesus, officially established in 1540, purposed to propagate the faith wherever the pope should want its members to go. Within a year, Xavier and four others left Europe for the East. Xavier had come as a missionary of the Portuguese *Padroado*, sent by the king of Portugal and invested with the authority of Papal Nuncio by the Holy See. His missionary activities, and those of his fellow Jesuits, began by relying upon Portuguese colonization. But his hopes of getting help and support from the civil authority led to bitter disappointment. He "fled," as he himself says,[14] from the sphere of Portuguese influence to Japan, where no European functionary, so harsh toward the natives, could undo what he so laboriously was building. While in India, Xavier had been more tolerant of local customs and practices than other missionaries, even though he had worked among poor fishermen and peoples of the lower castes who were willing to accept Christianity in its European garb.

In Japan, Xavier's approach took on a new dimension after he was challenged by the Buddhist monks. The Japanese response helped Xavier realize that for Christianity to succeed in Asia, missionaries had to reach the natives on their own terms: speak, read, and write the native languages; become an integral part of a particular civilization and behave like the natives of the country — or, as will be said later, "Become Chinese to win China for Christ." Thus, while trying to learn Japanese, Xavier wrote: "In these six weeks, by God's favour, we have got so far that we already give explanations in Japanese of the Ten Commandments."[15]

For a time, Xavier went so far as to equate the name *Dainichi*, "the great sun" (in Mahayana Buddhism the great Vairochana Buddha, the pantheistic deity of the Shingon sect), with the Christian concept of God. This was a singularly unhappy choice, for whatever else it may mean, *Dainichi* does not even remotely approximate the Christian concept of God. When he realized his mistake, he proscribed further use of the name. His Jesuit successors in Japan discussed this problem for the next fifty years and decided to employ traditional Portuguese or Latin terms to express Christian concepts. The word *Deus* later became *Deusu*, *Christiano* became *Kirishtan*, and so on, just as centuries later the Japanese adopted *beisuboro* (baseball), *aisukuremu* (ice cream), and so on. They got away with this because in the sixteenth century, during the *Sengoku* (country at war) period, Japan was an open society and was willing to accept Christianity in its Western garb, together with firearms and trade.[16]

To approach the daimyo and to debate the bonzes in front of them, Xavier put on an aristocratic appearance, donned expensive clothes with chains of gold, and had his attendants wait on him on their knees as he spoke to them. But all this royal display had only one purpose: to discredit the Buddhist monks whom he regarded as the deadliest enemies of Christianity.[17] In his debate with them, he became convinced of two things: one, that future missionaries to Japan would have to be learned men, "powerful intellects, practiced in dialectics . . . to unravel sophistical arguments, and to show the incoherence and mutual contradictions of false doctrines";[18] two, that the secret to the conversion of Japan was the conversion of China. The Japanese, Xavier wrote, try to make this "a principal point against us, that if things were as we preached how was it that the Chinese knew nothing about them."[19]

Xavier had already noticed, when he first landed in Japan, that the Japanese, like their Chinese masters, were led by reason and showed a great interest in the sciences. He wrote about the Japanese:

> They did not know that the world is round; they knew nothing of the course of the sun and stars, so that when they asked us and we explained to them . . . they listened to us most eagerly . . . regarding us with profound respect as extremely learned persons. This idea of our great knowledge opened the way for us to sow the seed of religion in their minds.[20]

Xavier was also impressed by the emphasis the Japanese and their Chinese masters placed on moral conduct. In this he thought he had discovered a close parallel between Eastern ethics and Christian morality. Consequently, future missionaries to East Asia would have to be men of high morals, learning, and science. Xavier was the first to realize the importance of science as an entrance to East Asian societies.[21]

Xavier decided to go to China, learn more about the sources of Japanese beliefs and values, and convince the emperor of the truthfulness of the Christian faith. He nourished the hope that once the Son of Heaven was converted, all the Chinese as well as the Japanese would follow suit, and soon all East Asia would be converted to Christianity. He did not succeed in penetrating the walls of China's self-imposed isolation, but in his attempt died (1552) on the small island of Shang-ch'uan (St. John's today) off the coast of China.

The innumerable voyages undertaken by Xavier must not be considered as the manifestation of the spirit of adventure in this man from Navarre. Neither can they be explained solely by his desire, as superior of the vast territories stretching from the Cape of Good Hope to Japan, to visit all his subjects and to inspect their work.[22] He never regarded himself as an individual missionary. His task was that of a pioneer, a pathfinder, destined to open the way for others. That was the work entrusted to him by the Holy See and by his own superior, Ignatius Loyola. Xavier was then only forty-five years of age, and there seemed to him ample time to plot the course of this mighty undertaking. He was urged on by his search for a vantage point from which the Christianization of the East could be accomplished. Relying, even temporarily, on a native clergy (in South India, Malacca, and the Moluccas) did not augur well for the future. Everywhere one encountered that soft, dreamy, and nonenterprising spirit which would never do. It was at this precise moment he was told that in Japan there was to be found a different type of man; as soon as he encountered the Japanese he saw that he had not been misled, and his hopes were fulfilled. The Japanese themselves told him, as we have seen, that their teachers and masters were the Chinese. Thus, after immense labors, he arrived at the conclusion that the conversion of East Asia had to be accomplished by first converting China.[23]

To put this plan into operation, however, an enormous obstacle had to be overcome. Sixteenth-century Ming China was still the very epitome of orderly government and political stability, but unwilling to come out of her self-imposed isolation — so unlike India and Japan, where warfare and turmoil and the open societies had enabled the Portuguese and the Jesuits to establish a foothold and even introduce Christianity in its European form. Before the Ming dynasty (1368–1644), China had been an open society.[24]

After the defeat and expulsion of the Mongols (Yüan dynasty), the emperors Hung-wu (r. 1368–1398) and Yung-lo (r. 1404–1424), the first rulers of the Ming (the last native Chinese dynasty), attempted to make the Middle Kingdom safe and impregnable from land and sea. Hung-wu led nine campaigns against the still-dangerous Mongols to push them as far away from the Great Wall frontier as possible. Under Yung-lo, the seven great maritime expeditions were undertaken, bringing China into contact with Southeast Asia and Africa. During at least the initial period of the Yüan dynasty, China had been part of the much larger Mongol world empire, and foreign "barbarians" came from all directions.

Having secured its borders on all sides by 1429, China closed her doors and withdrew into self-imposed isolation to cleanse herself and her civilization from this cosmopolitan contamination and to restore the purity of Sinic culture. This isolation was reinforced by the Japanese pirates, the *wako*, who endangered the coast of China. The Chinese in general often regarded the Portuguese as little better than the Japanese pirates, and rightly so as in the case of Simão Peres d'Andrade.[25]

Xavier was not deterred by the fact that it meant death or imprisonment for any foreigner attempting to land in China. He proposed to the Portuguese viceroy in the Indies that he appoint one of his fellow countrymen ambassador to the emperor of China, and with him he would travel as papal representative. He hoped that in this way he would be able to put forward his case to the highest authority. He would bring presents to the emperor, beg him to change the laws against the admission of foreigners, release from prison the Portuguese who were in the jails of Canton, and give him and his companions leave to preach the Gospel.

The viceroy thought the plan worth trying, for he already had witnessed Xavier's success against seemingly insurmountable obstacles. He, therefore, appointed Xavier's friend, Diogo Pereira, as ambassador, and Xavier was to accompany him. The whole effort, however, was frustrated by Álvaro de Ataíde da Gama, the captain-general of Malacca and the unworthy son of the great navigator, Vasco da Gama. When the ship carrying the ambassador stopped at Malacca, the captain-general would not permit it to leave unless Pereira's appointment was rescinded. A very greedy, materialistically minded man, de Ataíde wanted the very lucrative post for himself. Whatever success Xavier's pleading might have had with the emperor of China, it had none with Álvaro de Ataíde; so, abandoning all hope of an official introduction to China, the missionary decided to go on alone and be smuggled into the empire by boat. Before putting his plan into action, he wrote a farewell note to Ambassador Pereira, who had given him money for bribing his way into China. Xavier wrote that should Pereira visit him there, he would find him either in a Cantonese prison or in the palace in Peking where the Chinese emperor is said to have his residence.[26] Then, making his way in August 1552 to Shang-ch'uan island, off China's coast, together with a faithful Chinese interpreter, he made arrangements with a Chinese merchant to convey him to the mainland. The latter, however, never appeared, and Xavier died on the deserted island on 3 December, unsuccessful in his efforts to penetrate China's self-imposed isolation.

Although Xavier died before he could penetrate China, his spirit and method of accommodation survived; and for the next thirty-one years his confreres and successors tried with admirable tenacity to open the gates of China, but with little success. Even those who succeeded in entering — some twenty-five — were not permitted to stay but had to leave again in a short time. The story of the twenty-five is as follows: On 20 July 1555, Melchior Nunes Barreto (1519–1571), Portuguese provincial of the Jesuits in India, visited Shang-ch'uan island and celebrated Mass there on his way to Japan. He was accompanied by Father Gaspar Villela (1526–1572) and four Jesuit brothers: Melchior and António Dias, Luis Fróes (1528–1597), and

Estevão de Góis (1526–1588). On 3 August, he went to Lampação (*Lang-po-kao*) island,[27] twenty-eight leagues west of Macao, whence between August and November of the same year he went twice to Canton, on each occasion remaining there a month in an attempt to obtain the release from prison of three Portuguese and three native Christians.[28] He went to Canton a third time during Lent in 1556. Then, on 5 June, he continued to Japan, leaving Brother de Góis in China to learn the language, but the brother became ill and in 1557 returned to Goa.[29]

In late 1556, Gaspar da Cruz, O.P. arrived in Canton and remained there a month.[30]

On 21 November 1560, Baltasar Gago, S.J. (1515–1583), on his return trip from Japan, was forced, because of severe weather, to seek refuge on Hainan island until May 1561, whence after a trip of thirty days he reached Macao and remained there until 1 January 1562.[31]

On 24 August 1562, the Italian Jesuit, Giovanni Battista de Monte (1528–1587), together with his Portuguese companion, Luis Fróes, stopped in Macao and remained there until the middle of 1563.[32]

On 29 July 1563, the Jesuits Francisco Pérez (1514–1583), Manuel Teixeira (1536–1590), and André Pinto (1538–1588) arrived in Macao in the entourage of Diogo Pereira, the ambassador of the king of Portugal to the emperor of China. As indicated, this embassy failed.[33]

On 15 November 1565, the Spanish Jesuits Juan de Escobar and the above-mentioned Pérez came to Canton, and on 23 November Pérez asked permission from the authorities to remain in China, but was refused.[34]

In 1565, Pérez and Teixeira established a residence of the Society of Jesus in Macao.[35]

On 15 August 1567, the Spanish Jesuit Juan Bautista de Ribera (1525–1594) went to Macao with two companions and from there proceeded to Canton, arriving on 9 May 1568. He planned to move on to Nanking but was forced to return to Macao shortly after.[36]

Sometime before October 1568, Pedro Bonaventura Riera, S.J. (1526–1573) went to Canton with some Portuguese merchants.[37]

In 1569, another Jesuit, probably Bishop Melchior Carneiro (1519–1583), spent some time in Canton.[38]

In 1574, António Vaz, S.J. (1523–1573?) was in Canton from 7 February to about 20 March.[39]

In 1575, Cristóvão da Costa, S.J. (1529–1582) accompanied Portuguese merchants to Canton twice and stayed there on one occasion for two months and on another for a month but could not obtain permission to remain.[40]

Also around 1575, Bishop Carneiro tried to establish himself in Canton but without success.[41]

In 1575, two Augustinians, the Spaniard Martín de Rada and the Mexican Jerónimo Marín, came from the Philippines to Fukien province and returned to the Philippines on 14 September.[42]

In February 1579, some Jesuits visited Canton.[43]

On 23 June of the same year, four Franciscan friars and three members of the Third Order of Saint Francis dressed as Franciscans arrived in Canton. The priests were the Italian Giovanni Battista Lucarelli da Pesaro (1540–1604) and three Spaniards, Pedro de Alfaro (d. 1580), Augustino de Tordesillas (1528–1629), and Sebastiano de Baeza (d. 1579). The three Third Order men were two Spanish soldiers, Francisco de Dueñas and Juan Díaz Pardo (d. 1615), and the Mexican Pedro de Villaroel. They had to leave China after having spent fifty days in a Canton prison.[44]

For Easter of 1580 (3 April), Michele Ruggieri, S.J. (1543–1607) went to Canton and stayed in a house near the river. In 1581, he returned twice to Canton, the first time accompanied by Brother Pires (1563–1632) and the second time by Father André Pinto.[45] He remained the first time for three months, the second time for two months, being housed in the palace of the Siamese ambassador.[46] In April and May 1582, Ruggieri went to Canton for the fourth time and remained for a month and a half, and on 2 May he was joined by Alonso Sánchez, S.J. (1551–1614) and two Franciscans, one of whom was the Third Order member, Juan Díaz Pardo, for whom this was the second time. These men had come from the Philippines by way of a port in northeastern Kuangtung province. Sánchez remained in Canton from 2 May to 29 May.[47] From Canton, Ruggieri ventured on two occasions as far as Chao-ch'ing, vice-regal seat of the "two Kuangs" (the provinces of Kuangtung

and Kuangsi). On his first visit in June, he was accompanied
by Matías Panela, a judicial auditor, and on the second visit,
on 27 December, by Francesco Pasio, S.J. (1554–1612). Between
the two trips to Chao-ch'ing, he returned to Macao. From the
second trip, Ruggieri and Pasio returned to Macao in March
1583, while the two Franciscans returned to the Philippines
through Macao and Japan.[48]

In June 1582, the friars minor Jerónimo de Burgos (d. 1593),
Martín Ignacio de Loyola (nephew of Ignatius Loyola), Agostino
de Tordesillas (second time), Girólamo de Aguilar (d. 1591),
and Antonio de Villanueva, in their effort to reach Macao, landed
instead at Chuan-chou in Fukien province. They were accompanied by two lay brothers, Francisco de Córdova and Cristóforo
Gómez, together with three soldiers. From Chuan-chou, they
were all brought to Canton as spies but later were freed and
sent to Macao.[49]

In May 1583, another group of friars minor, Fathers Diego
de Oropesa, Bartolomé Ruíz, Francisco de Montilla, and Pedro
Ortiz Cabezas, landed on Hainan island, driven there by a storm
on their return trip from Annam to the Philippines. They were
accompanied by four Franciscan lay brothers, Cristóforo
Gómez, Diego Jiménez, Francisco Villarino, and a novice, Manuel
de Santiago. Taken for spies, they were all sent to Canton where
they were freed on a payment of alms given by the Portuguese.[50]

Thus, excluding the members of the Jesuit residence in
Macao, and counting each attempt of those who tried several
times to enter China, there were thirty-two Jesuits (twenty-four
priests and nine scholastics or lay brothers), twenty-four Franciscans (thirteen priests and eleven lay brothers or members
of the Third Order), two Augustinians, and one Dominican. If
we count only the individuals and not the times they tried to
enter China, there were twenty-five Jesuits, seventeen of them
priests and eight scholastics or lay brothers; twenty-two Franciscans,
of whom twelve were priests and ten lay brothers or members
of the Third Order; two Augustinians; and one Dominican. This
is by no means a complete listing. It is only a list of those who
tried unsuccessfully between 1552 and 1583 to penetrate
China's self-imposed isolation and establish permanent residence there.[51]

This is the story of missionary persistence with China, a country that remained hostile to the Western world. However, in return for Portuguese help in ridding the South China coast of an exceptionally troublesome pirate chief, Chinese authorities in 1557 had permitted Portugal to establish a trading post called Macao on the tiny tip of a peninsula in Kuangtung province.[52] At first, a barrier was built across the neck of the peninsula, and no one could cross it except twice a year by the carefully guarded gate in the middle, but after a time the gate became wider and means of getting around the wall more easily devised. As a result, more regular contact grew between the Portuguese and the Chinese authorities in Canton.

Enthusiasm for the effort to penetrate China never slackened, and it had the fullest support of superiors in Europe where it was also greatly stimulated by encouragement from an unexpected quarter. In the year before Xavier died (1552), a remarkable nobleman of Spain, Francis Borgia (1510–1572), Duke of Gandía, renounced his titles and property and was ordained a Jesuit priest. His previous position as well as his remarkable personality gave special authority to everything he said or did. In 1559, he visited Portugal, and because the East (from India to Japan) was in the Portuguese missionary zone and under the Portuguese *Padroado*, he had first-hand access to all that had been reported about the establishment of Macao and the efforts to penetrate China. He publicly stated that there was good hope for the opening of missionary work in China. This caused great excitement in Jesuit circles, and from all quarters petitions from priests, young and old, went to superiors asking to be allowed to participate in this undertaking.

An even greater opportunity to assist in this project came his way in 1565 when Borgia was elected general of the Society of Jesus. His interest in the missions was by no means confined to those of his own Order; it is on record that in a conversation with Pope Pius V in 1568 he suggested the formation of a special congregation to direct all activities pertaining to the conversion of those outside the Catholic faith; for, as things were then, the missions were to a degree subject to the secular powers who were no longer able to provide for their needs. This suggestion contributed to the establishment in 1622 of the Congregation of the Propagation of the Faith (Congregatio de Propaganda Fide).[53] As far as his own Order was concerned, one of the most useful things he did was to admit Alessandro Valignano (1539–1606) into the Society, the second great Jesuit missionary in the Orient.[54]

This remarkable young man was the son of a close friend of the reigning pope, Paul IV. He gained a doctorate in law with distinction at the University of Padua, and then began what promised to be a brilliant career in the legal service of the Holy See when at the age of twenty-seven he abandoned it and entered the Society of Jesus. Because of his previous studies, he was not long in being ordained to the priesthood and after five years was appointed assistant to the master of novices at San Andrea in Quirinale in Rome. In 1571, in the absence of the novice master, it was his good fortune to welcome to the novitiate another promising student of law, Matteo Ricci, then in his twentieth year. It was a significant meeting, for their lives were to be linked in a way that would have a deciding effect on the China mission.

Before young Ricci had finished his noviceship, he heard that Valignano, now rector of the Jesuit college in Macerata (the home of Ricci's family whose members Valignano must have met), had asked to be sent to the missions of the East. He got his wish but was sent not as a simple missionary but as official Visitor to inspect the whole of the mission and give guidance for the future. Valignano left Lisbon in March 1574 and arrived in Goa on 6 September. Until October 1583 he remained Visitor of the vast area stretching from the Cape of Good Hope; then he was appointed provincial of India. He retained this post until 1587, when he was again made Visitor of Asia until 1595, and thereafter Visitor of the Far East until his death in 1606. After his arrival in Goa, he took care of pressing Indian business and then embarked for Japan, but had to spend ten months in Macao (October 1577 to July 1578) waiting for the favorable monsoons. This was one of three trips he was to make to Japan. The other two were in 1590–1592 and 1598–1603, and each time he stopped in Macao. His ten-month delay in Macao, however, was providential, for here he was apprised of the persistent but unsuccessful attempts to enter China and saw for himself the pessimism of a number of his Jesuit brethren who were of the opinion that further attempts would be hopeless.

Valignano was a man who looked at everything with an open mind. This was his first meeting with the world east of India, and he set himself to learn everything he could about China. Like Xavier, he heard about the Chinese and made the acquaintance of some of them through personal dealings. He wrote of them in his letters to Europe as "a great and worthy people"[55] and came to the conclusion that the failure to lead them to a knowledge and acceptance of the Christian faith was due to the manner of approach that had been adopted. He wrote to Borgia, the general of the Society who had sent him, that the penetration of China would have to be completely different from the methods employed up to that time in all the other countries where the Society had missions. He believed that the Chinese respect for learning and their willingness to listen to anything that was put to them in an intelligent way would open their minds to the acceptance of Christianity, but he was equally convinced that they would reject anything that came from a civilization that claimed superiority to their own. Hence, he gave instructions that all who were assigned to missionary work in China must, as a necessary preliminary, learn to read, write, and speak Chinese and make themselves acquainted with Chinese culture, manners, and customs.

Having little hope that any of those already in Macao were fitted to do this because of the contrary views they expressed, he wrote to the Jesuit provincial in Goa, Vicente Rodrigo, to send him a young Italian priest, Bernardino de Ferrariis, the then-rector in Cochin. Why he chose this man and why he was not available is not clear, but the provincial sent in his stead one he thought would be a good substitute, Michele Ruggieri.[56]

Realizing, as Xavier had before him, that men of learning were needed, Valignano not only requested that such men be sent from Europe, but also took great care of the intellectual training of the young Jesuits, reorganizing studies in St. Paul's College at Goa, founding a college at Funai (Ōita), Japan, and building (1593–1594) the imposing structure of the college at Macao. Thus, Valignano not only inherited and further developed Xavier's method of cultural accommodation but also institutionalized it and implemented it in Japan, as his 1581 booklet *Il cerimoniale per i missionari del Giappone* shows.[57] He provided for China by assigning the men who were to implement it there. Valignano had three advantages over Xavier: He benefited from Xavier's pioneering insights, he had more time (thirty-two years compared with only ten for Xavier), and for the last eleven years he had only East Asia to worry about.

When Ruggieri, who had been called to the China enterprise, arrived in Macao in July 1579, Valignano had departed for Japan but had left minute instructions on how Ruggieri should prepare himself for the arduous task. He began his work with great zeal, composing first of all a catechism in Chinese and later on, with the help of interpreters, translating into Latin one of the Confucian *Four Books* (*Ssu-shu*), the *Great Learning* (*Ta hsüeh*.[58] He got little encouragement from the other priests in Macao. They were few in number, their work was among the soldiers and traders, and they wanted him to share in that work, as they entertained little or no hope of receiving permission to labor in China. Ruggieri nevertheless continued assiduously with his studies but found the study of Chinese something very different from that of an Indian dialect. Acquiring a command of it was very difficult for him, though he became quite accomplished in his grasp of the formalities of Chinese friends. He had few illusions about his progress with the language and therefore wrote to Valignano in Japan suggesting that Ricci, who had come with him to India, should be sent to join him. Valignano agreed and dispatched word to India that Ricci and Pasio, who had come with Ruggieri from Italy, should join Ruggieri in Macao. From there, Pasio was then to go to Japan. It took long for letters to travel in those days, and Valignano himself actually arrived at Macao before the two priests.

In the meantime, Ruggieri, determined to get as far as he could in the new approach to things Chinese, asked to be allowed to go to Canton with some of the Portuguese traders who had leave to pay two visits there each year. It was only during his second year in Macao that he was first able to go. On this occasion, he was scrupulous in his attention to everything required by Chinese etiquette, to which the visiting merchants paid no heed. This was noticed at once by the Chinese officials, and, after their first meeting with him, they asked that he be present at all the audiences granted to foreigners.

This successfully broke the ice. On his second visit the following year, Ruggieri was shown marked respect and was recognized not as a trader but as a foreign scholar. He was, therefore, allowed to stand during the audiences, while the others had to kneel. On his third visit, some of the civil and military officials attended his Mass.

Such was the situation when Valignano returned to Macao from Japan in 1582. He had seen the results of the method of cultural accommodation which he advocated in Japan; now he would be able to put it into operation with equal hope of success in China. Since there was little likelihood of winning over the missionaries who were settled in the old ways, he made a change of superiors in Macao and established the framework of a mission for China. It was to be quite distinct from the normal work among soldiers and traders.

Within a short time, Valignano had every reason to believe that the new method would succeed. The Philippine Islands, after their discovery by Magellan in 1522, had come under the Spanish crown and so became a new mission field. In 1578, a number of Spanish Jesuits were sent to join the other missionaries who were already laboring there.[59] Some of them, anxious to participate in the conversion of China, especially after 1580 when Philip II became king of Portugal (1578), went to Canton via Fukien, thus avoiding Macao. This was looked upon by the officials of Kuangtung province as an unwarranted use of facilities given only to special persons who came from Macao. The viceroy of the two provinces, Kuangtung and Kuangsi, who had his seat in the official capital, Chao-ch'ing, ordered the bishop of Macao to come to Chao-ch'ing where he would be apprised of the government's policy in this matter. In late 1582, Valignano sent Ruggieri to represent the bishop, and the courtesy and suavity of the young priest completely won over the viceroy with the result that on his return to Macao, he received an official invitation from him to return to Chao-ch'ing and settle there permanently. Valignano agreed at once and appointed Pasio, who had just arrived from India, to accompany Ruggieri. They were well received by the viceroy

who gave them a pagoda for their use, and when they were
settled he paid them a visit of courtesy and presented Ruggieri
with a Chinese scroll.

Their stay was unhappily short. The viceroy fell out of favor
and when summoned to Peking to answer charges, he thought
it wiser to ask the two Jesuits to leave. Sadly they returned to
Macao.[60] Ruggieri then wrote to the officials in Canton requesting their indulgence. Within a very short time he was given
permission to return, and, in accord with his request, was also
granted a small piece of land on which to build a house and
church. By this time, Pasio had gone on to Japan; so Ruggieri
brought Ricci, who had arrived in Macao on 7 August 1582,
to Chao-ch'ing as his companion. That was a significant date;
for though it was Valignano who had decided on the new approach to mission work in China and Ruggieri who first practiced it, it was Ricci who brought it to complete success. From
this time on, he became the principal Jesuit on the Chinese
scene.[61]

Ricci was born in Macerata, Italy on 6 October 1552, the
year of Xavier's death. The eldest of eleven children, he was
enrolled in the local Jesuit college at the age of nine. In 1568,
he was sent to the University of Rome to study law. Three years
later he joined the Society of Jesus, entering the novitiate of
San Andrea in Quirinale. After taking his first vows, and after
a short period of teaching at the Jesuit college in Florence, he
returned to Rome and entered the Roman College. Here he
studied philosophy and mathematics under the famous Jesuit
Christopher Clavius (1537?–1612), the associate and friend of
Kepler and Galileo and a leader in the Gregorian reform of the
Julian calendar promulgated in 1582. Ricci also studied Euclidean
geometry, physics, the Ptolemaic system of astronomy, map making,
and mechanics. Most of the scientific treatises on these subjects
were later translated into Chinese by him or under his direction.
He had practical talent as well; from the making of sundials
and astrolabes, he passed to the construction of clocks and
other appliances which he fashioned with exceptional ingenuity.

When he passed to the study of theology, he likewise showed
special ability. The Jesuit professor Robert Bellarmine (1542–
1621), today a Doctor of the Church, was then the great con-

troversialist of his day and "the hammer of heretics." Ricci attended his Course on Controversies and from it learned that clear exposition of doctrine which he put to such practical use in later years. Everyone predicted a great professorial career for the young student; but as his Renaissance training progressed, he was drawn to the foreign missions in the newly discovered world, the opening up of which had been one of the accomplishments of the Renaissance. In 1577, he was accepted for the Jesuit mission in India under the Portuguese *Padroado*. Going to Portugal, he prepared himself by continuing his study of theology at the University of Coimbra, and in March 1578 sailed from Lisbon. Except for a brief period at Cochin, he taught for the next four years at the Jesuit St. Paul's College in Goa, where he was ordained to the priesthood in July 1580. It was from here Valignano called him to Macao, where he arrived on 7 August 1582, a summons made, as noted earlier, at the suggestion of Ruggieri, who had been called to Macao in 1579 for the same China enterprise.

In the meantime, between 1580 and 1582, Ruggieri had made four trips to Canton and one directly to Chao-ch'ing, whither he was accompanied in December 1582 by Pasio. Ricci was still weak after a rough passage from India;[62] he would join them later.[63] However, Pasio and Ruggieri could not remain in Chao-ch'ing and had to return to Macao. However, some months later, on 10 September 1583, Ruggieri and Ricci succeeded in establishing themselves at Chao-ch'ing. Ricci never left China. In 1588, Valignano decided to send Ruggieri to Rome to explain the situation and to petition the pope to send an embassy to the emperor of China. The death of four popes within a year-and-a-half prevented consideration of an official mission, and by the end of that time the opportune moment had passed. In Europe, Ruggieri's health failed, and he never returned to China.

Ricci, having been left alone in Chao-ch'ing, remained there until 1589. In that year, the viceroy of the "two Kuangs" (Kuangtung and Kuangsi) died, and a new one was appointed. Three viceroys had sanctioned Ricci's stay, but this one took steps to have him expelled. By cleverness of argument, in which Ricci was now experienced from his dealing with officials, he got the decree changed on condition that he reside in another city. So he moved to Shao-chou, further north in Kuangtung province. He remained there until 1595, when one of his high-ranking friends, a member of the Imperial Board of War, was summoned to Peking in connection with the Japanese invasion of China; he invited Ricci to accompany him, at least part of the way. This was the opportunity he had been waiting for: to penetrate the heart of China. The official with whom he traveled was able to bring him as far as Nanking, where he hoped to settle for a time; but in the war atmosphere that prevailed, this was impossible, as Nanking was the second city of the empire. So after a few weeks he went back south to the capital of Kiangsi province, Nanchang, a city of many scholars. Here he stayed until June 1598, when he set out for Peking, the capital of the empire. Unable to establish himself there, he returned to Nanking until 19 May 1600, when he again set out for Peking — this time with success. He reached Peking on 24 January 1601 never to leave it again, dying there on 11 May 1610.

This is briefly the story of this extraordinary man. By the time Ricci died, missionaries of the Society of Jesus were all over the world, and different methods of evangelization were used in different countries appropriate to their culture and civilization, but the approach in China differed from others. The very old, deeply rooted, and sophisticated culture set China apart from other countries, and this honorable culture would have to be understood before the Christian faith could be grafted onto it.

It now remains to look at the method Ricci employed to accomplish this. Ricci's method of cultural accommodation was not a rigid policy but a mental attitude developed on a trial-and-error basis. He used ideas and practices inherited from his predecessors, but he used them selectively. Those that proved useful he retained; the others he modified or discarded. One of the most fundamental conceptions he inherited was that the Chinese were a very intelligent and reasonable people and placed high priority on moral principles and ethical behavior. They were also impressed by science.

The earliest Portuguese in China, as well as the first missionaries, including Xavier and Valignano, were convinced that if the emperor of China could be induced to grant them a hearing they would be able to persuade him to allow the Portuguese to trade with China and even to allow the propagation of the Christian faith among his subjects. This is why one of the first things the missionaries did was to translate the catechism. All that was necessary, in their opinion, was to get this translated work to the emperor or, failing that, to the officials who would bring it to the emperor's attention. The rest would follow. The problem as they saw it was to get to the emperor.

From their earliest contacts with the Chinese, the Portuguese also realized that one of the best means to this end was the sending of an embassy by the king of Portugal or the viceroy of India to the Chinese emperor. This could be either a diplomatic mission like the one of Tomé Pires in 1520, a papal mission like the one that Ruggieri, with Valignano's approval, was to urge the pope to send to China, or a trade mission like Diogo Pereira's which Xavier had promoted.[64] Missionaries would accompany these embassies and, seizing the opportunity, explain Christianity to the emperor. As difficulties and obstacles delayed the sending of embassies, some went so far as to advocate military action against China, a measure justified, in their opinions, by the unreasonable resistance of the Chinese to the Gospel. Mention of military action is found[65] not only in the very earliest Portuguese reports but also in the Spanish reports of the 1580s, when the number of Spanish missionaries entering China from the Philippines increased after the accession of Philip II to the Portuguese throne.

Ricci agreed with the basic assessment that the Chinese were an intelligent people guided by ethical principles and interested in science. But his greater perception and better understanding led him to draw quite different conclusions from those of his predecessors. He was the first to learn the language well enough not to have to rely on interpreters or the reports of former Portuguese prisoners. During his nine-year stay in Peking, he never once laid eyes on the emperor; but even before arriving at that city in 1601, he had already gained a profound insight into the sociopolitical structure of the Confucian state and had come to realize that the emperor's absolute power was theoretical, limited, and, in the cases of weak emperors, even usurped by officials, eunuchs, or both. He also came to understand the role of the gentry-literati official class. On the basis of all this, he gave up the idea of the efficacy of an embassy; at least he did not advocate it or place as high a priority on it as did Valignano and Ruggieri. As for the idea of military action against the Chinese, he ignored it completely; it is not even mentioned in his writings. He had seen the futility of the Korean invasion by Toyotomi Hideyoshi (1536–1598) in 1592.

When Ricci and Ruggieri first entered China together in 1583, they were dressed as Buddhist bonzes, a style of dress recommended by their predecessors, Xavier and Valignano; but when they realized the low esteem in which Buddhism was held by the literati and saw the lifestyle and ignorance of some of the Buddhist monks, they adopted, at the urging of some of their literati friends, the attire and lifestyle of the literati. This same advice had been given to Ruggieri earlier by the viceroy of Kuangtung and Kuangsi.[66] Besides, Ricci's interests were basically with the literati class, and it was to them he soon turned his attention.

Ricci's predecessors, Xavier, Valignano, and Ruggieri, having learned about the Chinese respect and admiration for science and technology, advocated using these as means or, as some say, as "bait," to attract the Chinese. Similarly, having come to know about the Confucian esteem for ethical behavior which seemed to harmonize with Christian morality, they thought they had found another means to attract the Chinese to Catholic teachings and dogmas. Ricci, with a deeper insight and a better understanding, realized that the Chinese world view was a global one, an ideology in which science, technology, ethics, and philosophical teachings formed an organic whole. Thus, he saw the need for presenting Christianity in a similar way, as an organic and global world view which his acquaintances, friends, and Chinese converts were to call Western Learning (*Hsi-hsüeh*) or Learning from Heaven (*T'ien-hsüeh*).[67] The original title of Ricci's magnum opus, xylographed for the first time in 1603, was *True Meaning of the Learning from Heaven* (*T'ien-hsüeh shih-i*) even though it became known under the more familiar title *True Meaning of the Lord of Heaven* (*T'ien-chu shih-i*).[68]

Ricci's attitude is best illustrated by his request to the viceroy of the two Kuang provinces in 1583 to be allowed to remain in Chao-ch'ing. In his petition, he said that having been attracted by the great fame of the government of China, he had come from a faraway country only to serve God (the Lord of Heaven, *T'ien-chu*, a term used by Ricci since 1583) in a small church and house he wanted to acquire. This modest request was granted after Wang P'an, the magistrate, had seen Ricci's map of the world. Ricci had not concealed his true purpose; he had clearly stated it, yet his request was granted because of the map. He never lost sight of the ultimate goal: the preaching of the Gospel and the conversion of China.[69]

This conversion was to proceed at the top and the bottom simultaneously, but it was to be effected primarily from the top down. Missionaries would work among the people, but some missionaries would serve the ruling class to maintain their good will toward Christianity. Ricci would, of course, concentrate his attention upon the emperor and the literati. Ricci fully recognized that things other than religious teachings would be the attraction at the top. Later on, he himself honestly acknowledged that among the six reasons for his renown, his religious teachings came last. They were outranked first by the fact that he as a foreigner had learned to speak, read, and write Chinese; second, by his fantastic memory and by the fact that he knew the *Four Books* by heart; third, by his knowledge of mathematics and other sciences; fourth, by the curious objects he had brought as presents; and fifth, by his alleged knowledge and experience in alchemy.[70] Among the ordinary people it was, of course, quite different.

To accomplish the conversion of China, a different method, a different approach, and different priorities were needed. To have Christianity or Learning from Heaven accepted both among the higher-ups and among the people, it had to become an integral part of Chinese culture and be taken off the list of foreign and pernicious doctrines. This "indigenization" was more important to Ricci than numbers. He knew this would take time. He was patient.

He also realized that "indigenization" among the higher-ups would require the written word: books. Also, the forum to accomplish "indigenization" at the top would not be the church or the house of worship but the academies (*shu-yüan*), highly popular during the Ming dynasty.[71] Here was where one had to get a hearing for Western Learning and all its facets and where ideas, even unorthodox ideas, could be exchanged. To the literati, before proceeding to the dogmas and the mysteries of the faith, those elements of the faith were to be explained first that could be proven by reason. This is the thrust of Ricci's *True Meaning of the Lord of Heaven.* Among the people, for whom the church would remain the place of worship, this gradation did not have to be as pronounced. This, however, does not mean that Ricci's approach was vitiated by duplicity. It only meant a difference in emphasis, never the suppression or elimination of vital elements of the faith.

"Indigenization" was to be accomplished with a four-faceted method: lifestyle, terminology (with underlying ideas and conceptions), ethics, and rites and customs inspired by the ideology. For a successful "indigenization," all four were equally important yet not equally difficult to implement. The least controversial was the first and the most controversial the fourth. Yet, the most crucial and difficult was the second. Let us look briefly at these methods of cultural accommodation.

Lifestyle. After his entry into China, Ricci became a Chinese with the Chinese.[72] He adopted Chinese manners, diet, sleep patterns, and clothing, down to cuffs, belt, sash, hat, and colors. He gave up grape wine for rice wine, no small matter for an Italian. When he died, one of the most important of his friends addressed a memorial to the emperor requesting that in view of the great merit of Li Ma-tou (Ricci's Chinese name), the Westerner who had become Chinese, a special place of burial should be designated to receive his remains.

Terminology and ideas. The principal problem Ricci faced was to translate Western words into Chinese. It was more than a simple matter of terminology. What was of utmost importance was to convey to the Chinese the ideas behind the words — e.g., that the world was created by a deliberate act of God (the Lord of Heaven). Ricci was convinced that the idea of the true God was not alien to the Chinese and that they had been recipients of divine revelation.[73] The more Ricci penetrated the intellectual life of China, the more he was astounded at finding in the oldest canonical books, the basis of Chinese learning, such a pure idea of God. In the classical writings, there simply was not the slightest trace of polytheism, nor did the Chinese have a pantheon as did the Greeks, Romans, Hindus, and Mahayana Buddhists. They recognized a Supreme Being as a personal being. The offering of sacrifices to this Supreme Being was reserved for the emperor, and ordinary citizens could not presume to arrogate this privilege for themselves. It is true that besides this Supreme Being the emperor offered sacrifices to the spirits of the mountains, rivers, and famous men and that the people were allowed and even urged to offer sacrifices to the tutelary spirits of their villages and individual families to their ancestors. But all these spirits were subordinated to the Supreme Being, so that the original religion of China before the advent of Taoism and Buddhism was monotheism. For this reason, Ricci and his successors, when speaking of the true God or Lord of Heaven (*T'ien-chu*), used the terms by which the Chinese Classics designated heaven (*t'ien*) and the Supreme Being, Supreme Lord, or Lord on High (*Shang-ti*). This was not too dissimilar from what the Apostles had done in not hesitating to use the Greek word *theos* to designate the true God of the Old Testament.

The Confucians of Ricci's day had lost the true idea of God because they equated the Lord on High and heaven with a concept of Sung Neo-Confucian creation, the Supreme Ultimate (*T'ai-chi*), a kind of impersonal, mechanical prime mover functioning by way of "act" and "potency" (*li* and *ch'i*). These concepts were created by the T'ang and Sung Neo-Confucians under the influence of Buddhism and Taoism in an attempt to provide Confucianism with a metaphysical superstructure. Confucianism, the official ideology of the Chinese state beginning with the Han dynasty (206 B.C.–A.D. 220), had lost credibility with the fall of the Han. As a result, Taoism and Buddhism rose to prominence during the ensuing period of disunion (220–618) before the rise of the T'ang (618–906) and Sung (960–1280) dynasties. To rehabilitate Confucianism and make it competitive with Buddhism and Taoism, which had their metaphysics, Confucianism had to acquire one. But in the process, as Ricci observed, they also corrupted Confucianism which evolved into, if not an atheistic and materialistic ideology, at least an agnostic one. Confucianism in its original form was basically a socioethical system. By equating his Lord of Heaven with the Lord on High of the Classics, Ricci joined battle with the Neo-Confucians of his day, the Lord of Heaven being a personal Supreme Being while the Supreme Ultimate was the immanent universal order in things.[74]

This very fundamental idea of a creator God also had many concomitant concepts, such as the dichotomy of soul and body, retribution, and so forth,[75] which had wide-ranging repercussions and created conflicts with prevalent Neo-Confucian views. But not only did this concept of a creator God provoke conflicts with Neo-Confucian ideas, it also raised some very thorny questions as far as traditional Confucianism was concerned. If the Lord of Heaven created the world and everything in it, he must also have created the Chinese race. How? This was not only a difficult question but a delicate and dangerous one, given the sensitivity and feeling of superiority of the Chinese. Then the enormity of the problem emerges when the explanations of the dogmas and the mysteries of the Catholic faith are added to this.

Ethics. While Ricci and his successors argued against and tried to discredit the metaphysical-cosmological world view of Neo-Confucianism, they retained the socioethical teachings of Confucius as not only not contrary to Christian morality but as complementing it. In his Treatise on Friendship (Chiao-yu lun), Ricci equated the Christian concept of love with the Confucian concept of humaneness (jen). He said that in true friendship the other person should be treated "like [one treats] oneself."[76] And he stretched the concept of humaneness even further when he said that the meaning of humaneness can perhaps be exhausted in two phrases: to love God above all things and to love men as one loves oneself. If one would do this, one would possess all virtues. God loves all men equally; and if one really loves God, is it possible then not to love all men? Confucius himself had said that a man of humaneness loves all others. "Not loving others, how could [one's] sincerity towards God be tested?"[77] Thus, Ricci's contention is obvious. If and when the Chinese regained the original notion of God, they would be transformed into truly virtuous men. Thus it is clear what he meant by complementing Confucianism with Christian morality. Instead of challenging the Confucian ethic of graded love (according to the Five Relationships), Ricci and his successors maintained that Christianity would perfect Confucianism.[78] China would then be able to create again a completely ethical and harmonious society under "original Confucianism," as it existed in ancient times.

Ricci offered the Confucians a method of testing the validity of his foreign teaching. By presenting Christianity as morally persuasive as Confucianism, if not more so, he confucianized Christianity or christianized Confucianism. Christianity was to be judged and evaluated by Confucian standards if it was to be accepted. It had to be morally effective. Hsü Kuang-ch'i (1562–1633), the best-known convert during the Ming dynasty, maintained that Christianity could "supplement Confucianism and displace Buddhism."[79] Hsü went so far as to state that in the West there were no terms for revolt and anarchy and that the Christian West was living in harmony under the guidance of God.[80] This exaggerated portrait of Europe in perpetual peace was not a case of the Jesuits' lying to their converts but of Hsü's insistence on judging Christian values in terms of their efficaciousness as a guiding force for moral reform, derived from God's revelation. Hsü and others considered Ricci and the early Jesuits true followers of the sages because their way (*tao*) was that of sincerity (*ch'eng*).

They were men of virtue (*te*) endeavoring to serve society. Many other Chinese were surprised that these barbarians lived by such high ethical standards, and in the end it was the unethical behavior of the later missionaries that hurt the mission more than anything else. Not all of them followed Ricci's exemplary life. This was probably his greatest miscalculation.

Rites. The core of the Chinese ethical system was, and to a certain degree still is, devotion and obedience toward parents and all legitimate authority. Part and parcel of these filial duties was also the veneration of ancestors. Their names were inscribed on wooden tablets, which were called the seat of the deceased souls, and before these they kowtowed (prostrated themselves, knocking the fronts of their heads against the

ground), lit candles, burned incense, offered food, and burned
paper money. These actions were supposed to be of service to
the deceased in another world. The officials and the literati
had to perform similar rituals to honor Confucius. To forbid
these rites would have made the conversion of China impossible
from the outset. The injunction of St. Paul to parents to care
for their children, and not the other way around, could not
even be mentioned in front of the Chinese without provoking
such a storm of indignation that it would be well nigh impossible for the missionary to say anything further.

Here Ricci found himself confronted by a seemingly insurmountable obstacle; if he forbade these rites, all he could hope
for was a few conversions. This problem had to be resolved.
It goes without saying that under no circumstances would it
be licit for Christians to believe that the tablets were the seat
of the deceased souls or that burned paper money could help
the dead in the hereafter. But then not all customs were of
this nature. Moreover, the Chinese literati in fact declared that
the prostrations to honor Confucius were only to pay him homage as teacher and exemplar of men and did not imply that
he was being prayed to for riches, talents, or honors. In other
worlds, the prostrations in front of Confucius were only signs
of courtesy and gratitude and not a religious rite. Similarly, it
seemed to Ricci and his followers that permission could be
granted to prostrate before the coffin of a deceased person or
before the tablet of Confucius on the occasion of the elevation
of a person to a higher official rank. Certainly among the common people there were those who, in return for this kind of
veneration, expected riches, progeny, and other favors. But in
the Chinese Classics, there are passages which show that the
original meaning of these rites was not that; therefore, in their
pristine form and meaning, these ceremonies could be practiced. Hence, one could consider the food offered to the dead —
food later on solemnly consumed by all the participants — a
simple way of making one feel in the company of the deceased
ancestors. This is especially confirmed by the fact that the word
for these offerings does not necessarily mean the same as our
word "to sacrifice."[81]

If it was necessary to be on guard about superstitions in connection with these rites, one also had to be careful about the explanation given them by the Neo-Confucian literati who, as followers of the teachings of Chu Hsi (1130–1200), were materialists. According to them, the soul of Confucius had long ago withered into nothingness and all that remained of him were the syllables of his name and his memory; and naturally the same was true about one's ancestors. Given this interpretation, it is evident that the ancestors could neither be invoked nor could anything be expected from them. Chu Hsi's interpretation of the Confucian Classics had been declared official by imperial edict as late as 1552; but one must not forget that although this atheism or agnosticism was the official doctrine, it was not necessarily the conviction of the individual literati. Nor did the masses share the ideas of the literati. Their veneration of the ancestors and the offerings made to them were religious acts. According to Ricci and his followers, both of these errors had to be rectified by a return to the original meaning in the Classics.

At first, Ricci had prohibited these rites, but when he saw that the kowtow was performed even to living beings, like the emperor and one's parents, he permitted the veneration of ancestors and Confucius. But even this initial hesitation had created a bad impression, and during the persecution of 1616, this was one of the gravest accusations brought against the missionaries.[82] Somewhat later, it appears the Jesuits considered the rites as neutral and the debate and conflict concerning them really developed only after the arrival of the mendicants.

Ricci and his successors realized that by making these concessions they were on dangerous ground; this can be seen from the fact that they intended to tolerate these rites only temporarily, even the most innocent ones. Ricci's directives of 1603 (a pioneer model of cultural accommodation), which initiated the Jesuit missiology of the rites, clearly testify to this fact. In other words, it was Ricci's intention to foster a cultural blending from the inside (Chinese rites) as a transition process to a permanent cultural blending from the outside (Western rites). His successors and the K'ang-hsi emperor, in his declaration of 1700, understood Ricci's intention in this manner.[83] This is called the "Jesuit thesis": the attitude of Ricci and his successors regarding the problem of certain immemorial non-Christian habits of thought and action that externally gave the appearance of illicit superstition. It has been defined by the French Jesuit Sinologist, Antoine de Beauvollier (1657–1708), in this terse formula: "There is danger in admitting the rites but a greater danger in suppressing them."[84]

Moreover, the Jesuits were content to give the Riccian method of cultural accommodation the theological note of "probability" (*probabile, immo valde probabile*). Ricci and his successors did not deny that the opposite opinion was "safer" (*tutior*), and that is why they, unlike their more militant adversaries, did not try to impose their views on those missionaries whose consciences were more at ease with the stricter religious ideas they had been taught. Let us not forget, however, that without the Jesuit method their adversaries would never have been able to set foot on Chinese soil. Thus, one may say that the Jesuit thesis was a balanced halfway dialectic based upon reasonable premises that were admissible by Catholic moral principles and made imperative in order to win a hearing for the Gospel. Although in the course of the century some few dissenters would sporadically turn up in Jesuit ranks and others would amplify the evidence beyond measure (the "certitudinalists"), the vast majority of Jesuit Sinologists judged Ricci's method of cultural accommodation as a "probability." The only one in disagreement with the entire method was Claude de Visdelou (1656–1738).[85]

Between the death of Ricci (1610) and the coming of the mendicants (1632), a lively debate was carried on among the Jesuits concerning just about every aspect of his method of cultural accommodation. The liveliest discussion revolved around Christian terminology and the meaning of words, particularly the terms used for God. In 1600, Valignano had approved Ricci's terminology. The first reservations about its use came from the Jesuits in Japan. There the problem arose at the very beginning of the mission. As indicated earlier, Xavier for a time used *Dainichi* (a pantheistic Shingon Buddhist term) for God. Other terms used were *jodo* (paradise), *jigoku* (hell), *tennin* (angel), and so forth. Xavier soon realized his mistake and proscribed further use of such terms, and the Jesuits in Japan for the next fifty years discussed the problem and decided to employ traditional Latin or Portuguese terminology to express Christian concepts.[86] After the unfortunate *Dainichi* incident, this Latin-Portuguese approach was safer, and in Japan at that time fairly easy to effect because the country was in the throes of internecine wars, creating an open society willing to accept Christianity in its European form, together with firearms and commerce.

China, however, was a closed society, an isolated country unwilling to open her doors until Ricci put his method of cultural accommodation into effect. Thus, it becomes understandable that, when he selected his terminology and his writings reached Japan, the Jesuits there were disturbed, not realizing that the problem in China was not the same as in Japan. They transmitted their apprehensions to Jesuit East Asian headquarters in Macao, and from there they became known to the Jesuits in China. Niccolò Longobardi (1565–1655), successor to Ricci as Jesuit superior of the China mission, agreed with the Jesuits in Japan and conducted an inquiry among the literati with regard to the validity of the Riccian terminology and meaning, and published a book containing his conclusions.[87] Another Jesuit in disagreement with Ricci was his colleague, Sebastiano de Ursis (1575–1620), although others, such as Giulio Aleni (1582–1649), Álvaro de Semedo (1586–1658), and Nicolas Trigault (1577–1628), supported Ricci. This debate lasted from 1610 to 1633. The term for God on which they all finally settled, because it could be used without damage to either orthodoxy or clarity, was Lord of Heaven (*T'ien-chu*), the term used by Ricci since 1583 and employed by Chinese Catholics ever since. This compromise, however, did not mean that Lord on High (*Shang-ti*) or heaven (*t'ien*) were unacceptable.

Noteworthy is the fact that Longobardi's book was banned between 1635 and 1641 by the Jesuit vice-provincial, Francesco Furtado (1589–1653), but it is preserved in the *Tratados históricos* of Domingo Fernández de Navarrete, O.P. (1618–1686), an opponent of the rites.[88] Longobardi's conclusions were not the same as Ricci's, but he accepted the Jesuit policy and method in the end — and not out of duress. It was an honest disagreement that was finally resolved. It was not too different from the case of Alfonso Vagnoni, S.J. (1568–1640), director of the mission establishment in Nanking, who, after Ricci's death, departed from his insistence on the indirect apostolate. Influenced probably by those outside China who could not be persuaded that mathematics and astronomy were apt means of propagating the faith, he had the first public church in China opened in the city and conducted the liturgical services with more display than was thought wise. This, and critical remarks about Buddhist monks which were attributed to him, created hostility that soon reached dangerous proportions. A new vice-president of the Board of Rites opened a campaign which resulted in 1617 in a proclamation by the board prohibiting the teaching and practice of the Christian religion in China.[89] The decree was strictly enforced in Nanking. Vagnoni and Semedo, the only Jesuits there at the time, were arrested; Vagnoni was condemned to the bastinado, and he and Semedo were brought to Canton in a cage and expelled from the country. In his brief exile, Vagnoni applied himself, among other things, to a further study of the Classics and to an improvement in his literary style. He succeeded in writing Chinese skillfully, and his works on Catholic doctrine were among the most effective of all those written by the early Jesuits.

There were also other Jesuits who, like Vagnoni, doubted that mathematics, astronomy, and the other sciences were fit means for propagating the faith and who objected to Ricci's Western Learning approach. For example, Valentim Carvalho (1559–1630), provincial of Japan, and André Palmeiro (1569–1635), Visitor to Japan and China, both forbade it for a time until the misunderstanding was cleared up.[90]

With the arrival of the mendicant friars in 1632, new elements enter the picture. The friars focused their attention on two other facets of cultural accommodation: lifestyle and rites. In the first case, they criticized the Jesuits' lifestyle, Christian practices, and missionary methodology, such as failure to promulgate the laws and commandments of the Church, the method of administering the sacraments, alleged failure to preach Christ crucified (the Jesuits emphasized his glorification), adoption of Chinese dress, refusal to say that Confucius was in hell (provable by a syllogism, as Friar Domingo Fernández de Navarrette tried to show). In the second case, the friars criticized certain rites observed by the Chinese in paying honor to their recently deceased family members, to their ancestors, and to Confucius, as well as to ancestral tablets and tablets on which the name of Confucius was inscribed. In due time, it was the question of the rites that became the focus of attention. Hence the term Chinese Rites (with a capital R).

But why were the friars so late in coming? Because on 28 January 1585, just two years after Ricci had successfully penetrated China, Pope Gregory XIII in his Brief *Ex Pastorali Officio* prohibited other religious Orders from entering China, so as to avoid disagreements and to permit the Jesuits to try out their method of cultural accommodation.[91] This decree, however, was short-lived, for on 15 November 1586, Pope Sixtus V rescinded it and gave the Franciscans permission to go to China.[92] This rescission was confirmed by Pope Clement VIII (12 December 1600), by Pope Paul V (1611), and by Pope Urban VIII.[93] Thus, the friars finally entered China in 1632. Antonio de Santa María Caballero, O.F.M. and Juan Bautista de Morales, O.P. arrived the following year. This marks the beginning of the Rites Controversy between the friars and the Jesuits based on their different methods of evangelization.

While the Rites Controversy is beyond the scope of this paper, let it be said in conclusion that in spite of the alterations it forced the Jesuits to make in Ricci's method of cultural accommodation, especially with regard to his cautious and gradual way of proceeding, enough of the essential elements remained to enable it to succeed for a brief period. In 1692, Christianity was finally taken off the list of pernicious doctrines and established as an indigenous religion, much like Buddhism (of Indian origin), which had become indigenized centuries earlier. This establishment of Christianity was due to the K'ang-hsi emperor's "Edict of Toleration"[94] (1692) and the "A Declaration concerning the meaning of the Chinese Rites or customs according to which the Society of Jesus up till now has permitted them, offered to the K'ang-hsi emperor on 30 November of the year of the Lord 1700."[95]

Originally, Ricci had hoped to meet the Wan-li emperor (r. 1573–1620) in person as soon as he reached Peking and to obtain from him direct permission to preach the Gospel in

China. But, by the time he was granted leave to reside there, he realized this was quite unnecessary, for permission to take up residence in Peking carried tacit approval for him and his companions to continue their way of life and to pursue their intellectual apostolate. The presupposition was that there would be no condemnation by the Jesuits of cherished Chinese beliefs or customs. Rather, every effort would be made to prepare the way, with sympathy and understanding, for the operation of divine grace in the hearts of those they hoped to convert. As already noted, the emphasis was to be entirely on quality of conversion, not on pride in numbers. This is what Ricci wrote to Macao at the time he was urged to seek explicit authorization from the emperor. He said, later on, that when the number of Catholics increased among the educated people, it would be possible to get permission for the practice of religion since there was no law against it in China; but until that took place, they should wait to see if such permission would be necessary. It became necessary some hundred years later during the last decade of the seventeenth century at the height of the Rites Controversy. Or so his successors felt and obtained the "Edict of Toleration" and the K'ang-hsi "Declaration."

China had officially accepted Ricci's method of cultural accommodation, but it was Europe that rejected it in the eighteenth century.[96] And it was the behavior of the Europeans during the Rites Controversy that exposed the greatest internal ideological weakness of Ricci's method of cultural accommodation, namely, the ineffectiveness of its ethical and moral system. He had painted a sanguine picture of the Christian moral code as something that could complement Confucianism. He was an optimist who believed that the rationality of human nature was able to transcend and overcome the irrationality of the self-imposed limitations of racial, national, and language prejudices. He followed the injunction of Jesus Christ: "Go, then, to all peoples everywhere and make them my disciples: baptize them in the name of the Father, the Son, and the Holy Spirit and teach them to obey everything I have commanded you, and I will be with you always, to the end of the age."[97] Is it now time for us to try Ricci's method of cultural accommodation again, in spite of its difficulties and shortcomings, and heed the warning of the Jesuit Pierre Teilhard de Chardin: "The age of nations is past. It remains for us now, if we do not wish to perish, to set aside the ancient prejudices and to build the Earth"?[98]

NOTES

1. Joseph Sebes, S.J., *The Jesuits and the Sino-Russian Treaty of Nerchinsk (1689): The Diary of Thomas Pereira, S.J.* (Rome, 1961), 83–86; two works by C. Raymond Beazley, *Prince Henry the Navigator: The Hero of Portugal and of Modern Discovery, 1394–1460 A.D.* (New York, 1895) and *The Dawn of Modern Geography*, 3 vols. (London, 1897–1906); three works by Joaquim Bensaude, *Lacunes et surprises de l'histoire des découvertes maritimes, 1ᵉ partie* (Coimbra, 1930), *A cruzada do infante d. Henrique* (Lisbon, 1942), and *Les Légendes allemandes sur l'histoire des découvertes maritimes portugaises: réponse a M. Hermann Wagner*, 2 vols. (Geneva, 1917–1920). See also Armando Cortesão, ed. and trans., *The Suma Oriental of Tomé Pires and the Book of Francisco Rodrigues*, 2 vols., (London, 1944); Adelhelm Jann, O.F.M. Cap., *Die katholischen Missionen in Indien, China und Japan. Ihre Organisation und das portugiesische Patronat vom 15. bis ins 18. Jahrhundert* (Paderborn, 1915); António da Silva Rego, *Ó Padroado Português do Oriente; esbôço histórico* (Lisbon, 1940).

2. Sebes, *Jesuits and Sino-Russian Treaty*, 84.

3. Ibid., 85.

4. Jacques Gernet, *A History of Chinese Civilization*, trans. J. R. Foster (Cambridge, England, 1985), 448–49.

5. Sebes, *Jesuits and Sino-Russian Treaty*, 85–86. Other European nations used (in various ways) their own euphemistic slogans with reference to territorial expansion. The Spaniards had "Gold, Glory, and the Gospel"; later there were "La Mission Civilisatrice" for the French and "Voyevat ili Torgovat" (War or Trade) for the Russians; "The White Man's Burden" originated with the British; "Manifest Destiny" was popular among the Americans; and in the twentieth century, Nazi Germany created "Lebensraum."

6. Sebes, *Jesuits and Sino-Russian Treaty*, 85–86.

7. Ibid., 90–91.

8. Sebes, *Jesuits and Sino-Russian Treaty*, 85–86. Jan J. L. Duyvendak, *China's Discovery of Africa* (London, 1949).

9. Sebes, *Jesuits and Sino-Russian Treaty*, 86.

10. Preface I for Sundays, *Roman Missal*, 1 Peter 2:9, elaborating from Exodus 19:6.

11. Chang Wei-hua, *Ming-shih Fo-lang-chi, Lu-sung, Ho-lan, I-ta-li-ya*

ssu-chüan chu-shih (A commentary on the four chapters on Portugal, Spain, Holland, and Italy in the history of the Ming dynasty), *Yenching Journal of Chinese Studies*, Monograph Series no. 7 (Peking, 1934), 139.

12. John D. Young, *East-West Synthesis: Matteo Ricci and Confucianism* (Hong Kong, 1980), 1–2.

13. António da Silva Rego, *Curso de missiologia* (Lisbon, 1956), 361.

14. Georg Schurhammer, S.J. and Josef Wicki, S.J., eds., *Epistolae S. Francisci Xaverii Aliaque Ejus Scripta*, nova editio, 2 vols. (Rome, 1944–1945), 2:61. See also Georg Schurhammer, S.J., *Francis Xavier, His Life, His Times*, trans. M. Joseph Costelloe, S.J., 4 vols. (Rome, 1973–1982).

15. Schurhammer and Wicki, *Epistolae*, 2:373; Henry J. Coleridge, S.J., *The Life and Letters of St. Francis Xavier, 2 vols.* (London, 1912), 2:241–42.

16. Michael Cooper, S.J., *Rodrigues the Interpreter. An Early Jesuit In Japan and China* (New York, 1974), 284–86.

17. Young, *East-West Synthesis*, 4–5.

18. Coleridge, *Life and Letters of Xavier*, 2:369.

19. Ibid., 2:300–301.

20. Ibid., 2:338.

21. Schurhammer and Wicki, *Epistolae*, 2:373; Young, *East-West Synthesis*, 5–6.

22. Ludwig von Pastor, *Geschichte der Päpste seit dem Ausgang des Mittelalters*, 16 vols. (Freiburg im Breisgau, 1891–1933), 15:284–85.

23. Schurhammer and Wicki, *Epistolae*, 2:373; Josef Wicki, S.J., ed., *Documenta Indica*, 17 vols. (Rome, 1948–), 13:5–13; Young, *East-West Synthesis*, 6–7.

24. Pastor, *Geschichte der Päpste*, 15:284–85.

25. Sebes, *Jesuits and Sino-Russian Treaty*, 39–42; Wicki, *Documenta Indica*, 4:106–8, 12:950–69. For the Ming dynasty, see Albert Chan, *The Glory and Fall of the Ming Dynasty* (Norman, 1982).

26. Schurhammer and Wicki, *Epistolae*, 2:483–88, 497–501, 513–15.

27. Pasquale M. D'Elia, S.J., ed., *Fonti Ricciane: documenti originali concernenti Matteo Ricci e la storia delle prime relazioni tra l'Europa e la Cina 1579–1615*, 3 vols. (Rome, 1942–1949), 1:139–40; Albert Herrmann, *Historical and Commercial Atlas of China* (Cambridge, 1935), 56, C3; Paul Pelliot, "Un Ouvrage sur les premiers temps de Macao," *T'oung Pao*, 31 (1934–1935):71 n. 2; Chang Wei-hua, *Chushih*, 138.

28. *Chronicon Societatis Jesu*, in Johannes Alphonsus de Polanco, S.J., *Vita Ignatii Loiolae et Rerum Societatis Jesu Historia*, 6 vols. (Rome, 1894–1898), 4 (anno 1554):652, 5 (anno 1555):715–23.

29. Emmanuel da Costa, S.J., *Rerum a Societate Jesu in Oriente*

gestarum ad annum usque a Deipara Virgine MDLXVIII, commentarius, trans. Giovanni Maffei, S.J. (Dillingen, 1571), fols. 107v–114v; Melchior Nunes Barreto in Macao, 23 November 1555 to brethren in India, Portugal, and Rome in *Diversi avvisi particolari dall'Indie di Portogallo ricevuti dall'anno 1551 fino al 1558* (Venice, 1558), fol. 271v. Also two letters from Nunes Barreto in Cochin to the general of the Society of Jesus: (1) 8 January 1558 in Archivum Romanum Societatis Iesu (hereafter cited as ARSI), Japonica et Sinica (hereafter cited as Jap.-Sin.), 4: fols. 82–89; (2) 13 January 1558, ARSI, Jap.-Sin., 4:fols. 90–94.

30. C. R. Boxer, trans and ed., *South China in the Sixteenth Century. Being the Narratives of Galeote Pereira, Fr. Gaspar da Cruz, O.P., Fr. Martín de Rada, O.E.S.A., 1550–1575* (London, 1953), lix, 122. Also *Chronicon* (1555) in Polanco, *Vita Ignatii Loiolae*, 5:723.

31. Gago to the fathers and brothers in Coimbra, 10 December 1562, ARSI, Jap.-Sin., 4:fols. 290–98v.

32. Monte (from Macao) to a Jesuit father in Rome, 29 December 1562, ARSI, Jap.-Sin., 4:fols. 311–12r.

33. Pérez (from Macao) to: (1) a Jesuit in Goa, 3 January 1564; (2) the Jesuit general, Diego Laínez, 3 December 1564; (3) Father Luis Gonsálvez, 3 December 1564. See also Texeira (from Macao) to the Jesuits in Goa, 3 December 1564. All this correspondence can be found in ARSI, Jap.-Sin., 5:fols. 101, 152r–56r, 161r–62v, 164r–69r; 6:fols. 93r–99v. Also Ibid., Goa 38:fols. 284r, 292r.

34. ARSI, Jap.-Sin., 6:fols. 86r–87v. For an Italian translation of Escobar's letter (from Canton) to Manoel Texeira, 22 November 1565, see Pasquale M. D'Elia, S.J., "Contributo alla storia delle relazioni tra l'Europa e la Cina, prima dell'arrivo di P. Matteo Ricci, S.J. (1582)," *Rivista degli studi orientali* 16 (1936):223–26.

35. D'Elia, *Fonti Ricciane*, 1:140.

36. Ribera (from Macao) to Father General Francis Borgia, October 1568, ARSI, Jap.-Sin., 6:fols. 236r–40r.

37. Wicki, *Documenta Indica*, 8:580 et seq. Riera had to go to Macao with Ribera.

38. Organtino Gnecchi-Soldo, S.J. (from Macao) to Luis Madrid, S.J., 29 October 1569, ARSI, Jap.-Sin., 6:fols. 257–58. Also Joseph de Moidrey, S.J., *La Hiérarchie catholique en Chine, en Corée et au Japon 1307–1914*. Variétés sinologiques, no. 38 (Zi-Ka-wei, 1914), 6. In January 1555, Carneiro was nominated bishop of Nicaea and coadjutor to the patriarch of Ethiopia. Like the patriarch, he never succeeded in reaching Ethiopia. In June (ARSI, Jap.-Sin., 6:fol. 240), he arrived in Macao as bishop of China and Japan but not as bishop of the diocese of Macao, which was not established until 1576. See D'Elia, *Fonti Ricciane*, 1:153 n. 5. Not long after his arrival in Macao, Carneiro tried to renounce his episcopal dignity and retire to a house of the Society but

was unable to do so until January 1582. He died in Macao on 19 August 1583. See *Catálogo de los documentos relativos a las Islas Filipinas existentes en el Archivo de Indias de Sevilla por D. Pedro Torres y Lanzas y Francisco Navas del Valle, y precedido de una erudita historia general de Filipinas por el P. Pedro Pastells, S.J.*, 8 vols. (Barcelona, 1925–1933), 2:CLIX.

39. Giovanni Francesco Stefanoni, S.J. (from Goto, Japan), 6 October 1574, ARSI, Jap.-Sin., 7, I:fol. 241r.

40. da Costa (from Macao) to Father General Everard Mercurian, 17 November 1575, ARSI, Jap.-Sin., 7, II:fols. 291–92v.

41. Ribera (from Lisbon) to Father General Everard Mercurian, 18 October 1575, ARSI, Jap.-Sin., 7, I:fol. 287r. See also Moidrey, *Hiérarchie catholique, 6.*

42. Boxer, *South China in the Sixteenth Century,* 19.

43. Annual letter of Francisco Chávez, S.J. (from Malacca), 20 November 1579, ARSI, Goa, 38:fol. 177r.

44. D'Elia, *Fonti Ricciane,* 1:141.

45. Domingo Álvarez, rector of Macao, to Father General, 25 October 1581, ARSI, Jap.-Sin., 9, I:fol. 49r.

46. D'Elia, *Fonti Ricciane,* 1:142, 156.

47. Alonso Sánchez (from Macao) to Father General Everard Mercurian, 3 July 1582, ARSI, Jap.-Sin., 9, I:fols. 87–93.

48. D'Elia, *Fonti Ricciane,* 1:142–67.

49. Ibid., 1:142.

50. Ibid.

51. Ibid.

52. Wicki, *Documenta Indica,* 13:195–201. See the two works by José Maria Braga, *O primeiro accordo Luso-Chinês realizado por Leonel de Sousa em 1554* (Macao, 1939) and *The Western Pioneers and Their Discovery of Macao* (Macao, 1949). See also two works by C. R. Boxer, *Fidalgos in the Far East 1550–1770: Fact and Fancy in the History of Macao* (The Hague, 1948), 1–9, and *The Great Ship from Amacan: Annals of Macao and the Old Japan Trade, 1555–1640* (Lisbon, 1959), 1–11.

53. Wicki, *Documenta Indica,* 7:504–6.

54. For Alessandro Valignano's life and work, see the three studies by Josef Franz Schütte, S.J.: (1) *Valignanos Missionsgrundsätze für Japan. 1 Band. Von der Ernennung zum Visitator bis zum ersten Abschied von Japan (1573–1582); I. Teil: Das Problem (1573–1580)* (Rome, 1951). II. Teil: *Die Lösung (1580–1582)* (Rome, 1951–1958); (2) *Introductio ad Historiam Societatis Jesu in Japonia, 1549–1650* (Rome, 1968); (3) *Die Wirksamkeit der Päpste für Japan im ersten Jahrhundert der japanischen Kirchengeschichte (1549–1650). Versuch einer Zusammenfassung* (Rome, 1967).

55. Henri Bernard-Maitre, S.J., *Aux Portes de la Chine. Les Missionaires du Seizième Siècle, 1514–1588* (Tientsin, 1933), 141.

56. ARSI, Jap.-Sin., 9, I:fols. 149–150v; Wicki, *Documenta Indica*, 11:550–51, 572–74.

57. See Alexandro Valignano, S.J., *Il cerimoniale per i missionari del Giappone*, ed. Josef Franz Schütte, S.J. (Rome, 1946).

58. Knud Lundbaek, "The First Translation from a Confucian Classic in Europe," *China Mission Studies (1550–1800) Bulletin* 1 (1979):1–11. About Ruggieri, see D'Elia, *Fonti Ricciane*, 1:141–49, and Louis Pfister, S.J., *Notices biographiques et bibliographiques sur les Jésuites de l'ancienne mission de Chine 1552–1773*, 2 vols. Variétés sinologiques nos. 59 and 60 (Shanghai, 1932–1934), 1:15–21.

59. The Jesuits were Alonso Sánchez and his companions. For Sánchez's own report (from Macao) to the Jesuit General, 2 July 1582, see ARSI, Jap.-Sin., 9, I:fols. 87–93v.

60. ARSI, Jap.-Sin., 9, I:fols. 149–50v.

61. For biographical data on Ricci, see D'Elia, *Fonti Ricciane*, 1:CICXXXV; Pfister, *Notices*, 1:22–42; Nicolas Trigault, S.J., ed., *China in the Sixteenth Century: The Journals of Matthew Ricci, 1583–1610*, trans. Louis Gallagher, S.J. (New York, 1953); Pietro Tacchi Venturi, S.J., ed., *Opere storiche del P. Matteo Ricci, S.J.*, 2 vols. (Macerata, 1911–13). From here on, this essay contains material from the present writer's "Matteo Ricci Chinois avec les chinois," *Études*, 357 (October 1982):361–74.

62. ARSI., Jap.-Sin., 9, I:fols. 112–13v.

63. Ibid., fols. 149–50v, 163–64r.

64. The idea of an embassy is a constant theme in the writings of Xavier and his successors. See Schurhammer and Wicki, *Epistolae*, 2:358–64, 453–63, 468–75, 483–88, 497–501, 513–16, 516–21. See also Wicki, *Documenta Indica*, 2:510–20; 3:119–28, 163–69, 245–54, 449–51; 5:160–88, 238–46, 250–65, 315–18, 398–423, 481–87, 693–99, 719–22, 722–25, 737–47, 752–58; 6:69–77, 103–28, 508–18, 522–29, 660–62; 7:207–12, 486–94; 11:727–41; 12:950–69. See also ARSI, Jap.-Sin., 4:fols. 76–81v, 90–94v, 290–98v, 311–12; 5:fols. 101r–v, 152–56, 161–62v, 164– 69v; 6:fols. 93–99v; 9, I:fols. 58–61v, 112–13v. The distinction between diplomatic and trade missions was made by Ruggieri. In his opinion, former embassies had failed because they were trade missions. He urged a diplomatic mission. See Ruggieri (from Macao) to Father General Everard Mercurian, 12 November 1581, ARSI, Jap.-Sin., 9, I:fols. 58–61v.

65. Wicki, *Documenta Indica*, 4:160–88, 673–714; 7:207–12, 486–94; 9:661–69, 696–708; 10:662–83; 13:1–134, 134–319. ARSI, Jap.-Sin., 6:fols. 211r–v, 234–35v, 236–40; 7:fols. 241–43v; 8 I:fols. 280–82v; 9, I:fols. 49–50v, 130–32v. War between Spain and Portugal

over the East Indies also caused concern. See Wicki, *Documenta Indica*, 7:157–61; 9:644–49, 669–71; 10:509–15. See also C. R. Boxer, "Portuguese and Spanish Rivalry in the Far East during the 17th Century," *Journal of the Royal Asiatic Society of Great Britain and Ireland*, part 3 (December 1946):150–64, part 4 (April 1947):91–105.

66. ARSI, Jap.-Sin., 9, I:fols. 137–41v.

67. Jacques Gernet, *Chine et Christianisme. Action et réaction* (Paris, 1982), 36, 54, 81–89.

68. Ibid., 16–17. See also *Ssu-k'u ch'üan-shu tsung-mu t'i-yao* (Summary reviews of the general bibliography of the great encyclopedia of the four treasuries) (Imperial Catalog), 24, part 2. For an article about the summary review given the *T'ien-chu shih-i* in the latter work, see the present writer's "The Summary Review of Matteo Ricci's *T'ien-chu shih-i* in the *Ssu-k'u ch'üan-shu tsung-mu t'i-yao,*" *Archivum Historicum Societatis Iesu* 53 (1984):386–91.

69. D'Elia, *Fonti Ricciane*, 1:180–83.

70. Tacchi Venturi, *Opere storiche*, 2:206–9; Gernet, *Chine et Christianisme*, 29.

71. Emil Zürcher, "The First Anti-Christian Movement in China (Nanking 1616–1621)," in *Acta Orientalia Neerlandica*. Proceedings of the Congress of the Dutch Oriental Society held in Leiden on the occasion of its 50th anniversary, 8th-9th May 1970, ed. P. W. Pestman (Leiden, 1971), 192–93.

72. Pedro Gómez, another Jesuit on his way to Japan, expresses this spirit well. He writes: "I am almost fifty years of age, and I confess to Your Paternity that I am learning everything anew as if I were entering the world: I am learning how to eat, to drink, to sit, to lie down, to dress, to put on shoes, to receive and be received; learning the courtesies, the alphabet, the language, and life. May it please the Lord that I truly become a child for His love who, being the Wisdom of the earth, for my sake became a child unable to speak. According to what I understand, those going to Japan also have to divest themselves of the customs and clothes they bring from Europe and put on the clothes and new customs of Japan, so that we do not [try to] transform the nature of the Japanese into ours but ours into theirs in order to bring them to our spirit and our holy faith." Gómez (from Macao) to Father General of the Society of Jesus, 5 June 1582, ARSI, Jap.-Sin., 9 I:fols. 85–85v.

73. Some later Jesuit missionaries, the Figurists, tried to prove this in a unique way. See John W. Witek, S.J., *Controversial Ideas in China and in Europe: A Biography of Jean-François Foucquet, S.J. (1665–1741)* (Rome, 1982), 143–44, 148–51, 179–80, 300–308, 332–35. This was important to counteract the feeling of racial superiority on the part of the Europeans and their feeling of superiority as the sole

recipients of divine revelation. The early Jesuits maintained that the Chinese and Japanese belonged to the white race. Xavier asserts this in two letters from Cochin, 29 January 1552: one to Ignatius Loyola and the other to the members of the Society. See Schurhammer and Wicki, *Epistolae,* 2:291–92, 277, respectively. Also Valignano in his Indian summary written in Malacca, 8 December 1577. See Wicki, *Documenta Indica,* 13:5. The others followed their lead.

74. Gernet, *Chine et Christianisme,* 261-90.

75. Ibid., 198–230.

76. See Li Ma-tou [Matteo Ricci], *Chiao-yu lun,* 1b, as cited in Young, *East-West Synthesis,* 46. See also two articles by Pasquale M. D'Elia, S.J.: (1) *"Il Trattato sull'Amicizia.* Primo Libro scritto in Cinese da Matteo Ricci, S.J. (1595). Testo Cinese. Traduzione antica (Ricci) e moderna (D'Elia). Fonti, Introduzione e Note," *Studia Missionalia* 7 (1952):425–515; (2) "Further Notes on Matteo Ricci's *De Amicitia,"* *Monumenta Serica* 15 (1956):356–77.

77. Ricci, *T'ien-chu shih-i, hsia-chüan,* 46–48, as cited in Young, *East-West Synthesis,* 44–45.

78. Ibid., 48.

79. Ibid., 44, 68 n. 11: *pu ju i-fo.*

80. Ibid., 48.

81. James Legge, *The Religions of China. Confucianism and Taoism described and Compared with Christianity* (New York, 1881), 53. Legge also states: "The Chinese character tsî (祭) covers a much wider space of meaning than our term sacrifice.... The most general idea symbolised by it is — an offering whereby communication and communion with spiritual beings is effected" (66).

82. Zürcher, "First Anti-Christian Movement," 192–93.

83. *New Catholic Encyclopedia,* s.v. "Chinese Rites Controversy" (by Francis A. Rouleau, S.J.).

84. Antoine Beauvollier, S.J., "Éclaircissements [sur la Controverse] de la Chine (1702)." Unpublished manuscript in the Archivum Societatis Iesu Parisiense (Chantilly, France), Fond "Rites Chinois" (Article 3, 33–126). For this reference, the present writer is indebted to the late Francis A. Rouleau, S.J.

85. *New Catholic Encyclopedia,* s.v. "Chinese Rites Controversy." See also Francesco Brancati (Brancato), S.J. (1607–1671), *De Sinensium ritibus politicis acta seu responsio apologetica ad R. P. Dominicum Nava-rette Ordinis Praedicatorum,* 2 vols. (Paris, 1700), 2:185. Quoting Johann Adam Schall von Bell, S.J. (1592–1666), Brancati writes: "Quamquam illud quod hactenus Paternitates Vestrae [Patres Dominicani] secutae sunt, et magis probabile est et tutum, nostrum tamen probabilitate non caret, atque omnino illud sequi convenit." Brancati adds: "Nemo ex nostra Societate umquam condemnavit practicam opinionem Patrum

aliorum, nam bene novimus nostram opinionem non esse demonstrationem, sed contineri intra limites *opinionis probabilis.*" This information was also provided by Father Rouleau from his files, which are housed at the Institute for Chinese-Western Cultural History at the University of San Francisco in California.

86. Cooper, *Rodrigues the Interpreter,* 284–86.

87. Gernet, *Chine et Christianisme,* 19. Longobardi's book was entitled *Traité sur quelques points de la religion des Chinois.*

88. Gernet, *Chine et Christianisme,* 19. Note that all missionaries in China, Jesuit and non-Jesuit, including the Dominican Domingo Fernández de Navarette, reached an agreement on the "Praxes" (Jesuit practice of the Rites) at the Canton Synod (29 November 1669) during the Canton internment of the missionaries; this internment resulted from the persecution provoked by Yang Kuang-hsien (1597–1669) and known as the persecution of the "Four Regents" during K'ang Hsi's minority (1669–1671). About this event, see the present writer's unpublished colloquium paper, presented 6 October 1977, "History of the Jesuits in the Old China Mission, 17th and 18th Centuries: An Attempt at Cultural Accommodation," 14–15; excerpts from this paper were published as "China's Jesuit Century," *The Wilson Quarterly* (Winter 1978), 170–83.

89. Regarding this persecution, see Zürcher, "First Anti-Christian Movement," 188–95.

90. Gernet, *Chine et Christianisme,* 34.

91. Jann, *Die katholischen Missionen,* 125–26; Otto Maas, O.F.M., *Die Wiedereröffnung der Franziskanermission in China in der Neuzeit* (Münster, 1926), 77; George H. Dunne, S.J., *Generation of Giants: The Story of the Jesuits in China in the Last Decades of the Ming Dynasty* (Notre Dame, 1962), 231.

92. Maas, *Franziskanermission in China,* 77: Dunne, *Generation of Giants,* 234.

93. Maas, *Franziskanermission in China,* 77; Dunne, *Generation of Giants,* 234–35.

94. "The Edict of Toleration" or "Edict in Favor of the Catholic Religion," 17 March to 20 March 1692. See Huang Po-lu, S.J., *Chengchiao feng-pao* (Public praise of the true religion) (Shanghai, 1904), 115b–116b.

95. Two copies can be found in ARSI, Jap.-Sin., 165:fols. 188 et seq.

96. The four specific occasions were: (1) the decree *Cum Deus Optimus,* issued by Pope Clement XI on 20 November 1704; (2) the 1707 condemnation in Nanking by Charles Thomas Maillard de Tournon (1668–1710), the papal legate, of the Chinese Rites; (3) Clement XI's papal Bull *Ex illa die,* of 19 March 1715, approving Tournon's

action; (4) the 1742 Bull of Pope Benedict XIV, *Ex quo singulari*, peremptorily condemning the Chinese Rites.

97. Matthew 28:19–20.

98. "L'âge des nations est passé. Il s'agit maintenant pour nous, si nous ne voulons pas périr, de secouer les anciens préjugés, et de construire la Terre." Pierre Teilhard de Chardin, S.J., *Oeuvres de Pierre Teilhard de Chardin*, Vol. 6, *L'Énergie humaine* (Paris, 1962), 46.

3

Understanding the Chinese:
A Comparison of Matteo Ricci and
the French Jesuit Mathematicians Sent by Louis XIV

JOHN D. WITEK, S.J.

THE SIXTEENTH AND SEVENTEENTH CENTURIES in European history were dominated by the emergence of nation states, religious disputes from the beginning of the Protestant Reformation to the Thirty Years' War, and a quest for overseas expansion. To the observer of China's history in that same period, internal and external changes contributed to the gradual decline and overthrow of the Ming and the rise of the Ch'ing dynasties. After the Ming dynasty was established in 1368, a brilliant renaissance of Chinese civilization began as an antidote to the heavily controlled state under the preceding Yüan dynasty. The Ming regime encouraged Cheng Ho (1371–1433) to undertake a series of voyages that extended to Southeast Asia, India, and even the coasts of East Africa. There is no totally satisfactory explanation for the abandonment of these voyages after 1433, but a sense of isolation later penetrated the Ming court and, indeed, the common people. Once the ancient policy of forbidding its ships to leave Chinese coastal waters was revived by the government, the result "unquestionably changed the course of history."[1] The Chinese lost their former influence in the Indian Ocean to the Arabs and about seven decades later to the Portuguese.

By the Treaty of Tordesillas (1494), a line of demarcation was drawn between the colonial activities of Spain and Portugal. Within three decades, the Portuguese sent an embassy under Tomé Pires (1468?–1524?) to Peking. By 1557, Macao had become a Portuguese enclave on the doorstep of China. Just a few years earlier, Francis Xavier (1506–1552) worked first in India and then in Japan.[2] The longer he lived in Japan, the more he became aware of China, which several Japanese urged him to visit if he really wanted to penetrate Japanese thought and customs. In his efforts to enter China, however, he got no further than the offshore island of Shang-ch'uan, where he died 3 December 1552, a few months after his arrival.

Although Xavier had begun to understand the need for using different methods in Japan than he had employed in India, it was not until Alessandro Valignano (1539–1606) arrived in Macao in 1574 as Visitor to the Jesuit mission that a new policy of evangelization was constructed. Convinced that the Portuguese Jesuits in Macao were too Eurocentric and unwilling to try different approaches, he sent first for Michele Ruggieri (1543–1607) and then later for Matteo Ricci (1552–1610), both of whom were in India, to come to Macao where they were ordered to learn how to read, write, and speak Chinese.[3]

Valignano's command might be considered commonplace today, but the idea was quite new at that time. As a missionary arrives at a foreign station in a non-Christian land, he can adopt two general attitudes toward those he seeks to convert. The first might be called a tabula rasa approach by which the total life of the people from beginning to end — the circumstances of the individual, of the family, and of society — is considered so imbued with idolatrous and superstitious practices that complete abandonment of the past tradition is demanded for the development of a new Christian. The second approach, a method of accommodation, is much more difficult, for it presupposes a thorough knowledge of the people one seeks to convert and is predicated on working with them as they are. It is an acceptance that not all in their lives is evil even though the missionary clearly realizes that the people are far distant from what he considers the true religion. Thus, certain practices and customs of a people that are clearly not superstitious may be tolerated and even adapted to Christian customs. Such an attitude was Valignano's, although he depended heavily on the patience and discernment of Ruggieri and Ricci for its implementation.[4] China, with its estimated population of 150 million steeped in a culture that almost no Westerner as yet understood or appreciated, was not about to change its ways. The Westerners had to change theirs, for only by respecting Chinese culture could an entry into China be achieved.

Within this essay, neither a thorough study of Ricci's method of accommodation nor its comparison to missionary experiences in the nineteenth and twentieth centuries is envisioned,[5] but a short discussion about the term *accommodation* might be in order. In the social sciences, especially in anthropology, there is a continuing growth of literature about culture contact, cross-cultural communications, and culture change, but mostly centering on the contemporary world. Less attention has been paid to experiences of Westerners vis-a-vis non-Western cultures in centuries past, especially, for our purposes, Westerners entering China from the sixteenth to the eighteenth centuries. One of the seminal studies about Ricci's method of accommodation distinguishes six types: external, linguistic, aesthetic, social behavioral, intellectual, and religious.[6] Whether such divisions are accepted by all scholars is not of particular concern at this point. In fact, another essayist viewing Ricci's missionary efforts has devised a paradigm of eight prescriptions that evolved by trial and error as Ricci became more thoroughly acquainted with Chinese civilization.[7] Even today accommodation has also been discussed in terms of "missionary adaptation," "nativization of local churches," or the "principle of cultural relevancy."[8]

But no matter what specific term might be used or, indeed, how the topic might be divided and subdivided for presentation, it was only in the Age of Discovery when missionaries accompanied traders and merchants to non-Western lands that the Catholic Church had to face the problem of inculturation.[9] In the first centuries of its history, the Church had to adapt to Hebrew, Greek, and Roman customs; but by the Middle Ages it had become so ethnocentric that good and civilized were identified with Europe, whereas evil and superstitious were identified with foreign lands. Because of the Protestant Reformation, the Catholic Church became even more defensive and as an institution could not readily adapt to new lands then being discovered. Since missionaries, however, from the middle of the sixteenth century worked in these newly discovered (from the European viewpoint) lands, discussion of missiological methods arose. Within this context, Ricci's attempt to understand Chinese civilization in its own right and to present Christianity to the intellectual elite and to the general population stands as a contribution to that discussion. Part of the focus of this essay centers on Ricci's study of the Chinese Classics and his understanding of the three teachings of Confucianism, Buddhism, and Taoism (*san-chiao*). This then led Ricci to write two influential Chinese works that offered the Chinese and also the Japanese a new way of understanding the world.

The absence of a general history of the Jesuit presence in China from 1582 (the arrival of Ricci in Macao) to 1793 (the death of Jean-Joseph Amiot) has not allowed the beginning student of that topic to appreciate the important stages of its development. A substitute is available at least in the chronology in the *Répertoire des Jésuites de Chine de 1552 à 1800* of Joseph Dehergne, S.J.[10] A glance at its charts indicates that not only did Ricci lay the groundwork of the Jesuit presence in the capital and elsewhere in China in the first decade of the seventeenth century, but in the last dozen years of the same century, five French Jesuits created an impact that lasted well into the next century and beyond and reoriented the character of the mission.

This chapter does not retell the well-known story of Ricci's entry into China and his eventual labors in Peking nor trace in detail the story of the first French Jesuits' departure from Paris and their arrival in Peking, even though the latter is not as thoroughly portrayed in English-language studies as the former. But inasmuch as the approach of both Ricci and the French Jesuits necessarily included an understanding of the Chinese as a means of evangelization, it is this topic that is the focal point of this study. Understanding the Chinese means more than a superficial acquaintance with some Chinese people that a three-week stay in contemporary China offers a tourist. It includes at least a serious, long effort to know their language, to read their Classics and the commentaries, to try to penetrate their religious views, and to study their customs and their political administration. Many of these traits may ultimately constitute accommodation, but such an appreciation of the Chinese was first needed before accommodation could be attempted.

In studying the Chinese language, Ricci progressed far more rapidly than Ruggieri. Neither Jesuit had to be convinced of the value of their undertaking. In 1580, when Ruggieri (Ricci was still in India) accompanied Portuguese merchants to the Canton trade fair, he carefully followed Chinese etiquette formalities. This was quickly noticed by the Chinese who wanted Ruggieri to appear at all public audiences.[11] Learning spoken Chinese was, of course, much more readily attained than a mastery of the written language, especially because of a lack of bilingual dictionaries. Eventually, both Ruggieri and Ricci were permitted to live in Chao-ch'ing, west of Canton, owing to the kindness of the governor-general of Kuangtung and Kuangsi, Kuo Ying-p'ing (1529–1586, *chin-shih* 1550).[12] After their arrival in September 1583, they continued their language studies. Within two years, Ricci was able to carry on a conversation without an interpreter, though Ruggieri still had not attained such proficiency by the following year. In 1588, about one hundred Cantonese petitioned an imperial censor to remove both missionaries from Chao-ch'ing, and when the censor ruled in favor of Ricci, Valignano sent Ruggieri to Rome to try to organize an embassy to Peking to get imperial approval for missionaries to preach in China.[13] When a new governor-general, Liu Chi-wen (*chin-shih* 1562, d. 1592), took office after the death of his predecessor, Ricci's efforts to remain in China seemed lost. He turned his meeting with Liu, however, to the advantage of both sides, for Liu allowed Ricci to settle in another city, Shao-chou. After several years there, he was asked to accompany Shih Hsing (1538–1599, *chin-shih* 1559) to Peking where the latter, as a member of the Board of War, had been called during the Japanese invasion of Korea in 1592. This helped Ricci reach Nanking, but his stay there lasted only two weeks. He then decided to settle in Nanchang, the capital of the province of Kiangsi.

Ricci's reputation for learning had preceded him. At Nanchang, scholars visited him and, in turn, invited him to meet others. With the approval of his superiors, Ricci no longer appeared in Buddhist garb but adopted the dress of the Confucian scholarly class. His familiarity with the Chinese Classics and his knowledge of mathematics excited much admiration. Many were amazed at his prodigious feats of memory — e.g., repeating after a single reading more than four hundred characters written at random by Chinese scholars. Since he could reproduce these characters forward and backward, he was urged to write an essay on his techniques. This was his *Western Memory Techniques* (*Hsi-kuo chi-fa*), published in 1595. At Nanchang he developed a warm friendship with Chang Huang (1527–1608), a famous scholar and author of the *Encyclopedia of Geography* (*T'u-shu pien*). In 1595, aware that the Chinese frequently discussed the five relationships that Confucius had taught, Ricci wrote the *Treatise on Friendship* (*Chiao-yu lun*) and dedicated it to Chu To-chieh (d. 1601), the prince of Chien-an, then residing in Nanchang. Several scholars asked Ricci for permission to copy the essay; others, however, printed and distributed it without his permission. By the time Ricci reached Nanking again in 1598, he was aware that the short essay had established the Jesuits' reputation as "scholars of talent and virtue,"[14] and, indeed, gained credit for European civilization as well. The essay, reprinted several times during Ricci's life, helped convey to the Chinese reader the realization that Europeans were actually more than "barbarians."

Invited by the Nanking minister of rites, Wang Hung-hui (*chin-shih* 1565, d. 1601), to accompany him to Peking, Ricci gladly accepted the offer. However, because the second Japanese invasion of Korea in 1597 had aroused suspicions among the scholars who were reluctant to admit a foreigner as a guest in the capital, Ricci was forced to return to Nanking, where he became acquainted with Hsü Kuang-ch'i (1562–1633), Li Chih-tsao (1565–1630), and Feng Ying-ching (1555–1606).[15] Through the efforts of these famous scholars, who became converts to Catholicism, Ricci reached Peking under new auspices in 1601 and worked there until his death nine years later.

Besides the *Treatise on Friendship*, there are two other significant Chinese works by Ricci that merit attention: *True Meaning of the Lord of Heaven* (*T'ien-chu shih-i*) and *Complete Map of the Myriad Nations of the Earth* (*K'un-yü wan-kuo ch'üan-t'u*).[16] Although the map was first published in Chinese before Ricci

was thoroughly acquainted with the Classics, it was one of the
last works he reedited in his later years in Peking. Since his
writing of a new explanation of Catholicism in Chinese was
connected with his need to study the Classics, this latter topic
is considered first.

At Shao-chou, toward the end of 1591, Ricci's knowledge of
classical Chinese reached a turning point; Valignano, dissatisfied
with the first Chinese exposition of Christian doctrine, the *True
Record of God* (*T'ien-chu shih-lu*) by Ruggieri, asked Ricci to
translate the *Four Books* (*Ssu-shu*) into Latin and then to write
a new essay about Catholicism. Ricci had read the *Four Books*
earlier in his career and thus became acquainted with the Sung
Neo-Confucianism of Chu Hsi (1130–1200), but by translating
the work into Latin, he was forced to consider this ideology
more thoroughly. He thus distinguished the original doctrine
of the Confucian Classics from the interpretations later joined
to the texts by the commentators of the Chu Hsi school. For
Ricci, the school of nature and principle (*hsing-li hsüeh*) had
created a metaphysics too rationalistic and materialistic and
thus in his view opposed to Christianity. In the teachings of
Confucius and Mencius, however, he found a moral system not
unlike that found in the West, and on this foundation he could
create a presentation of Catholic beliefs. To what extent his
view coincided with or flowed from a similar movement of a
"return to the Classics" in the late Ming and then in the early
Ch'ing periods cannot be answered in sufficient detail at this
point.[17]

From his knowledge of the Classics, Ricci was persuaded that
in "heaven" (*t'ien*) or "Lord on High" (*Shang-ti*) the early Confucians had worshipped God who, omniscient and omnipotent,
rewarded virtue and punished evil.[18] Noting that the literati in
Kwangtung tended to deny the immortality of the soul in contrast to the scholars in central China, Ricci observed that the
Neo-Confucian school had substituted a theory of an impersonal
universe of principle and material force (*li* and *ch'i*) to replace
the earlier Confucian theistic conception of heaven. In this context, then, he wrote his celebrated *True Meaning of the Lord
of Heaven.*

As early as 1593, Ricci had written the first draft of this essay and four years later submitted it to his superiors for approval. After his arrival in Peking in 1601, he decided to incorporate into the essay the debates he had in Nanking with the Buddhist San Huai (Huang Hung-en, 1545–1608) and those he had in Peking with Huang Hui (*chin-shih* 1589), an outstanding scholar of Buddhism and tutor of Chu Ch'ang-lo (1582–1620), the crown prince. From these discussions, Ricci began to understand how Chinese argumentation was not constructed in absolute definitions but in an evolving description of reality.[19] Quite conversant with the *Analects* (*Lun-yü*), he decided to use the dialogue form of questions and answers in his treatise.

Divided into two volumes (*chuan*) with four sections each, eight topics are thus covered in the dialogues: (1) God's creation and governing of the universe; (2) man's false ideas about divinity; (3) man, with an immortal soul, and his basic difference from animals; (4) man's ability to reason about spirits and the soul of man; (5) the Buddhist paths of existence and the prohibition of killing animals; (6) the motives of fear and of hope for the future needed for an understanding of a hell and of a paradise after death; (7) the nature of man as good in itself; and (8) religion in Europe, missionary celibacy, and God's incarnation.[20] Essentially, then, the *True Meaning of the Lord of Heaven* is a treatise of natural theology, the culmination of over a decade's reflection and experience by Ricci in China. Its intent was not to present all the mysteries of the Catholic faith, as the author expressly pointed out, but to answer "the opinions of the Chinese which contradict those truths."[21]

Perhaps one of the clearest examples of Ricci's challenge to the Chinese Buddhists and Taoists was his statement in the seventh chapter of this essay. The religion of Buddha was based on nothing, that of Lao Tzu on emptiness, and that of Confucius on the real. He asked if there was not in the universe anything more opposed than these fundamentals.

> Is it possible to reunite the real with nothing, the void with the solid? If so, it would be putting together fire and water, the round with the squared, the east with the west, heaven and earth ... Is it not better not to have any religion than to have three? ... The truth is one; all doctrine is based on truth and must sustain itself. If then the doctrine is not one, the principles

are not solid and the consequences are not certain, so that faith
is no longer firm and whole. But without unity of doctrine, without solidity of principles, without integrity of faith, is there
religion?[22]

Ricci's argumentation affirmed the acceptance of the principle of noncontradiction on which the Buddhists challenged him
shortly after the publication of the essay. Moreover, the Buddhist
preacher, San Huai, had discussed some of these same issues
with him in Nanking, as the Buddhist scholars in Peking well
understood. Nor, indeed, did Ricci's comments on Buddhism
go unheard, for Chu-hung (1535–1613), a Buddhist monk
known for the formation of a lay Buddhist society in the late
Ming period, energetically led the movement to expose heretical teachings (p'i-hsieh yün-tung) in Hangchow and Fukien.
Ricci centered his attack on nonkilling and on the release of
life (e.g., setting captured animals free), but Chu-hung stead-
fastly held to the doctrine of transmigration. As two recent
studies have shown, Chu-hung did not merely superimpose
"Buddhist ethics on a Confucian structure" but took a Confucian
virtue, like filial piety, and reinterpreted it according to Buddhist
views.[23] In this way, Chu-hung was apparently co-opting Ricci's
method of accommodation, albeit for his own purposes.

Another dimension of Ricci's method of intellectual accommodation was his contribution to the development of cartography in China. In 1583, at Chao-ch'ing, he had put a European
map of the world on the interior wall of his residence. With
the literati who visited him, it soon became a conversation
piece, not least of all because the location of China was off to
one side on the map and thus did not indicate what China
claimed to be, namely, the Middle Kingdom. Ricci, however,
used the map as a basic tool to explain his origins in Italy and
his travels from Rome to Macao.

Although lacking a solid command of literary Chinese, Ricci
printed the first edition of his Chinese map entitled *Complete
Map of the Earth, Mountains, and Seas* (*Yü-ti shan-hai ch'üan-
t'u*). This time China was depicted in the center. No copies of
this edition are extant, but Chang Huang, whom Ricci had be-
friended in Nanchang, included a reproduction of this 1584 map
in his *Encyclopedia of Geography* that did not appear until

1613.[24] Ricci published a second edition of his map in 1600 in Nanking at the request of a Chinese official there. Again, no copies of this map are extant. After his arrival in Peking, several Chinese officials who had learned about the earlier maps urged him to publish more editions. This he did in 1602 and 1603. Only five copies of the third (1602) edition are extant, so that most of the literature on Ricci's cartography has focused on this edition, entitled *Complete Map of the Myriad Nations of the Earth*.[25]

The impact of Ricci's map on Chinese geographical knowledge cannot be doubted. Ricci described to the Chinese the use of meridians and his own fieldwork observations made on his trip from Europe.[26] The Chinese, of course, had some idea about various localities and the relative position of important places, but they lacked sufficient data for accurate calculation. Ricci indicated the latitude of such cities as Peking, Nanking, and Ningpo, among others. His translation and his transliteration of geographic names — e.g., Asia (*Ya-hsi-ya*), Rome (*Lo-ma*), etc. — consitituted a notable achievement, for the map had more than a thousand such terms, many of which are commonly used today not only by the Chinese but also by the Japanese and the Koreans. Perhaps the most fundamental theme he presented to the Chinese was a unified conception of the entire world. To them this was new, not only in their learning about the continents of North and South America across the Pacific Ocean, but also about the world's limits. Ricci clearly understood the Chinese views of the world were being challenged by the publication of his map.

Whatever success Ricci attained in his missionary enterprise depended in no small measure on his years of patient efforts in Macao as he began to understand the Chinese and as he kept adapting himself to changing circumstances on the mission. At his death in 1610 in Peking, only a nucleus of a mission had been established. Yet, as he claimed, a door was now open to great merits, but it was not without perils and labors.[27]

The extension of the Jesuit presence in China through the efforts of Johann Adam Schall von Bell (1592–1666) and Ferdinand Verbiest (1623–1688) has been the focus of other studies. It is, of course, an oversimplification to consider only these two individuals without taking into account Niccolò Longobardi (1565 – 1655), Giulio Aleni (1582 – 1649), Martino Martini (1614 – 1661), Gabriel de Magalhães (1610 – 1677), and many others in their continued work not only as pastors in areas outside the capital, but above all in their Chinese writings which led a number of Chinese to become converts to Catholicism. But ten years before his death in 1688, Verbiest, then vice-provincial, reflected on the lack of personnel entering China. In his 15 August 1678 letter that was widely disseminated in Europe, he urged his fellow Jesuits to consider the China mission and added that such volunteers should be well-versed in philosophy and theology and above all be ready to adapt themselves to Chinese customs. Since only seven Jesuits had actually entered China during the decade before this letter was written, Verbiest's concern cannot be considered an exaggeration.[28]

When Verbiest's letter arrived in Europe in 1680, a possible answer was already on the horizon from an unexpected proposal in France. The director of the astronomical observatory in Paris, Jean-Dominique Cassini (1625 – 1712), had approached French government authorities about the possibility of sending some Jesuits as royal mathematicians to make astronomical observations in the Orient. For a variety of reasons, however, the plan did not reemerge until 1684, when Philippe Couplet (1622 – 1693), a Belgian Jesuit missionary from China, visited Louis XIV and also discussed with the Jesuits in Paris the matter of procuring personnel. Later that year, envoys from Siam arrived at the court of Versailles, so the king and his advisers were now convinced that a way was available to get the Jesuits to the East. Six were recruited: Joachim Bouvet (1656 – 1730), Jean de Fontaney (1643 – 1710), Jean-François Gerbillon (1654 – 1707), Louis Le Comte (1655 – 1728), Guy Tachard (1648 – 1712), and Claude de Visdelou (1656 – 1737).

In the late autumn and early winter of 1684 – 85, hasty preparation had to be completed for this French project, a venture important both for the Jesuits and the French government. In fact, since only four Jesuits were initially accepted for the voyage, they alone were admitted as *mathématiciens du Roy* at the Académie Royale des Sciences. Later, the two other Jesuits

were added to the group whose purpose was to make astronomical observations and to study Chinese literature in order that
some of them might return to Paris where they would translate
the Chinese books they were to collect for the Royal Library.
Fontaney, a professor of mathematics and physics who had desired to go to China for a long time, was perhaps the most
qualified. Tachard had been in South America for a short period.
The others were still completing various stages of theological
studies. In fact, although two of them, Bouvet and Visdelou,
were ordained to the priesthood in January 1685, neither of
them ever completed the required fourth year of theology.[29]
Additional details on the selection of astronomical instruments
and the attempt to get passports from Portugal added to the
rather hectic pace of last-minute preparations for sailing by
early March.

What becomes fairly clear from the documents discovered
thus far is that before their departure, the "royal mathematicians" were limited in their knowledge of China and can
scarcely be described as possessing an empathy for and an understanding of Chinese beliefs and customs. From the death of
Ricci in 1610 until the arrival of these French Jesuits in 1687,
several important Western-language works on Chinese civilization had appeared. Apart from the *De Christiana Expeditione
apud Sinas* that had an impact on Europe, the Augustinian Juan
González de Mendoza (1545–1618) had published his *Historia
de las cosas más notables, ritos y costumbres* in Rome in 1585,
just a few years after Ricci entered Macao. French translations
of both these works were available before 1685.[30] Other possible sources of information for the French Jesuits were the
printed editions of the Jesuit *Litterae Annuae* and the study of
the missions in the East by Daniello Bartoli, S.J. (1608–1658).
In contrast to Ricci's and Mendoza's works, these last were fairly
general sources about missionary endeavors, with some emphasis on China. Moreover, one can point to Martino Martini's
Sinicae Historiae Decas Prima, a translation of Chinese history
sources, and the *Dernières nouvelles de la chrétienté de la
Chine.*[31]

Although many more titles could be extracted from bibliographical lists by Henri Cordier and the Jesuits Louis Pfister and

Carlos Sommervogel that reflect works published before the
French Jesuits left Brest in 1685, there appears to be no evidence that they read any of them. It could be argued that knowledge of missions was simply general knowledge of the status
of the Jesuit Order that any member could be expected to
possess. But any historian seeking documentary support for
such a position will be quite dissatisfied. There is, nonetheless,
the clear possibility that Couplet had discussed some details
with Fontaney, Bouvet, and others during his visit to Paris. Yet,
his sojourn in France on his way to Rome was very brief, and
quite likely he lacked the time to explain many significant
points about the China mission.[32]

To determine the incipient views about the Chinese that the
French Jesuits gradually developed, one must turn to their writings during their first years in Asia. Several of these unpublished
sources are incomplete diaries and letters sent more to parents
and relatives than to Jesuit superiors to describe the French
Jesuits' travels and their responses to the new surroundings in
which they lived. Such materials present data that, in turn, not
infrequently complement their published works.

French governmental sponsorship of the royal mathematicians assured passage only to Siam, for the French had no direct
commercial relations with China until the last years of the
seventeenth century. The Jesuits accompanied the French envoy
to Siam, where they were expected to find some means of entering China either through Macao or some other port. The
closer they got to China, the greater was their opportunity to
experience some Chinese customs. At the Cape of Good Hope,
which they reached in May 1685, the Dutch offered Fontaney
and Tachard some tea as an introduction to that custom in
China. But it was in Batavia that the Jesuits met their first
Chinese — four to five thousand who lived alongside Muslims,
Malays, Japanese, many natives, and Europeans. Catholicism was
banned in Batavia by the Dutch, who certainly did not want
any Jesuits preaching there or even visiting among the local
populace; however, Bouvet and Tachard at least had a chance
to visit a Chinese Buddhist temple.[33] Witnessing the ceremonies
led by six or seven priests who offered sacrifices for the dead,
the Jesuits announced themselves as priests of the Lord of

Heaven who were on their way to China to preach the law of God. The Buddhists treated them politely and gave them a betel and an areca, as was customary. The Jesuits declined the offer, however, on the pretext that it was not their custom; in reality, it was because the items had been offered to idols.

An important aspect of the French envoy's mission to the Siamese monarch, Phra Narai (r. 1657–1688), was to convert him to Catholicism. Just a few years earlier, Antoine Thomas (1644–1709), a Jesuit already in Peking by the time his French confreres arrived in Siam, assisted in the conversion of Constantine Phaulkon (1647–1688), the prime minister to the Siamese monarch. Through his envoy, Louis XIV hoped that Phra Narai's conversion would lead to that of the entire country. This never happened. In fact, the king's refusal to become a Catholic at the behest of the French envoy should not be surprising, for Bouvet himself remarked that the number of Buddhist pagodas in the capital could well equal the number of churches and chapels in Paris. Magnificent statues forty to fifty feet tall were so skillfully decorated with gold that the goldsmiths in France did not surpass the quality of workmanship in Siam.[34] Implicitly, Bouvet recognized that Buddhism in Siam was so widespread and so intimately connected with the government that the spread of Christianity would not be that easily achieved.

Deeper acquaintance with Chinese customs resulted from the Jesuits' rather lengthy stay in Siam, which lasted from September 1685 to June 1687; in fact, as they began remote preparations in June 1686 for their departure, Phra Narai discussed the customs, religions, and history of China and Tartary. He had ordered an outline history of China and a history of Hindustan to be translated into Siamese. Moreover, Phra Narai promised to send a skilled Chinese to France to translate Chinese and Siamese books into French, and two days later he issued an order to this effect; it was written "in Chinese characters, the king anticipating that language as our natural language," Bouvet noted.[35]

It was not in Siam but in Macao that they were expecting to learn Chinese and at the same time to await a reply to the letters they had written to Verbiest.[36] Although Chinese was very difficult because of the different tones in its spoken form and because there were "as many different letters as words," yet in one year one could learn enough to give catechetical instructions. The Siamese envoys who traveled to Peking proved to be quite helpful to the French Jesuits who anticipated working in the Chinese capital. Phra Narai also gave each Jesuit twelve silk suits cut according to Chinese fashion.[37]

From several letters that Antoine Thomas sent to his French Jesuit colleagues in Siam, they acquired valuable information about certain aspects of Chinese customs, especially those in Peking, and the types of discussions on mathematics and science that the Chinese held with Verbiest, Thomas, and others. So far as is known, the only account of these discussions can be found in an extract of a letter from Bouvet to a Jesuit confrere in France, one striking detail of which merits attention. The K'ang-hsi emperor (r. 1661–1722) asked a Christian eunuch if the Catholic religion allowed veneration of Confucius and if a Catholic could show it by prostrating himself to the ground. The eunuch denied this, saying that Confucius, a man like anyone else, could not come to man's aid, so that such signs should not be shown to him. But the emperor pressed on by asking if the eunuch did not show a similar homage to his parents at the beginning of the new year without demanding or expecting anything from them. If this was so, why then was he not able to show the same customary signs of respect to Confucius? Bouvet commented that "the authentic witness of the emperor" showed that "the veneration that the Chinese have for Confucius is purely political and is by no means a cult," but had "some simple marks of adoration."[38] Written before Bouvet set foot in China, this letter clearly demonstrates his own conviction and support of Ricci's interpretation in the Chinese Rites controversy.

Changes in plans had to be made to continue the good relations Phra Narai had developed with the French envoy's party, both merchants and missionaries alike. He requested that Tachard return to France and bring twelve Jesuits as Phaulkon had earlier suggested. In addition, he prevailed on Le Comte to stay in Siam until Tachard returned. The other four Jesuits set out for Macao in early July 1686, but a violent storm forced them to return to Siam. Unable to sail again until the following

June, the five (Le Comte had been allowed to rejoin his confreres) finally arrived in Ningpo, Chekiang province, on 23 July 1687.[39]

Communication difficulties developed among the French Jesuits in Ningpo, Verbiest in Peking, and the Chinese officials who were with the emperor in Tartary. The dilatory tactics of Chin Hung (*chin-shih* 1652), the governor of Chekiang, in refusing for two weeks to relay the imperial orders to proceed to the capital, showed the French Jesuits the type of hostility to Christianity that prevailed among some officials in the provinces. This hostility was quite in contrast to the favorable impression made on them by the nascent Chinese Church they were shortly to visit. The group's imperial clearance to enter Peking was shown by banners on the junks that brought them to the various cities. Leaving Ningpo on 26 November, they arrived four days later in Hangchow, where they stayed until 21 December. They were also impressed by a young Christian, a prospective Jesuit novice, who aided them throughout their stay in Hangchow, where they met the Jesuit vice-provincial, Prospero Intorcetta (1625–1696).[40] Later in Soochow, they met another Jesuit and also a number of important Chinese Christians, descendants of Hsü Kuang-ch'i. In viewing the churches of these cities, both in terms of buildings and as communities of worship, the French Jesuits were able to get a quick overview of the steady progress the Church was making. But without a knowledge of the language, this understanding was effected through the eyes of their confreres, not necessarily through those of the Chinese Christians.

Having reached the outer limits of Peking by 1 February 1688, they learned of the death of the empress dowager, the grandmother of the emperor, on 27 January and that of Verbiest the next day. Not until 7 February did they enter Peking itself, where all official business halted until the mandatory mourning period ended. Verbiest's death fundamentally altered the positive hopes that the French Jesuits had experienced until then. After an examination by the Board of Astronomy conducted by Tomé Pereira, S.J. (1645–1708), the emperor ordered Gerbillon and Bouvet to work in the court, whereas the others were allowed to live in the interior of the country according to their

choice.[41] As a result, Le Comte, Visdelou, and Fontaney went
to Shansi, though Fontaney then proceeded to Nanking. The
location of the new arrivals in China gave them excellent
perspectives from which they could view the Chinese: one from
the capital, the other from the provinces. This dual perspective
emerged and developed during the first years of their living in
China.

As the superior of the French Jesuits, Fontaney was kept busy
during his initial years in China, since the emperor allowed
him and his two companions to live anywhere they chose. He
interpreted that permission to mean that they could take their
scientific instruments and use them in their mission stations.
In addition, he sought a port city through which the French
could have postal access to Europe, since Macao was not considered amenable for this purpose.[42] Fontaney was fully cogni-
zant of the reasons why Louis XIV had sent them and realized
that above all the Académie Royale des Sciences expected
periodic reports on their astronomical observations. So, after
sojourning in China and diligently studying the language for
more than a year, he devised a plan by which the French Jesuits
could continue their astronomical observations and still work
for the salvation of souls.

To work in Peking was not conducive to his plan because
of the misleading opinion in that city that the calculations based
on European tables were so accurate that they were immune
from error. As a result, when an eclipse or some other similar
event happened, more attention was given to show the accuracy
of the calculations than accepting the possibility of error in
the instruments. In his view, all the observations made in Peking
were only "pure ceremonies" and could not fulfill the plans
for comparative work that the Paris observatory wanted.[43] For
this and other reasons, he considered Peking an unpropitious
place for his purposes and for corresponding with Paris about
astronomical observations; hence, he rejected the idea of living
there. Because the emperor allowed him to reside wherever
he desired, he could, with the astronomical instruments he still
had, set up in another part of China an observatory no less
durable than the one in Paris. The tower would not have a
platform because the Bureau of Astronomy would not approve

such a plan. But the members of the Académie knew that a platform was not essential; well-equipped rooms were sufficient. In China, there were no high buildings to obstruct the view of the heavens. He envisioned setting up three such sites: one in Shansi, another in Nanking, and a third somewhere in the southern part of China. Then, if Louis XIV would ask the Jesuit general for more recruits, each site could have three or four Jesuits, and each house would continue to belong to the vice-province.

To this general plan, Fontaney added some specific proposals that were intended to assist the development of the sciences in China. First, he urged the recruitment of some Christian schoolmasters, perhaps ten or twelve, to teach young Chinese pupils in tuition-free schools to be set up in major cities and near Jesuit houses. He realized that some Christian parents no longer permitted their children to attend school: some because of straitened financial circumstances, others because of their reluctance to send their children to "idolatrous masters" who put "pernicious books" in their hands and would not allow them to attend Mass on Sundays and feast days even for one hour. Providing them with Christian teachers would aid in preserving their faith and, at the same time, give them an opportunity for a Christian education. Even if non-Christian children wanted to take advantage of such an education, Fontaney saw no difficulty in their attendance. The exact origins of this proposed school system are obscure, although Fontaney may have observed the impact of Buddhist temples on the teaching of youth in Siam.

Another proposal was that some of the Chinese students might be lodged in Jesuit houses. The better students from the school were to be eligible for this status. With ten or twelve in each house, they could serve in the Church and become acquainted with Christian living. An excellent Chinese master was to supervise their studies so that their entire occupation was to be nothing but study. Some of the students quite possibly would seek entrance into religious life, but even if this did not happen, they would at least leave the Jesuit houses well prepared to take the official Chinese examinations for the literati degrees. In the long run, this would have far-reaching and important

consequences for Christianity in China. Both proposals were
to be realized through royal foundations supported by Louis
XIV. For the Jesuits, this would be an excellent means of learning
spoken and written Chinese. These educational centers were
to become additional sites for collecting noteworthy Chinese
scientific data for transmission to the Royal Library in Paris.
Then, once this arrangement became effective, Visdelou, Le
Comte, and Fontaney could ask the emperor for permission to
go to Tartary and Korea, especially since Bouvet had been prevented before from going there. This would constitute a fourth
station among a people who did not know the true God. Indeed,
Fontaney added, it would fulfill the prophecy of Antoine Verjus
(1632–1706), who told them before they left France that they
were to become the restorers of the China mission.[44]

Fontaney also envisioned a "second stage" over and beyond
the implanting of the Catholic faith in China, a stage that would
demand additional personnel. By no means a visionary, he entertained hopes for the formation of a Chinese Jesuit province,
or even an assistancy, with perhaps two or three hundred Jesuits
to be drawn from France, Spain, and Portugal. Convinced that
this project would be quite feasible if these countries would
act cooperatively, he felt that the time for action was ripe, especially now that the routes to China through the Caspian Sea
and Moscow were about to be opened. He found it more than
ironic that the Turks and the heretical English and Dutch allowed missionaries to travel through their territory but that
the Portuguese alone preferred to see the loss of souls rather
than allow passage to a missionary who had not come by way
of Portugal.[45] This type of nationalistic dispute Fontaney alone
could not resolve, but one cannot help admire his splendid
vision for the missions. His plans were not conceived before
entering China, but were based on his practical, though relatively short, experience of traveling and working on the mission; yet, except for his opening a French Jesuit residence in
Canton in 1692, they were not to be realized, partly because
the Portuguese vice-provincial limited the opportunities of the
French Jesuits and partly because no letters from France arrived
in China for nearly four years.

Fontaney's companion, Le Comte, published his views of

China in his *Nouveaux Mémoires*, a compilation of various letters addressed to French savants. His efforts in understanding the Chinese are perhaps best illustrated in the second volume. In discussing the politics and government of China, Le Comte clearly was interested in appreciating the basic moral principles of the Chinese and the maxims of government that China followed. Among the Chinese there were three principles of morality. The first concerned individual families in which love, kindness, and respect of children for their fathers was so set that neither bad treatment, advanced age, nor superior rank one had acquired could ever change this relationship. One could not know to what perfection "this first sentiment of nature" had been carried among the Chinese.

The second moral principle was to accustom the people to regard the mandarins as the emperor himself, for they represented his person. To attain this goal, they always appeared in public "with a retinue and an air of authority capable of inspiring veneration." Borne in sedan chairs, they were allowed immediate passage wherever they went; the people were to move to the right or left. If a judicial matter was brought before them in their palaces, the people had to speak to them on their knees. Since they had the right of using a bastinado, it was always in fear that anyone approached them. Called the benefactor, conserver, and father of the people, the mandarin, who was to be transferred to another post at the end of his tour of duty, was expected to shed some tears at seeing the tender marks of affection that the people showed him at his farewell. Le Comte added that this profound respect of the children for their fathers and the veneration the people had for their mandarins preserved more than anything else "peace in the families and tranquility in the towns." He was convinced that good order among such a large population came principally from these two sources.[46]

The third principle of morality was quite important, for it was to instill in the people "civility, modesty, and a certain air of politeness" capable of inspiring meekness. By this characteristic, the Chinese held, men differed from beasts and the Chinese differed from other men. They claimed that ferocious behavior in certain peoples infallibly disturbed their countries. The source of such behavior was domestic quarrels when no respect was given to anyone, and thus the elements of revolt were engendered. But the Chinese, Le Comte noted, knew how to suffer, to conceal and to smother resentment. No class of people among them was exempt from this third principle, for artisans, domestics, and peasants (and he was astounded to see a thousand times even footmen) bent their knees before one another in saying farewell. Even villagers paid more compliments to one another at their feasts than Frenchmen paid to one another in their public ceremonies.[47]

Among the ten maxims of government that Le Comte discovered in Chinese political administration, one particularly caught his attention as a foreign missionary. The Chinese never allowed foreigners to settle down in their empire,[48] for they were convinced that mixing with barbaric peoples would debase the Chinese and lead to corruption and disorder. Moreover, the differences among peoples necessarily included a diversity of customs, languages, moods, and religions. These were sources of quarrels that led to revolts, for such people were not members of the same family, sharing the same ideas. Le Comte did not fault this Chinese policy when it dealt with false religions, for, in his view, they almost always inspired ideas of revolt, formed as they were by a spirit of cabal and trouble. On the other hand, the Christians, with their humility, meekness, and obedience to sovereign authority contributed to peace, union, and love among peoples. This trait the Chinese began to recognize after an entire century of examining the Christian religion.[49]

Of the three French Jesuits in the provinces, Visdelou perhaps is the most elusive, since few of his letters or other manuscripts from his early years in China appear to be extant. This stands in direct contrast to his lengthy translations from Chinese texts that he completed in the last decades of his life and which have remained unpublished. There is but one incident related by Bouvet that shows Visdelou's knowledge of Chinese literature. Fontaney and Visdelou arrived in Peking in June 1693 in answer to an imperial summons first issued in February. Since the emperor was ill, Yin-t'i (1672–1734), the emperor's oldest son, met them. After he returned to his father's apartment, Yin-jeng (1674–1725), the heir apparent, acting in his official capacity as the substitute for his father, received them. The meeting was quite cordial, for Yin-jeng was interested in learning more about Fontaney's mathematical capabilities.

Upon hearing of Visdelou's progress in Chinese literature, Yin-jeng was surprised that he could not name any book of ancient Chinese literature that Visdelou either had not already read or did not personally know. Yin-jeng pressed further by asking Visdelou to explain passages from the Five Classics. Visdelou's precise and facile answers led Yin-jeng to declare that Visdelou was the most skillful European to have come to China until then. Yin-jeng asked if the doctrine of Confucius was quite different from Christianity. Visdelou replied that there was perfect harmony between the two, except for the *Book of Changes* (*I Ching*), which was purely superstitious. Yin-jeng was delighted to hear Visdelou's reply, except for his comments on the *Book of Changes*. He told Visdelou that no one had yet fully comprehended the exact meaning of that work.[50] In his first five years in China, Visdelou had thus definitely advanced in the study of Chinese literature and was recognized for his efforts by the heir apparent, who, in turn, explained the incident to his father, the K'ang-hsi emperor.

It must be stressed that Bouvet and Gerbillon, the two French Jesuits assigned to the capital, had to adapt to a lifestyle neither of them had initially sought. Bouvet's real desire was to be a missionary in Tartary, whereas Gerbillon had already indicated his aversion to staying at the royal court in Siam since he wanted to be a missionary somewhere in China. The diaries and letters of both Jesuits contain a wealth of information about their experiences at the imperial court, but only a few incidents can be selected for this study.

One of the most immediate needs was for both Jesuits to become fluent in Chinese and Manchu. They were not the first, for Schall and Verbiest, among others, had done so beforehand. But for Gerbillon, who spent more than five months in 1688 on the first negotiation missions to Seleginsk and then an additional four months at Nerchinsk in 1689, there was little leisure time for such language study. Bouvet, however, progressed sufficiently within that period. The K'ang-hsi emperor insisted during February 1690 that both Jesuits must attain proficiency in

Manchu. On one occasion the emperor found them along with Antoine Thomas and Joseph Suarez (1656–1736) at an imperial hall (*Yang-hsin tien*). To the emperor's inquiry about Gerbillon's progress in Manchu studies, they replied that their advancement was due in no small measure to the imperial tutor. Noting that Manchu was very suitable for explaining all Western sciences, they said that they had already begun such a project. When asked if they had written anything, they answered affirmatively, but added that they had left the short essay in one of the offices. The emperor ordered Gerbillon to get it. When he returned, the emperor read it and found that its viewpoints agreed with a Chinese book that dealt with the same subject. Showing that he was quite pleased with the essay that explained the digestion of food, the circulation of blood, and basic nutrition, he told Bouvet and Gerbillon that he could understand them very well but that their accent was "still uneven and different.[51]

Familiarity with the emperor and with the Manchu language backfired on these Jesuits. Through Chao Ch'ang, a Manchu court official, the emperor warned Pereira and Thomas to "take serious steps and to be extremely circumspect in their conduct"; otherwise, they might experience the same fate that befell Schall, Verbiest, and the other fathers.[52] Moreover, there were three types of people in China they could befriend: the Manchus, the Mongols with their lamas, and the Chinese with their bonzes who did not wish them any good. The emperor added, through his deputy, that he found nothing blameworthy among the Jesuits. Yet, at the very end of his discourse, he warned them never to write anything in Manchu at the bureau about Western sciences; if they wanted to translate some material, it should be done only in their rooms in the Jesuit residence. Thomas and Pereira were told to instruct the others on this matter. Bouvet indicated his surprise that a sheet of paper which had only a short explanation about nutrition and the circulation of blood should occasion such a serious admonition.[53] By this time, Bouvet and Gerbillon had been in the imperial service almost three years; yet, they were still in the process of learning to become more sensitive to Chinese and Manchu customs.

Upon learning about an incident in the province of Shantung, Bouvet and Gerbillon envisioned their role as intermediary on behalf of Christians outside the capital. Their confrere, Jean Valat, S.J. (1614?–1696), who worked for years in Tsinan, discovered on a visit to Peking in April 1690 that a Tsinan district magistrate (*chih-hsien*) had imprisoned eight or nine Christian men and women and extorted money from them as followers of a false sect condemned in China. In addition, the district magistrate had torn up a letter that Pereira had sent him and, in the mistaken belief that the letter's courier was a domestic servant of Pereira, had berated him. Another district magistrate in a neighboring area had also arrested several Christians.[54]

To help settle the issue, Chao urged the Jesuits to visit the emperor under the pretext of inquiring about his health. After Euclidean geometry lessons and dinner, the emperor, hearing from Chao about the incident, wanted to see the letters recounting these events. He recalled the Jesuits for more lessons but did not appear disconcerted. Upon their departure, Chao told them not to speak about the affair in Shantung, that it was enough that he knew about it, that the episode would not redound to the credit of the Chinese, and that the district magistrate apparently sought nothing but money.

The next day, when the emperor offered Chinese tea to Pereira and Thomas, he asked the latter to work on a mathematical problem. Calling Pereira aside, he showed him a note with some Manchu words that Pereira did not immediately understand. The emperor explained the message: He had written the governor of Shantung about the arrest of the Christians, but when he saw that Pereira intended to keep the note, he pulled it from his hands and told him not to speak about the issue to anyone.[55]

After continuing to give geometry lessons to the emperor and answering his numerous questions about Europe, the Jesuits learned from Chao a few weeks later that the emperor planned to have all their scientific works translated into Manchu for wide dissemination throughout China. If this were done, there was every reason to hope that Christianity would gradually establish itself so that one day it would prevail in China. Chao added that he did not believe it would take two centuries for Christianity to shed its fear of opposition from the Chinese or even the Manchus; but, in the meantime, he counseled patience.[56]

Two days later, after the Euclidean geometry classes with the
emperor, Chao asked the Jesuits if they had any further news
from Shantung. They replied in the negative, but the following
day a domestic sent by the Shantung governor arrived in Peking
with information the emperor had ordered collected for his
perusal about the district magistrate and the Christians. Not
long after, Chao told the Jesuits that the emperor personally
wrote his decision in Manchu. But according to Bouvet, even
though the accuser of the Christians was to be punished, the
decision did not affect the district magistrate who had imprisoned the Christians as followers of a false and seditious sect.
Moreover, the district magistrate had charged that Valat was
the head of a mutinous people. When Chao asked for their
opinion, the Jesuits stated that they had expected more from
the emperor. But Chao told them that the emperor did not
want them to speak about the matter, neither to Valat nor to
anyone else so that no one could claim the emperor was the
protector of the Europeans. Beyond that level, the emperor
did not want to become involved. This last statement saddened
the Jesuits, as Chao clearly realized. In reporting to the throne,
Chao declared that though the Jesuits were very grateful for
past imperial generosity, they appeared to be waiting for some
favorable imperial gesture in favor of the Christian law. When
the Jesuits saw the emperor at the next geometry session, he
appeared gay and contented, although they entertained little
hope of gaining their objective. Bouvet admitted that his enthusiasm for writing short essays in Manchu for the emperor
cooled considerably.[57]

The attitude of the Jesuits did not change the emperor's decision, although he seems to have maintained his interest in
the status of Christianity in China. This became clear when
Chao pointed out to him that the fine Nestorian monument at
Sian-fu in the province of Shensi was a witness that Christianity
in times past had flourished in China and had been treated
honorably by his predecessors. Chao's statement so aroused
the emperor's curiosity that he asked for a copy of the monument's inscription.[58]

On 29 April 1690, the emperor completed his customary
geometry lessons and later questioned the French Jesuits about

various customs in Europe — e.g., burial practices, punishment of criminals, the cure of smallpox and other illnesses. Afterward, Chao notified the Jesuits about the reply he had given to the emperor, who had questioned him about their reaction to the emperor's conduct toward them. He pointed out that the Jesuits had left Europe to preach the law of God publicly, and although they were most grateful for past imperial favors, they were deeply pained by the fact that their law was treated as false in China and that the bonzes and lamas continued to belittle it with impunity. To the Jesuits, it was very grievous to see their holy law considered in such a way that they, in turn, were viewed as professing and publishing a false law. In fact, the Jesuits added, they were ashamed to appear in the presence of the emperor, for if there was something reprehensible in their law, they were ready to submit to such a judgment and suffer punishment according to the laws of the Chinese empire. But if their law was true, they questioned why it should be on the same level as that of the bonzes and lamas.[59] According to Bouvet, this was but one of several occasions in which Chao expressed such views to the emperor.

As the French Jesuits were becoming more accustomed to the mode of working in the imperial court and living in Peking, they also had the opportunity to witness the emperor's sensitivity to European customs. On 30 June 1690, after the usual geometry lessons, he explained that just as his father, the Shun-chih emperor (r. 1644–1661), had posthumously honored Schall, so too had he raised Verbiest after his death to the rank of mandarin of the first order. This fact was totally unknown to Thomas, Gerbillon, and Bouvet until the emperor mentioned it. He wanted to send some court attendants to Verbiest's grave to give, in his name, the usual honors reserved for those raised to such a dignity. Not wanting to do anything contrary to the practices of the Christian law, the emperor asked if offering a cup of wine and then pouring it out would be against Christian principles. The three Jesuits replied that if one claimed nothing else than that the ceremony would honor the person in a civil way, this was not contrary to reason and consequently not contrary to the Christian law. Several days later, the ceremony in honor of Verbiest was conducted at the cemetery of Chala.[60]

The Westerners, increasingly aware of the customs of the Manchus and the Chinese, were to some degree rewarded by the emperor's appreciation of their own.

On 13 January 1691, the youngest brother of the emperor arrived unannounced at the Jesuit house in Peking.[61] Only Giandomenico Gabiani (1623–1694) and Bouvet were there, so they had to entertain him. After briefly visiting Pereira's room, the prince sat down in Gabiani's room where they offered him tea three times. He asked to see some maps. After showing him a new map of the world, they then displayed a three-volume atlas. The prince glanced at a number of the maps but spent some time over those of Italy and France, which they had to explain. This occasioned several questions from him about Christianity, especially if the Christian law was universally followed throughout Europe and if there were Christians everywhere in the world. To his query about the part of the world and the specific place where the Son of God became man, they answered in detail. Reflecting on their reply, he observed that the spot was accurately located in the middle of the world as it was known in the past and that it was also far from the extremity of Europe as well as of China. The prince asked if this religion was not the same as had entered China in the past. The Jesuits agreed and then explained that the Nestorian monument at Sian-fu was proof of this fact. Further discussion included the need for governmental protection of Christian believers and of Chinese books that explained Christian beliefs. Although Bouvet does not explicitly state this, he had been in Peking long enough to realize that their conversation would be reported to the emperor. He had experienced this in the past and knew the impact his words and those of Gabiani, his confrere, could have in the capital.

By reason of his participation in two missions with the Russians, Gerbillon was becoming an expert among the Westerners on Manchu affairs. In late January 1691, Gerbillon explained six Euclidean propositions to the emperor, who easily understood and showed great joy in this. Then, taking out a map of Asia on which he had marked the latitudes of some sites in Tartary, as the emperor had requested several days earlier, Gerbillon explained the route the Russians took to enter China and

pointed out other possible routes from Peking to Europe. He
then added that the four royal mathematicians sent by Louis
XIV had been refused passage by the Russians and thus took
another route, and the Jesuit Father General earnestly desired
to see the Russian overland route open. Further, Verbiest had
asked the General to send Jesuits for imperial service, and the
General had chosen the four who were skilled in mathematics.[62]
The emperor welcomed this news and said that without doubt
the Russians would no longer create difficulties for the Jesuits
to travel overland to Peking. Gerbillon pressed the importance
of the land route, adding that the sea route had many perils,
even though vessels coming directly from Europe needed only
eight months for a one-way trip. Gerbillon was thus returning
to the chief reason why the Jesuits were working at the Peking
court, that is, to use their contacts to promote a climate in
which they could openly preach Christianity. In fact, several
months later the emperor himself publicly showed his satisfaction with the astronomical coil the Jesuits gave him and added
a eulogy of Gerbillon, praising him above all for his candor.[63]

The French Jesuits' attempt to understand the Chinese during
their first years on the mission was rewarded by the Edict of
Toleration of March 1692. By no means were they alone responsible for this imperial decision, but the two French Jesuits in
Peking contributed significantly toward its issuance. In many
ways, the edict was the culmination of the persistent efforts
of Ricci and others to appreciate Chinese customs and habits.
To illustrate the French Jesuits' role, a short overview of the
background of the edict is pertinent.

In 1691, the Dominican Petrus de Alcalá (1640?–1705)
bought a house in Lan-ch'i, situated in the province of Chekiang.
Although such an establishment was contrary to the edict of
1669 against Christianity, the Chinese official there did not oppose him until he heard some comments from the domestics
of Alcalá. Deciding to pressure him juridically, the official asked
Alcalá how he dared to move into the city, why he preached
a foreign law, and whether he had the right to be in China.
Alcalá replied that the official had not raised any objections at
the time of the purchase of the property. He added that since
the emperor retained five Europeans whom he called to Peking

and allowed three to live in China wherever they wanted, he had bought the house in Lan-ch'i for one of them. Moreover, when the emperor allowed the missionaries to return from exile in 1671, their names were recorded in the local registers. Alcalá asked the official to check the records in Lan-ch'i.

This incident led a Chinese official in another part of Chekiang to proscribe Christianity, posting notices to that effect in all areas under his jurisdiction. Prospero Intorcetta foresaw the consequences of this move if it was not checked. He knew that the emperor a few years earlier had, with his own hand, deleted several lines from a book that otherwise put the Christian law among the numerous dangerous sects and popular heresies.[64] This book was an important work customarily read to the people several times a year. Thus, in Intorcetta's judgment, the incident was a question of a Chinese official's condemning on his own what the emperor had apparently approved. He felt obliged, therefore, to write to the governor of the province of Chekiang, Chang P'eng-ko (1649–1725), requesting that the subordinate Chinese official be made to retract his decree proscribing Christians. Chang, however, sent Intorcetta's letter to the subordinate official who, affronted by the Jesuit's move, asked him by whose authority he lived in Chekiang and ordered him to leave at once after he had burned not only all Christian books but also the bookplates. Intorcetta retorted that he lived in Hangchow (province of Chekiang) by the same authority that allowed the Chinese official to be there, namely, the emperor himself. He reminded the official that in 1688, when the emperor visited the area, he (Intorcetta) had accompanied the imperial entourage and that the emperor, noticing his advanced age, told him to return to his church where he could pass the rest of his days in peace. Thus, the official should realize, Intorcetta cautioned, that ordering him out of Chekiang would be an affront to the imperial will.[65]

Intorcetta's next move was to contact the missionaries in Peking, who, in turn, wrote to Gerbillon, then accompanying the emperor on a hunt in Tartary. Gerbillon believed it was best not to approach the emperor directly but to ask Songgotu (d. 1703), his friend, for assistance. The latter wrote to Chang P'eng-ko, who was highly honored to get a letter from such an influential' official at the court; but so displeased was he at its contents and so piqued that a foreigner counted more at court than he did, that he ordered all the churches seized, their statues and other accessories broken, and several Christians, including Intorcetta, chastised. Songgotu was not to be out-done, however, and wrote Chang and Intorcetta. He demanded that Chang take three steps: (1) deliver the letter that he (Songgotu) had addressed to Intorcetta, (2) stop persecuting Intorcetta but rather use his good offices, and (3) end all harass-ment of the missionaries and Christians. He assured Chang that a third letter, one of thanks, would be sent as soon as he learned of a change in his conduct; otherwise, this was the last letter he would receive.[66]

Despite Songgotu's efforts, nothing changed. Intorcetta, learn-ing about this correspondence, wrote the Peking Jesuits that the situation remained the same. His confreres addressed the court eunuchs who approached the emperor, since dealing di-rectly with the anti-Christian Board of Rites (*Li-pu*) was useless. Having decided to write secretly to Chang, the emperor told the Jesuits to write a secret memorial to him. In this document, the missionaries listed their past services to the throne: the work of Verbiest, the trip of Claudio Filippo Grimaldi (1638–1712) to Europe on the emperor's behalf, the Jesuit labors at the Nerchinsk negotiations, and Bouvet's and Gerbillon's geometry and philosophy lessons to the emperor. This memo-rial the emperor translated into Manchu and returning it, he told them to add or delete anything they saw fit.[67]

In early February 1692, the Jesuits presented another memo-rial reviewing the entire issue of the persecution of Christianity. The emperor sent it to the Board of Rites, but the onset of the Chinese New Year delayed a reply for two weeks. When the board met, however, its members scarcely discussed the memorial and satisfied themselves with confirming the old edicts against Christianity. This meant that no native Chinese could become Christians, even though the officials in Chekiang were warned not to confuse Christianity with the seditious sects of China. Chagrined by the board's reply, the emperor took no action for several days but reluctantly signed the document presented by the board. The Jesuits contacted Chao Ch'ang who pleaded their case with the emperor. In Chekiang, meantime, the governor, Chang P'eng-ko was elated and, after issuing even more stringent orders against the Christians, sent a memorial to the emperor asking him to get rid of them altogether. But the memorial arrived too late. By the time it was presented, circumstances in Peking had changed.

Songgotu again raised the issue with the emperor. Reminding him of the Jesuit services to the imperial court, he stressed that what the Jesuits wanted was a condemnation of their law, if it was dangerous. But Songgotu immediately asked if there was any law as wholesome as theirs or more useful for governing people?[68] The emperor replied that although the case was closed, he would still continue to favor the missionaries but that the rage of the officials against them did not allow him to follow his inclinations. Songgotu then asked him if he was not master in China and whether he could not exert his authority when dealing with such subjects, distinguished as they were. Impressed by Songgotu's remarks, the emperor wrote to the officials of the Board of Rites on 19 March and explained the services that the Jesuits had consistently performed for the good of China. Moreover, he declared, since their law was not seditious, it seemed good to permit its acceptance by anyone wishing to embrace it. Ordering that all edicts against Christianity were to be burned, he directed the board to deliberate on the question and report its answer.

For the initial deliberations, only the Manchu members of the board convened as a separate committee. Songgotu very forcefully defended Christianity by comparing it to the freedom that the lamas of Tartary and the bonzes of China enjoyed in their exercise of religion. Muslims had even built a mosque in Hangchow that dominated all the public buildings. When the Europeans asked for the same liberty to preach, the government rejected them as if the laws proscribing Europeans from entering China had also proscribed the truth. Interrupted at this point by his audience, Songgotu countered that if they could find one vice that Christianity allowed or one virtue that it did not admit, then its condemnation was in order; otherwise, it should be approved. After the Manchu committee eventually endorsed Songgotu's recommendation, the emperor ordered the Chinese members of the Board of Rites to assemble with their Manchu counterparts. They deliberated for some time and presented a memorial to the emperor stating that the Europeans admired Chinese culture, had performed valuable services to China — e.g., calendar making, negotiations with the Russians, etc. — and had not committed any crimes. Since the Chinese could worship in the temples of lamas and Buddhists, it was unfair that Christianity should be prohibited. Thus, the Chinese were allowed to attend the churches for worship. The Board of Rites added that the edict would be sent to all the officials throughout China.[69] The emperor signed and approved the edict at once and ordered that copies be sent to all governors and governors-general who were to make copies for distribution to all subordinate officials in their area.

Imperial support of Christianity continued after the Edict of Toleration of 1692, and the following year the emperor granted the French Jesuits a residence near the palace. An increase of Jesuit personnel necessitated additional living quarters; and, what is more, he wanted some of them to be more readily available rather than have them shuttle across Peking from the South Church (*Nan-t'ang*).[70] This residence and the adjacent North Church (*Pei-t'ang*), which was opened in 1703, were positive external signs of imperial favor not to be overlooked by officials who, though scattered in China, depended for their authority on the emperor.

During the two centuries in which the early Jesuit mission in China perdured, it is noteworthy that neither Ricci, the founder of the mission, nor the French Jesuit mathematicians were well prepared before going to China. Despite the efforts of his predecessors to enter that empire, Ricci succeeded primarily because of his willingness to adapt himself to a different civilization. As China was a country relatively unknown to late sixteenth-century Europe, Ricci had to learn as a pioneer in Macao and in China itself. But the French Jesuit mathematicians, despite more sources from which to understand China, came almost equally unprepared as Ricci. The need for quick decisions by Jesuit superiors in France to fulfill Louis XIV's desire to send a number of Jesuits to the East and especially to China hardly allowed them much time for reading about the country. Then, too, the language training that Ricci faced differed from that of the French Jesuits because the nature of the mission had changed. Ricci struggled to master Chinese and became very successful, as even his detractors had to concede. The French Jesuit mathematicians who worked in Peking were required to learn Chinese and Manchu since both languages were mandatory for imperial service. Bouvet and Gerbillon, for instance, had to spend many hours preparing translations from Chinese and Western languages into Manchu. Moreover, many Manchu converts lived outside Peking, as Le Comte noted, so that proper care of them obligated these early French Jesuits in the provinces to learn Manchu.

When Ricci lived in Peking, his service at court was considerably different from the lifestyle the French Jesuit mathematicians were expected to follow. Ricci was not a personal tutor to an emperor. Schall had such a role, as did Verbiest later, but both developed this over time by meeting the rigorous demands of the imperial court. Gerbillon and Bouvet, however, were thrust into such a position despite their youth and inexperience. Besides astronomy, they had to teach geometry, medicine, and philosophy to the emperor, whose curiosity was by then becoming legendary. Ricci had translated several works into Chinese and written a number of essays on Christianity in order to attract, above all, the Chinese scholarly class; therefore, due to Ricci and others on the mission, by the time the French Jesuit mathematicians arrived in Peking in 1688, a significant body of Christian literature in Chinese was already available.

To try to claim that Ricci understood the Chinese better than the French Jesuit mathematicians or vice versa would be a disservice to both. Faced with formidable obstacles in mastering the language, Ricci had the fortitude and openness that won many Chinese to listen to him, although few became converts. The French Jesuit mathematicians, however, had different hurdles to overcome. The best mathematician among them, Fontaney, never worked in Peking, though one of the chief purposes of the group was to carry on astronomical observations. His attempts to do so elsewhere in China were not successful. Le Comte left Amoy in late 1691 to return to France and then to Rome to report on the status of the mission, but he never returned to China. His writings, however, became important in the Chinese Rites Controversy that was rekindled in 1693 and later. Visdelou became highly competent in ancient Chinese literature and history, but more research is needed before further assessment of his role in his first years in China can be made. Of the original five mathematicians, Bouvet and Gerbillon were most responsible for laying the groundwork on which later French Jesuits, who entered China under Bouvet's direction in 1698, could expand. Representative of this group were such men as Dominique Parennin (1665–1741), Joseph Marie Anne de Moyriac de Mailla (1669–1748), Jean-Baptiste Régis (1663–1738), and Joseph Henri de Prémare (1666–1736).

From the Sino-Manchu perspective, the Jesuits served the empire by their constant efforts to appreciate Chinese civilization. Christianity became tolerated in China in 1692 not because all the government officials accepted it or because a significant number of scholars became converts. Rather, it was considered to be a promoter of general harmony in Chinese society as exemplified in the conduct of the missionaries who had for more than a century continued to understand Chinese civilization in its own right. The Edict of Toleration became at least in part the Chinese and Manchu response to that Jesuit effort of understanding the Chinese.

NOTES

1. L. Carrington Goodrich, *A Short History of the Chinese People* (New York, 1959), 195. For a biography of Cheng, see L. Carrington Goodrich and Chaoying Fang, eds., *Dictionary of Ming Biography 1368–1644*, 2 vols. (New York, 1976), 2:192–94.

2. Georg Schurhammer, S.J., *Franz Xaver. Sein Leben und seine Zeit*, 2 vols. in 4 (Freiburg, 1955–1963), 2, part 3:597–682.

3. For a discussion of Valignano's views, see Pasquale M. D'Elia, S.J., ed., *Fonti Ricciane: documenti originali concernenti Matteo Ricci e la storia delle prime relazioni tra l'Europa e la Cina 1579–1615*, 3 vols. (Rome, 1942–1949), 1:lxxxix–xcix.

4. Pasquale M. D'Elia, S.J., "Il metodo di adattamento del P. Matteo Ricci, S.J. in Cina," *Civiltà Cattolica* 3 (anno 107) (July 1956):174–75.

5. Essential materials for understanding Ricci are: Pietro Tacchi Venturi, S.J., ed., *Opere storiche del P. Matteo Ricci, S.J.*, 2 vols. (Macerata,

1911–1913); D'Elia, *Fonti Ricciane;* and Nicolas Trigault, S.J., ed., *China in the Sixteenth Century: The Journals of Matthew Ricci, 1583–1610,* trans. Louis Gallagher, S.J. (New York, 1953). Two assessments by Henri Bernard-Maitre, S.J. are still noteworthy: *Le Père Matthieu Ricci et la Société Chinoise de son temps, 1552–1610,* 2 vols. (Tientsin, 1937) and *Matteo Ricci's Scientific Contribution to China,* trans. E. C. Werner (Peking, 1935). See also Wolfgang Franke's biography of Ricci in *DMB,* 2:1137–44. A compilation not cited by Franke is Chou K'ang-hsieh, ed., *Li Ma-tou yen-chiu lun-chi* (Collected essays on Matteo Ricci) (Hong Kong, 1971). A list of contents and an assessment of the latter work appear in the present writer's review in *Archivum Historicum Societatis Iesu* 44 (1975):186–88.

6. Johannes Bettray, S.V.D., *Die Akkomodationsmethode des P. Matteo Ricci S.J. in China* (Rome, 1955), vi.

7. George Harris, "The Mission of Matteo Ricci, S.J.: A Case Study of an Effort at Guided Culture Change in China in the Sixteenth Century," *Monumenta Serica* 25 (1966):158–59.

8. *New Catholic Encyclopedia,* s.v. "Missionary Adaptation" (by Louis J. Luzbetak).

9. The issue did not arise for Protestants in Europe until Gottfried Wilhelm Freiherr von Leibniz began to show an interest in the Jesuits working there. See R.F. Merkel, *Die Anfänge der protestantischen Missionsbewegung. G.W. Leibniz und die China-Mission* (Leipzig, 1920), and David E. Mungello, *Leibniz and Confucianism: The Search for Accord* (Honolulu, 1977).

10. Joseph Dehergne, S.J., *Répertoire des Jésuites de Chine de 1552 à 1800* (Rome, 1973), 324–25.

11. George H. Dunne, S.J., *Generation of Giants: The Story of the Jesuits in China in the Last Decades of the Ming Dynasty* (Notre Dame, 1962), 18.

12. Ibid., 19–21; *DMB,* 2:1137.

13. Ruggieri's efforts were not successful in part because of the death of four popes within a year and a half, as George Dunne explains in his article on Ruggieri in *DMB,* 2:1148–49. See also Dehergne, *Répertoire,* 235–36.

14. Dunne, *Generation of Giants,* 44. For a discussion of Ricci's essay on friendship, see Fang Hao, "Li Ma-tou Chiao-yu lun hsin-yen" (A new study on Matteo Ricci's *Chiao-yu lun*), in *Fang Hao liu-shih tzu-ting kao* (The collected works of Maurus Fang Hao revised and edited by the author on his sixtieth birthday) 2 vols. with Supplement (Taipei, 1969), 2:1849–70. A reply to some of the problems that Fang Hao raised in this essay, which first appeared in 1948, was made by Pasquale M. D'Elia, S.J. in "Further Notes on Matteo Ricci's *De Amicitia,*" *Monumenta Serica* 15 (1956):356–77.

15. Dunne, *Generation of Giants,* 94–98. For biographies of Hsü and Li, see Arthur W. Hummel, ed., *Eminent Chinese of the Ch'ing Period (1644–1912),* 2 vols. (Washington, D.C., 1943–1944), 1:316–19, 452–54, respectively. For data on Feng, see *DMB,* 2:1141.

16. A comprehensive study of the map is that of P. Pasquale M. D'Elia, S.J., *Il mappamondo cinese del P. Matteo Ricci, S.I. (terza edizione Pechino 1602) conservato presso la Biblioteca Vaticana, commentato tradotto e annotato dal . . .* (Vatican City, 1938). The map is reproduced in T. Severin, *The Oriental Adventure. Explorers of the East* (Boston, 1976), 78–79.

17. Ruggieri's catechism marks a step in the adaptation efforts in the Chinese context. See Jacques Gernet, "Sur les différentes versions du premier catéchisme en chinois de 1584," in *Studia Sino-Mongolica. Festschrift für Herbert Franke,* ed. Wolfgang Bauer (Wiesbaden, 1979), 407–16. On the movement to return to the Classics, see Henri Bernard-Maitre, S.J., "Whence the Philosophic Movement at the Close of the Ming?" *Bulletin of the Catholic University of Peking* 8 (1931):67–73; Paul Demiéville, "The First Philosophic Contacts between Europe and China," *Diogenes* 58 (Summer 1967):75–103; and Jacques Gernet, "A Propos des contacts entre la Chine et l'Europe aux XVIIe et XVIIIe siècles," *Acta Asiatica* 23 (1972):78–92. As Donald Treadgold has remarked: "Whether Jesuit influence on modern Chinese philosophy was marginal or substantial, it deserves further careful study." *The West in Russia and China: Secular and Religious Thought in Modern Times,* 2 vols. (Cambridge, England, 1973), 2:33. Further discussion is in John W. Witek, S.J., *Controversial Ideas in China and in Europe: A Biography of Jean-François Foucquet, S.J. (1665–1741)* (Rome, 1982), 146 n. 5.

18. D'Elia, *Fonti Ricciane,* 1:108–9; Harris, "Mission of Ricci," 107–8.

19. On the rather heated discussion in which San Huai lost his temper but Ricci remained calm, see Dunne, *Generation of Giants,* 62; D'Elia, *Fonti Ricciane,* 2:75–77.

20. Matteo Ricci, *T'ien-chu shih-i,* in *T'ien-hsüeh ch'u-han* (First collection of writings on Learning from Heaven), comp. Li Chih-tsao. Reprinted in Wu Hsiang-hsiang, ed., *Chung-kuo shih-hsüeh ts'ung-shu* (Collectanea of Chinese historical studies), 23 (Taipei, 1965), 351–636; for titles of the sections, see 399, 421, 450, 491, 521, 562, 602.

21. D'Elia, *Fonti Ricciane,* 2:292.

22. Ricci, *T'ien-chu shih-i,* in Li, *T'ien-hsüeh ch'u-han,* 599–602.

23. Kirsten Yü Greenblatt, "Chu-hung and Lay Buddhism in the Late Ming," in *The Unfolding of Neo-Confucianism,* ed. Wm. Theodore de Bary (New York, 1975), 113–16; Yü Chün-fang, *The Renewal of Buddhism in China: Chu-hung and the Late Ming Synthesis* (New York, 1981), 87–90. The *p'i-hsieh yün-tung* lasted well into the early Ch'ing

period. Jacques Gernet's *Chine et Christianisme. Action et réaction* (Paris, 1982) is a recent attempt to understand this late Ming movement, but it relies heavily on Buddhist, not necessarily Confucian, anti-Christian writings.

24. For an illustration of Ricci's map in Chang Huang's *Encyclopedia of Geography* (*T'u-shu pien*), see D'Elia, *Fonti Ricciane*, 2:plate 8; also Joseph Needham, *Science and Civilisation in China*, 7 vols. to date (Cambridge, England, 1954–), 3:plate 90.

25. Kenneth Ch'en, "Matteo Ricci's Contribution to and Influence on Geographical Knowledge in China," *Journal of the American Oriental Society* 59 (1939):325–59, and the corrigenda, 509. See also Hung Wei-lien, "K'ao Li Ma-tou te shih-chieh ti-t'u" (A study of Matteo Ricci's world map), in Chou, *Li Ma-tou yen-chiu*, 67–124. Wada Sei considered Ricci's map and the beginnings of cartography in China "the most important event in the history of culture during the Ming dynasty." See Albert Chan, *The Glory and Fall of the Ming Dynasty* (Norman, 1982), 390.

26. For an extensive study in Japanese, see Ayuzawa Shintarō, "Matteo Ricci no sekaizu ni kansuru shiteki kenkyū" (A historical study of Matteo Ricci's world map), *Yokohama shiritsu daigaku kiyō* (*Journal of Yokohama Municipal University*) 18 (August 1953):1–239.

27. D'Elia, *Fonti Ricciane*, 2:540.

28. Witek, *Controversial Ideas*, 21–22.

29. Ibid., 24–33.

30. The *De Christiana Expeditione apud Sinas* is the extensively edited Latin translation of Ricci's journals by Nicolas Trigault, S.J. (1577–1628). For details, see Trigault, *China in the Sixteenth Century*, xvii–xxii. A recent reprint of the French translation is Nicolas Trigault, S.J., *Histoire de l'expédition chrétienne au royaume de la Chine, 1582–1610* (Paris, 1978). For earlier translations, see Henri Cordier, *Bibliotheca Sinica*, 5 vols. (Paris, 1904–1924), 2:809–11. The French Jesuit mathematicians were not the first French Jesuits to enter China, for in 1654–55 a number of them responded to the call of Alexander Rhodes, S.J. (1591–1660) to work in Tonkin, Cochin China, and China; only a few French Jesuits worked in China under the patronage of the Portuguese crown. See Louis Pfister, S.J., *Notices biographiques et bibliographiques sur les Jésuites de l'ancienne mission de Chine, 1552–1773*, 2 vols. Variétés sinologiques, nos. 59 and 60 (Shanghai, 1932–1934), 1:294.

Mendoza's *Historia* was reprinted in Madrid in 1944. For various other editions and translations, see Cordier, *Bibliotheca*, 1:7–15. A Japanese translation has also appeared: Yazawa Toshihiko, ed., *Gonsāresu de Mendōsa Shina daiō kokushi* ([Juan] González de Mendoza's account of the great kingdom [China]) (Tokyo, 1965).

31. For lists of the *Litterae Annuae* about the China and Japan missions, see Cordier, *Bibliotheca*, 2:795–815. See also Joseph Dehergne, S.J., "Les Lettres annuelles des missions jésuites de Chine au temps des Ming (1581–1644)," *Archivum Historicum Societatis Iesu* 49 (1980):379–92. Daniello Bartoli, S.J., *Dell'istoria della compagnia de Giesù. La Cina. Terze parte dell'Asia* (Rome, 1663) contains an extensive account comprising more than a thousand pages. Martini's *Sinicae Historiae Decas Prima* (Munich, 1658) was not translated into French until 1692, in contrast to many of the early works by Europeans about China. For the contents of *Dernières nouvelles de la chrétienté de la Chine* (Paris, 1668), see Cordier, *Bibliotheca*, 2:830–31.

32. Carlos Sommervogel, S.J., *Bibliothèque de la Compagnie de Jésus*, 12 vols. (Brussels, 1890–1932). On Couplet's visit to France, see Joachim Bouvet, S.J., *Voiage de Siam du Père Bouvet*, ed. Janette C. Gatty (Leiden, 1963), 10–11. Besides trying to get financial support from the Sun King for the mission, Couplet was also delivering Verbiest's letter inviting Fontaney to come to Peking.

33. Ibid., 45, 75, 85–86.

34. Ibid., 108. On the conversion of Phaulkon, see Mme. Yves de Thomaz de Bossièrre, *Un Belge mandarin à la cour de Chine aux XVIIᵉ et XVIIIᵉ siècles. Antoine Thomas, 1644–1709. Ngan To P'ing-che* (Paris, 1977), 20–22.

35. Bouvet to his mother, 20 June 1686, "Voiage de Siam" Manuscripts, fols. 335–36, Wason Collection, Cornell University Library, Ithaca, New York.

36. Gerbillon to his father, 5 June 1686, in Henri Cordier, "Cinq lettres inédites du Père Gerbillon. S.J.," *T'oung Pao* 7 (1906):444. Bouvet, in a letter to his sister 21 June 1686, refers to their hope of getting to Macao, "Voiage de Siam" MSS., fols. 341–42, Wason Collection, Cornell University Library, Ithaca, New York.

37. Gerbillon to his father, 1 July 1686, Cordier, "Cinq lettres," 448. This letter is a postscript to his letter of 5 June.

38. Bouvet to Claude Bertrand Tachereau de Linières, "Voiage de Siam" MSS., fols. 404–5, Wason Collection, Cornell University Library, Ithaca, New York. Bouvet, *Voiage de Siam*, xcvii, suggests that the date of this letter is between November 1685 and July 1686.

39. Phra Narai put pressure on Gerbillon to stay, but he said his vocation was to go to China and added that he did not foresee himself working in the royal court. Gerbillon to his mother, 19 June 1686, Cordier, "Cinq lettres," 451.

40. Intorcetta labored first in Kiangsi province and later in Hangchow, Chekiang province. For his biography, see Pfister, *Notices*, 1:321–28 and Dehergne, *Répertoire*, 129–30.

41. Witek, *Controversial Ideas*, 42–48.

42. Fontaney to François de La Chaise, the confessor of Louis XIV, 30 September 1688, "Relation d'un voyage depuis Siam jusqu'à la Chine et de ce qui s'est fait au commencement à Ning-po" Manuscripts 1246, fols. 131–35, Bibliothèque de Chambre des Députés, Paris.

43. Ibid., fol. 131.

44. Ibid., fols. 135–36. A number of French Jesuits at the time viewed Portugal as unable to send enough personnel to China. Verjus was the procurator of the missions, that is, a liaison agent in Paris for the missionaries overseas. See Dehergne, *Répertoire*, 316–17. On Verjus's work in the humanities, see Sommervogel, *Bibliothèque*, 8:598–602.

45. Fontaney to La Chaise, "Relation" MSS. 1246, fol. 137, Bibliothèque de Chambre des Députés, Paris.

46. Louis Le Comte, S.J., *Nouveaux mémoires sur l'état présent de la Chine*, 2 vols. (Paris, 1701), 2:35–45.

47. Ibid, 45–46.

48. Ibid., 62. The phrase is "de ne point souffrir que les estrangers s'establissent dans leur Empire." But the English translation states: "Never to suffer strangers to have any share in their administration," and thus inaccurately portrays the author's intent. See Louis Le Comte, S.J., *Memoirs and Remarks Geographical, Historical, Topographical ... Made ... in Travels through the Empire of China* (London, 1737), 288.

49. Le Comte, *Nouveaux mémoires*, 2:62–63. Some of the other maxims included: (1) not to give anyone jurisdiction in his native province; (2) to retain at court the children of the most influential officials who govern the provinces under the guise of teaching them but really to keep them as hostages; (3) not to sell any post in government but to grant it on merit; (4) not to establish a hereditary nobility. Ibid., 56–75.

50. Joachim Bouvet, S.J., "Journal des voyages du Père Bouvet, jésuite missionaire, envoyé par l'empereur de la Chine vers Sa Majesté très Chrétiene," Codex Gallicus 711, fols. 17–20, Bayerische Staatsbibliothek, Munich. For additional references, see Witek, *Controversial Ideas*, 59–61.

51. Bouvet's Diary (untitled) Manuscripts français 17240, fols. 263–64, Bibliothèque Nationale, Paris. The date, based on the Chinese calendar, is 12 February 1690.

52. Ibid., fol. 264v. A member of the imperial household (*Nei-wu fu*), Chao Ch'ang, acted as a liaison agent with the Jesuits. See Antonio Sisto Rosso, O.F.M., *Apostolic Legations to China of the Eighteenth Century* (South Pasadena, 1948), 161 n. 32, and Witek, *Controversial Ideas*, 41 n. 8.

53. Bouvet's Diary MSS. français 17240, fol. 264v, Bibliothèque

Nationale. After completing the treatise on anatomy several years later, the Jesuits were not allowed to publish or even disseminate it in Peking. Only a few select scholars were allowed by the emperor to make notes from extant copies. See Pierre Huard and Ming Wong, *Chinese Medicine* (New York, 1972), 118−23, and T. Kue-hing Young, "French Jesuits and the 'Manchu Anatomy' — How China Missed the Vesalian Revolution," *Canadian Medical Association Journal* 111 (21 September 1974):565−68. Some of the data on the background of the French Jesuits in China need correction in the latter article.

54. Bouvet's Diary MSS. français 17240, fol. 269, Bibliothèque Nationale. For Valat's biography, see Pfister, *Notices*, 1:279−82, and Dehergne, *Répertoire*, 278−79.

55. Bouvet's Diary MSS. français 17240, fol. 269, Bibliothèque Nationale.

56. Ibid., fol. 271.

57. Ibid., fol. 272.

58. Ibid., fols. 272v−73. For a translation of the inscription on the monument at Sian-fu and a study of its historical significance, see P.Y. Saeki, *The Nestorian Documents and Relics in China* (Tokyo, 1951), 11−112.

59. Bouvet's Diary MSS. français 17240, fol. 273, Bibliothèque Nationale.

60. Ibid., fol. 279. That Bouvet and the other Jesuits did not know about the imperial grant of the posthumous status to Verbiest two years after it occurred seems puzzling, since it was considered a public document. See *Ta Ch'ing Sheng-tsu jen (K'ang-hsi) Huang-ti shih-lu* (Veritable records of the K'ang-hsi reign), 6 vols. (Taipei, 1964), 3:1802. There is a short description of this text in Lo-shu Fu, *A Documentary Chronicle of Sino-Western Relations, 1644−1820* (Tucson, 1966), 99.

61. Bouvet's Diary MSS. français 17240, fol. 286, Bibliothèque Nationale. The prince apparently was Ch'ang Ning (1657−1703), who defeated Galdan. For his biography, see Hummel, *Eminent Chinese*, 1:69−70.

62. Bouvet's Diary MSS. français 17240, fol. 287, Bibliothèque Nationale. But other sources show that the French provincial presented the general with a fait accompli. See Witek, *Controversial Ideas*, 34−35.

63. Bouvet's Diary MSS. français 17240, fol. 301v, Bibliothèque Nationale. The date is 17 November 1691.

64. For a short biography of Alcalá, see Anastasius van den Wyngaert, O.F.M., ed., *Sinica Franciscana* (Quaracchi-Florence, 1942), 4:188 n. 4. The incidents are related in Le Comte, *Nouveaux mémoires*, 2:301−5.

65. The identity of the subordinate Chinese official is not clear.

Chang P'eng-ko was governor of Chekiang from 1689 to 1694. For his biography, see Hummel, *Eminent Chinese*, 1:49–51.

66. Le Comte, *Nouveaux mémoires*, 2:319–20. Since Gerbillon had worked with Songgotu (also called Sosan) at the negotiations for the 1689 Sino-Russian treaty in Nerchinsk, the basis of a friendship had been established. For a biography of Songgotu, see Hummel, *Eminent Chinese*, 2:663–66.

67. Le Comte, *Nouveaux mémoires*, 332–33.

68. Ibid., 346. For an overall survey of events, written shortly after the edict was granted, see Charles Le Gobien, S.J., *Histoire de l'édit de l'empereur de la Chine, en faveur de la religion chrestienne* (Paris, 1698).

69. Fu, *Documentary Chronicle*, 105. The Chinese text is in Huang Po-lu, S.J., *Cheng-chiao feng-pao* (Public praise of the true religion), 2 vols. (Shanghai, 1904), 115b–16b.

70. During the few years the French Jesuit missionaries worked in the imperial court, they knew the emperor had read several Christian treatises, especially Ricci's *T'ien-chu shih-i*. For details, see Joachim Bouvet, S.J., *Histoire de l'empereur de la Chine* (The Hague, 1699; reprint, Tientsin, 1940), 112. For a study of the recent Chinese and Japanese translations of Bouvet's book, see John W. Witek, S.J., "Transmission of a Comparison: Father Joachim Bouvet's View of the K'ang-hsi Emperor and Louis XIV," in *Chi-nien Li Ma-tou lai hua ssu-pai chou-nien Chung-Hsi wen-hua chiao-liu kuo-chi hsüeh-shu hui-i lun-wen chi* (Collected essays of the international symposium on Chinese-Western cultural interchange in commemoration of the 400th anniversary of the arrival of Matteo Ricci, S.J. in China), ed. Lo Kuang (Taipei, 1983), 841–60, and in revised form in *Tonga Yon'gu* (East Asian Studies), no. 3 (December 1983), 107–30. Regarding the emperor's desire to have the Jesuits live closer to the palace, see Bouvet's Diary MSS. français 17240, fol. 285r–v, Bibliothèque Nationale; and also his letter, written in Surat, 21 September 1695, to Jean Bomier, French assistant to Father General, Archivum Romanum Societatis Iesu, Japonica et Sinica 166, fols. 94–95.

4

Chinese Art and the Jesuits in Peking

HARRIE VANDERSTAPPEN, S.V.D.

THIS CHAPTER TOUCHES ON A VARIETY of art forms connected with the presence of Catholic missionaries in China in the late Ming and early Ch'ing periods. This Western contact with China took various forms; illustrated books, engravings, and crafts were imported, and paintings and architectural designs were executed by the missionaries for the court.

The first and most tangible evidence one has to consider are the illustrated books. Religious as well as secular book illustrations were introduced into China in fair numbers beginning with the requests made by Michele Ruggieri, S.J. (1543–1607) in 1580. The practice continued with Matteo Ricci (1552–1610) and other missionaries into the seventeenth and eighteenth centuries. A useful guide listing many of these books is Michael Sullivan's contribution to the International Symposium on Chinese Painting held in Taipei in 1970.[1] Even though records are incomplete, studies by Johannes Laures, S.J. and Hubert Verhaeren, C.M. show that the early Jesuit libraries in China were extensive, and if the number of seven thousand Western books in China mentioned by Yang Ting-yün (1557–1627) in 1623 cannot be verified, it is at least an indication of an impressive presence of Western printed material in China at that time. Fang Hao mentions that 750 titles of the original collections were still in the Pei-t'ang library in Peking in the 1940s.[2]

Some of these publications brought by the missionaries entered into Chinese publications. Probably the best-known instance is Ch'eng Ta-yüeh's *Ink Impressions of Ch'eng* (*Ch'eng-shih Mo-Yüan*), a 1606 book with illustrations taken from ink stones; among the illustrations, there appeared, at least for a short period, four engravings portraying biblical motifs: Lot in Sodom, a standing Madonna with Child, Peter walking on the water, Christ and the disciples of Emmaus.[3] The original engravings of the latter two were made by the brothers Hieronymus (1551–1614) and Antonius Wierix (1555–1603) after a design by Martinus de Vos (1532–1603) and published by Eduardus Van Hoeswinkel (fl. ca. 1600); the first was made by Crispin de Passe (ca. 1560–1637), and the Madonna is by inscription identified as the Virgen de la Antigua of Seville. The European sources for the engravings refer to northern traditions for the Emmaus engraving and to southern traditions for the others. For all but the Madonna engraving, Ricci provided the author of the book with explanations, which were added to the illustrations both in Chinese and in a romanization supplied also by Ricci. In addition, a lengthy composition dedicated to Ch'eng, signed and dated by Ricci in 1605, eulogizes the importance of printed books for the spread of culture and religion.

Paul Pelliot compares the *Ink Impressions of Ch'eng* with *Fang's Ink Index* (*Fang-shih Mo p'u*), another collection of stone rubbings. He notes that many of the illustrations in these two collections were the same. The illustrations in *Fang's Ink Index* cover a variety of strange phenomena relating to the heavens, beings of the earth, precious things, Confucianism, Buddhism, and Taoism. Pelliot also mentions that in the edition of Ch'eng's book available to him, the four Western engravings appeared with text.[4] Hsiang Ta reports that these four engravings with Christian subject matter were not paged in the first edition but appeared at the end after the sections on Buddhism and Taoism.[5] Rather than stressing the importance of interest in religious ideas, it would seem that books such as those by Ch'eng and Fang catered to the curiosity in things strange and exotic. When Ricci, introduced by Chu Shih-lu (*chin-shih* 1589) from Nanking, presented the engravings, Ch'eng must have been happy to put them in his book even though it was finished, or quite possibly he added them as a postscript so they could be removed should official restrictions cause difficulties. This precaution

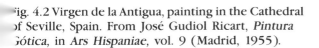

Fig. 4.1 Virgen de la Antigua, engraving. From Berthold Laufer, *Christian Art in China* (Peking, 1939).

Fig. 4.2 Virgen de la Antigua, painting in the Cathedral of Seville, Spain. From José Gudiol Ricart, *Pintura Gótica*, in *Ars Hispaniae*, vol. 9 (Madrid, 1955).

proved well founded since later editions do not have the text
and some appear without the illustrations as well.

The inscription on the Madonna mentions the conquest of
Seville by Ferdinand III of Castile in 1248. The tradition is that
a painting of a Madonna was found on the wall of the church
which had survived the Moorish occupation and that the name
Virgen de la Antigua derives from this.[6] A comparison with the
extant painting (figs. 4.1 and 4.2) shows how faithful the engraving reproduces the original.[7] Holding a rose in her right hand
and the Child in her left, Our Lady stands under a crown held
by two angels; a third angel holds and reads a scroll. The small
attending figure (Leonor de Albuquerque, wife of Ferdinand I
of Aragon, r. 1412–1416) in the lower right corner of the painting is left out in the engraving, and in the halo of the Madonna
the inscription "Ave Maria Gratia Plena" has been added. This
Madonna is an example of a wide-spread Byzantine and medieval type called the *Odigitria* (pointing the way) Madonna, indicated by the right hand gesture. The abbreviated part of the
caption on the lower right corner, with the date 1597, refers to
a school of painting in Japan. This school was established
in 1592 in the city of Shiki, and later in Arima, by Giovanni
Niccolò (Cola), S.J. (1560–1626).[8] Suggestions have been made
that the engravings in Ch'eng's book were done by the well-
known artist Ting Yün-p'eng (d. 1638) and the carver Huang
Lin (fl. ca. 1635). The awkward details may be explained by
the fact that they did not work from the European originals
but from copies made in Japan.

In 1640, Johann Adam Schall von Bell, S.J. (1592–1666) presented the last Ming emperor (Ch'ung-chen, r. 1628–1644)
with a sheepskin album containing forty-eight pictures of the
life of Christ and sixty-four pages of writing. The illustrations
show definite Chinese facial characteristics not present in the
ones used by Ch'eng in the *Ink Impressions of Ch'eng;* the generally sketchy execution retains the European layout, garments,
and architecture. The album was accompanied with a set of
painted plaster statues of the Adoration of the Magi, and Schall
had made Chinese annotations to each of the illustrations. In
the anti-Christian writing of Yang Kuang-hsien (1597–1669),
three illustrations from Schall's album were reprinted. Hsiang

Ta in a very informative article reproduces all three illustrations and cites Yang's introductory note to the pictures.[9] In his work, Yang uses the illustrations, especially the crucifixion scene, to demonstrate that it will show to all the world that Jesus was a subversive rebel leader who was convicted and executed.

From a variety of sources on the early Jesuit mission in China, Johannes Bettray[10] collected references to illustrations with Christian themes as they were used as gifts and in churches in the spreading of the gospel, but significant evidence of these in Chinese works remains elusive. Still, certain ideas had an impact on the visual arts of China. Some of the images came to the attention of Chinese art historians; and the "Portrait of Our Heavenly Lord" and "Two Portraits of Our Holy Mother," mentioned in Ricci's memorial to the Wan Li emperor (r. 1573–1620) in 1601, may well be the ones described by Chiang Shao-shu (fl. ca. 1615). He writes about a "Portrait of Our Heavenly Lord" and remarks that the facial features and the lines of the clothing look like real things in a mirror, vividly alive; the dignity and elegance of the figures are beyond the technical ability of Chinese painters.[11]

Related to these analyses are statements on shading and on plasticity of form. James Cahill quotes Ku Ch'i-yüan (1565–1628) as an example of the impression made on the Chinese by shading in Western painting, especially in portrait painting. That lifelikeness fascinated Ku is evident in such phrases as "arms and hands seem to protrude tangibly from the painting" and "concavities and convexities of the face are visually no different from a living person's."[12] Ku then quotes from Ricci's own explanation: "Chinese painting emphasizes *Yang* the light but not the dark *Yin*. Therefore, it is flat. In the west, a combination of shadows and lights are used . . . recessed parts of eyes, ears, nose and mouth have dark shadows . . . so they can make their portraits indistinguishable from living persons."[13]

Similar descriptions by Chinese authors abound. Chao I remarks on the image of Christ in the Catholic church in Nanking: "the portrait was painted on the wall but it looks like a round body, protruding from the wall."[14] Observations occur in which a painting of a figure is said to look like a statue with nose and ears as if they were in relief. In his article on Western influence on Chinese painting, Hsiang Ta devotes a section to portrait painting in late Ming and early Ch'ing times.[15] The most notable artist in this branch was Tseng Ch'ing (1568–1650), from Fukien. Chiang Shao-shu praises him for his lifelike portraits, "every inch of beauty or ugliness in his portraiture resembled the real person"; and on his technique, Chiang remarks that he would never tire of adding washes and shades and that "his portraits were all like images reflected in a mirror."[16] This reads as if Chiang is discussing Western shading since the same words are used for the description of Western images. However, Western influence is not mentioned in the earliest sources on Tseng Ch'ing, and only later writers make that point. In a comparison with a portrait of the Ch'ien-lung emperor (r. 1736–1796) of later date by Giuseppe Castiglione, S.J. (1688–1766), Tseng Ch'ing's portrait seems very Chinese.[17] The emphasis on line eclipses whatever roundness may have been suggested by the shading. In contrast, Castiglione puts minimum emphasis on line and relies on very technically subtle shading for an effect of modeling. He refines Western modes to suggest vaguely an approach to a Chinese manner, but the Chinese manner remains very different through its emphasis on the dynamic line to produce lifelikeness.

In addition to shading, the novelty of Western perspective is mentioned in several places as another aspect of Western technique introduced into China of the late Ming. Ricci is said to have introduced Ku Ch'i-yüan to the rules of perspective. Luigi Buglio, S.J. (1606–1682) arrived in Peking in 1648 and demonstrated the rules of perspective at the court. In his essay *Responses to Questions on Painting (Hua Ta)*, Francesco Sambiasi, S.J. (1582–1649) discussed questions on perspective.[18] It is further reported that Ferdinand Verbiest, S.J. (1623–1688) taught perspective to Chiao Ping-chen (ca. 1680–1720) who is well known for his *Illustrations of Rice and Silk Culture (Keng Chih-t'u).*[19] In this connection, the books with a variety of illustrations brought into China still seem to be the most useful source of possible Western influence: *Biblia Regia, Civitates Orbis Terrarum, Evangelicae Historiae Imagines,* and *Theatrum Orbis Terrarum* are the most important ones.[20]

Most recently, the whole question of the importance of Western

pictorial sources on some late Ming artists has received special
attention in Cahill's studies.[21] The evidence he presents in the
text and especially in the illustrations leaves no doubt in the
present writer's mind that aside from curiosities, such as smok-
ing chimneys, reflections in water, and cast shadows, some
other pictorial devices were used; these devices are most evident in topographical renderings. A most convincing example
is the comparison of a view of Frankfurt (taken from the *Civitates
Orbis Terrarum*) with a view by Chang Hung (1577–post-1652)
of the Chih Garden (from the Vannotti Collection, Switzerland).
In the latter, the curious placement of the garden in the bend
of the river and the unusually angled view surely compares
closely with the view of Frankfurt.[22] Equally thought provoking
is the comparison of Chang Hung's district of Yüeh scene (from
the Moriya Tadashi Collection, Kyoto) with the view of the
Dutch city of Kampen (from *Civitates Orbis Terrarum*).[23]

However, the comparison made between Wu Pin's (ca. 1580–
1626) "Lohan" (1601; from the National Palace Museum, Taipei)
and "Christ Praying in the Garden of Gethsemane" (from
Evangelicae Historiae Imagines)[24] seems less convincing (figs.
4.3 and 4.4). Cahill suggests that Wu Pin's use of shading in
the clouds can be compared with the shading in the clouds as
it appears in a similar setting in the Western biblical scene.
Rather, a good example of the Chinese tradition to which Wu
Pin's painting belongs is a Lohan painting reflecting a fourteenth-century style (fig. 4.5). Clearly, Wu Pin closely follows
the standard tradition. Both paintings deal with the same subject matter; that is, the use of the dragon descending on a cloud
is the same, and the arrangement of the figure and the tree is
very similar. In this context, the use of shading is to be credited
to the traditional Buddhist practice. This is the case especially
here where Wu Pin stays very close to the tradition, including,
it would seem, the mannerisms of the shading. The same is
true of the strange tree, well defined in Cahill's words as shaded
for unnaturally neat cylindricality and twisted into bizarre
shape. Such trees are also standard types in Lohan paintings.

Different though it is in date and detail of execution, the
tree in the Lohan painting signed by the fourteenth-century
painter Chao Chiung (fig. 4.6) is clearly more likely part of

Fig. 4.3 "Lohan" by Wu Pin, hanging scroll, ink and colors on paper, 1601. Photograph courtesy of National Palace Museum, Taipei.

ORAT CHRISTVS IN HORTO.   107
Matth. xxvi. Marc. xiiij. Luc. xxij. Ioan. xviij.   lxxx

A . *Torrens Cedron .*
B . *Hortus Gethſemani .*
C . *Rupes concaua; qui eſt primus locus;*
   vbi octo diſcipuli ſubstiterunt .
D . *Secundus locus ſuperius ad dextram:*
   vbi tres reliqui .

E . *Specus ad Iactum lapidis à tribus diſcipulis*
   diſtans: vbi orauit IESVS .
F . *Apparet illi Angelus è cœlo confortans eum .*
G . *Locus quo ſemel* ℞ *iterum venit*
   IESVS *ad tres diſcipulos .*
H . *Iudas cum cohorte properat ad hortum .*

Fig. 4.4 "Orat Christus in Horto" (Christ Praying in the
Garden [of Gethsemane]), engraving. From Gerónimo Nadal,
Evangelicae Historiae Imagines (Antwerp, 1593). Photograph
courtesy of The Newberry Library, Chicago.

Fig. 4.5 Vajraputra. Anonymous. One of eighteen
Lohans, ink and colors on silk. One of the
paintings in the set carries an inscription
signed I-shan I-ning (1247–1317). Ryukō-in,
Koya-san, Japan.

Fig. 4.6 Lohan by Chao Chiung.
Fourteenth century. One of sixteen
Lohans painted on a pair of eight-fold
screens in ink and colors on silk.
Hokekyō-ji, Chiba, Japan.

the prototype for the treatment of the tree in Wu Pin's work than Western ideas. Similarly, the painting entitled "Piled Snow on Old Cliffs" (1616) of Chao Tso (fl. ca. 1620), which suggests to Cahill Western models in handling light and shade, could as well be explained by references to snow landscapes such as "Traveling in a Snowy Mountain" (1572; from the National Palace Museum, Taipei) by Ch'ien Ku (1508–1572) and various paintings in the academic manner by T'ang Yin (1470–1523) and Hsieh Shih-ch'en (1488–post-1567).

There are other points one might make. In his discussion on the relationship between Tung Ch'i-ch'ang (1555–1644) and Chao Tso, Cahill writes that Tung's "River and Mountains on a Clear Autumn Day" (from the Cleveland Museum of Art), when compared with the "Vale of Tempe" engraving (from *Theatrum Orbis Terrarum*), may have depended upon sources other than Huang Kung-wang (1296–1354), sources Tung Ch'i-ch'ang would be less willing to admit. Cahill adds that for the kind of composition used in Tung's "River and Mountains" painting, no Chinese precedent can be convincingly brought forward. It would seem, however, that similar compositions could be lifted from Wen Cheng-ming's (1470–1559) paintings, such as his "Heavy Snow in the Mountain Passes" (1532; from the National Palace Museum, Taipei).[25] Such matters can be argued. The point remains very elusive, and it is quite true what Cahill says, namely, that once a thing is seen it can never be made unseen, try as one may. Where the borderline is between being influenced outright by what one sees, even after one buries it in one's subconscious, and between being reminded by what one sees of similar things in one's own past is forever going to be difficult to define. Surely Chinese artists could hardly have been unaware of Western illustrated books in their midst. And equally sure is it that Chinese painting of the past offered limitless pictorial models to match the newly seen or to put the new into acceptable Chinese formats.

Another aspect of Western impact on Chinese artistic traditions should be mentioned. Decorative arts of various kinds were brought into China by the missionaries. During the seventeenth and eighteenth centuries, there are numerous occasions on record of gifts to the emperors of China from European rulers, officials, and the popes. Of special importance was the appearance of painted enamel. In 1684, on one of his inspection tours to the southern parts of China, the K'ang-hsi emperor received the Jesuits Giandomenico Gabiani (1623–1694) and Jean Valat (1614?–1696) in audience. Chang Lin-sheng reports that this is the first instance officially recorded of contact between the emperor and the Jesuit missionaries where snuff is mentioned.[26] Snuff was among the gifts presented to the emperor on that occasion, and while he returned the other gifts to the fathers he kept the snuff — in a painted enamel container. Through the services of French Jesuit missionaries, Louis XIV presented the K'ang-hsi emperor with enamel paintings and other enameled wares.

Developed in Belgium and perfected in Limoges in France, painted enamels on both sides of a piece of copper without the application of copper ridges to hold the enamel in place were unknown in China, in contrast to cloisonné where ridges are attached to the copper to hold the enamel to the bordered patterns. The continued interest in this particular craft during the K'ang-hsi period and through that of Yung-cheng (r. 1723–1736) and Ch'ien-lung was in no small measure responsible for the establishment of the Tso-fang ssu studio in 1693 for the K'ang-hsi emperor's own education in the arts and sciences. Some thirty different workshops produced clocks, glassware, and enamels, of cloisonné as well as of the painted enamel type. In 1697, Joachim Bouvet, S.J. (1656–1730) returned to France, and K'ang-hsi asked him, among other requests, to find more artisans, especially enamelers. None of the latter was found, and in 1617, Castiglione and the diocesan priest Matteo Ripa (1682–1745) were ordered to start enameling for the emperor. When Castiglione did not produce satisfactory results, the emperor gave up. Apparently fearing that he would be burdened with excessive demands, Castiglione did not exert himself very much. In 1719, the enameler Jean Baptiste Gravereau arrived at the court but left shortly because of ill health.

In the succeeding period of Yung-cheng, enamel remained a highly desired commodity, and the quest for an enameler at the court even found its way into the minutes of the Sacred Congregation of the Propaganda de Fide of 23 September 1729 where

Domenico Perroni, O.M.D. (1674–1729), procurator general of
that Congregation in Canton, is reported stressing the need for
an enameler at the Yung-cheng court.[27] The same tradition continued into the Ch'ien-lung period. Examples of this particular
Western-inspired enamel are illustrated in Chang Lin-sheng's article.[28] A bottle with a watch on its top is most likely of European origin. Other examples showing Western-style figures in
a combination of cloisonné and painted enamel date from the
Ch'ien-lung period, as are some of the enamel painted glass
bottles. Obviously, this tradition had interactions with the production of porcelain, and some of the names, such as Famille
Verte, Rose, and Noire, may in part derive from this tradition
at the court.

There is also some interest in the ceramic ware with Christian
motifs produced in China in the imperial Ching-te-chen porcelain kilns, in the province of Kiangsi, in the seventeenth century
and later in Canton. There is little if any evidence that the
missionaries were in any way involved, and the ceramic ware
is most likely connected only with Western trade companies.

In 1715, Castiglione arrived in Peking.[29] In religious vows
since 1707 and already known as a painter of religious subjects
executed in the chapel of the novices in Genoa, he was presented to the K'ang-hsi emperor the year he arrived, together
with the Italian Jesuit lay brother and physician Giovanni da
Costa (1679–1747). On the occasion of Castiglione's introduction to the court, Ripa wrote a letter which gives an impression
of the prevailing circumstances. The sense of restrictions imposed on the missionaries surfaces when Ripa complains about
the eunuchs' impatience with foreigners whose faces are all
alike and who do not understand Chinese, the unrelenting insistence upon formalities of the court, the waiting and the rep-
etitious and minute observance of etiquette. The position of
the Church itself was equally tense and precarious. This atmosphere can be summarized from some of the remarks published
by Jonathan Spence in his book on the K'ang-hsi emperor.[30]
K'ang-hsi's response in 1705 to the papal legate, Charles Thomas
Maillard de Tournon (1668–1710), leaves no doubt about the
position of the foreigners. No outside jurisdiction is tolerated,
not even over the foreigners themselves. To the delegate's claim

that only someone familiar with the Curia in Rome and in the confidence of the pope could head the Church in China, the emperor answers that China has no common concern with the West. Missionaries have no concern beyond their own mind and their own doctrine. Besides, the foreigners must follow Ricci's attitudes toward the Rites. The situation did not improve during the Yung-cheng reign or under Ch'ien-lung; the missionaries were put under even stricter supervision and control. The presence of Castiglione and the other Jesuits working at the court must be seen against such a background.

In his more than fifty years of experience at the court from 1715 till his death in 1766, Castiglione was involved in many projects, from the development of various crafts to architectural designs, from painting portraits of emperors and concubines to painting horses and large-scale imperial hunts and outings; his brief involvement in enamel work has already been mentioned. His principal architectural work was building the Yüan-ming Yuan, the imperial summer residence some six miles to the northwest of Peking.[31] It was completely destroyed in 1960 by joint British and French forces, but we can get an impression of this complex of buildings, gardens, and fountains from surviving engravings and from some meager descriptions. From the engravings, one gets an impression of very decorative and slightly exotic mixtures of Chinese ornament put onto French-related structures. Embellished with majolica and colorful tiles, intricate mouldings, and recessed panels, the buildings were set in manicured gardens and surrounded by the fountains hydraulically operated to indicate the time of day. Apparently, the Ch'ien-lung emperor especially admired the fountains, designed principally by Michel Benoist, S.J. (1715–1774). The artful gardens, terraces, and walkways bordered by striking balustrades are instructively illustrated in a painting by Castiglione himself. In this painting, "The Garden of Extended Spring" (fig. 4.7), the emperor, accompanied by servants and the famous concubine Hsiang Fei from Yarkand in Central Asia, is seated on a tiled terrace in front of a belvedere accompanied by the inscription "Garden of Harmonious Amusement" (*Hsien-ch'ü Yüan*). There is undoubtedly a sterile quality in the precision of the setting, the arranged form of leisure, and the meticulous and

Fig. 4.7 "The Garden of Extended Spring" (detail) by Giuseppe Castiglione, handscroll, ink and colors on silk, after 1761. Private collection, Japan.

technically finished execution. One is reminded of buildings and gardens made for the occasion of a fair. The importance lies in the facade, and the buildings, without apparent substance, would seem ready to crumble after a very short period of neglect.[32]

Another project for which Castiglione and other Jesuits like Denis Attiret (1702–1768), Ignatius Sickelbart (1708–1780), and the Augustinian Damascene Salusti (d. 1781) are well known were engravings they designed to illustrate the Chinese war campaigns and the conquest of Chinese Turkestan. Sixteen scenes of these exploits were painted as memorials on the walls of the memorial hall, Tzu kuang ko, on the western shore of Central Lake in Peking. These paintings pleased Emperor Ch'ien-lung, who issued a decree in 1765 that they be reproduced in engravings to be made in Europe based on sketches by the Jesuits working at the court. These sketches were sent to France and executed on copper plates at the Académie Royale de Peinture under the supervision of Charles Nicholas Cochin (1715–1790). Accompanying the order were the instructions of the emperor that the best artists were to be chosen so that they might render each of these prints perfectly in all its parts. There was also a letter by Castiglione with detailed instructions that the prints should be executed with the greatest delicacy and the greatest possible exactitude and precision. These engravings have historical interest, but whatever the sketches showed of the personal style of the missionaries at the Chinese court has been overlaid with a technical uniformity following academic principles of the French academy.[33]

Finally, there are the paintings for which Castiglione is best known. Several Western and Japanese scholars have written on this material. The difficulties he faced in trying to please his patron and at the same time to adhere to the principles of painting which he must have firmly believed in were great. In 1757, Castiglione painted a scroll depicting the Kazaks presenting horses to the Ch'ien lung emperor in tribute (fig. 4.8). Written by Ch'ien lung, the inscription on the painting reads in part: "Swift as lightning these horses are veritable dragons and the Emperor has asked Castiglione [Lang Shih-ning] to paint them."

In order to highlight the differences between the Western

Fig. 4.8 "The Four Steeds of Ai-wu-han" (detail) by Giuseppe Castiglione, handscroll, ink and colors on silk, 1762. National Palace Museum, Taipei.

Fig. 4.9 "The Lean and the Fat Horse" (detail) by Jen Jen-fa (1254–1327), handscroll, ink and colors on silk. Palace Museum, Peking.

approach by Castiglione in the painting of horses and the method used by Chinese artists, a comparison can be made between the last section of Castiglione's scroll and a detail of a painting attributed to the famous fourteenth-century Chinese horse painter Jen Jen-fa (fl. ca. 1335) (fig. 4.9). Even though over four centuries separate these two works, the comparison makes a point that does not essentially depend upon historical changes of style. The controlled, even surfaces with subtle gradations of tones stand out in the painting by Castiglione. An emphasis on contained linear definitions in the Jen Jen-fa painting is in contrast with the tonal preference in Castiglione's work. The lines in which muscles and mane are defined in the Chinese painting are predictable because they are part of a long-standing tradition. The strength of such a painting depends upon the individual execution of well-known forms, and the inventiveness of the artist is confined to the skill and sensitivity he puts into these conventions. Castiglione's horse derives from a tradition of solidly treated and rounded forms of plastically executed and physically well-functioning organisms. The resulting weight of the animal is convincingly supported by the ground on which it stands, and, since these interact well, the horse retains a balanced presence. The Chinese horse is not placed in any definable locale. It exists without physical corporeality and without bodily weight. The lines and the pose are vivid, and they define the horse as an animal that has gained an accepted reputation as a speedy, reliable companion.

If it were not for the horse, we would be held to the slow pace of walking, and the horse helps men overcome part of his physical limitations. From there it is a small step to place the horse on the level of a cult and in the realm of dragons, a privilege the horse has retained throughout Chinese history. The technically smooth and impeccably clean horse by Castiglione is physically weakened by this insistence on the attractiveness of surface. That polish surely pleased the emperor's taste, and it may at the same time have been an attempt to accommodate the manner of painting to Chinese traditions; but the painting neither retains the strength of muscular flexibility of superior power nor approaches the venerable quality of the superhuman associated with the Chinese depiction.

To conclude this brief survey of Western impact on Chinese art caused by the presence of the missionaries in China during the seventeenth and eighteenth centuries, one has to bear in mind the basic dichotomy between the spiritual message the missionaries were intent on bringing and the framework in which it was presented. Part of the framework was the gifts, the technical skill, and, certainly in the eyes of the Chinese, the strange, exotic, and, in many ways, admirable mental and practical ability of the missionaries. Surely, the framework surrounding the spiritual message was much more easily appreciated than the complexities of divine revelation and human redemption. We should also be aware that the Chinese were never exposed to great works of Western art, and neither did missionaries consider themselves agents of secular art and culture. They used art to illustrate Christian doctrine, and whatever artistic merit these illustrations had was, in the eyes of the Chinese, easily overshadowed by the strange and new technical qualities they saw. That seems borne out by the emphasis in Chinese reactions to the use of perspective and to modeling in light and dark combined with lifelikeness, and by the fascination they developed for cartography, topography and maps, and, finally, the measurements of distance and time in astronomy, clock work, time pieces, and configurations of the calendar.

This led to an emphasis upon the framework itself rather than the purely spiritual. It seems quite clear that later in the seventeenth and eighteenth centuries, the court in Peking had little interest in employing missionaries other than to arouse further its own fascination with technical matters, to embellish court life, and to enhance the physical surroundings of the palace and its inhabitants. The missionaries, on the other hand, tenaciously clung to the idea that no matter how onerous and, at times, humiliating, they were still using their skills as a means to bring home their spiritual message. In fact, this attitude may have been counterproductive because the emperor and the court could easily and with good traditional conscience downgrade the moral and religious ideals of the missionaries who by their very existence as craftsmen, decorators, and engineers were nothing but old-fashioned and morally incorruptible servants. There are a number of incidents which show that the emperors had a personal respect and affection for the missionaries; certain titles given to them attest to that. But when it came to decisions of consequence in public policy, any influence the missionaries had was easily ignored or, at best, exercised quietly, outside the normal route of bureaucracy.

In all, it would appear that the impact of Western artistic traditions was mainly limited to technical matters. In some areas of topography, refinements in portraiture, and works of decorative art, Western ideas survived for some time. The novelty, however, wore off when imperial and other court-connected patronage waned or ceased to exist. The traditional Chinese artistic heritage was barely, if at all, touched by Western ideas.

NOTES

1. Michael Sullivan, "Some Possible Sources of European Influence on Late Ming and Early Ch'ing Painting," in *Proceedings of the International Symposium on Chinese Painting* (Taipei, 1970), 595–633.

2. See two articles by Johannes Laures, S.J. : "Die Bücherei der älteren Jesuitenmission im Pei-t'ang zu Peking Erinnerungen an P. Adam Schall, S.J.," *Katholische Missionen* 65 (1937):76, 100–102, 129–30, and "Die alte Missionsbibliothek im Pei-t'ang zu Peking," *Monumenta Nipponica* 2 (1939):128–31. See also Hubert Verhaeren, C.M.,"L'Ancienne bibliothèque du Pei-t'ang," in *Bulletin Catholique de Pékin* 27 (Peking, 1940):82–96. Fang Hao mentions that about ten percent of the original collection was still in the Pei-t'ang library in the 1940s; consult his *Fang Hao liu-shih tzu-ting kao* (The collected works of Maurus Fang Hao revised and edited by the author on his sixtieth birthday), 2 vols. with Supplement (Taipei, 1969), 2:1843. For information on Yang T'ing-yün, see ibid., 1845.

3. Bertold Laufer, "Christian Art in China" (Peking, 1939), reprinted from *Mitteilungen des Seminars für Orientalische Sprachen an der k. Friedrich-Wilhelm-Universität zu Berlin* 13 (1910):100–118, XX plates; the four biblical engravings are reproduced in Laufer. Paul Pelliot, "La Peinture et la gravure européennes en Chine au temps du Mathieu Ricci," *T'oung Pao* 20 (1920–1921):2 n. 2. For more on Ch'eng Ta-yüeh, see L. Carrington Goodrich and Chaoying Fang, *Dictionary of Ming Biography 1368–1644*, 2 vols. (New York, 1976), 1:212–15.

4. Pelliot, "La Peinture et la gravure," 2.

5. Hsiang Ta, "European Influences on Chinese Art in the Later

Ming and Early Ch'ing Period," trans. Wang Teh-chao, in *The Transla-tion of Art: Essays on Chinese Painting and Poetry.* Renditions No. 6, Special Art Issue (Hong Kong, 1976), 157; this article was originally published in Chinese in *Tung-fang Tsa Chin* (Studies of the East) 27 (1930) and was later collected into *T'ang-tai Ch'ang-an yü Hsi-yü Wen-ming* (Ch'ang-an and West areas culture in the period of T'ang) (Peking, 1933). Hsiang Ta also reports that the four Western engravings were republished in 1927 by Ch'en Yüan.

6. Laufer, "Christian Art," 110.

7. See *Ars Hispaniae: historia universal del arte hispánico,* 14 vols. (Madrid, 1946–1957), 9:194, pl. 160. The present writer thanks Pro-fessor E. Rosenthal for his help in locating this painting.

8. Georg Schurhammer, S.J., "Die Jesuitenmissionare des 16. und 17. Jahrhunderts und ihr Einfluss auf die japanische Malerei," in *Gesam-melte Studien,* 4 vols. (Rome, 1963), 2:769–79. (Vol. 21 of Bibliotheca Instituti Historici Societatis Iesu) This article was first published in *Jubiläumsband herausgegeben von der Deutschen Gesellschaft für Natur-und Völkerkunde Ostasiens anlässlich ihres 60 jährigen Bestehens 1873–1933.* Teil I (Tokyo, 1933), 116–26.

9. Hsiang Ta, "European Influences," 159–61. The Bayersiche Staatsbibliothek, Munich, owns a book with fifty-seven woodblock il-lustrations; it is listed as Ai Ju-lüeh (Giulio Aleni, S.J., 1582–1644), *T'ien chu chiang sheng Ch'u hsiang ching chieh* (The life of Our Lord, Jesus Christ, Savior of men, drawn from the four evangelists), Codex sinicus 23. The preface is dated 1637. These woodblocks illustrate the life of Christ, and they may be a Chinese copy of the illustrations of the life of Christ handed to the Chinese emperor by Johann Adam Schall von Bell. For more detailed information, see Jane Hwang,"The Early Jesuits-Printings [sic] in China in the Bavarian State Library and the University Library of Munich," in *Chi-nien Li Ma-tou lai hua ssu-pai chou-nien Chung-Hsi wen-hua chiao-liu kuo-chi hsüeh-shu hui-i lun wen-chi* (Collected essays of the international symposium on Chinese-Western cultural interchange in commemoration of the 400th anniver-sary of the arrival of Matteo Ricci, S.J. in China), ed. Lo Kuang (Taipei, 1983), 281–93.

10. Johannes Bettray, S.V.D., *Die Akkomodationsmethode des P. Mat-teo Ricci, S.J. in China* (Rome, 1955), 51–65.

11. Hsiang Ta, "European Influences," 156.

12. James Cahill, "Wu Pin and His Landscape Painting," in *Proceed-ings of the International Symposium on Chinese Painting* (Taipei, 1970), 651–56; see also James Cahill, *The Compelling Image* (Cam-bridge, 1982), 71–80.

13. Cahill, "Wu Pin," 653.

14. Chao I, *Yen-pao Tsa-Chi* (Miscellaneous notes from under the

exposed eave), as quoted in Hsiang Ta, "European Influences," 164 n. 23.

15. Hsiang Ta, "European Influences," 164–66. Also Cahill, *Compelling Image*, 116–25. A Western manner of painting in portraits and horses is also attributed to the Manchu painter Mang-ku li (1672–1736). See Sally W. Goodfellow, ed., *Eight Dynasties of Chinese Painting, with Essays by Wai-kam Ho, Sherman E. Lee, Laurence Sickman, Marc F. Wilson* (Cleveland, 1980), fig. 260, pp. 352–53.

16. Hsiang Ta, "European Influences," 165.

17. For illustrations, see Goodfellow, *Eight Dynasties*, pl. 262, p. 677; and Cahill, *Compelling Image*, pl. 4, p. 18.

18. See Pelliot, "La Peinture et la gravure," 1–6.

19. Consult the older and still very informative publications: Otto Franke, "Zur Geschichte des *Keng Tschi T'u*," *Ostasiatische Zeitschrift* 2 (1914):169–200; and Paul Pelliot, "A Propos du *Keng Tche T'ou*," *Mémoires concernant l'Asie orientale (Inde, Asie centrale, Extrême-Orient)* 1 (1913):65–122.

20. Sullivan, "Some Possible Sources," 604–7.

21. Cahill, *Compelling Image*, secs. 1 and 3.

22. Ibid., figs. 1.22 and 1.20, pp. 21, 20. The view of Frankfurt is from Georg Braun and Franz Hogenberg, *Civitates Orbis Terrarum* (Cologne, 1572), vol. 1.

23. Cahill, *Compelling Image*, figs. 1.18 and 1.19, pp. 18, 19. The view of Kampen is from Braun and Hogenberg, *Civitates Orbis Terrarum*, vol. 2.

24. Cahill, *Compelling Image*, figs. 3.21 and 3.20, pp. 89, 88. "Christ in the Garden" is from Gerónimo Nadal, *Evangelicae Historiae Imagines* (Antwerp, 1593).

25. Cahill, *Compelling Image*, figs. 2.21 and 3.3, pp. 54, 73. "Vale of Tempe" is from Abraham Ortelius, *Theatrum Orbis Terrarum* (1579). For Wen Cheng-ming, "Heavy Snow in the Mountain Passes," see *Wu-p'ai Hua Chiu-shih Nien Chan* (Ninety years of Wu School painting) (Taipei, 1976), pl. 141.

26. Chang Lin-sheng, "The Enamel Snuff Bottles in the Palace Museum Collection," *National Palace Museum Bulletin* (Taipei) 15 (1980):6–7. See also Zhu Jiajin, "A Study of the Manufacture of Painted Enamelware of the Qing Dynasty," *Gugong Bowuyuan Yuankan* (Peking Palace Museum Records) 3 (1982):67–76, 96. From the archives of the Palace Museum and from the Historical Archives Collection, Mr. Zhu has culled the entries relating to the making of enamelware between 1725 and 1738; the limited involvement of Castiglione in enamel painting on copper seems confirmed since he is mentioned only in one entry in 1725.

27. George Loehr, "Missionary-Artists at the Manchu Court," *Transac-*

tions of the Oriental Ceramic Society (London) 34 (1962–1963):59. For the information on Domenico Perroni, O.M.D., the present writer expresses gratitude to Sinologist Antonio Sisto Rosso, O.F.M. of Rome.

28. Chang Lin-sheng, "Enamel Snuff Bottles," 11.

29. George Loehr, *Giuseppe Castiglione (1688–1766) pittore di Corte di Ch'ien lung, Imperatore della Cina* (Rome, 1940).

30. Jonathan Spence, *Emperor of China: Self-Portrait of K'ang-hsi* (New York, 1975), xvii–xix, 75–84.

31. For a brief survey and additional bibliography, see Cécile and Michel Beurdeley, *Giuseppe Castiglione: A Jesuit Painter at the Court of the Chinese Emperors*, trans. Michael Bullock (Rutland, 1971), 65–75.

32. *Minshin no Kaiga* (Paintings of the Ming Ch'ing dynasties), Exhibition Catalogue with text by Kawakami Kei (Tokyo, 1964), pl. 122, pp. 49–50.

33. The most extensive study in Western languages is still Paul Pelliot, "Les 'Conquêtes de l'Empereur de la Chine,'" *T'oung Pao* 20 (1920–1921):183–274.

PART TWO

Chinese Reaction to the Jesuit Missionaries

Why Did They Become Christians?
Yang T'ing-yün, Li Chih-tsao, and Hsü Kuang-ch'i

WILLARD J. PETERSON

Posing THE QUESTION OF WHY they became Christians is not intended to imply that a comprehensive answer is possible, anymore than would analogous questions of why, for example, Ku Hsien-ch'eng (1550–1612) and Kao P'an-lung (1562–1626) became involved in the revival of the Tung-lin Academy during the same years that some of their contemporaries became Christians. The minds and hearts of Yang T'ing-yün (1557–1627), Li Chih-tsao (1565–1630), and Hsü Kuang-ch'i (1562–1633) would not be fully accessible even if one could subject them to all sorts of prying interrogations. Available sources do not provide sufficient evidence to analyze any profound religious experience they may have undergone. This essay also leaves aside the theological and sociological problem of whether they were adherents rather than converts. The question is taken here in the context of Chinese intellectual history.

The "why" of the question is an appeal for an answer that is explanatory, an answer that makes historical sense of the conduct of certain men nearly four hundred years ago. The pronoun in the question is straightforward. "They" — Yang T'ing-yün, Li Chih-tsao, and Hsü Kuang-ch'i — are well known in the secondary literature as the Three Pillars of Christianity in China.[1] There are many reasons for treating them together. They were born within eight years of each other and died within six. Their homes were on the edge of Chiang-nan, the region that was economically most advanced and intellectually most active in late Ming China. They were well-educated men who achieved the highest civil examination degree status of *chin-shih* in their thirties or early forties. They each served more than ten years in government positions and advanced to relatively high posts. They were financially secure. They wrote books on their own and were also involved in the translation and publication of books in Chinese by Jesuit missionaries. In taking these three as examples, we are at the center of the literati's experience of Christian teachings in the early seventeenth century.

It might be superfluous to clarify what is meant here by to "become Christians" except that Professor Jacques Gernet in his stimulating book, *Chine et Christianisme*, argues that Chinese in the seventeenth century did not have a sufficient comprehension of Christianity and were only apparently Christians. Gernet's point is not under dispute here. The question can be restated: Why did they become involved in Christianity to the extent they did? For our purposes here, it is sufficient to follow the judgment of the missionaries in late Ming times, and they mainly accepted that Yang, Li, and Hsü were Christians.[2]

Although there does not seem to be any direct, unambiguous evidence that shows Hsü or Li or Yang themselves testifying they had been baptized, which is accepted as a minimal definition of "becoming a Christian" in that context, missionaries reported they had been. They used the new names they were given at the time of baptism. They, and their critics, said they "followed" the "Holy Religion" (*sheng chiao*) and the "Way of the Lord of Heaven" (*T'ien-chu chih tao*). They devoted effort to living by the precepts they learned from the missionaries and to influencing others to accept those precepts. They induced close members of their families to receive baptism. More generally, the public manifestations of their continuing commitment to the missionaries and to what was being taught in China by the missionaries warrant calling them "Christians" here.

HOW YANG T'ING-YÜN BECAME A CHRISTIAN

The stages by which Yang "became a Christian" are detailed in the well-known account of his life, the full title of which is usually given as *Manifestations of the Surpassing Character of*

Yang Ch'i-yüan (*Yang Ch'i-yüan hsien-sheng ch'ao hsing shih chi*).[3] The account was written down by Ting Chih-lin after the death of Yang in 1627. Ting says in a postscript that he had heard many times about Yang from Giulio Aleni (1582–1649)[4], and Aleni knew Yang, of course. He stayed with him in Hangchow, and they worked together on the *Account of Countries Not Listed in the Records Office* (*Chih-fang wai chi*), which was printed in 1623. Because their friendship began a few years after Yang had been baptized in 1611, Aleni was not giving Ting a first-hand description of affairs leading up to that event. Moreover, the account obviously is intended for a public audience. It portrays *how* Yang became a Christian — with the hope, which Ting expressed in his postscript, that he might be taken as a model by others. The following is primarily a paraphrase of the stages of Yang's progress as recorded by Aleni and Ting. Also, direct comments of the present writer are interspersed parenthetically.

The account begins conventionally with information on Yang's names, his place of origin (Hangchow), and his illustrious character, fondness for learning, and desire to be known as good. In 1592, Yang becomes a *chin-shih* and then holds a succession of provincial and capital appointments. (Yang is thus established for the readers of the account as a successful man in late sixteenth- and early seventeenth-century terms).

Yang resigns in 1609 (in his fifty-third year) from the office of Education Intendant at Nanking and returns to Hangchow where he devotes his energies to reading books. He is admired by the provincial governor, who arranges for him to give lectures on Neo-Confucianism (*Tao-hsüeh*) at a scenic place on West Lake. (Like many of his contemporaries who were also interested in reviving the intellectual vigor of Ch'eng-Chu teachings,) Yang organizes a study group called the Truth Society (*Chen shih she*). At the same time that he is becoming well known for his efforts on behalf of Neo-Confucianism, he is supportive of local Buddhist clerics who press Ch'an doctrine on him, and he contributes to the reestablishment of local Buddhist temples. Yang has already learned something about the "Way of the Lord of Heaven" which Matteo Ricci had been expounding in Peking, but he "did not understand it." (Here we have

a summary of Yang's intellectual and religious involvements in
1610 and 1611. Out of office for the first time in years, he was
actively and publicly promoting the moral self-cultivation side of
Neo-Confucianism. He also was supportive of Buddhists, not just
generally interested in Buddhist doctrine, at the time when the
monk Chu-hung [1535–1615] was enjoying great success in
promoting lay Buddhist societies and reinvigorating the monas-
tic rule at the Yün-ch'i temple complex near Hangchow.[5] At this
stage, Yang was serious about moral and religious values, and
he was aware of Christian teachings.)

(In the next stage, Yang made a sudden turn toward Christian
teachings.) In the fourth month of 1611, Yang's friend Li Chih-
tsao (who had been baptized by Ricci in Peking in the spring
of the previous year) resigns from office in Nanking to attend
his ailing father. Li invites the two Jesuits Lazzaro Cattaneo
(1560–1640) and Nicolas Trigault (1577–1628) to accompany
him back to Hangchow. When Yang goes to offer his condo-
lences on the death of Li's father, he meets Cattaneo and Trigault
and is pleased to find out more about their religion. When he
sees an image of the Lord (*chu*), he is reverential toward it
and feels as if he were in the presence of a great lord (*ta chu*)
who gives him a command. He then invites Cattaneo and
Trigault to visit him at his own home. (Although there is no
clear indication here as to why he was so attracted to them,
he was now deeply interested in what the missionaries had to
teach.)

(Ready to learn more,) Yang cuts himself off from all other
concerns to concentrate on fathoming the fundamentals of the
Learning from Heaven (*T'ien-hsueh*). Cattaneo and Trigault
teach him about the Lord's grace and other precepts of their
religion. He understands that the ten thousand things in heaven
and earth are created and sustained by the Lord of Heaven
(*T'ien-chu*). He acknowledges to the missionaries that the Lord
of Heaven is to be served as the Lord of the ten thousand things
in heaven and earth but wonders what harm there might be
in also serving the Buddha. He assents to the missionaries' answer to this question. In further discussions with them, he wonders why the omnipotent Lord of Heaven would endure such
sufferings when he descended to live as a man, and he expresses

his view that it is disrespectful to the Lord of Heaven to speak of these sufferings. Again, the missionaries explain the reasons for all of this and he applauds their answer.

One day, Trigault and a Chinese convert from Kuangtung named Chung Ming-jen (also given as Chung Nien-chiang), whom the Jesuits called Brother Sebastian (1562–1622), are expounding the meaning of Christian rituals to Yang, and they think that he does not quite believe that the Lord of Heaven is actually present in the consecrated communion bread. With some agitation, Yang says: "How is this something for me to cogitate over? My Lord's love for the world is boundless. [The notion of] His grace in descending to atone for the world's [sins] does not derive from an unconsidered doctrine, so how would I revert to doubts about this?" He then makes a commitment to be a servitor of the Lord. (In short, he was now willing to believe.)

When Yang expresses his desire to receive baptism, Trigault does not permit it. The reason is that in addition to a wife, Yang has a concubine who is the mother of his two sons. He hesitates over what to do and discusses the matter with his friend Li (who, as we shall see shortly, had experienced the same difficulty). Yang says that the missionaries' attitude bewilders him. Here he, a former high official, is willing to serve *them,* but they do not allow it because he must not have a single concubine. Buddhist monks, Yang avers, certainly would not act like this. And that, Li explains, is precisely why the missionaries from the Far West and the monks are not comparable. The Western religion (*hsi-chiao*) has its rules, which were received from the Lord of Heaven. Following them is virtuous, neglecting them is punishable; the distinction is clear. How could the missionaries assent to what you like, Li asks, when the rules prohibit it? The missionaries want to save others, but they are unwilling to compromise on this to receive you. They want to reform this degenerate world, but they do not dare dishonor the rules of their religion. If you know you are wrong and do not change, Li asks Yang, what point is there in following them? Yang is suddenly awakened. He changes from his former wrong ways, sends away his concubine, and puts into practice the rules of the religion. The missionaries witness his sincerity, and he is baptized in the sixth month of 1611 with the new name of Michele.[6]

(Yang has become a Christian, and the account written down by Ting Chih-lin makes it clear that he lived the remaining years of his life [1611 – 1627] doing Christian works in close association with Jesuit missionaries. Here are a few examples of his works, as described by Ting.) Yang has a hall, which held a statue of a Bodhisattva; this hall is turned into a chapel for the missionaries. His mother is a pious Buddhist and does not listen to him about the Western religion. For years he worries and prays, and when he is about sixty (and his mother is eighty), he eats sparingly and becomes noticeably haggard. Under his mother's persistent questioning, he tearfully says he feels he is culpable because she is deluded by false teachings (hsieh shuo) and rejects true religion (cheng chiao). Should his mother fall into eternal suffering, her son could not be redeemed. Through her son's suffering, she understands, says she believes, and receives the rite of baptism. Yang builds a church and supports missionaries (whom he also harbored at his own risk during the anti-Christian prohibitions beginning in 1616).

As an alternative to the Buddhist lay societies that concentrate on releasing live fish and birds purchased from the market place, Yang organizes a charitable society to help the needy. (The Societies for the Release of Life [fang sheng hui] were popular in Hangchow at the time owing largely to the inspiration of the monk Chu-hung.)[7] When Aleni tells him it is good that he succors the poor and the sick of body, but he should also have pity on those who are sick of heart, Yang begins to spend money and effort on the printing of books about the Learning from Heaven. He personally writes *In Place of Doubt* (*Tai i p'ien*) and other short books "to make clear the Way of the Lord of Heaven." (He becomes, in short, a pillar of the Church in China.)

WHY YANG T'ING-YUN BECAME A CHRISTIAN

Yang is not presented as experiencing any great personal stress or crisis during his approach to Christianity. What can be inferred from the account of his life is that he was troubled about what he, and many of his concerned contemporaries, perceived as a pervasive moral decay. Perhaps this was associated with his resignation from government office in 1609, when the emperor's willfulness and the factional disarray at court and throughout the bureaucracy were undermining confidence. His efforts on behalf of Neo-Confucianism are evidence of a deep concern with values and a desire to restore a sense of "right" to a society adrift. What seems clear from the account of Yang's life is that he sought to identify what is "right," as when he organized the Truth Society. The opportunity was present for him to find it in Neo-Confucianism; this was presumably the subject of the books he read so assiduously when he returned to Hangchow. He also sought it in Buddhist teachings, provided by the clerics to whom he gave contributions. They both failed him.

Yang's turning away from Neo-Confucianism and Buddhism came when he visited his friend Li in the fourth or fifth month of 1611. The account does not say so, but Western sources[8] tell us Li encouraged his friend Yang to embrace Catholicism. What can be inferred from the account is that Yang became interested when he perceived how Li, back in Hangchow with Cattaneo and Trigault after his baptism in Peking the previous year, had entrusted so much to the missionaries. This is the only context we are given for Yang's reaction to the sight of an image of the Lord. If it is correct to suppose that he was seeking a moral certainty, then it seems to follow that when he discovered his friend Li had it, he was then willing to find out more about the source of the certainty.

There are five main points in the account of Yang's growing understanding of Christianity. First, as he read and discussed with Cattaneo and Trigault, Yang understood that the Lord, whose image affected him so, was the Lord of Heaven who is behind all the ten thousand phenomena in the realm of heaven and earth; this Lord is not "of the Far West" but stands external to any particular time and place.

Second, they explained to him that the Lord of Heaven was the one and only Lord. Any talk of the Buddha "supporting the heaven and enveloping the earth" was dismissed as stupid for not recognizing the omnipotence of the Lord of Heaven. The missionaries said the Buddhists were guilty of something akin to the *lèse majesté* of a person wanting to be his own emperor or his own king. Cattaneo and Trigault, according to the account, told him, "The Buddhists want to venerate their own hearts and natures [as the source of "knowing"] and deny the omnipotence of the Lord on High (*Shang chu*)." The missionaries' accusation that the Buddhists rely on their own hearts and natures as the source for their values (and this is certainly an implication of the dominant Ch'an teachings at the time) can be extended to much of late Ming Neo-Confucianism, particularly the followers of the Wang Yang-ming school, in which there was a similar tendency to "venerate the moral nature" (*tsun te hsing*). The issue was whether one's own heart, or nature, was to be the source on which one's values were grounded or whether there was an external source. The missionaries insisted exclusively on the latter.

Third, in response to Yang's view that it is disrespectful to speak of the sufferings of the Lord of Heaven, the missionaries explained that among the attributes of their Lord is "extreme good" and a concern for all human beings. This was manifested by his taking a body "to atone for the sins of all peoples and all times." The point for Yang, and the readers of the account, is that this external source of knowing is a moral source and one accessible to humans.

Fourth, once Yang understood this, then he had no need to go on generating doubts; he could immediately grasp the significance of the consecrated bread. Not incidentally, ten years later when he produced his own book on doctrinal questions, he called it *In Place of Doubt*. Doubt, of course, is the opposite of certainty or truth, which it seems is what he thought he was embracing.

Fifth, Yang learned from the obstinacy of the missionaries about his concubine that the moral rules were not susceptible of compromise; one had to submit to them. They were not made up by humans and thus subject to a situational interpretation relative to the particular time or place of their origin. They came from the Lord of Heaven.

If Yang is seen as searching in effect for an externally determined source of moral values as an alternative to the relativism and introspection which prevailed among many of his contemporaries, then it is explicable why he grasped at the complex ambiguities of the "heaven" and "Lord of Heaven" depicted by the missionaries. It was precisely when he moved the step beyond understanding to submission to this "higher authority" that he could be baptized, that he "became a Christian." The whole process was accomplished in the space of about two months.[9]

LI CHIH-TSAO'S PROGRESS TO CHRISTIANITY

Li took about nine years. He was baptized in Peking early in 1610, about two months before Matteo Ricci (b. 1552) died.[10] In contrast to Yang, who had only brief direct contact with missionaries prior to the two months leading up to his baptism, Li had first called on Ricci in 1601 and developed an enduring, admiring relationship with him. Ricci himself described the beginning as follows:

> Li Wo-ts'un [i.e., Li Chih-tsao] is from the city of Hangchow in the province of Chekiang. At the time I first arrived in Peking, he was a high official in the Tribunal of Works and was a doctor of great intelligence. [Highly placed in the *chin-shih* examination of 1598, Li was called a "doctor" by the Jesuits, as were other *chin-shih*.] In his youth he made a "Description of All China" with the fifteen provinces shown in great detail; he thought it was the whole world. When he saw our "Universal World Map," he realized how small China was compared to the whole world. With his great intelligence he easily grasped the truths we taught about the extent and sphericity of the Earth, its poles, the ten [concentric] heavens, the vastness of the sun and stars compared to the Earth, and other things which others found so difficult to believe. From this a close friendship developed between us, and when the duties of his office allowed it, he liked to learn more of this knowledge (*questa scientia*).[11]

Years later, Li recalled: "In 1601, when Ricci had come [to Peking], I went with several associates to call on him. Hanging on his wall was a map of the world with finely drawn lines of degrees [longitude and latitude]. Ricci said, This was my route from the West."[12] In a sense, the map pointed to Li's route *to* the West. It initiated his involvement with Ricci. His interest in the map grew to the point that Ricci gave him credit for his assistance, which resulted in an enlarged version of the map being printed in 1602.[13]

In turn, Li's appreciation of Ricci and the new ideas from the West only increased. They worked together on arithmetical and astronomical books and instruments,[14] and in 1607 Li wrote a preface to a revised printing of Ricci's *True Meaning of the Learning from Heaven* (*T'ien-hsüeh shih-i*) under the new title of *True Meaning of the Lord of Heaven* (*T'ien-chu shih-i*). Critical of both Buddhism and Neo-Confucianism, Li was explicitly sympathetic to the religion of the Lord of Heaven (*T'ien-chu chiao*) which he found had much that was in accord with the Classics.[15]

The progress of Li's admiration for Ricci is summarized most neatly in his preface of 1608 to Ricci's *Ten Essays on the Extraordinary Man* (*Chi-jen shih p'ien*). Herein Ricci recorded his discussions on religious and moral questions with eight Chinese interviewers, including Li and Hsü Kuang-ch'i. Li wrote in the preface that when he first met this person who had braved all sorts of hazards in making the tremendously long journey to China and who was friendly and generous to others without seeking anything in return, he thought Ricci was "a strange man" (*i jen*). Observing that he did not marry or hold office, that he only sought to be virtuous and to serve the Divinity on High (*Shang-ti*), Li considered Ricci to be a man of independent conduct (*tu hsing jen*). Next, he thought Ricci was a broadly learned man who had special arts (*po wen yü tao-shu chih jen*) because he venerated what was right and opposed false teachings, was assiduous in learning, memorized texts so facilely, and knew so much about metaphysics, astronomy, geography, geometry, and arithmetic — subjects about which Confucians (*ju*) in earlier generations had not been clear. Now, in 1608, after knowing Ricci familiarly for nearly ten years, Li realizes that when he is about to do something and it accords with Ricci's words, then he knows he should do it, and if it does not, then he knows he should reject it, and thus Li recognizes Ricci as the perfected man (*chih jen*). "The perfected man," Li wrote, "is compatible with Heaven, but not foreign (*i*) to other men."[16]

The reader of Li's preface might well infer that, with this degree of identification with Ricci, he was ready to be baptized in 1608. He probably would have been, but as Ricci said in a letter written in the spring of that year, he could not yet be a Christian because of a "certain impediment."[17] In his journals at about this time, Ricci wrote of Li, "He is very well instructed in matters of our Holy Faith and stood ready to be baptized if the Fathers had not discovered the impediment of polygamy, which he promises to rid from his house."[18] When this same impediment of having a concubine as well as a wife confronted Yang in 1611, he consulted Li and, as noted above, received the direct advice that he should abandon the concubine. Li, on the other hand, still had not been baptized at the beginning of 1610, whatever the fate of his concubines.

Our source for what then happened is again Aleni.[19] He said that when Li became severely ill in Peking with no relatives at hand, he was attended to day and night by Ricci for weeks. When the illness was at a critical point, Li made a will and asked Ricci to execute it. Ricci urged him to accept the faith at this life-and-death moment. In contrast to Yang, Li was experiencing a great personal crisis when he was baptized. Given the name Leone, he donated a hundred taels of silver for the Church's use, and with the aid of the Great Lord, Li recovered. Ricci died in May of that year.[20]

With Ricci gone, Li maintained his commitment to Christianity. In the spring of 1611, he invited Trigault and Cattaneo to go with him to his home in Hangchow. There, as we have seen, he probably stimulated Yang's interest in Christianity; he certainly encouraged him to follow the faith.[21] The account of Yang's life says of Li at this time: "When his father's illness was so severe, he [Li] thenceforth entrusted matters relating to the rites of death to them [the Church in general and the missionaries in particular]."[22] It was apparently this trust that inspired Yang.

When the mourning period was over in 1613, Li resumed his official career and accepted appointments for the next seven years. He simultaneously continued his involvement in the translation and publication of books on the heavens and mathematics. His efforts culminated in 1628 with his publication of the *First Collection of Writings on Learning from Heaven* (*T'ien-hsüeh ch'u han*). It included nearly all of the important books by the missionaries printed in China up to that time, nineteen titles in all, plus two of his own. In the years just before his death, Li was also instrumental in having Jesuit missionaries officially involved in imperially sponsored calendrical reforms based on the newly introduced Western theories of the heavens.

THE ATTRACTION FOR LI CHIH-TSAO

Why did Li become a Christian? The "public" evidence briefly sketched here allows two inferences, and they often appear in the secondary literature. The first inference is that he and a number of other literati at the time were attracted to the "science" (a term not closely defined in these contexts) brought to China by the missionaries.[23] Trigault gave one of the earliest expressions of this interpretation when he observed that all of the study and publication by Li and Ricci on mathematics and astronomy "was not Father Matthew's principal interest, though it did serve as an allurement, as it were, to attract Leo [Li Chih-tsao] into the fisherman's net."[24]

The second inference is that Li, like many others, was attracted to Christianity by Ricci's strengths of character. D'Elia drew on both of these inferences when he observed of three friends of Li, who also wrote notes which were printed on the 1602 version of the map of the world, that they each praised "the science and the virtue of Ricci."[25] The three had attained higher degrees before or at the same time as Li, and as officials at the capital they had called on Ricci and been interested in the map. They did *not*, however, become Christians. Thus, it does not contradict the two inferences to notice that they simply push the question of "why" back one step: Why was Li so attracted to Western science and to Ricci that he moved beyond that attraction and became a Christian?

According to both Li and Ricci, when Li first met the missionary in Peking in 1601, what struck him was the map of the world. Ricci credited him with a youthful interest in geography, with the implication that such an interest accounts for his response to the map. But Li does not seem to refer to it, even in his 1623 preface to the *Account of Countries Not Listed in the Records Office*, and it is noteworthy that this most significant contribution to the expansion of Chinese knowledge of world geography was the result of a collaboration between Aleni and the non-numerical Yang rather than Li.

Li's fascination in 1601 was with the new model of the world rather than with the geography of the countries of the world. It was not so difficult for him to accept that there were many countries not previously known in China. The world map, or, more specifically, the two-dimensional rendering of a sphere the missionaries called the earth, directly challenged the prevailing Chinese assumption that the earth was a relatively flat square under a canopy or an encapsulating heaven. This is what Ricci meant when he said that Li easily grasped what others found so difficult to believe. Li stressed in his 1623 preface that after seeing the map in 1601 he made calculations to confirm that the earth was a sphere the size Ricci said and that it was a sphere located in the midst of the great sphere of the heavens.[26] Ricci recorded on the 1602 map that Li held it was an everlasting, immutable law (*wan shih pu k'o yi chih fa*) that the degrees of latitude and longitude should correspond to orbital paths in the heavens, and he devoted a year to making calculations to fathom this pattern or principle (*li*).[27] In his own note printed on the 1602 map, Li related the material on the map to Chinese precedents for the idea of a round earth divided into degrees, and he expressed his acceptance of both the concept of a spherical earth larger than previously known and also the associated model of the heavens.[28] Perhaps at his instigation, the map printed in 1602 was supplemented not only with small maps of the northern and southern hemispheres with the poles at the center but also with small figures showing the nine concentric heavens, orbital paths on the celestial sphere, and the relative positions of the sun, moon, and earth for eclipse-produced shadows.

Of course, the material in which Li was interested fits under the general rubric of "science," and Ricci recorded in his journals that in 1601 Li sought to learn more of *questa scientia*, which was translated above as "this knowledge." "This knowledge," with which Li was occupied for years afterward, can be labeled more precisely as the "Learning from Heaven." If it is called science, then an important ambiguity is lost, for Learning from Heaven was also an alternative means of referring to the religious ideas being introduced by the missionaries. That there need be no demarcation is implicitly still recognized in 1628, when Li published "scientific" as well as religious writings together under the title *Learning from Heaven*.[29]

Yang resolved his search for "an externally determined source of moral values" by accepting heaven and the Lord of Heaven. From a quite different intellectual orientation, Li's quest for "an immutable law" on a small scale led him through numbers and calculations involving the heavens and through the realization that there are "the same minds and the same principles in the Eastern and Western seas,"[30] to a willingness to accept the eternal, universal "Lord of Heaven."

Li's appreciation of Ricci proceeds in steps almost exactly comparable to his broadening understanding of heaven, and culminates in seeing Ricci as "compatible with heaven." As Li testifies, Ricci manifested morality and confidence. If his personal strengths were to be accessible to others, such as Li, they had to be portrayed as derived from the discipline of submitting to heaven. Li may not have let go of his concubines and submitted to the moral rules until he faced death; but however much he and Yang contrast in personality and intellectual orientation, they found in the ambiguous "heaven" a source of knowing and a source of discipline that was external and universal. Li was indicating this when he drew the term "perfected man" (*chih jen*) for Ricci out of the *Chuang tzu*. The term occurs throughout the text of the *Chuang tzu*, and most of the contexts are apt, but two are especially appropriate for Li's perception of Ricci in association with heaven. In the first chapter of the *Chuang tzu*, one reads: "The perfected man has no self" (*chih jen wu chi*). This contrasts with the late sixteenth-century preoccupation with self-centered "inner" realms. And in the final chapter of the *Chuang tzu*, there is this definition: "He who does not depart from what is true is called the perfected man" (*Pu li yü chen, wei chih chih jen*).[31] Li appreciated that Ricci's virtue as well as his science were based outside of his own "self" and also outside of his own society.

HSÜ KUANG-CH'I'S BAPTISM

Hsü was every bit as attracted to Ricci as was Li, but the

missionary does not seem to have played as preponderant a role in the events leading up to Hsü's baptism in Nanking in 1604. Ricci's journals are, however, the primary source for the story.[32]

Hsü was born in Shanghai in 1562. His father was a merchant, sometimes quite poor. His mother was from a local literati family and is portrayed in strongly moral terms in Hsü's funeral biography of her.[33] When Hsü passed the prefectural examination in 1581 at the age of twenty, a marriage was immediately arranged for him.[34] He failed in four successive attempts at the triennial provincial examination, and in 1592 his mother died. After mourning her, he failed again in 1594.

In great despair, according to Ricci, Hsü went south to Kwangtung, where he supported himself by teaching in Shaochou. There he visited the newly established Catholic chapel and was shown a painting of the Savior. His host was Cattaneo. The following year, 1597, he sat again for the provincial examination. The chief examiner this time was the famous literatus Chiao Hung (1541–1620), who was deeply involved in Buddhism.[35] Hsü was ranked first, but the next spring he failed in the metropolitan examination. Ricci wrote that years later Hsü attributed his first failure in the *chin-shih* examination to divine intervention, for if he had passed in 1598 he probably would not have had the opportunity to spend time with the fathers. He also probably would have taken a concubine, as was common practice among new *chin-shih,* and he would have been loath to part with her because at the time he had only one young son.[36] Thus, the "divine intervention" of his failure saved him from the "impediment" which later troubled both Yang and Li.

In 1600, on his way from Shanghai to Peking, Hsü stopped in Nanking and met Ricci for the first time. They spoke of the faith, about which Hsü already knew something; but because Hsü was in a hurry, Ricci said, he learned only a little about serving "the Creator of heaven and earth and author of all things." Ricci recorded that a short while after their meeting, Hsü dreamed he was in a temple with three chapels. In one he saw a statue, which, a voice said, was God the Father (*Iddio Padre*); in another chapel was a crowned statue, which was said to be God the Son (*Iddio Figliuolo*); the third chapel was empty. Hsü did obeisance to the two statues and then woke up. He did not understand his dream until a few years later when he was instructed in the mysteries of the Holy Trinity. Because the fathers had cautioned against believing in dreams, he did not say anything about his until 1605, when Ricci happened to mention that God sometimes revealed things in dreams. At that point he recounted his experience.[37]

In the spring of 1601, Hsü failed the *chin-shih* examination in Peking a second time.[38] In the winter of 1603, he went from Shanghai to Nanking. Ricci was still in Peking, and Hsü called on João da Rocha, S.J. (1565–1623), who showed him the mission's chapel. There he paid reverence to a painting of the Madonna and Child and then stood talking with da Rocha about the religion until night fell. He went back to his lodging with manuscript copies of *Christian Doctrine* (*Dottrina cristiana*) and the *Catechism* (*Catechismo*), which he read through the night. The next day he returned to da Rocha with some parts memorized and asked for further explanation. Because he had to return to Shanghai for the New Year, he pressed da Rocha to start the process of baptism immediately. Da Rocha told him that he would have to come to receive instruction once a day for each of the remaining eight days he had in Nanking. Hsü went not once but twice a day, and if da Rocha was not available, he received explanations of doctrine from the Chinese students who were there. On the eighth day he was baptized with the name Paolo and left the same day for his family in Shanghai.[39]

On his way up to Peking in the spring of 1604, Hsü again made the detour to stop in Nanking, where he lodged with da Rocha and heard Mass every day.[40] When he arrived in Peking, he made contact with Ricci and received communion. He then passed the *chin-shih* examination and embarked on an official career in which he rose from Hanlin compiler to grand secretary.[41] He simultaneously started working closely with Ricci on translating and publishing books on mathematics and astronomy.[42] In ways large and small, Hsü supported and promoted the Church in China for the next thirty years with his wealth, political influence, and intellect. He became, as Ricci stated, a "great pillar" for Christianity in China.[43]

The preceding incidents, mostly drawn from Ricci's journals, tell us several things about Hsü's becoming a Christian. First, the juxtaposition of his fortunes in the examinations with stages in his interest in Christianity suggests that an uncertain Hsü found he derived some confidence from the missionaries' teachings. Second, it appears that he was persuading himself more than he was being persuaded. Third, before his baptism in 1604, the attractive force for him does not seem to have been either science or Ricci's character, although clearly he became inextricably connected with both. Why, then, did Hsü take the initiative in seeking baptism?

WHAT HSÜ KUANG-CH'I FOUND

In the summer of 1604, after he was baptized in Nanking and had become a *chih-shih* in Peking, Hsü wrote a postscript for a booklet by Ricci entitled *Twenty-Five Discourses (Erh-shih-wu yen)*. Hsü began by recalling that when he was traveling in the South, he respectfully looked up to an image of the Lord of Heaven which had been brought by ship from Europe. Next, he recalled that he had already seen a printed map of the world and thus knew of the existence of Ricci. He happened to meet him in Nanking and, generally sympathetic to his ideas, considered him to be a gentleman with a comprehensive understanding of a wide range of things. (Note that here is some basis for the two inferences about the attractiveness of science and Ricci's character.) Shortly after this, Ricci went to offer gifts to the emperor in Peking and was himself treated as a guest of the state. Thus, people from all over knew about the missionary, and anyone who was anybody was eager to meet him. When they became acquainted with his ideas, they found them both pleasing and original. When Hsü himself learned about Ricci's more important ideas, he realized that the ones which had first attracted readers were merely dregs or ashes. And this booklet, Hsü wrote, is only a small fraction of these dregs and ashes.

Hsü told the readers of his postscript that Ricci's learning touched on every subject, but the main precept was to serve continuously and openly the Divinity on High. All emotions and desires, as well as extraneous words and actions, are to be cleansed away as one seeks what is called "a body which

has received the whole." Hsü combed through everything the
missionaries said and searched for even one word that was not
in accord with the great teaching of being loyal to one's ruler
and filial to one's father or even one word not beneficial to
the minds of individuals or the good of society. He could not
find any. Moreover, their books contained no such thing either,
and the rules of their religion prohibited it. He wrote that during his entire life he had tended toward scepticism, but this
was like a cloud lifting. There could be no doubting. When
he himself was able to provide explanations based on their
theories, it was like roaming in profound depths. There could
be no doubting. Thus he took it to heart and asked to serve.[44]
In this postscript, he has summarized the process of his deciding
to become a Christian.

A few years later, in his preface to Ricci's and his translation
of a geometry textbook, Hsü told his readers what his hope
for them was:

> My urging [Ricci] to transmit the lesser aspect [of his teaching
> in this translation] is out of a desire to put first what is easy to
> believe, thereby causing others to become involved in these
> texts, perceive the pattern of these ideas, and understand that
> this learning can be believed and not be doubted.[45]

He stressed that only the less important aspect of Ricci's learning involves "investigating things and fathoming principles,"
while the more important aspect involves "cultivating one's self
and serving heaven."[46] He expected readers of the geometry
book to move from the lesser aspect of Ricci's Learning from
Heaven to its greater moral and religious aspects. We may infer
that Hsü himself had been similarly moved.

Hsü's professed quest for certainty is congruent with the
three points extracted from the incidents leading to his baptism.
He was searching for something, and he found it somewhere
else than in "science" or Ricci's character.

A phrase of Hsü's has been made into a slogan which appears
in much of the secondary literature on him.[47] It is usually given
as "Supplements Confucianism and Displaces Buddhism" (*pu
ju i fo*), with the implied subject either Christianity or Western
learning in general. It is worthwhile to quote the phrase in the
context in which Hsü used it in a preface he wrote in 1612.

After praising Ricci and his teachings, more or less in the fashion of the 1604 postscript, he wrote:

> I have often said that his [or our] religion certainly can "supple-ment Confucianism and displace Buddhism," and the remainder [of the teachings] also has a type of learning involving "investiga-ting things and fathoming principles" [a phrase central to Ch'eng-Chu Neo-Confucianism],[48] so that whether it is a question about within or outside of the realm of human society, whether about a principle of the ten thousand affairs [in man's social world] or of the ten thousand things [in the realm of heaven and earth], they can endlessly respond with extremely detailed explana-tions, and when one thinks them over, whether for months or for years, he increasingly sees the necessity and immutability of their theories.[49]

What Hsü found was a mode of learning, the Learning from Heaven, which, as exemplified by the missionaries, added an earnest quality and a discipline to the moral values he inherited from his tradition. The Learning from Heaven was a corpus of certain knowledge based not on one's own mind but on the external world epitomized in the word "heaven" (*t'ien*). At the same time, the knowledge was subject not to the sanctions of authority but one's own investigatory confirmation.

WHY DID THEY BECOME CHRISTIANS?

Hsü Kuang-ch'i, Li Chih-tsao, and Yang T'ing-yün approached Christianity in different ways, with different needs and ques-tions, but they each found in it a moral discipline based upon an external, universal source. Like many of their contem-poraries, they can be understood to have been looking for new intellectual bases to fortify traditional values which were widely perceived to have been eroded. Unlike most of their contem-poraries who did not become Christians, Hsü, Li, and Yang had the Learning from Heaven come into their purview and found its answers persuasive. As Hsü implicitly acknowledged, how-ever, there was nothing inevitable about their choice.

NOTES

1. Matteo Ricci called Hsü Kuang-ch'i the "great pillar" of Christianity in China. See Pasquale M. D'Elia, S.J., ed., *Fonti Ricciane: documenti originali concernenti Matteo Ricci e la storia delle prime relazioni tra l'Europa e la Cina 1579–1615*, 3 vols. (Rome, 1942–1949), 2:308 (N712). For biographical material on Yang T'ing-yün, Li Chih-tsao, and Hsü Kuang-ch'i, see the pertinent footnotes in D'Elia as well as the following works: (1) Hsü Tsung-tse, *Ming Ch'ing chien Yeh-su hui-shih i-chu t'i-yao* (An annotated bibliography of Jesuit translations and writings during the late Ming, early Ch'ing periods) (Taipei, 1958); (2) Yang Chen-o, *Yang Ch'i-yüan hsien-sheng nien-p'u* (Chronological account of the life of Yang Ch'i-yüan) (Shanghai, 1944); (3) Fang Hao, *Li Chih-tsao yen-chiu* (Research on *Li Chih-tsao*) (Taipei, 1966); (4) Lo Kuang, *Hsü Kuang-ch'i chuan* (Biography of Hsü Kuang-ch'i) (Hong Kong, 1953); and (5) Liang Chia-mien, *Hsü Kuang-ch'i nien-p'u* (Chronological account of the life of Hsü Kuang-ch'i) (Shanghai, 1981); also the articles on these Chinese literati in Arthur W. Hummel, ed., *Eminent Chinese of the Ch'ing Period 1644–1912*, 2 vols. (Washington, D.C., 1943–1944), 1:316–19, 452–54; 2:894–95. For the spelling of the missionaries' names, see Joseph Dehergne, S.J., *Répertoire des Jésuites de Chine de 1552 à 1800* (Rome, 1973). Detailed summaries on a place-by-place basis of missionary activity, drawn from a survey of most of the early Western-language materials, are provided by Joseph Dehergne, S.J., "Les Chrétientés de Chine de la Période Ming (1581–1650)," *Monumenta Serica* 16 (1957):1–136.

2. Gernet stresses that some missionaries, particularly Niccolò Longobardi, S.J. (1565–1655), expressed doubts over whether the persons who had been baptized were in fact well instructed in the faith. Jacques Gernet, *Chine et Christianisme. action et réaction* (Paris, 1982), 46–47. Notice that the views ascribed to Longobardi, who is frequently cited, come to us in a version that seems to have passed through the hands of the Franciscan Antonio de Santa María Caballero (1602–1669) before being published in French in Paris (1701) as a contribution to the Rites Controversy. Ibid., 19–20. See also Paul Demiéville, "The First Philosophic Contacts between Europe and China," *Diogenes* 58 (Summer 1967):94–95.

3. A copy of what appears to be a late Ming printing of this work is held in the Bibliothèque Nationale in Paris, Courant No. 3370. It is this version that is followed.

4. Fang Hao, in his introductory notes to Yang Chen-o, *Yang nien-p'u*, says (p. 2) that Aleni dictated the account to Ting, who put it into its written form. See also data on Yang T'ing-yün in Hummel, *Eminent Chinese*, 2:894.

5. Chün-fang Yü, *The Renewal of Buddhism in China: Chu-hung and the Late Ming Synthesis* (New York, 1981), 23–28.

6. Yang Chen-o, *Yang nien-p'u*, 26; Fang Hao, *Li yen-chiu*, 36.

7. Chün-fang Yü, *Renewal of Buddhism*, 76–90.

8. Yang Chen-o, *Yang nien-p'u*, 27.

9. For the year of Yang's baptism, see ibid., 26; Fang Hao, *Li yen-chiu*, 36; and D'Elia, *Fonti Ricciane*, 3:13 n. 3. Also "Yang T'ing-yün," in Hummel, *Eminent Chinese*, 2:894, where the date 1612 is given. L. Carrington Goodrich and Chaoying Fang, eds., *Dictionary of Ming Biography 1368–1644*, 2 vols. (New York, 1976), 33, give 1613. Gernet observes that "Yang T'ing-yün, baptized at age 54, passed almost without transition from the Buddhist faith to Christianity." Jacques Gernet, "La Politique de conversion de Matteo Ricci et l'évolution de la vie politique et intellectuelle en Chine aux environs de 1600." *Archives des sciences sociales de religiones* 36 (1973):86.

10. Fang Hao, *Li yen-chiu*, 30.

11. D'Elia, *Fonti Ricciane*, 2:168–71 (N628). For a slightly different version, see Nicolas Trigault, S.J., ed., *De Christiana Expeditione apud Sinas* (Rome, 1615), 435–36. See also the translation of the latter work by Louis J. Gallagher, S.J., *China in the Sixteenth Century: The Journals of Matthew Ricci, 1583–1610* (New York, 1953), 397.

12. See Li Chih-tsao's 1623 preface to Aleni, *Chih-fang wai chi*, in *T'ien-hsüeh ch'u-han* (First collection of writings on Learning from Heaven), comp. Li Chih-tsao; reprinted in Wu Hsiang-hsiang, ed., *Chung-kuo shih-hsüeh ts'ung-shu* (Collectanea of Chinese historical studies) 23 (Taipei, 1965), 1a, p. 1269.

13. See Ricci's prefatory note on the 1602 map reproduced and published under the title *Li Ma-tou k'un-yü wan-kuo ch'üan-t'u* (Ricci's complete map of the myriad nations of the earth) (Peking, 1936).

14. See D'Elia, *Fonti Ricciane*, 2:173–78 (N631); Trigault, *De Christiana Expeditione*, 436–37, and *China in the Sixteenth Century* 398.

15. Fang Hao, *Li yen-chiu*, 22–23.

16. See Li Chih-tsao's 1608 preface to Ricci, *Chi-jen shih p'ien*, in Li, *T'ien-hsüeh ch'u-han*, 1a–2a, pp. 101–3. Li was making an allusion, as was Ricci's title, to the chapter in the *Chuang-tzu* entitled "Great and Venerable Teacher" where it has Confucius defining the "extraordinary man" as one who is "extraordinary to others but compatible with heaven." See *Chuang-tzu*, Harvard-Yenching Institute Sinological Index Series (Peking, 1947), 18/6/73. The *Chuang-tzu* is a text attributed to the philosopher Chuang-tzu of the fourth century B.C.

17. D'Elia, *Fonti Ricciane*, 2:178 n. 3 (NN631–32).

18. Ibid. Trigault was less sympathetic to Li over the issue of his concubines. He commented: "It seems as if the man had more light to recognize the truth than courage to accept it." Trigault, *De Christiana Expeditione*, 437, and *China in the Sixteenth Century,* 398.

19. Fang Hao, *Li yen-chiu,* 29. Fang notes that Aleni's biography of Ricci includes the only early account in Chinese of Li's baptism. See Giulio Aleni, S.J. (Ai-ju-lüeh), *T'ai-hsi Hsi-t'ai Li hsien-sheng hsing-chi* (The career of Ricci from the Far West), ed. Hsiang Ta (Peking, 1947), 19.

20. See Fang Hao, *Li yen-chiu,* 29, where he quotes Aleni. Also D'Elia, *Fonti Ricciane,* 2:501 (NN926–27). Trigault's version of events seems to conflict with Aleni's, for Trigault has Li still ill when Ricci himself is stricken. Consult Trigault, *De Christiana Expeditione,* 611, 614, and *China in the Sixteenth Century,* 562, 564. A tael was a unit of value; as a unit of weight, in late Ming, it was approximately 1.3 ounces.

21. Fang Hao, *Li yen-chiu,* 36.

22. Ting Chih-lin, *Yang Ch'i-yüan hsien-sheng ch'ao-hsing shih-chi* (Manifestations of the surpassing character of Yang Ch'i-yüan) (N.p., n.d.), 1b, p. 3.

23. For a summary account of the Jesuits' publications on "science" in Chinese during Ming times, see Willard J. Peterson, "Western Natural Philosophy Published in Late Ming China," *Proceedings of the American Philosophical Society* 117 (August 1973):295–322.

24. Trigault, *De Christiana Expeditione,* 437, and *China in the Sixteenth Century,* 398.

25. D'Elia, *Fonti Ricciane,* 2:172 n. 3 (N629).

26. See Li Chih-tsao's 1623 preface to Aleni, *Chih-fang wai chi,* in Li, *T'ien-hsüeh ch'u-han,* 1b–2a, pp. 1270–71.

27. See Ricci's prefatory note on the 1602 map reproduced and published under the title *Li Ma-tou k'un-yü wan-kuo ch'üan-t'u* (see note 13 above). Li was apparently trying to correlate the "fields" in the sky with those on earth.

28. See Li Chih-tsao's note (in the mid-Pacific) on the 1602 map in Ricci's *Li Ma-tou ch'üan-t'u.*

29. This point is also made by Gernet, *Chine et Christianisme,* 93, 265. He translates *t'ien-hsüeh* as *études célestes.* The six mathématical, four astronomical, and one water conservancy books were grouped in a section called "Compilations on Concrete Phenomena" (*Ch'i pien*). The titles on mores, religion, and geography come under the heading "Compilations on Principles" (*Li pien*).

30. Se Li Chih-tsao's note (in the mid-Pacific) on the 1602 map in Ricci's *Li Ma-tou ch'üan-t'u.*

31. *Chuang-tzu,* Harvard-Yenching Institute Sinological Index Series, 2/1/21 and 90/33/3.

32. In addition to a summary of what Ricci wrote, as contained in D'Elia, *Fonti Ricciane,* 2:250–55 (NN680–83), see supplementary material in Lo Kuang, *Hsü Kuang-ch'i chuan,* and Liang Chia-mien,

Hsü Kuang-ch'i nien-p'u. With some variation, the story is also given in Trigault, *De Christiana Expeditione,* 471–73, and *China in the Sixteenth Century,* 429–31.

33. See Hsü Kuang-ch'i, *Hsü Kuang-ch'i chi* (Collection of writings of Hsü Kuang-ch'i) (Peking, 1963), 527–28.

34. Liang Chia-mien. *Hsü Kuang-ch'i nien-p'u,* 44: Lo Kuang. *Hsü Kuang-ch'i chuan,* 6; D'Elia, *Fonti Ricciane,* 2:250 n. 3 (NN679–80). The straitened circumstances of the Hsü family can be inferred from the late marriage arrangement.

35. Ricci said that Chiao Hung, of whom Hsü Kuang-ch'i was by convention an acknowledged follower because he was passed in the provincial examination by Chiao, later tried to dissuade Hsü from following the missionaries' faith. See D'Elia, *Fonti Ricciane,* 2:489 (N912).

36. Ibid., 2:252 (N680). By 1604, when Hsü did pass the examination, his son had already provided him with two grandsons. Ibid., 253.

37. Ibid., 253–54 (N681).

38. The story Ricci gives of Hsü's name being deleted from the list of successful candidates at the last minute in 1601 is puzzling. See Ibid., 253 (N680). Without regard for Ricci's testimony, Liang Chia-mien surmises that Hsü did not sit for the 1601 examination and suggests illness or family affairs as a reason. See his *Hsü Kuang-ch'i nien-p'u,* 65, 67.

39. D'Elia, *Fonti Ricciane,* 2:254–55 (N682). No historian, it would appear, has been able to find testimony by Hsü himself about these events. See Goto Motomi, *Min-Shin shisō to Kirisuto-kyō* (Ming Ch'ing thought and Christian religion) (Tokyo, 1979), 144–45. The account of Hsü's life by his son does not mention that they became followers of the Western faith. See Hsü Kuang-ch'i, *Hsü Kuang-ch'i chi, 551–63.*

40. D'Elia, Fonti Ricciane 2:255 (N683).

41. Ibid., 308 (N714). Also Liang Chia-mien, *Hsü Kuang-ch'i nien-p'u,* 193; and "Hsü Kuang-ch'i," in Hummel, *Eminent Chinese,* 2:316–19.

42. See Trigault, *De Christiana Expeditione,* 520, and *China in the Sixteenth Century,* 476, where it is stated that Hsü suggested the strategy of publishing books on Western science. Certainly none had been published before Hsü became involved with Ricci, but Li Chih-tsao had been working on mathematics and astronomy for at least a year.

43. D'Elia, *Fonti Ricciane,* 2:308 (N712).

44. Hsü Kuang-ch'i, "Pa Erh-shih-wu yen" (Postscript to the twenty-five discourses), in *Hsü Kuang-ch'i chi,* 86–87. See also Li, *T'ien-hsüeh ch'u-han,* 325–27.

45. Hsü Kuang-ch'i. "K'o Chi-ho yüan pen hsü," (Preface for the

printing of the elements of geometry) in *Hsü Kuang-ch'i chi,* 75. See also Li, *T'ien-hsüeh ch'u-han,* 1927–28.

46 Ibid.

47. An early example is by Trigault: "The reply made by Doctor Paul, when he was asked, in company, what he considered to be the basis of Christian law, might be quoted here, as being very timely. He defined the whole subject in four syllables, or rather in four words, when he said, Ciue, Fo, Pu, Giu, meaning, it does away with idols and completes the law of the literati." Trigault, *De Christiana Expeditione,* 489, and *China in the Sixteenth Century,* 448. In Trigault, the four words Ciue, Fo, Pu, Giu probably transliterate 解佛補儒 . Also Gernet, *Chine et Christianisme,* 94; Demiéville, "First Philosophic Contacts," 89–90; and Wang Chung-min, *Hsü Kuang-ch'i* (Shanghai, 1981), 25.

48. See Willard J. Peterson, "Fang I-chih: Western Learning and the 'Investigation of Things,'" in *The Unfolding of Neo-Confucianism,* ed. Wm. Theodore de Bary (New York, 1975), 377.

49. Hsü Kuang-ch'i, "T'ai-hsi shui fa hsü" (Preface for the Western methods of water control), in *Hsü Kuang-ch'i chi,* 66. See also Li, *T'ien-hsüeh ch'u-han,* 1506–7.

Late Ming Society and the Jesuit Missionaries

ALBERT CHAN, S.J.

W HEN MATTEO RICCI (1552–1610) arrived in China, the great days of the Ming dynasty (1368–1644) had long passed, but the empire was still an imposing structure. An unfortunate succession of emperors had done, and was doing, great harm, yet there were still men and movements that gave grounds for hope.

On Ricci's arrival, the empire was then under the rule of the Wan-li emperor (r. 1573–1620), who had come to the throne at the age of ten and inherited a country the treasuries of which had been almost exhausted by his grandfather, the Chia-ching emperor (1522–1566), a fanatic Taoist worshipper and builder of temples and palaces. The latter had started his reign with a great effort to cut down the expenditure of the imperial household to one-tenth of what his predecessor, the Cheng-te emperor (1506–1521), had spent. But in the later part of his reign, he outdid the Cheng-te emperor in extravagance. *The Ming History (Ming shih)* says that toward the end of his reign, the country was restless both within and without.[1]

Between these two spenders came the Lung-ch'ing emperor (1567–1572) who succeeded his father at the age of thirty. He was placid and retiring and never had much ambition for governing. Unlike his father, he was not able to exert authority. During the six years of his reign, the power of the government was left in the hands of his ministers, who fought unceasingly among themselves.

In his boyhood, the Wan-li emperor had the good fortune to

have as his tutor and guide the renowned minister Chang Chü-cheng (1525–1582), probably the most talented grand secretary that the Ming dynasty ever had. Unlike many of his colleagues, Chang was a man of great determination. As head of the government, he set out to reform the administration and to repair the damage done by the Chia-ching emperor. He demanded strict discipline and efficiency from all who were subject to him. As tutor to the emperor, he fixed a course of studies which the boy had to follow regularly and diligently. He tried to cut down all unnecessary expenses both in the imperial household and in the government. Under his vigilance, corruption was greatly reduced and the people treated more justly.

By the time of Chang's death in 1582, the situation of the empire had improved greatly. In particular, it was financially sound and even prosperous. The government granaries in the capital had a ten-year supply and the Court of the Imperial Stud had a reserve of silver amounting to over four million taels.[2]

Unfortunately, these years of prosperity did not last very long. The decline of the dynasty began to manifest itself in the behavior of the emperor and in the weaknesses of the government. Even the reputation of Chang suffered posthumous disgrace. He was stripped of all the honors granted by imperial decrees and was accused of many crimes. Seemingly, the emperor resented the severity of his former tutor who had not allowed him freedom to do what he wished. The ministers, on the other hand, cherished a mortal hatred of Chang because of his high-handed manner and because he had them always at his mercy.

Chang's greatest mistake perhaps was that he had governed alone and single-handedly. By concentrating power in his own person, he made himself absolute. The officials most affected were the censors (Yü shih), who held an important place in the central government of the Ming dynasty. A special characteristic of the censors was that, although they were subordinated to a higher authority, they were independent of that authority when exercising their powers. Perhaps because they were the "eyes and ears" of the emperor, they were directly responsible to him alone. Not a few of them had the courage to criticize the emperors themselves, and they often escaped the penalties of audacity. In some way it was sensed that they were backed by public opinion. It was, moreover, their duty to admonish and to criticize. For this reason, emperors of different dynasties were chary of ill-treating their censors and thereby won a reputation for small-mindedness.[3]

In the last ten years of his life, Chang manifested great severity toward the censors, probably because of conflicts of power among them. He took every occasion to humiliate them and often removed them from office. Shortly after his death, he became the target of their attacks.

Chang had never thought of training a successor. Now that he was gone there was no one to take his place. Chang's successors were men of mediocre ability. Their great desire was to keep their positions, and in order to do this they bowed before the emperor. The emperor, on the other hand, had little interest in the government. Consequently, he paid little attention to what the grand secretary or the censors said or did. The emperor, who was close to twenty, desired feverishly to assert himself — but not for the good of the empire. Instead of seeking advice and help from his ministers, whom he distrusted, he turned to the eunuchs, who were men of no education and, as a rule, of obscure origin. Their greed for wealth and their ambition for power naturally influenced the emperor to seek his own interests.[4] He was so absorbed in his private affairs that he neglected the duties of his office. His last New Year meeting was held in 1588. After that he never appeared before his ministers for the Chinese New Year ceremonies and gradually limited his audiences with his ministers. Even memorials sent to the throne were kept in the palace without reply. These negligences of the emperor eventually led to many vacancies in important offices in the government.[5] Further, political factions were soon formed among the censors and their followers. Instead of uniting to fight against the General Secretariat, they turned against each other. Like most scholars of those days, they possessed little knowledge of politics, and their polemic disputes were centered on speculative problems — on the imperial household.[6]

When Matteo Ricci arrived in China, he witnessed the rise of the Tung-lin party. Ku Hsien-ch'eng (1550–1622), founder of this party, was a native of south Chihli. In 1594, he was dismissed from government and returned to his home town, Wu-hsi. There he and a few friends rebuilt the Tung-lin academy (*shu-yüan*) where the renowned Sung scholar Yang Shih (1053– 1135) had taught. From the beginning, great numbers of scholars attended their meetings, some of which were not purely speculative. There was an active interest in public affairs: "Those who are serving at the court should be mindful of the people, and those who are residing far away [from the court] must not forget their monarch."[7] This perhaps can be taken as the motto of the Tung-lin party. In a word, the party set out to bring together government officials and such of the common people as had a sense of honor and justice to fight openly against dishonesty and injustice.

Under the Sung dynasty (960–1279), the academy system (*shu-yüan*) had flourished greatly among the Neo-Confucian scholars. In the Ming period, it was equally popular among the scholars. Chao Nan-hsing (1550–1628), one of the prominent members of the Tung-lin party, stated that the purpose of the academy was to gather together instructors and friends for discussions. According to him, truth exists throughout the universe and is handed down through traditions, from teachers to disciples. Unless one meets the right instructor, one can spend years going through books and still be ignorant of the truth.

Ku made it clear how important it was to have good friends for mutual help. He said that it had never been heard that anyone had succeeded in becoming a sage by shutting himself behind doors; likewise, it had never been told that sages could live alone, cut off from society. If one tries to associate with virtuous scholars of the village, one benefits by receiving all the good virtues of the village; and the spirit of these good virtues will fill the whole village. In the end, if one tries to associate with virtuous men of the whole world, one will undoubtedly reap the good virtues of the whole world and fill it with this spirit.[8]

In 1582, the Wan-li emperor took over personal control of the government. Soon his court began to fill with undesirable characters, many of whom tried to persuade him of the advantages of mining. The emperor was quite ready to yield to their persuasion, but a group of faithful government officials opposed the project so strongly that the emperor, still a young man, reluctantly gave in to their weighty advice. After that, however, his rule began to deteriorate, and toward the end of his reign the country was in a precarious state. Financially, the empire was at a very low ebb. The war against the Mongols in the north and the defense of Korea against the Japanese invasion had cost the government huge sums. To add to the financial burden, the audience and residential palaces were burnt down in 1596 and 1597, respectively. The cost of reconstruction embarrassed the imperial treasury. The proposal for opening silver mines was brought up again as a means of meeting the crisis. The emperor, interested solely in raising funds, approved this suggestion, disregarding the opposition of grave ministers. The emperor's eunuch commissioners set out at once to carry out the orders of the emperor. And as noted earlier, their ambition for power and their greed for wealth had made them unscrupulous and cruel.

Abuses developed in the summer of 1596 when a mine was opened in the capital itself under the supervision of a eunuch. Wastrels and vagabonds very soon took advantage of this to enrich themselves. This is the turmoil Ricci described and lamented in his journals (see note 4). Chinese history in this period records a large number of revolts against the eunuchs all over the country.[9]

It is easy to understand why the Tung-lin members in these circumstances stressed the importance of a union of forces between government officials and the common people if they wanted to come out victorious over evil influences. The riot of 1627 (7th year of the T'ien-ch'i reign [1620–1627]) is a good example of the union of forces between the literati and the townspeople of Soochow. We are told that after this riot the chief eunuch and his advisers recognized the limits of their power, and imperial guardsmen were no longer sent to the south to make arrests.[10]

Ever since his arrival in Peking in 1601, Ricci had been making friends with numerous government officials, many of them members of the Tung-lin party. He himself claimed to have come from Europe to make friends with the Chinese, and this was the time when the Tung-lin members were trying to make true friends all over the country. His book, the *Treatise on Friendship* (*Chiao-yu lun*), gave them abundant inspiration. Even the eccentric philosopher Li Chih (1527–1602) was so impressed by Ricci and his writing that he had the book copied out and sent to his friends in different provinces.[11]

Despite certain individual and social differences, there was a good deal of similarity between Europeans and the Chinese in intellectual capacity and morality. Both had high civilizations. If the two could unite through mutual communication, it would be possible to form a family with a single spirit. This was the ideal cherished by Ricci: to join the East and the West into one family. Through his writings and his scientific works he had won a name among the scholars. It now remained to win their confidence and to establish permanent friendship.

How could foreigners gain the confidence of the Chinese, who from time immemorial had regarded all foreigners as barbarians and as necessarily lower in culture and in everything else? Furthermore, the fact that foreigners were bellicose was a sign that they were not peace lovers or law-abiding people. Recent events had been discouraging. Ever since the beginning of the dynasty, Japanese pirates had been causing great trouble along the coast, and the Mongols had invaded the Chinese borders in the north and northwest. Toyotomi Hideyoshi (1536–1598) had invaded Korea (1597), and the Japanese had become a menace to China. Moreover, the Manchus, a small tribe long subject to China, were showing signs of unrest.

From Southeast Asia it was reported that the Spaniards had occupied the Philippine archipelago and that the Dutch had conquered Java. Time and again Spanish and Dutch ships appeared along the Fukien coast trying to trade with people of the province. Above all, there was Macao. The Portuguese had been using Macao as a trading post since the middle of the sixteenth century. In 1580, it had come under Spanish dominion when Philip II enforced his claim to the crown of Portugal and her dominions. Owing to commercial relations, Macao had attracted a large number of foreigners, not always men of good character. Under these circumstances, the Chinese had reason to suspect foreigners coming into China and tried to keep them out whenever they could do so. Otherwise, the foreign inhabitants were always under the vigilant eyes of the Chinese.[12]

Ricci was not only well educated and virtuous but also possessed great personal charm and great adaptability to Chinese customs. At first, of course, people took him for a foreigner — a barbarian; but he tried to have himself accepted as one of the Chinese. When they suspected him of being a foreign spy, he strove to win their confidence and make himself a friend of everybody. He captivated them by his Western learning, which was new and by no means inferior to Chinese learning. In every respect he was a gentleman, never giving offense and never offended. Unlike the foreign merchants, he was not looking for worldly gain but was always ready to help. He was admired by many of his Chinese friends.[13] The supervising secretary of Nanking, Chu Shih-lu (1539–1610), became acquainted with him through the *Treatise on Friendship*. Speaking later of Ricci's taking up residence in Nanking, he remarked that he knew he had been in Kiangsi and other parts of the empire and he was, therefore, no longer an alien to China. Why then should he not live in Nanking where there were so many Mohammedans?[14]

In his *Treatise on Friendship*, Ricci seems to have followed the ideas of Cicero's *On Friendship*. First, friendship is not egoistic but looks rather for something that satisfies the soul; hence, there is no admixture of worldly interests. Secondly, there can be no true friendship without true virtue. Virtue and friendship fortify one another. We should, therefore, make friends only with good men; they alone deserve our affection, and they alone are capable of mutual love and respect. The *Treatise on Friendship* points out that if one makes friends with a view to benefit oneself rather than mutual help, one must be regarded as merely a tradesman and not a friend. And further, "it is only among the virtuous that constant friendship is established." In a way, many of Ricci's ideas were quite close to those of the leaders of the Tung-lin party, and this gave them something in common.

From his early days in China, Ricci had made his own the advice in the *Analects*, "to meet friends through literary discussions and to cultivate virtue through friendship."[15] This idea was seen in practice especially in the academies throughout the Ming period and in literary societies toward the end of the period. Ricci seems to have made good use of it from his earliest days in China. Was not his house full of guests in Chao-ch'ing, Shao-chou, Nanchang, Nanking, and later in Peking? Did he not often go to visit mandarins and scholars and take part in their discussions? Li Chih observed that Ricci was so self-possessed that even in a boisterous crowd he was able to deal with each person with great calmness of mind. That is, in no way was Ricci disturbed by a disorderly multitude. This led Li to exclaim:

> Among all the people I have come across, I have never met one equal to him [Ricci]. Some of them are too insolent, others too cringing: either they are too ostentatious or too retiring. Indeed, he is a gifted man: inwardly he is very intelligent, outwardly he is simplicity itself.[16]

In 1608, Ricci published his *Ten Essays on the Extraordinary Man (Chi-jen shih-pien)*. This is a book on philosophical and ethical questions in the form of ten short dialogues between Ricci and some of the scholars and ministers. The dialogues were in the form of discussions, very much like those carried on in the academies. The style was elegant and the subjects interesting, full of paradoxes and of philosophical wisdom taken from Western authors who up to then were unknown in China. The book aroused much questioning among the literati; as a result, some of them were converted to the Christian faith. Ricci himself testified that among all the books he had written in Chinese none had caused a greater sensation than the *Ten Essays on the Extraordinary Man* or had been so readily accepted by the literati.[17]

In his report to his superior on the situation of the mission in China, written in the spring of 1609, Ricci mentioned among other things that the success in Chinese studies by his fellow Jesuits had won them the reputation of being learned and virtuous scholars. This he considered more important than the conversion of ten thousand pagans. To his mind it was a foreshadowing of the conversion of the whole empire.[18]

Speaking of Italians, the *Ming History says*: "These who came to the East were intelligent and were men of great capacity. Their only purpose was to preach religion, with no desire for government honors or for material gain. For this reason those who were given to novelties were greatly attracted to them."[19] Conversation with the missionaries showed clearly that in the West, people were concerned not only with intellectual problems but also with the practical side of life. In a word, they were realistic. Serious-minded Chinese scholars saw that the attitude of the West was in sharp contrast with the attitude of the Chinese of their time who concentrated chiefly on philosophy and moral problems. Such realization gave them the answer to their questions about what was needed in their country. This was a significant point. It can be said that it was the beginning of what the Ch'ing scholars advocated later: [Let us] adhere to our [traditional] studies [and at the same time] apply the Western methods (*Chung-hsüeh wei ti, hsi-hsüeh wei yung*).[20]

This movement started with a small group of men who were close friends of the missionaries. Naturally, it was they who advocated reform, that is, the application of Western methods. They collaborated with the missionaries in translating books from European languages into Chinese, and they themselves wrote on what they knew about Western sciences. In treating of social problems, they were equally in favor of reform, though they were careful not to offend against the old traditions of the country. They tried to begin with themselves and their families, hoping to lead others by their good example.[21]

Those who advocated a total reform according to the Western method thought it necessary to seek the full collaboration of Westerners. In 1610, for the first time in the history of the Ming dynasty, a court minister, Chou Tzu-yü, presented a memorial to the Wan-li emperor pointing out that since the Chinese calendar was becoming very inaccurate, it would be a wise experiment to summon the foreigners from the Great West to institute the reform. However, it was not until the second year of the T'ien-ch'i reign (1622) that a house was set up in the capital for calendar reform purposes. It was known as the Calendar Bureau of the Great West, and European missionaries were given charge of it.

The late Ming period saw great enthusiasm for the study of things European, especially of firearms. The study of firearms was fostered by the government, which was working desperately to win the war against the Manchus. Pi Mao-k'ang, author of the *Book on Firearms with Illustrations (Chün-ch'i t'u-shuo)*, says in his preface that there were over three hundred kinds of firearms in his day. Besides European models, he makes mention of models that had been modified along European lines by the Chinese. These modified types, he says, produced even greater effect than the European types. However, not all who wrote on firearms possessed adequate knowledge of them. Hence, what they said was ridiculed by Sung Ying-hsing (b. ca. 1660) as nonsensical talk whose sole and illusory purpose was to gain the talkers an entry to the government.

A notable number of books written in this period bore the title *World Improving (Ching-shih)* or at least implied such an idea. Thus, Feng Ying-ching (1551–1610) wrote *A Practical Manual for Daily Life (Ching-shih shih-yung-pien)*, and Cheng Ta-yü published *A Grand Scheme for State Administration (Ching-kuo hsiung-lüeh)*. The *Book on Chinese Technology (T'ien-kung kai-wu)* of Sung Ying-hsing (b. ca. 1600) and the *Thesaurus of Agriculture (Nung cheng ch'üan-shu)* of Hsü Kuang-ch'i (1562–1623) both reflect the *Ching-shih* idea. The *General Encyclopedia (San-tsai t'u-hui)*, though compiled largely in the traditional way, gives the impression that it was influenced by the *Ching-shih* idea. The *Japanese-Chinese General Encyclopedia (Wa-han sansai tokai)*, published later in Japan, clearly indicates that it had been influenced by the writings of the West.

While European sciences were beyond the grasp of some, others found in them a source of inspiration and an object of pursuit. This was so especially at the end of the Ming and the beginning of the Ch'ing periods when the translations and writings of the Jesuit missionaries and their followers were spread all over the empire. Among the works by scholars who wrote on diverse aspects of Western studies are the *Encyclopedia on Miscellaneous Subjects (Wu-li hsiao-chih)* of Fang I-chih (d. 1671?) and the *Miscellaneous Notes by Kuang-Yang-tsu (Kuang-yang tsa-chi)* of Liu Hsien-t'ing (1648–1695). Let it suffice to mention these authors and their works.

In conclusion, let us recall that the sixteenth century was the period of Spanish and Portuguese expansion in both the West and the East Indies. It was the age of the conquistadores.

Martín Alonso in his dictionary points out that the word *conquistar* had its origin in the Middle Ages, between the twelfth and fourteenth centuries. He gives two very brief definitions: (1) to win by arms (*ganar con las armas*); (2) used figuratively, to capture the will (*captar la voluntad*).[22] Whereas the soldiers tried to conquer by arms, religious missionaries tried to capture the will of the conquered by spreading the Gospel. It was inevitable that Western culture should also be introduced where they went. But when they came to China and Japan, they began to realize that these two nations had high cultures of their own, quite different from those of the West. There was no question of conquering them by arms, nor was it easy to introduce them to anything new.

Francis Xavier (1509–1552), who worked for a number of years in Japan, saw the necessity of evangelizing the Chinese first if he was to convince the Japanese of the truth of Christianity. His untimely death prevented him from formulating a policy for these two missions, but he was determined that the method of dealing with the Chinese and Japanese should not be the same as that in use in other mission countries. Missionaries to China and Japan should be carefully chosen, and they should be well qualified in learning and in virtue. Ricci, the man who really should be considered the founder of the Chinese mission, was just the type of man that Xavier would have looked upon as ideal for this mission. He was not only learned and virtuous but also possessed great personal charm and great adaptability to Chinese customs. His methods were slow but sure.

NOTES

1. See *Ming shih* (Ming history), comp. Chang T'ing-yü and others, 28 vols. (reprint edition, Peking, 1974), chuan 18, 2:250–51.
2. Ibid., chuan 213, 19:5645. A tael was a unit of value; as a unit of weight, in late Ming, it was approximately 1.3 ounces.
3. Kao I-han, *Chuan-kuo yü-shih chi-tu te yen-ke* (Development of the censorial system in China) (Shanghai, 1933), 29–31.
4. In his journals, Matteo Ricci had this to say: "The eunuchs, as a class, are unlettered and barbarous, lacking shame and piety, utterly

arrogant and very monsters of vice. What with these semimen in command, and with their greed developing them into savages, the whole
kingdom was in a turmoil within a few months, and in a worse state
than it was during the Korean war. The war was external. This evil
was from within, and greater, because of the fear it developed. Pilfering,
cheating, and robbery were everywhere common. The tax and customs bureaus were veritable dens of thieves, and the royal treasury,
entrusted by the King to the eunuchs, was thoroughly despoiled. The
tax collectors found gold mines, not in the mountains, but in the
rich cities. If they were told that a rich man lived here or there, they
said he had a silver mine in his house, and immediately decided to
ransack and undermine his home. This method of collection resulted
in the payment of large sums of money by unfortunate victims before
the collectors appeared, in order to save their properties. Sometimes,
in order to secure an exemption from being robbed, the cities and
even the provinces bartered with the eunuchs and paid them a large
sum of silver, which they said was taken from the mines for the royal
treasury. The result of this unusual spoliation was an increase in the
prices of all commodities, with a corresponding growth in the general
spread of poverty. Unlike the King's degraded servants, the Magistrates
remained loyal to him and to the public charge they administered.
They sent frequent notices warning the King that the people were
being treated unjustly, that there was danger of a public uprising,
and not only danger but that serious outbreaks had already happened
in several places. When the King paid no attention to their warnings,
they wrote to him, reprehending his conduct in no uncertain terms,
and some of them, outside of the royal city, openly opposed the rav-
ages of the eunuchs. But His Majesty was growing fat on the daily
provender brought to his palace by his henchmen, and he resolved
not only to pursue his policy, but to punish with heavy penalties the
critics and censors of the royalty, and all those who dared to interfere
with the work of the eunuchs. As a result, some of the judges were
deposed from their high offices, and others were sent to prison in
Peking to serve long terms in chains. With the King's authority renewed, the robbers became more insolent in their attitude and more
daring in their depredations." Nicolas Trigault, S.J., (1577–1628), ed.,
*China in the Sixteenth Century: The Journals of Matthew Ricci, 1583–
1610*, trans. Louis Gallagher, S.J. (New York, 1953), 343–44. For a
fuller account from Chinese sources, see Ku Ying-t'ai (d. after 1689),
Ming-shih chi-shih pen-mo (History of the Ming dynasty in topical
form), 2 vols. (Shanghai, 1935), B:chuan 65, 73–86. In his journals,
Ricci gives an account of his own dealings with Ma T'ang, the eunuch
tax collector, whom he calls Mathan. Trigault, *China in the Sixteenth
Century,* 359–69.

5. Toward the end of 1607, the grand secretary, Yeh Hsiang-kao (1559–1627), reported: "Today most of the important government offices are vacant and the situation is most lamentable. There is only one official in each court; some of these have asked for permission to resign on account of sickness, others because of criticism. Only three great officials now remain in office: Li Hua-lung [1554–1612], president of the Board of War, Yang Tao-pin, vice-president of the Board of Ceremonies, and Liu Yüan-lin, vice-president of the Board of Works. Of these, Yang has asked for leave, and Li is absent because of his health, so that in the capital one can find hardly a trace of an important official. Moreover, the president of the Board of Revenue, Chao Shih-ch'ing, is in such distress that he seems to have lost his interest in life, solely because he is unable to provide the salaries of the troops on the borders. The Board of Works finds it difficult to supply rewards for the foreigners. Both the Board of War and the Court of Entertainment, owing to lack of resources, have petitioned for leave to borrow from the Boards of Revenue and Works, and, in their discouragement, they are beginning to find fault with each other." Chuang T'ing-lung (ca. 1650), *Ming-shih ch'ao-lüeh* (A glimpse of the history of the Ming dynasty), 2 vols. (reprint edition, Shanghai, 1935), (ts'e 1):29b.

Nor was this an isolated case. In 1609, the Boards of Revenue, Ceremonies, and Punishment were left vacant, and when the grand secretary sent in a petition to have officials appointed, the petition was pigeon-holed. Even the office of the grand secretary, one of the most important, perhaps the most important of government offices, was no better treated than the others. Fang Ts'ung-che (d. 1628) found himself the solitary custodian of the office, and when he petitioned for new appointments to fill office vacancies, the emperor said that one man was enough. Fang was so discouraged that for forty days he refused to carry out his duties and did not return to them until after repeated requests from the emperor. See Ch'a Chi-tso (1601–1677), *Tsui Wei-lu* (A complete history of the Ming dynasty), 2 vols. (reprint edition, Shanghai, 1928), 14 (ts'e 6):36b; Kuo Shang-pin (ca. 1598), *Kuo chi-chien shu-kao* (Draft of the memorials to the throne by the censor Kuo Shang-pin), in *Ts'ung-shu chi-ch'eng ch'u-pien* (First series of the collection of collectanea), 5 vols. (Shanghai, 1935), 1 (ts'e 0, 908):19–20; Chao I (1727–1814), *Erh-shih-erh-shih cha-chi* (Miscellaneous notes on the twenty-two dynastic histories), 2 vols. (Shanghai, 1963), B:731.

6. Hsia Hsieh (ca. 1850), *Ming t'ung-chien* (A chronological history of the Ming dynasty), 3 vols. (Shanghai, 1959), 3:2654; Meng Sen, *Ming-tai shih* (A history of the Ming period) (Taipei, 1957), 276; Hsieh Kuo-chen, *Ming Ch'ing chih chi tang-she yün-tung k'ao* (A study of

factions and cliques in the late Ming, early Ch'ing periods) (Taipei, 1967), 15–39.

7. Kao P'an-lung (1562–1626), *Kao-tzu i-shu* (Posthumous works of Kao P'an-lung), late Ming edition (ts'e 8, 164):2–8; see Huang Tsung-hsi (1610–1695), *Ming-ju hsüeh-an* (A systematic historical survey of all the important schools of thought throughout the Ming period) (Shanghai, 1933), 50, where a similar statement by Ku Hsien-ch'eng is given. Huang goes on to say that in the Tung-lin meetings, government personnel as well as government affairs were brought up for discussion. It was expected that in this way the authorities might be moved to make necessary changes. As a result, the Tung-lin party was backed by public opinion, and the government gave weight to its views.

8. Chao Nan-hsing, *Wei-po-chai wen-chi* (Essays by Chao Nan-hsing), in *Ts'ung-shu chi-ch'eng*, 5 (no. 2443, ts'e 5):181; Hou Wai-lu, comp., *Chung-kuo ssu-hsiang t'ung-shih* (A general history of Chinese thought), 7 vols. (Peking, 1949–1960), Book 4B (Peking, 1960):1101, 1103.

9. Ku Ying-t'ai, *Ming-shih chi-shih pen-mo*, B:chuan 65, 73–86; Kuo, *Kuo shu-kao, in Ts'ung-shu chi-ch'eng*, 1 (ts'e 0, 908):28–30, 34; 2 (ts'e 0, 908):38; Chao I, *Erh-shih-erh-shih cha-chi*, 35 B:729–31; Chou Shun-ch'ang (1584–1626). *Chou-chung chieh-kung chin-yü-lu* (Some incomplete writings of Chou Shun-ch'ang), in *Ts'ung-shu chi-ch'eng*, 1 (ts'e 2, 165):1–7. Similarly, the eunuchs were commissioned by imperial orders as tax collectors. Since they were strangers to the provinces to which they were assigned, they had to depend upon the natives of those localities for information, and many ne'er-do-wells offered their services, helping the eunuchs to make great profits. Protected by the eunuchs, many locals went about exploiting the people audaciously. The *Ming shih* relates that they set up numerous custom stations along both land and water routes. They laid hands on merchants and confiscated their goods, searching even their personal belongings. They also made their way into small villages and imposed taxes on such common necessities as rice, salt, chickens, and pigs. Their atrocities sometimes became all the more intolerable in that they followed one another in quick succession. See *Ming shih*, chuan 81, 71978–79.

10. The riot of 1627 was caused by the arrest of Chou Shun-ch'ang, a retired government official and a Tung-lin member, by order of the notorious eunuch Wei Chung-hsien (1568–1627). Several tens of thousands of townspeople of Soochow were involved. When violence broke out, the presiding officials escaped with little dignity; two guards were killed and many injured. Subsequently, five Soochow commoners were executed as ringleaders (a son of a wealthy merchant,

a salesman, a haberdasher, a sedan-chair bearer, and one unkown). Others were subjected to corporal punishment or sent into exile. Chou Shun-ch'ang was brought secretly to Peking where he died in the palace prison under cruel torture. See Chang P'u (1602–1641), "Wu-jen mu-pei chi" (The tombstone inscription of five [martyrs]), in *Ming-wen-hui* edition (Ming literature collection) (Taipei, 1958), 1094–95. From this narrative, one can see that members of the Tung-lin party were involved in this riot.

11. *Chiao-yu lun* was the first book written (in 1595) in Chinese by Ricci. He was then in Nanchang, Kiangsi province, as the guest of Chu To-chieh, the Chien-an prince (d. 1601), who was curious to know what Europeans had to say about friendship. Ricci's little book was based on the writings of Greek and Roman authors as well as on well-known Catholic writers. The *De Amicitia* of Cicero is quoted frequently. Likewise, the writings of Seneca and St. Augustine appear several times. Some of the ideas seemed so new and so beautiful to the Chinese scholars that they were quite captured by them. Before it was published, many besides Li Chih had it copied and sent to friends all over the country. Since then it has gone through many editions down to our day. See Pasquale M. D'Elia, S.J., ed., *Fonti Ricciane: documenti originali concernenti Matteo Ricci e la storia delle prime relazioni tra l'Europa e la Cina 1579–1615*, 3 vols. (Rome, 1942–1949), 1:368–70; Fang Hao, "Li Ma-tou Chiao-yu lun hsin-yen" (A new study on Matteo Ricci's *Chiao-yu lun*), in *Fang Hao liu-shih tzu-ting kao* (The collected works of Maurus Fang Hao revised and edited by the author on his sixtieth birthday), 2 vols. with Supplement (Taipei, 1969), 2:1849–70.

Chiao-yu lun seemingly was still quite popular in the circle of the literati at the beginning of the Manchu period when it inspired Martino Martini (1614–1661) to write his own work on friendship, *Chiu-yu pien* (A treatise on making friends) (1661), two *chuan* in one volume. Somehow he felt that Ricci's book was too short and not exhaustive on the subject. While Ricci's booklet is in the style of proverbial phrases, Martini's book is a full textbook on ethics. It is interesting to note from the preface of *Chiu-yu pien* that Hsü Er-chüeh (1605–1683), grandson of Hsü Kuang-ch'i (1562–1633), cautions against the ill effect that may come from making friends, namely, the formation of factions, which may eventually lead to party strife. He was hinting at the damage done by party strife in the late Ming period. At the time he wrote the preface (1661, the eighteenth year of the Shun-chih reign [1664–1666]), the forming of parties and private academies was strictly forbidden by the Manchus. See Teng Chih-ch'eng, *Chung-hua erh-ch'ien-nien shih* (Two thousand years of Chinese history), 5 vols. (Hong Kong, 1964), 5B:249–55; Hsieh Kuo-chen, *Ming Ch'ing chi tang-she*, 250–55; Hsü Tsung-tse, *Ming Ch'ing chien Yeh-su-hui-shih i-chu t'i-yao* (An annotated bibliography of Jesuit translations and writings during the late Ming, early Ch'ing periods) (Shanghai, 1949), 345–48.

12. Commerce had developed greatly since the middle of the Ming period. As a result, big cities had begun to appear. Soochow and Hangchow were the centers of silk production. Sung-king became the center of cotton weaving, and Ching-te chen was the center of the porcelain industry. According to Li Ting, who lived at the beginning of the Wan-li period, merchants traveled to the south day and night with the products of the northern provinces; likewise, merchants traveled to the north with goods from the south. Those along the coast where the soil was poor often risked their lives by sailing the high seas in search of a better living in neighboring states. Such voyagers reached Korea, Japan, the Pescadores, the Philippines, Annam, Cambodia, Malacca, and Siam. Many made their fortunes in this way. Despite prohibitions issued by local authorities, foreign trade went on without interruption. See Hsieh Chao-che (1567–1642), *Wu tsa tsu* (Encyclopedic notes), 2 vols. (Shanghai, 1959), A:107, 115–16; see also Hsieh Kuo-chen, ed., *Ming-tai she-hui ching-chi shih-liao hsüan-pien* (Selected materials for the socioeconomic history of the Ming dynasty), 3 vols. (Fukien, 1980), B:61–121, where quotations are cited from first-hand sources.

In the second half of the Ming period, a number of Confucian scholars changed their views on commercial transactions; traditionally, Confucian scholars would never involve themselves in business transactions since they considered that by so doing they would lower their social standing. Tsao Shu-ming mentions a number of these scholar families that went into business and became quite wealthy as a result. Even the grand secretary, Hsü Chieh (1503–1583), it is reported, kept a considerable number of women weavers in his native place in order to produce for the market. Tsao Shu-ming, *Hsin-an Hsiu-ning ming-tsu chih* (Records of the eminent families of Hsin-an and Hsiu-ning), in Hsieh, *Ming-tai shih-liao*, B:68, 96–97.

Trading by these great families was not confined to their native country. It often extended to foreign states despite repeatedly issued imperial decrees forbidding foreign trade. Ch'en Jen-hsi (1579–1634), in his *Huang-Ming shih-fa lu* (Collection of government documents of the Ming period), 4 vols. (reprint edition, Taipei, 1965), 4:2005–6, gives a number of cases that occurred in different Ming reigns. In the Wan-li period, it seems to have become quite common for rich families in Fukien to trade with neighboring countries through their servants; they supplied the capital and ships, and their servants made the voyages and carried out business transactions. Earlier in the Chia-ching period, Chu Wan (1494–1549), governor of Fukien, attempted to stop foreign trade. Both the common people and the gentry felt the blow. Their protests and their complaints to the court eventually brought about the governor's removal from office. Later, he was thrown into prison and committed suicide. See *Ming shih*, chuan 205, 18:5403–5, for the biography of Chu Wan. Chang Hsieh (ca. 1600) summed up the conditions of the time briefly but clearly: "As a rule, we used to find foreigners coming to China for trade and it must be admitted that there never was a time in which so many Chinese went abroad for trade as go in our day." Chang Hsieh, *Tung-Hsi-yang k'ao* (A maritime geography of South Asia) (Shanghai, 1937), 103.

13. In one of his letters, Ricci wrote: "We are dressed in Chinese gowns; our speech, our food and drink, and the house we live in are all according to the Chinese custom ... and for this reason it seems to us more solidly fruitful and better advised to adopt this plan. Little by little we shall win the confidence of this people and remove all their suspicions, and then we will deal with their conversion." Pietro Tacchi Venturi, S.J., ed., *Opere storiche del P. Matteo Ricci, S.J.*, 2 vols. (Macerata, 1911–1913), 2:247. Elsewhere, Ricci wrote: "The higher authorities, having good relations with us, are losing the fear they had for foreigners, and many say that we are very much like them, something not to be overlooked in a country so hard to communicate with and so proud. In everything we yield to them except in the law of God." Ibid., 2:57. A contemporary remarked that "recently some foreigners from the Great West came here by sea. They preach the doctrine of worshiping heaven. The terminology they use is very precise, their teachings are very logical, and their behavior very proper. They refute Buddhism and Taoism but favor Confucius. There are people who have taken a fancy to them. They even say that sages had been born." Ch'en Hou-kuang, *Pien-hsüeh ch'u-yen* (Philosophical writings of Ch'en Hou-kuang), n.p., n.d., 16

In the preface to *Chao-tai chi-lüeh* (A brief history of the contemporary Ming period), 6 vols. (late Ming edition), 5 (ts'e 5):70b, Chu Huai-wu relates that, after the death of Ricci in 1609 (read 1610), his follower Pang Wo-ti (read Pang Ti-wo; i.e., Diego Pantoja, S.J. [1571–1618]) remained in Peking; Wang Feng-shu (i.e., Alfonso Vagnoni, S.J. [ca. 1568–1640]) and others were in Nanking. They so attracted scholars and commoners that these gathered like clouds. Ch'en Lung-cheng (1568–1645), in *Chi-ting wai-shu* (Miscellaneous writings of Ch'en Lung-cheng), 6 vols. (late Ming edition), 2 (t'se 2):28b–29b, describes Ricci as a very clever man who, after his arrival in China, learned to speak and read Chinese. Even his writings were above the ordinary. After his death, his followers were able to carry on his teaching, but none of them could compare with him intellectually. Shen Te-fu (1578–1642), in *Wan-li yeh-huo pien* (Miscellaneous notes written on the late Wan-li period) (Shanghai, 1959), p. 30, C. 785, relates that Ricci did not take offense when he was contradicted, was generous in almsgiving, and always came to the relief of those in urgent need. As a result, his earnestness and kindness were always appreciated and he was highly respected. Li Chih-tsao (1565–1630), in his preface to Ricci's *Chi-jen shih p'ien*, says: "Sometimes I consulted him on diverse problems, and if I followed his advice I always came out right. But if I did otherwise, I always had cause for regret."

14. D'Elia, *Fonti Ricciane*, 2:46–47 (N536).

15. Ch'eng Shu-te, *Lun-yü chi-shih* (A collection of commentaries on the *Analects* of Confucius), 2 vols. (Taipei, 1965), B:763–64.

16. Li Chih, *Hsü Fen-shu* (Second series of Li Chih's collected works) (Shanghai, 1959), 36. In the year 1610, over 5,000 students from all over the country came to the capital for the examinations, besides a number of officials who had come to report on the performance of their official duties. Many of these officials had heard Ricci's name and others were old acquaintances, and they took this opportunity to pay him a visit. This kept Ricci very busy receiving visitors and returning visits. It was during Lent, the season for fast according to Church law, and Ricci often had to leave his supper to receive visitors; then when the visits were over, he forewent his supper. See Henri Bernard-Maitre, S.J., *Le Père Matthieu Ricci et la Société Chinoise de son temps, 1552–1610*, 2 vols. (Tientsin, 1937), 2:366–67. This shows clearly the success of Ricci. In his mission, he had to exercise great self-denial and make heavy sacrifices. The same author refers to the experiences of an eighteenth-century French Jesuit missionary in China, Jean de Fontaney (1643–1710). According to Fontaney, to be a missionary in China, one must have full control of one's natural disposition and tendencies. It is the nature of a European to be lively and passionate and to forge ahead vigorously. Once he came to China, he would have to make a thorough reform. He must be gentle, cheerful, patient, and polite to all his visitors. He must listen to them with great patience, his expression should be graceful, and he should not raise his voice or behave without regard to decorum. Ibid., 1:242.

17. This book cost him two years (1606–1608) of hard work. Shortly after it was published, Ricci was able to write: "We have received news that the book has been printed in two or three other provinces, and requests for copies have come from different places. I have already given away hundreds of them." The following year he wrote: "Not only have the fathers here asked for many hundreds of copies in order to make presents to their friends, but many others have

had numerous copies of it printed at their own expense for distribution to their friends." In that same year (1609), the book was printed twice by the Chinese literati, once in Nanking and once in Kiangsi. D'Elia, *Fonti Ricciane*, 2:304 (N711) (NN1819, 1856).

The success of *Chi-jen shih p'ien* led to the composition by later-period missionaries of a few works in the form of academic discussions, or in the *yü-lu* style, that is, the lecture style of writing especially characteristic of the Neo-Confucian scholars of the Sung dynasty (960–1279). Such Jesuit works are: (1) *San-shan lun hsüeh chi* (Learned conversations at San-shan [Foochow]) by Giulio Aleni, S.J. (Ai Ju-lüeh [1582–1649]). This is a dialogue between Aleni and Yeh Hsiang-kao, the former grand secretary, on God as the creator and governor of the universe. (2) *K'ou-to jih-chao* (Daily records taken from dialogues between Jesuit missionaries and some Chinese scholars in Fukien). The missionaries were Aleni and Andrius Rudamina, S.J. (Lu An-te [1596–1631]), who dialogued about questions of faith, the natural sciences (physics and mathematics), and contemporaneous events. The conversations and discussions were taken down by several Christian literati. (3) *Hsü k'ou-to jih-chao* (A second series of the *K'ou-to jih-chao*) by Wu Li (Simon-Xavier a Cunha, S.J. [1632–1718]). This book is very similar to the *K'ou-to jih-chao*. The conversations and discussions of Wu Li were recorded by Chao Lun, who, according to Pfister (*Notices*, 1:397), was Wu Li's catechist. See also Fang Hao, *Chung-kuo T'ien-chu-chiao shih jen-wu chuan* (Biographies of eminent persons in the history of the Catholic Church in China), 3 vols. (Hong Kong, 1967–1973), 2:234–37.

18. Bernard-Maitre, *Père Ricci*, 2:230.

19. *Ming shih*, chuan 326, 28:8461.

20. Ch'en Tien (1849–1921) says correctly that "after Hsü Kuang-ch'i passed the *chin shih* examinations, he learned astronomy, mathematics, and firearms from Matteo Ricci and learned them thoroughly. He seems to have foreseen the good fruit that Western studies would bear in China three centuries later. At the same time, he made studies of national defense, military settlement, hydraulics, salt production, etc. This shows that his interests were not confined solely to Western studies. As a man of flexibility and common sense, he is indeed worthy of the praises of men of wisdom." *Ming-shih chi-shih* (Miscellaneous annotations to the poems of the Ming period), 10 vols. (Shanghai, 1936), Keng-chien, chuan 21 (ts'e 8), 2475.

21. For instance, at the end of *Ch'ung-i-t'ang hsü-pi* (Miscellaneous writings of Wang Cheng), there is a public confession by Wang Cheng (1571–1644) that shows the great openness and sincerity of the man. One can but admire his courage. The confession tells us that when he was baptized a Catholic, he made up his mind never to take a

concubine. On the day he passed his government examinations, he wrote home reminding his family of his determination. Since he had no son by his first wife, his family held that he would have to take a concubine. He yielded to pressure from his father. Later, he repented and tried to send the concubine away. "My wife wept and begged me to tolerate the concubine, and we nearly had a quarrel. The concubine too was so distressed that she nearly lost her life. She would on no account remarry, and she expressed her wish to become a Christian and observe chastity." Remorse finally caused Wang to make up his mind. "Throughout the whole night I reflected (saying to myself) that I am nearly seventy, and my behavior is no better than that of a youth of seventeen. . . . Now I promise before God that in future I will treat the concubine as a friend . . . and if afterward I again commit sin with her, the angels (will be my witness) and I am willing to die the penalty of death." This confession by Wang Cheng was made on the tenth day of the twelfth month in the ninth year (1636) of the Ch'ung-chen reign (1627–1644). See Bibliotheca Vaticana: Borgia Cinese 336 (3).

22. Martín Alonso, *Enciclopedia del Idioma*, 3 vols. (Madrid, 1958), 1:1184.

7

A Serious Matter of Life and Death: Learned Conversations at Foochow in 1627

BERNARD HUNG-KAY LUK

"EAST IS EAST, and West is West, and never the twain shall meet," wrote Rudyard Kipling in 1889; and the poet proceeded with a ballad about how an Indian horse thief and a British army officer met in pursuit and came to develop a kind of respect for each other in the mutual code of machismo.

But is it only in feats of physical daring that people from different cultures can meet? Can there not be mutual appreciation and respect in ethical, religious, and intellectual endeavors? Contemporary writers critical of the age when the white man was an unabashed burden on the subject peoples of more than half the world have many faults to find with the attitudes and assumptions of Kipling and his like, not the least of which is the stereotyping of East and West, and the preconception of unbridgeable chasms in the intellectual and spiritual realms.

But the European expansion was not uniformly arrogant. During the centuries of the ascendancy of the West, there were, now and then, here and there, genuine efforts at understanding, appreciation, and mutual respect between Europe and the cultures in its path. One of the most dramatic and significant of these efforts was the Jesuit mission in China in Ming-Ch'ing times. While the crossing of philosophical and doctrinal barriers was difficult for the Jesuits and for the Chinese literati, both

The author is indebted to Philip West, Hin-cheung Lovell, and Willard J. Peterson for invaluable suggestions that have enhanced this essay.

of whom were often imprisoned by their respective modes of thinking, mutual esteem for the ethical and spiritual attainments of one another's tradition did develop out of their contact.

Under the leadership of Alessandro Valignano, S.J. (1539–1606) and Matteo Ricci, S.J. (1552–1610), the Jesuits developed a policy of accommodation with Confucianism as an approach to proselytizing Chinese scholar-officials. In the intellectual sphere, the Jesuits took the position that there was nothing incongruous between Catholic doctrines and what they held to be the "pristine" Confucianism of the Classical texts. Anything in contemporaneous Confucianism that conflicted with their teaching, the missionaries attributed to a corrupted transmission of the doctrines of the Chinese sage. They equated the heaven of the Classics with the Christian God, and rejected Taoism, Buddhism, and the Neo-Confucian metaphysics that grew out of the Sung synthesis of these schools with older forms of Confucianism. Confucius thus became, so to speak, a Chinese John the Baptist, preparing the way for the coming of the Lord. The Jesuits contended that they were attempting to restore the original Confucianism and to bring it to its fruition. In this way, they hoped to ease the acceptance of Christianity by the Chinese literati. Liturgically, the Jesuits also granted, or obtained papal permission for, corresponding concessions to Chinese customary practices.[1]

Operationally, Ricci and his confreres proceeded with the work of proselytization by cultivating individuals or small groups of literati with learned conversations and discussions rather than by public preaching. The latter would all too easily attract unfavorable attention or lead to breaches of the public peace in the late Ming milieu, while learned conversations were an accepted part of literati culture and of the philosophical tradition.[2] Thus, dressed and speaking as a Chinese literatus, a Jesuit missionary would seek to be first an adjunct, later a member, of the intellectual circles of a locality. He might use his knowledge of Western science or his travel experiences in a kind of pre-evangelization; then he would raise and answer questions of a philosophical or religious nature, pass around literature, pay courtesy calls, attend literary gatherings or banquets, and do most of the other things an upright and serious-minded literatus would do. Quietly and modestly, he would allow his broad learning and virtuous behavior to be known. Soon people would make further inquiries, and then the more direct work of doctrinal instruction could begin.

The accommodation policy never enjoyed universal acceptance; the mendicant rivals of Jesuit missionaries, and even some Jesuits themselves, attacked this accommodation as itself a corruption of Catholic faith and morals.[3] From a different perspective, literati in the seventeenth century, as well as Sinologists of more recent times, have cast grave doubts on the Jesuits' understanding of Chinese philosophy and their interpretation of Chinese intellectual history.[4] Nevertheless, the views of Ricci and his followers prevailed in the mission, and a number of late Ming scholar-officials, including a few of the best minds of the age, did embrace the Catholic faith without apparently giving up much of their Confucianism, thereby demonstrating that the Jesuits' theories did make sense to at least some of their intended audience.

It is not the intention here to review the arguments for or against the accommodation policy. Rather, this is an attempt to examine in some depth a learned conversation between a missionary and a Confucian in order to observe the policy in action and to aid in evaluating the effectiveness of the Jesuits in their grand enterprise of bridging continents.

The first and most famous of the published encounters between Confucianism and Christianity in conversational form was written by Ricci himself: the *True Meaning of the Lord of Heaven (T'ien-chu shih-i)* (1603), in which a Chinese scholar and a Western scholar engaged in dialogue on philosophical and religious topics.[5] While this was a key document of the accommodation policy, and the topics are systematically developed, it was not a record of any one historical conversation, although it was based on numerous discussions Ricci and his associates experienced. Rather, it was a constructed dialogue, much like the ones in contemporaneous Europe written to present philosophical, political, or scientific debates. It could neither convey the actual give and take and personal factors an account of a real conversation would have, nor show how an actual learned conversation between missionary and literati might end. For the purpose of this essay, another kind of source is required.

In June 1627, an amiable but unremitting discussion on philosophy and religion took place at Foochow among the Jesuit Giulio Aleni (Ai Ju-lüeh [1582–1649]), Yeh Hsiang-kao (1562–1627), the former grand secretary, and the Intendant Ts'ao. An account of the conversation was published soon afterward by Aleni under the title *Learned Conversations at San-shan* [*Foochow*] (*San-shan lun hsüeh chi*).[6] The style of this booklet is too literary to have been a verbatim record of the conversations and must have been edited. Since Aleni published it to aid his proselytizing work, its fidelity as a record may be questioned. However, the status and prestige of Yeh and Ts'ao, and Yeh's position as Aleni's patron in Fukien, should guarantee (even if Aleni's honor did not) that this would be a reasonably faithful account of what transpired during the discussions. Indeed, in a foreword to the booklet written some time after the conversations by one Huang Ching-fang (who might or might not have been converted to Christianity), the writer testified that Yeh, as here recorded, spoke the minds of many literati in the difficulties he raised with Aleni's teachings.[7] In this as well as in another foreword by one Su Mou-hsiang (probably a Christian), Yeh was considered to have argued the Confucian position very well, and Yeh and Aleni were each judged equal to the challenge of the other.[8] Thus, the general credibility of the *Learned Conversations at San-shan* [*Foochow*] was attested by contemporaries.

In the discussions, the issues raised included the Jesuit's rejection of Buddhism, comparisons between Neo-Confucian and Christian cosmologies, the omnipotence of God, the problem of evil and the justice of God, free will, moral self-cultivation, retribution and afterlife, salvation and the incarnation of Jesus, and Christianity in Chinese history. The booklet contains some ten thousand characters and was not by any means a systematic catechism. Rather, the points raised by Yeh reflected deep and urgent political and existential concerns, many of which were shared by other literati of the time.

In what follows, the three conversationalists are introduced and the booklet examined.

GIULIO ALENI

The protagonist of the conversations, Giulio Aleni, was one of the most distinguished successors of Ricci in China. Laboring mostly in the south and far from the center of power in Peking, he never served any emperor as clock maker, astronomer, diplomat, confidant, surveyor, or court painter. He remained in the provinces, made friends among the scholars and officials, and won converts. He was well enough respected by his Chinese contemporaries in an epoch of spiritual quest to have been known as a sage reborn.[9]

Aleni was born in 1582, the year Ricci arrived in China, in the northern Italian city of Brescia. Brescia was then going through the rigors of the Catholic Counter Reformation, and young Giulio was educated in a Jesuit school where he "acquired the sciences, devotion, and the holy fear of God," so much so that in 1600 he entered the Jesuit novitiate. During the course of his philosophical studies, his missionary vocation matured. In his letters dating from this period, in which he applied to his superiors to be sent to the "East or the West Indies," he already displayed that combination of a strong sense of mission with deep personal humility. It is readily evident in the prefaces and postscripts of his Chinese books and made an immense impression on his Chinese acquaintances. Eventually, after his theological studies and priestly ordination, he was assigned to the China mission. He arrived at Macao in late 1610, a few months after Ricci had died in Peking. Thus, he might be considered one of the second generation of China Jesuits.

Aleni entered the mainland of China in 1613 and stayed with Hsü Kuang-ch'i (1562–1633) in Shanghai. In 1616, when the first anti-Christian persecutions broke out following the impeachments by Shen Ch'üeh (15??–1624), he and several other Jesuits sought refuge in the house of Yang T'ing-yün (1557–1627) in Hangchow. He probably spent much of this period of confinement in studying and polishing his Chinese style under

Yang. His Chinese diction, as evinced in his publications, is impressive indeed.

When the troubles subsided, Aleni became more active in Hangchow. In 1619, according to a letter he wrote to a relative in Italy, he baptized 265 converts. Later, he traveled in the entourage of one of his converts to Shansi province where he introduced the mission.

By the end of 1621, he was back in Hangchow where he stayed for two years. During this time, he wrote a book-length global geography, a comprehensive description of Western learning, and an Aristotelian-Thomistic psychology; these were the first on these topics published in the Chinese language.[10] He also won a number of converts among the literati.

In 1624, Aleni met Yeh Hsiang-kao at Hangchow. Yeh had just retired from office as grand secretary and was on his way back to his native Fukien. He invited Aleni into that province. The Jesuit mission was thus brought into the province, and from 1625 on Fukien was the scene of Aleni's activities.

INTENDANT TS'AO

Aleni's fellow guest at Yeh's house during the learned conversations, and in a way the Buddhist antagonist to the Jesuit, was identified in the booklet only as Intendant Ts'ao. He was most probably Ts'ao Hsüeh-ch'üan (*tzu* Neng-shi) (1574–1646), a friend of Yeh's.[11] Ts'ao was a native of Foochow. He obtained the *chin-shih* degree in 1595 and, after a number of official appointments, became the intendant of the Kuei-p'ing circuit in Kuangsi in 1624. While at that post, he incurred the wrath of the eunuch faction headed by Wei Chung-hsien (1568–1627) because of his controversial book on recent palace politics. The book was suppressed and the author dismissed from office. He returned home in 1626 to devote himself to studying and compiling a literary encyclopedia. He had a good reputation as a poet, and Yeh enjoyed his company when sightseeing.[12] He is not known to history as a devotee of Buddhism, but was probably as eclectic in his religious approach as were many of his contemporaries.

YEH HSIANG-KAO

Aleni's main interlocutor in the Foochow conversations, Yeh Hsiang-kao, was a bitterly disillusioned man who had lost the will to live. After a long and successful career as a scholar-official, he saw his life's work and his reputation ruined as a result of the corruption of the court and the confused factional politics.

Yeh was born in 1562, the son of a minor scholar-official from Fu-ch'ing, a coastal county within the prefecture of Foochow.[13] After passing the examinations for the *chin-shih* degree in 1583, he made, by and large, steady if unspectacular progress in the official hierarchy. For a number of years, he was the acting head of the Imperial Academy at Nanking. It was during this period that he first met Ricci and made his first acquaintance with Christianity.[14]

In 1608, Yeh was recalled to Peking to become minister of rites and concurrently grand secretary. As the only attending member of the Secretariat under a slothful though intelligent emperor, he was virtually a prime minister, although he was not able to be very effective. During his six years in office, he repeatedly memorialized the Wan-li emperor (r. 1573–1620) to reform the imperial household and the government, but to no avail — except in at least one area. He strenuously opposed the penalty of flogging scholar-officials in court, and that punishment was seldom used so long as his influence lasted with the throne. The emperor respected and favored him as a man who could reconcile the views of the outer court of Confucian officials and the inner court of the sovereign and his household. But the emperor would not exert himself to approve Yeh's proposals for more positive reforms.

Yeh was by all accounts an honest man. His career was that of a competent but not too brilliant or forceful official who found himself in a political situation more difficult than he was able to handle. He adhered to his Confucian principles with courage but was temperamentally inclined to conciliate rather than to controvert. Although he was sympathetic toward the Tung-lin faction, and friendly with many of its members, he avoided factional conflicts. In the late Wan-li controversies arising from the question of imperial succession, Yeh championed the legitimate rights of the crown prince (whom he had tutored in 1598) but did so in such a way that he eventually won the respect even of the mother of that prince's rival. In 1614, after repeated requests, the emperor granted him permission to retire. He returned to Fukien to edit and publish his memorials, essays, and poems.

Intellectually, Yeh seems to have been a man of rather broad and eclectic interests and beliefs but not a very profound thinker. His extant writings include the *Grand Secretariat Papers* (*Lun fei tsou ts'ao*) and literary efforts such as a book on the history of countries surrounding China, entitled *Study of the Barbarians of the Four Quarters* (*Ssu-i k'ao*); a commonplace book called *Categorized Collection of Anecdotes from Ancient and Modern History* (*Lei-pien ku-chin shih-chien ku-shih ta-fang*); and the *Ch'ü Annals* (*Ch'ü pien*), his autobiographical annals.[15]

The *Study of the Barbarians of the Four Quarters* he probably wrote in connection with his official work. The commonplace book was compiled for an educational purpose; to broaden the minds of young students who were too much immersed in preparing for the civil service examinations. Its categories were very diversified, and the anecdotes were Buddhist and Taoist as well as Confucian. The *Ch'ü Annals* were largely political and peripherally personal. They reveal that in philosophy and religion, although Yeh was educated in the Neo-Confucian tradition and retained its outlook, he was not above folk beliefs. For instance, he noted several incidents in his youth which he took to be indicative of heaven's protection over a family destined to attain eminence through his own career in the emperor's service; and in 1616, he built a Kuan-yin shrine to commemorate the fulfillment of an auspicious dream he had had many years before.[16] He also believed firmly in geomancy and was a rather self-confident geomancer himself.[17] Further, as we shall see, whether he believed in Yen-lo, the divine judge of the underworld in Chinese folk religion, Yeh at least took some account of this myth. Thus, although he was favorably impressed by the missionaries and remained a good friend for many years, it did not necessarily imply that he was on the verge of conversion.[18]

In 1620, Yeh was recalled to the Grand Secretariat as soon as his former pupil mounted the throne. That monarch died after a reign of less than a month, however, and Yeh served his teenage son, the T'ien-ch'i emperor (r. 1620–1627), in the capacity of senior grand secretary. In the outer court, the Tung-lin faction was in ascendancy, and Yeh was generally considered to be their protector. Two Tung-lin leaders, Tsou Yüan-piao (1551–1624) and Fêng Tsung-wu (1556–1627?), founded the Shou-shan academy (*shu-yüan*) in Peking, and asked Yeh to write a commemorative essay for them.[19] Yeh was earnest in praise for the learning and virtue of the founders and recommended both the Chu Hsi orthodoxy of the academy and the institution of academies in general as superior to both the Wang Yang-ming school and cramming for examinations. While a good deal of this might have been polite compliments, the essay reflected the general direction of Yeh's thought.

If Yeh had found service under the Wan-li emperor frustrating, he came to experience much worse during the T'ien-ch'i reign.[20] Chief eunuch Wei Chung-hsien, who had the emperor in his power, looked upon the Tung-lin as the main obstacle in the path of his aggrandizement. Struggles between the Tung-lin and other cliques, now associated with Wei, intensified, and Tsou was dismissed at Wei's instigation. Yeh had no taste for partisan politics. He also recognized that Wei was too influential with the frivolous and ignorant sovereign to be easily removed. Thus, he cautioned the impetuous Tung-lin leaders against any precipitate action, and soon lost their impatient respect. When in the summer of 1624 Yang Lien (1571–1625) impeached Wei and brought down imperial wrath on the heads of his faction, Yeh was unable to save them.

His own reputation had already suffered as the result of a frontier disaster. His protégé Wang Hua-chen (?–1632) quarreled with Hsiung T'ing-pi (1569?–1625), the two sharing authority for defenses against the Manchus. When the disputes led to the routing of the Ming army in 1622, Yeh was widely criticized by other officials.[21] Now, in the factional crisis, Wei brought false charges against the Tung-lin leaders as having received bribes from Hsiung. A mob of eunuchs also besieged and searched Yeh's residence for a fugitive Tung-lin official. This unprecedented outrage on Yeh and on the dignity of his office completely disillusioned him. His health also declined; he had been an insomniac for years, and now other symptoms appeared.[22] He resigned most insistently and once more returned to Fukien. It was during this journey that he met Aleni in Hangchow in late 1624 and invited the Jesuit to his home province.

With Yeh's departure from the Secretariat, the "upright elements" lost their most influential protector, and there was no one else who could even attempt to hold the balance between the Tung-lin and its enemies. Wei and his allies enjoyed a complete and brutal triumph among the scholar-officials. The Tung-lin men were successively purged, detained, tortured, and martyred. Yang Lien and others were tortured to death in jail. The confused politics of the Ming court sank to its nadir, while the megalomaniac Wei had temples erected throughout the empire to his own honor on par with Confucius.

Yeh was blamed by many of his former friends and associates for not having stood his ground against Wei and for allowing matters to deteriorate to such a state. Other officials whose whim he had thwarted previously now launched personal attacks against him. He expressed fears that the eunuch faction might not leave him in peaceful retirement.[23] He was a very unhappy man.

In his personal life, other misfortunes befell him. His only son and a very dear half-brother had both died shortly after his first retirement. Now within two months of his arrival at home (January 1625) for his second retirement, his wife also died.[24] As bad news upon bad news reached him from Peking, he became gravely ill in the summer of 1626, excreting large quantities of blood and suffering from abdominal pains.[25] He talked of preferring death to life.[26] Meanwhile, he spent his time searching for auspicious grave sites for his family, enlarging his ancestral temple, and putting his papers together. When editing for publication the state papers of his second term as grand secretary, he recalled talking with Tsou Yüan-piao about having to render an account of his official deeds to Yen-lo, the divine judge of the underworld.[27] Whether or not he had meant this literally, citing the conversation in the preface to his papers was certainly indicative of his mood. He also compiled a second literary anthology, and in the preface to this book, the lonely and distressed old man implied that since both virtue and meritorious service had eluded him, his only remaining claim to immortality as a Confucian lay in his literary accomplishments, meager as they were.[28] He also updated his autobiographical annals with the depressing events of the past few years.

Late in 1626, Yeh's illness abated. And in the fourth month of the following year, he was able to travel from his home in Fu-ch'ing to enjoy the sights of Foochow. In the *Ch'ü Annals,* he recorded his mood as follows: "I am an old man who has given up on things. I have found disfavor with the times, and that still weighs on my mind. So I decided to let go of myself in front of the beauty of the hills and waters. No longer do I feel constricted by rank. People are glad to see me so easy to get along with, and they befriend me."[29] It was during this temporary easing of tensions, amidst the encircling gloom, that Yeh shared with Ts'ao and Aleni the serious conversations on life and death.

THE LEARNED CONVERSATIONS: THE FIRST DAY

During Yeh's stay in Foochow from late May to late June, 1627, Aleni called one day on his patron. He found Intendant Ts'ao also present. The host steered the conversation onto a religious track with the question: "Both you gentlemen have your minds set on the otherworldly. But one follows the Buddha, and the other is against Buddhism. Why is that?"

Aleni went straight to the point with his response: "We probably both devote our attention to the serious matter of life and death." But Ts'ao was more circumspect. He answered that he just followed what he found to be good in Buddhism, and had not been able to trace all its arguments. For him, following religious teachings was like copying examples of fine calligraphy by famous ancient masters. Many specimens had been eaten through by insects, and he just imitated those parts which remained undamaged. So he picked out for himself those Buddhist doctrines essential for virtuous living.

With Ts'ao's catholic approach, Aleni could not agree. So far as the Jesuit was concerned, those Buddhist doctrines essential for virtue were similar to Christian teachings, but he believed that one had to trace a school of learning to its origin before one could tell whether it was true or false. He pointed out that separatist states in Chinese history had institutions that aped those of the imperial dynasties, but were in fact all usurpations. The Lord of Heaven honored in the West was the true Lord and Creator of all things, and was the great parent of humankind who ordained everything. Without him, who would have given humans the lives of body and mind? Humans should worship him. Aleni further asserted that Sakyamuni, a prince of India, was just like any other man made by the Lord of Heaven. If even the Confucian sages of the superior realm of China were only honored as teachers and not as lords of the myriad things, how could the followers of Sakyamuni afford not to believe in the Lord of Heaven and act as if it were enough just to rely on the Buddha for their fate?

Human minds and lives were given by the Lord of Heaven who should be the beginning and end in one's study of the human mind and human nature. The Buddhists, in denying this, had denied the root and origin of human nature and mind. The Jesuit observed that those people who followed Buddhism just wanted to be delivered from suffering after this life, but they had been misguided in their quest. On his part, he had traveled to China through the lands of cannibals and many other dangers, lest people fail to recognize the great merciful Lord and choose the wrong turn at the juncture of life and death. Finally, he confessed that it wrung tears of sorrow from him even to talk of the fatal errors of others. He echoed Mencius in saying that he asserted his beliefs not in order to win arguments but because it was necessary for the benefit of others.[30]

At the end of this long speech, Ts'ao was puzzled by the missionary's point that the Chinese did not know about honoring heaven. Even the Buddhists, he said, also honored heaven. At festivals and on solemn occasions, the people performed obeisance first to heaven and earth, then to their ancestors and gods. Were there indeed people who did not know about honoring heaven?

Aleni's approach was radically different:

> Just as there are not two supreme lords and not two paths on the most exalted way, the human mind cannot follow two directions. How can it venerate heaven and yet honor Buddha? . . . Besides, you are talking about the material heavens and earth; how can they receive your veneration? Can the material heavens exist by themselves? Can all the wonders that take place between heaven and earth be spontaneous?[31]

In these opening remarks between Aleni and Ts'ao can be perceived an immediate clash between the much more eclectic Chinese approach to the transcendent and the Christian's single-minded devotion to one approachable truth. These two different ways of viewing implied different attitudes to another person's faith. For Aleni and the other Jesuit missionaries, the policy of rejecting Buddhism and accommodating with Confucianism, already evident in the above exchanges, really meant subsuming agreeable elements of Confucianism under Catholic dogma, and not an equal merging of the two doctrines. To yield on points of dogma would be heretical, as the Jesuit Roberto di Nobili (1577–1656) had found out in his accommodations with Hinduism. But on the part of the literati, the attitude was often that expressed in Ts'ao's analogy of studying calligraphic specimens — taking from diverse masters what was uncorrupted and suited to one's own practice. The one emphasized the accurate formulation of truth, the other was more pragmatic and aesthetic.

The conversation continued. Ts'ao answered Aleni's cosmological challenge with two rhetorical questions: "Is it not the motions of yin and yang that causes everything to happen? Or is it Principle (*li*) ?"

Aleni disagreed. For him, yin and yang were no more than ingredients which transformed to become the form and matter of things, while Principle was nothing but the law of things that resided within things. There must first be things before there could be principles, not vice versa. And just as the laws and ordinances of a country were not its sovereign, for the sovereign must be a person who gives commands, so there must be an intelligent Lord of Heaven who was the creator. Before the creator made all the myriad things, his unlimited intelligence must first have comprehended the principles of all the myriad things — then he made the things accordingly. This was (to take an example familiar to his literati friends) like composing an essay for which there must be an author to formulate a theme or principle into coherent writing. Thus, one knew that the principles in created things could not create things, and that there must be a creating Lord.[32]

To Ts'ao's suggestion, after the Sung philosophers, of an impersonal Great Ultimate, Aleni offers a scholastic proof for the existence of a personal God. For a Neo-Confucian, the universe was formed by the continuous and spontaneous divisions from the Great Ultimate into the cosmic force of yin (passive) and yang (active), which in turn went through the five evolving phases of metal, wood, water, fire, and earth, and combined during one phase or another to give rise to the myriad things. This Principle or Great Ultimate was the highest good, but was devoid of personality or of juristic content.[33]

For a Thomist, on the other hand, everything came about through the operation of the "four causes": material, formal, efficient, final. The material cause was matter. The formal cause was the nature and shape of a thing that combined with amorphous matter to become a definite thing. But such a "transformation" did not happen at random; rather, it took place for a purpose, which was the efficient cause. Purpose implied intelligence, which was the final cause. All things had their four causes, and such a teleological scheme required an ultimate Final Cause to have brought about and to sustain the universe. This Final Cause was the Creator, the scholastics' personal God. The rationality of the Creator guaranteed the rationality of nature. This could be observed and formulated by humans as natural law, and was derived from the purpose (or efficient cause) for which the Creator made all things. This was the schema behind Aleni's challenges and explanation to his Neo-Confucian interlocutors.[34] He was suggesting that yin and yang were probably formal and material causes, that Principle was natural law, and that Neo-Confucian cosmology needed a Final Cause. Did he succeed in putting across his view? If for Aleni to talk of yin and yang and Principle without positing a Creator would be to behead the universe, for Ts'ao the universe would not have required a head at all. In this discussion between representatives of two traditions, neither side seemed to have grasped the basic assumptions of the other.

Yeh intervened to ask the missionary:

> Now you say there is a Lord of Heaven who made and rules all things. I have not heard of such a theory before. I guess there must first have been my body before there was my spirit to be the body's master. Before this body came into existence, there could not have been its spirit. So there must have been first heaven and earth, before they could have a Lord of Heaven to be their master. Before heaven and earth came into existence, how could there have been their master?[35]

While Yeh was thinking of an immanent force that was part and parcel with being alive, Aleni insisted on his four causes. He argued that something with no beginning must have come before that which had a beginning; that which had no body must have come before that which had a body; and that which caused to be must have come before that which was caused to be. Before the existence of one's body, there must have been one's parents to give one birth; and there must have been a Lord of Heaven to confer what was within one. Otherwise, where would one's spirit and body come from? If indeed there had been no almighty great Lord before there was heaven and earth, and he came into being after them, then out of what came heaven and earth? And who set up this lord to be the lord (*chu*)?[36]

Yeh stood his Neo-Confucian ground. He replied, "It is the Great Ultimate that is the origin (*chu*) from which heaven and earth divided."[37] Although Aleni and Yeh used the same Chinese word *chu*, they attached such divergent meanings to it that two separate English words have to be used in translation, respectively "lord" and "origin." Aleni disagreed with Yeh's impersonal "origin"; he argued that the Great Ultimate theory did not go beyond principle (*li*) and matter (*ch'i*). Never had anyone suggested that the Great Ultimate had intelligence and perceptions. Without these qualities, how could it govern all creation (*wan-hua*)? Actually, was not the Great Ultimate just the primary matter (*yüan-chih*) of things? As such, it was bound up with things, and could not be the Lord of Heaven and Earth. That is why Chinese people never talk about serving the Great Ultimate.[38]

Aleni's persistent effort to personify Yeh's "origin" (*chu*) probably reflected his misunderstanding (stemming from the preconceptions of his confreres) of the other's position. Perhaps there is no more succinct illustration of the conceptual chasm between immanent suchness and supreme lawgiver, between so many principles that added up to and derived from an ultimate origin, and an omniscient, omnipotent lord. That chasm remained unbridged in these conversations.

The discussion continued. Yeh was willing to grant for the sake of the discussion that a creator ought to be above principle and matter in order to create and govern heaven and earth. But if the Lord of Heaven created all things, did he create the bad as well as the good? In view of Yeh's recent experiences, such a question would naturally arise at this point.

Aleni replied that the Lord of Heaven did create all things, that he created humans and started them toward good. All that was bad came from humans who disobeyed the Lord. So one could not say that he created the bad as well as the good. On the contrary, he rewarded those who did good and punished those who did ill. Aleni cited the Confucian Classics for corroboration.

Yeh said: "That may well be. But heaven and earth are so vast, and there is such a variety of things. If the Lord of Heaven made them all, and governs over them, would it not be too petty and tiresome for him?"

Aleni pointed out that the myriad things, be they big or small, high or low, did not differ in the facility with which they were made, and that all this rich variety only served to show the wonder of the great Lord's work of creation. The Lord of Heaven was most high and nothing was too petty for him; he was most intelligent and nothing was too troublesome; he was most capable and nothing could weary him. Unlike the ordinary artisan who needed tools and materials, he created the myriad things out of nothing. Like the sun which brightened up even the lowliest and dirtiest nook and cranny with no effort, he took care of all creation without exhausting himself.

Yeh could neither agree nor disagree with this.[39] The logical necessity of what Aleni just said would hold only within the Thomistic system. Yeh and Ts'ao did not know that system, nor did they share the Jesuit's faith. Ts'ao confessed that he did not understand the intricacies of Aleni's doctrines but was curious to know more. He also had a more personal question to ask the missionary: "You have forsaken your own country to come eastward. You are not tangled with any earthly desires, and move freely between heaven and earth. Is that most enjoyable?" To this, Aleni insisted that he was only a humble traveler who had gone through many mortal dangers for the propagation of the teachings he held. He had come to this land of superior culture to seek out persons in the right Way to learn from them, so that together they might further this serious business of avoiding perdition. How dared he think of enjoyment?[40] With such a remark, the serious discussion ended for the day. Some late Ming literati would have considered this remark so ascetic as to be inhuman, but other literati would have found it reminiscent of the famous Neo-Confucian motto of the Sung reformer Fan Chung-yen (989–1052): "to be first in feeling concern for the world's problems, and the last in enjoying its pleasures." Most likely, the conversation drifted on to some lighter topic, tea was passed around, and dinner was served.

THE LEARNED CONVERSATIONS: THE SECOND DAY

The next day, the grand secretary called upon the missionary, and the two resumed the discussion. Intendant Ts'ao did not take part. The problem of evil, as one may expect, did not give Yeh rest. He returned to where they were on the previous day, asking: It might well be as Aleni had said that the Lord of Heaven created everything without effort for the sake of humans, but then why would he make fierce and harmful creatures in the hundreds and thousands? In reply, Aleni urged that there was nothing between heaven and earth which was not ultimately beneficial to humankind, and that it was only human ignorance that prevented the proper utilization of all things. Some creatures supply us with our food or clothing; other creatures carry our burdens or supply us with cures for diseases. Yet other creatures provide us with amusement or with ennobling examples. As for fierce beasts of prey, very often they attack people out of self-defense. But even if they harm our bodies, they can do no harm to our inner selves. If such outward injuries were taken as signs from heaven to teach greater veneration and repentance, one would in fact gain much in eternal blessing. This last was just like a loving mother who weaned her child by putting something of bitter taste on her breast. Aleni insisted that the Lord of Heaven made the myriad things to support humans, and made humans to serve himself. There was in the beginning nothing that could hurt people. It was only when the first humans disobeyed his commands that he allowed other creatures to punish the guilty and to warn the innocent.[41]

This teleological answer did not satisfy Yeh. The political and personal situation in which he found himself was too acute, and there was no relief or vindication in sight. Why should a God who was all good, all knowing, and all powerful, allow Wei Chung-hsien to rank himself with Confucius and murder honest men without being stopped and without retribution? He could explain it in the Neo-Confucian terms in which he was trained but could find little consolation there. Was Aleni's religion able to offer him solace? He raised this question: "The Creator may indeed reasonably use other creatures to punish guilty people; but why should the good and innocent be allowed to come to harm as well? We Confucians consider that to be the unreasoned operation of fate. If you ascribe it all to heavenly principles, you may not be able to explain away all the unjust things. And if you cannot resolve this question, I fear that you will not be able to convince the world and win its reverence and faith."

Aleni's response stressed faith in God. He pointed out that the Creator's Way was unlimited, and the limited human intelligence could not possibly comprehend the great power of the Lord. Besides, one could never adequately judge the goodness or badness of a person just by his public behavior. Goodness was completed only in perfection, while a single bad inclination in the innermost self was enough to make one a bad person. Only the Lord could see everything and judge fairly. Also, the Lord of Heaven might grant misfortunes and tribulations to a good person to test one's endurance. All this was certainly not the same as fate.[42]

Yeh was unsatisfied with these explanations. He protested: "If the Lord of Heaven would even punish the infringements of those who still do a certain amount of good, then what about those who are well known to do wrong!? Why are they on the contrary given hereditary honors? Does he intend to punish their descendants? Or are their bad reputations and troubled minds sufficient as penalty?"[43] Perhaps he was asking: Why am I allowed to be so unfortunate, while Wei and his henchmen have so much success? A few months before, Wei had been made a duke and his nephew a count. Wei was still building temples to himself.[44] Yeh was deeply concerned about the turn taken by public affairs.

Aleni's answer brought out the immortality of the soul. He first noted that descendants were not held responsible for the virtues and vices of their ancestors, only their own. He explained to Yeh that our lives came from our souls given by the Lord of Heaven, and that the soul was not destroyed upon the death of a human being. Rather, it returned to the Lord and was judged. From the beginning of the universe, there had not been one person who was born without a command from the Lord to do good and avoid evil; and not one who was not judged at death, and then, most fairly, sent to the heavenly kingdom for eternal reward or to the prison of the underworld for punishment. Tribulations suffered by good persons in this life were often a purification process; worldly blessings enjoyed by the bad may be an inducement to reform. In conclusion, Aleni stressed that in matters of reward and punishment, the Lord of Heaven kept his own scales and time; he was always just and never wrong.[45]

Whether Yeh was consoled or satisfied with this answer, Aleni did not report implicitly or explicitly. It was inevitable that the immortality of the human soul should have arisen in such a discussion because it was, on the one hand, a cornerstone of Catholic belief and, on the other, an area in which the Chinese intellectual tradition differed fundamentally from that of the West. The image of the divine judge who metes out sentences to the dead according to their merits is of course not unique to Christianity. Indeed, in Chinese popular religion, there is a somewhat similar belief in the judgment of Yen-lo, head of an underworld bureaucracy patterned after the mundane officialdom of the Chinese empire. Although as an educated man Yeh was not supposed to take the "vulgar" myth seriously, he might not have been indifferent to what the judge would pronounce about the record of his life on earth. As noted above, not long before these conversations, when compiling his official papers, he spoke of rendering an account to Yen-lo. How literally he meant this is not known, but his questions to Aleni here must have arisen from an eschatological anxiety as well as from his concern for the affairs of state.

Meanwhile, Yeh's next question again reflected the recent history of bad rulers that was weighing heavily on his mind. He wanted to know why the Lord of Heaven did not make more good people and fewer bad ones; or, failing that, why he did not provide us with plenty of worthy and wise rulers whose virtuous examples would bring peace and order to all under heaven for ten thousand generations.

Aleni presented the idea of free will: "The Lord of Heaven is all good, and does not endow anyone with an evil nature. At birth he gives everyone intelligence to tell between good and ill, and the ability to desire and hence to approach or avoid certain things. He then leaves one to choose on one's own." However, people make different choices because of original sin, which clouded the intellect and desire, and because temperament and upbringing vary. The Lord of Heaven leaves us free to choose so that we can earn our merits and rewards.

> As for earthly rulers, they have intellect and choice like everyone else.... It is not the Lord of Heaven who decides whether they are to be good or bad rulers. Now, where our Teachings are practiced, there are sages and wise persons in every generation to teach and influence the people, so that policies are just and the way of life is admirable, and all classes live together in harmony and happiness. Is it because the Lord favors the people there over those of other parts? No, it is because high and low all respect and follow the Sacred Teachings, and are unwilling to do wrong.[46]

Aleni was saying, in effect, that sage kings were not born

but self-made and that the Christian religion could guarantee their making. This claim would appeal directly to the heart of a Confucian, whose idea of good government was centered around personal virtues: virtuous behavior radiating from a good ruler downward to illuminate the several ranks of good subjects. If the ruler's virtue was great, harmony would prevail. If the Christian Way could indeed generate such virtue with greater certainty, so as to provide Christendom with durable peace and righteousness, it would certainly be worthy for the Confucian to follow, especially in view of the failure of the Chinese schools to generate virtuous government in late Ming times.

But was Aleni's claim believable? He had written a world geography to demonstrate that an ideal society did exist in the Christian West.[47] In view of the actual condition of Europe at the time — where the Thirty Years' War was raging even as Aleni and Yeh were holding their discussion — what he said is ironic indeed. On the question whether Aleni's literati friends accepted his claim, Yeh made no comment. But he was interested in the practice of virtue. He pointed out that, to be sure, to reform one's behavior from doing ill to doing good was an essential part of reverence. Aleni elaborated on this point with a metaphor:

Let me compare differences in endowment to two people riding on horseback. One of the horses is tame, the other untame. The tame horse is no trouble to control. If the other rider uses the bridle skillfully, the two could still proceed abreast; if not, the wild horse will run away, which would not be just the fault of the horse, but the rider's as well.

The soul is to the body like the rider to the horse. One could choose to practice control over oneself and transform one's natural endowment, or one could indulge in breaking the Ten Commandments and in following the Three Enemies. If one is unwilling to repent, and rather doubts that one can transform one's life, that is mistaken indeed.[48]

For the first time in the dialogue, the two men were in agreement. If the full implications of Aleni's metaphor were alien to Yeh's mind (as Yeh indeed was going to have difficulties with the dualistic notion of body and soul), the emphasis on self-cultivation, on directing one's inner life or one's entire being, toward what was perceived as the good — that at least was firmly held in common. In fact, the Jesuits' moral concern and attainment, more than any doctrinal formulation, was what held the esteem of the literati.

Meanwhile, Yeh raised more questions about the problem of evil, which do not require elaboration here. Aleni's answers still center on the immortality of the soul and heaven and hell.[49] Yeh's own mortality was very much on his mind, and this should have provided Aleni with a favorable opportunity. But Yeh had his doubts.

He had heard that the soul was just a collection of energies (*ching ch'i*). When they gathered, there was life; when a person died, they dispersed. So how could the soul receive reward or punishment after bodily demise? Besides, even if in some cases the energies did not disperse, without a body how were sufferings or pleasures or happiness to be perceived?[50] For Yeh, there was no serious theory of a body-soul division in the human being. Rather, he probably shared the usual Chinese belief that there were elements within the human organism which were not altogether anatomical or physiological. These were the closest equivalent to the Western soul, and there may be as many as ten of them in one person. Three were derived from the yang force, and were called *hun*; the other seven were from the yin, and were called *p'o*. Their exact function during life was never made clear. At death, the *hun* and the *p'o* would disperse and, except in very uncommon circumstances, never re-collect. The *p'o* were sometimes believed to stay in the corpse until decomposition was complete, when they would return to the earth, which was yin. The *hun* were supposed to go out of the body at the last breath; some of the *hun* might stay in the commemorative tablets of the dead person and receive sacrifices, but no part was expected to survive outside the body for more than a few generations of the descendants of the deceased. In certain situations, especially where grave injustice had been perpetrated, *hun* or *p'o* might linger in this world and appear as ghosts (*kuei*) seeking revenge or vindication, but they were ephemeral. Some of these popular ideas had been assimilated into Neo-Confucian metaphysics and were given expression here by Yeh.

There were, of course, other schools of thought in Chinese tradition. Certain Taoists sought the attainment of physical immortality in this world through bodily exercises, meditation, or disciplined sexual practices. Some Buddhist sects, on the other hand, preached karmic reincarnation or the existence of a heaven and a hell with concrete physical rewards and penalties. This last belief was fused in the popular mind with the myth of the Yen-lo bureaucracy of the underworld and might have had some hold on Yeh. Be that as it may, the climate of opinion among Confucians admitted of no body-soul dichotomy. The emphasis was definitely physical, aiming at the attainment of fulfillment in this world and this body, rather than in eschatological expectations of personal immortality of the soul.

Aleni's position, on the other hand, was definitely dualistic. It was based upon Thomistic hylomorphism, a theory upheld by the authority of the Roman Church, namely, that the soul as "form" actualized the body ("matter") which otherwise only had life in potentiality. His lengthy explanation, laden with illustrations, need not take up too much space here. Suffice it to say that he started out by identifying the energies (*ch'i*) that Yeh mentioned as "breath" or "air" (*ch'i*), that is, as a physical substance and one of the four Aristotelian elements, thereby confusing the issue and revealing that he misunderstood Yeh's point.[51] At this juncture as well as many another juncture, it is evident how difficult it is for two comprehensive and sophisticated systems of thought to be compared point for point without calling in the entire systems. Possibilities for misunderstandings and distortion are boundless. Perhaps the point to be noted about these conversations was not that there were so many misunderstandings and distortions but that the discussion and communication went as far as they did. For this, much of the credit lay with the Jesuits. In the present case, Aleni eventually managed to make clear to Yeh his own belief by citing the phenomenon of dreams to support that the soul could exist independently of the body and that eternal reward and punishment involved not physical sensation but spiritual happiness and pain.[52]

Granting that all this might perhaps be true, Yeh was still

not satisfied. He had earlier agreed with Aleni on the need for self-cultivation. He now pointed out: "Good is what we should practice even without expectation of reward; wrongdoing is what we should avoid even without fear of punishment. To talk of rewards and punishments sounds too much like the Buddhist theory of karma. We Confucians do not accept that." Aleni emphasized that this was a serious matter of life and death. The Buddhists had earned the disgust of the Confucians with their absurd theory of karma, but that theory was not the same thing as the truth of heaven and hell and should not be confused with it.[53]

If Yeh had doubts about Christianity because its eschatology appeared too much like the Buddhists' karma, he had even more doubts about why Aleni's Almighty God had to become incarnate in order to save the world, why the fact of divine incarnation had never been mentioned in the Chinese Classics, and, last but not least, why, if the Incarnation had happened, it did not take place in China. Aleni's answers were firm in assertion and possessed a certain persuasive power. But nowhere did Yeh give any indication that he was convinced by what the Jesuit had to say.[54] By life-long habit, Yeh was not one to hound an abstract issue to its logical extremity to win a debate; by recent inclination, he was "an old man who had given up on things." It is likely that he had far more doubts and disagreements with Aleni's teachings than he was prepared to voice for the missionary to acknowledge and record. But in any case the learned conversations ended on a hopeful note for the Jesuit when the grand secretary told him that he found the teachings of the Lord of Heaven to be very illuminating and asked to be given books to read. The two men parted on Aleni's promise to supply some literature for both Ts'ao and Yeh.

THE AFTERMATH

The learned conversations took place in June 1627. By the end of the month, Yeh was back in Fu-ch'ing to put his family temple in order for purposes of honoring his dead ancestors and in particular to commemorate his dead parents and siblings. His illness was taking a turn for the worse; there was a hard lump near his diaphragm, and he lost his appetite. In early August, he was in Foochow again to consult physicians. But they could not do very much for him. There was something gravely wrong with his liver or gall bladder. Around mid-autumn, his entire skin became golden yellow in color. He died on 7 October. He had not been baptized.[55]

In Peking, the young emperor had died a few days before Yeh, and his younger brother came to the throne. Wei and his henchmen were purged, and the martyrs and Yeh came to be vindicated. But it was a hollow victory because the Ming court had become so weakened by corruption and factionalism that it was unable to meet the dual challenge of Manchu expansion and peasant rebellion. Within twenty years, the dynasty was to fall.

After the first day of discussions, Ts'ao apparently did not enter the China Jesuit story again. If indeed he was Ts'ao Hsüeh-ch'üan, then he stayed at home in Foochow for twenty years, declining official appointments and devoting himself to literary and scholarly pursuits. During the war of the Manchu conquest, he organized support for the resistance in Fukien and died a martyr to the Ming cause.[56]

As for Aleni, he spent the rest of his life in Fukien. A relatively stable residence allowed him to make many friends and become a noted local personality. The conversations with Yeh were probably typical of many other unrecorded discussions he had with the literati. Although he experienced certain setbacks, he was by and large very successful in spreading his influence and establishing the mission. Chapels were set up in all the major cities in Fukien. When in 1641, Aleni was made vice-provincial and superior over all the Jesuits in South China, there were some sixty thousand Christians in the empire, and Fukien was one of the most flourishing mission fields. He died in 1649 in western Fukien during the war and was buried in Foochow.

Aleni's career conformed to the accommodation policy and was in may ways parallel to Ricci's experiences in the 1590s and early 1600s. Aleni's Chinese name, Ai Ju-lüeh, a clever transcription which means literally "Ai of Confucian talent," reflects the Jesuit policy. His broad learning and virtuous behavior won the respect of friend and enemy alike.[57] But was he by writing and in conversations successful in communicating his Catholic faith?

THUS THE TWAIN DID MEET?

It would be interesting to see what Yeh might have said about the discussions after examining Aleni's record of their learned conversations. Unfortunately, there is no mention of the conversations in Yeh's surviving writings. In fact, he made no mention of the Jesuits at all in his autobiography and said very little about them in his literary works. This omission could only suggest that he did not consider the missionary episodes of his life to have been very significant. That we cannot document Aleni received baptism should not be surprising in view of the meager literary record.

Dunne mentions that Yeh was not converted because he saw an essential incompatibility between the notion of the Incarnation and the majesty of God.[58] It was noted above that he indeed entertained such doubts during the conversations. But was this the only major difficulty? It can be seen from the previous pages that in most topics there were wide chasms separating the Hellenized formulations of Christian dogmas and the Neo-Confucian minds, and that much of the time missionary and literatus were talking past each other. There were immense obstacles to the meeting of the philosophies, and scholastic doctrines did not provide much solace to Yeh in his political and existential tribulations.

Yet, on one point Yeh and Aleni were in complete agreement: the need for more moral self-cultivation. In this matter much more than with philosophical or theological formulations, it was possible for the meeting of hearts without doctrinal convergence. And was not the impressive personal virtue of the Jesuits acknowledged by friend and foe alike?

In the only two short pieces of writing by Yeh on Aleni, the latter's teachings are mentioned but vaguely. In his preface to Aleni's geography, Yeh stressed the limitations of traditional Chinese geographical knowledge and how the Jesuits might be heralding an expansion of earthly horizons. He said little about the religion of the Westerners and nothing at all about Aleni's idealized European society. But he revealed himself to be impressed with the courage and honesty of the Jesuits who had traveled through so many lands to tell of their experiences.[59]

Again, in a poem addressed to Aleni (See Appendix), which the missionary used as a frontispiece to the *Learned Conversations at San-shan* [*Foochow*], Yeh made little note of the teachings, except that "He [Aleni] concurs deeply with our Confucian principles"; but he is full of praise for the personal qualities. As for his own reactions to Aleni's ideas, he said simply, "I have studied with this man/And have been jolted with deep insights."[60]

For Yeh and many another literatus, being jolted with deep insights (*leng jan te shen chih*) might have been the most significant experience when confronted with Scholastic arguments. In the learned conversations, Aleni posed many questions and raised many points completely new to Ts'ao and Yeh. They could not have been easily answered in Neo-Confucian terms because of the difference in concepts and approaches between the mental frameworks represented by the two sides. The literati must have felt as though they were being confronted by a Ch'an master's riddle (*kung-an*) and would have felt frustration, doubts, or sudden realizations. These, of course, do not add up to an understanding of or conversion to Christian doctrines but should add to the reputation of the Jesuits as thoughtful, learned men.

The moral and intellectual virtues of the Jesuits and the leading Chinese Christians were greatly admired by Yeh. Whether or not the Christian philosophical formulations were adding anything to Chinese philosophy and bringing Classical Confucianism to its fulfillment, as the accommodation policy claimed to do, Yeh could see with his own eyes that Christian self-cultivation was adding to the Confucian self-cultivation in the moral growth of a number of virtuous men. One of them was Yang T'ing-yün. In 1624, Yeh wrote in the preface to Yang's book on the Ten Commandments (see Appendix):

> Mr. Yang . . . often spoke to me about the essential points of this doctrine. I had just gained some appreciation when I resigned my office and left Peking. Mr. Yang then showed me his book. . . . I read it and was touched, saying, This is the orthodox Confucian learning of reverence and trepidation toward heaven. Our people are so set in their ways as to have been unaware of [the proper path]. Little does one expect that Westerners could expound on it.

And he cited Yang's evident peacefulness and simplicity as proof of the goodness of this doctrine. But if Yeh was impressed with the moral aspects of Christianity, the Jesuits would not have been consoled by his interpretation of their theology, for Yeh considered the rewards of heaven as a product of the mind of the virtuous and Jesus as on par with Confucius and the sage kings of ancient China — all incarnations of the Lord on High.[61]

But, then, Yeh was offering these ideas just by way of suggestions. He was not seriously interested in following the path of inquiry and study (*tao-wen-hsüeh*) of the Westerners; what impressed him was their honoring the moral nature (*tsun te-hsing*). And so Aleni's Thomistic formulations could offer him no kindly light out of his encircling gloom.

Did the twain meet under the Jesuits' policy of accommodation with Confucianism? If the learned conversations at Foochow in 1627 were any indication, then most of the time the minds did not overcome the very high conceptual barriers to attain clear and accurate understanding, but the hearts did meet in mutual appreciation.

APPENDIX

Yeh Hsiang-kao's *Ode to Mr. Ai Ssu-chi* (Giulio Aleni) (*Tseng Ssu-chi Ai hsien-sheng shih*).

> Heaven and earth are truly without limit
> And not graspable by our small minds.
> New there comes a Westerner
> From a distance of eighty thousand *li*
> Across desert sands he did tread,
> Over fabled waters he set sail.
> Professing to admire Chinese culture,
> He concurs deeply with our Confucian principles.
> His books are full of quotable sayings,
> His friends all noted scholars of the age.
> He boasts not of his achievements,
> But contemns mundane bustle.
> Our sage ruler's influence covers all nine corners of the world;
> All lands reveal themselves as following the same path.
> Pedantic Confucians may confine themselves to pipe-wide vision,
> But the broadminded naturally regard his teachings as equal to ours.

> I have studied with this man
> And have been jolted with deep insights.

Yeh Hsiang-kao's preface to *A First Explanation of the Ten Commandments of Western Learning (Hsi hsüeh shih-chieh chu chieh)* by Yang T'ing-yün (1557–1627).

There are many paths to learning, and even in our Middle Kingdom they have never been unified. During the time of Confucius and Mencius, there were Lao-tzu, Chuang-tzu, Yang Chu, and Mo tzu to rival the sages. Later, there came also Buddhism. Confucians have attacked all these schools but have not vanquished them.

Recently, there have come among us persons from the Great West, some tens of thousand *li* away. Their learning is rooted in the veneration of heaven, and they practice mortification and observing commandments. In general, their teachings are similar to our Confucianism, and they are strenuous in refuting Buddhism.

These persons are as intelligent as any to be found in the world. They read all the books that they come across, and have translated nearly all the Chinese Classics and histories. Their crafts and arts are so sophisticated as to surpass those of the Middle Kingdom.

Many scholars and officials have studied with them, but relatively few admire them so profoundly and believe them so wholeheartedly as to think they have truly found out about human nature and solved the problem of life and death.

I too once made my acquaintance with the Western Learning, but did not have the opportunity to delve into it deeply. Mr. Yang T'ing-yün, the metropolitan prefect, often spoke to me about the essential points of this doctrine. I had just gained some appreciation when I resigned my office and left Peking. Mr. Yang then showed me his book entitled *A First Explanation of the Ten Commandments.* I read it and was touched, saying, This is the orthodox Confucian learning of reverence and trepidation toward heaven. Our people are so set in their ways as to have been unaware of [the proper path]. Little does one expect that Westerners could expound on it. Indeed, do not Eastern and Western barbarians, and early as well as later sages, all hold the same tenets!

Some people would object that [the Western scholars'] theory of heaven and hell are the same as Buddhist doctrines. They do not realize that the Buddhists base their theory on karmic retribution, while the Westerners found theirs on righteous principles. That point has been distinguished at length in this book.

As for the other criticism, that the Western Learning is intan-

gible and unsupported by evidence, I would suggest that if one
concentrates one's energies and mind on something, that something would form a realm of its own. The Sung painter Li Kung-
ling loved to paint horses so much that with his preoccupation
he would descend to the realm of horses after his death. So if
one's preoccupation is heaven, would one's spirit not return to
heaven?

Ever since the world formed out of chaos, everything has
been made by heaven, and there is nothing greater than heaven.
But the Buddhists hold that heaven is only an emperor, and
that the Buddha is superior to it. This is no doubt absurd, and
that is why the Westerners exert themselves to refute Buddhism.

On the other hand, the Westerners' claim that the Lord of
Heaven came down to earth and was born in their country does
sound like a weird story. But then all the sages who have been
born to us had their origins [from above]. If even minor sages
who benefited humankind were [the gods of] mountains and
stars, then the major sages who presided over creation and
brought peace to ten thousand generations, such as Yao, Shun,
and Confucius, could not have wielded the immense strength
that they did unless they were born as the descension on earth
of the Lord on High. Now, if the Lord on High had come down
to us in the East, how would we know that He did not do so
in the West as well?

Ordinary Confucians do indeed talk frequently of heaven, but
they behave as if heaven is far away. The Western scholars, on
the other hand, speak of heaven as connected intimately with
us, and communicating with us in our every breath. This is most
appropriate for awakening the world.

That is why Mr. Yang has found their doctrines so much to
his taste. Mr. Yang's learning is the most genuine self-cultivation;
it is peaceful, simple, and not tainted with worldliness. He can
truly be called a disciple of heaven. The depth of his learning
is of course not exhausted in this *Explanation*. Yet, the *Explanation* is well worth reading indeed.

(From Yeh's *More Azure Sky Verses* (*Ts'ang-hsia yü ts'ao*),
chuan 5, 22a—23b.

NOTES

1. George H. Dunne, S.J., *Generation of Giants: The Story of the Jesuits in China in the Last Decade of the Ming Dynasty* (Notre Dame, 1962), esp. 4–14, 17–18, 26–28, 86–89, 227–28, 269–302. See also (1) Fang Hao, "Ming-mo Ch'ing-ch'u T'ien-chu-chiao shih-ying Ju-chia hsüeh-shuo chih yen-chiu" (A study of Catholic accommodation with Confucianism during the late Ming, early Ch'ing periods), reprinted in *Fang Hao liu shih tzu ting kao* (The collected works of Maurus Fang Hao revised and edited by the author on his sixtieth birthday), 2 vols. with Supplement (Taipei, 1969), 1:203–54; (2) Ch'en Shou-yi, "Ming-mo Yeh-su-hui-shih ti Ju-chiao kuan chi ch'i-t'a" (The late Ming Jesuits' view of Confucianism etc.), in Pao Ts'ung-p'ang, ed. *Ming-tai tsung-chiao* (Studies on Ming religion) (Taipei, 1968), 67–123; (3) Chu Ch'ien-chih, "Yeh-su-hui-tui-yü Sung Ju li-hsüeh chih fan hsiang" (The Jesuit response to Sung Neo-Confucianism), in Pao, *Ming-tai tsung-chiao,* 125–80.

2. Dunne, *Generation of Giants,* 245–68. Donald Holzman, "Conversational Tradition in Chinese Philosophy," *Philosophy East and West* 6 (October 1956): 223–30.

3. Dunne, *Generation of Giants,* 282–301. Also J. S. Cummins, ed. and trans., *The Travels and Controversies of Friar Domingo Navarette, 1618–1686.* (Cambridge, England, 1962), introduction.

4. For example, Hou Wai-lu, Comp., *Chung-kuo ssu-hsiang t'ungshih* (A general history of Chinese thought), 7 vols. (Peking, 1949–1960), Book 4B (Peking, 1960):1189–1290.

5. See Ricci's work in the photo-reprint edition by Liu Shun-te (Taichung, 1966).

6. This work was reprinted in Wu Hsiang-hsiang, ed., *T'ien-chu-chiao tung ch'uan wen-hsien hsü-pien* (Documents on the Catholic Church in China: second collection), 3 vols. (Taipei, 1966), 1:419–93. For a printing history of Aleni's book, see Fang Hao's introduction in Wu, *Tien-chu-chiao tung ch'uan,* 1:17–18. The exact date of the first publication is not known, but it was most probably very soon after the conversations took place, since Yeh was referred to as if he were alive; he died a few short months after the event.

7. Text in Hsü Tsung-tse, *Ming-Ch'ing-chien Yeh-su-hui-shih i-chu t'i-yao* (An annotated bibliography of Jesuit translations and writings during the late Ming, early Ch'ing periods) (Shanghai, 1949), 152–53.

8. Ibid., 153–54. See Wu, *Tien-chu-chiao tung ch'uan,* 1:421–24.

9. This account is based on Fang Hao, *Chung-kuo T'ien-chu-chiao shih jen-wu chuan* (Biographies of eminent persons in the history of the Catholic Church in China), 3 vols. (Hong Kong, 1967–1973), 1:185–97. See also M. Santambrogio, "Il Confucio dell'Occidente: P.

Giulio Alenis [sic], gesuita bresciano, missionario e scienziato in Cina, 1582–1649, "*Memorie storiche della diocesi di Brescia* 17 (1950): 21–54; and two works by Joseph Dehergne, S.J.: *Répertoire des Jésuites de Chine de 1552 à 1800* (Rome, 1973), 6–7, and "Le Premier Voyage missionaire d'est en ouest dans la Chine des Ming," *Bulletin de l'Université l'Aurore* (Shanghai) (1942):618–42.

10. See Giulio Aleni, *Chih-fang wai-chi* (Account of countries not listed in the Records Office) and his *Hsi-hsüeh fan* (A summary of Western learning), both in *T'ien-hsüeh ch'u-han* (First collection of writings on Learning from Heaven), comp. Li Chih-tsao, reprinted in Wu Hsiang-hsiang, ed., *Chung-kuo shih-hsüeh ts'ung-shu* (Collectanea of Chinese historical studies), 23 (Taipei, 1965). Also Aleni, *Hsing-hsüeh ts'u shu* (An outline of human nature) (Hangchow, 1623; woodblock edition, Shanghai, 1873). See also Bernard Hung-kay Luk, "And Thus the Twain Did Meet? — The Two Worlds of Giulio Aleni" (Ph.D. diss., Indiana University, 1977).

11. This account is based upon *Ming shih* (Ming history), comp., Chang T'ing-yü and others, 28 vols. (reprint edition, Peking, 1974), chuan 288, 24:700; and upon the article on Ts'ao in L. Carrington Goodrich and Chaoying Fang, eds., *Dictionary of Ming Biography, 1368–1644,* 2 vols. (New York, 1976), 2:1299–1301.

12. Yeh Hsiang-kao, *Ts'ang-hsia yü ts'ao* (More azure sky verses), a microfilm copy of the late Ming edition in the library of The Chinese University of Hong Kong, chuan 14.

13. This account is based upon *Ming shih,* chuan 240, 20:6231–38; Wang Hung-hsü, *Ming shih kao* (Draft history of the Ming dynasty) (reprint edition, Taipei, 1962), lieh-chuan 95, 12a–21a; and Yeh Hsiang-kao, Ch'ü pien (Ch'ü annals) (Taipei, 1977).

14. Dunne, *Generation of Giants,* 60.

15. See Chou Tao-Chi's bibliography of Yeh in *DMB,* 2:1570. The *Lei-pien ku-chin shih-chien ku-shih ta-fang* was consulted in a rare late Ming woodblock edition in the library of The Chinese University of Hong Kong. The word *ch'ü* as used by Yeh in the title of his autobiography can have at least three meanings: (1) It could refer to the grass *Dianthus superbus Linn.,* which resembles wheat but has no edible grain; it has certain medicinal uses and is bitter in taste. (2) It could suggest awakening from a dream, the *locus classicus* of which sense is in *Chuang-tzu:*" Once I, Chuang Chou, dreamed that I was a butterfly and was happy as a butterfly; I was conscious that I was quite pleased with myself, but I did not know that I was Chou. Suddenly I awoke, and there I was, visibly Chou [*ch'ü-ch'ü-jan Chou yeh*]. I do not know whether it was Chou dreaming that he was a butterfly, or the butterfly dreaming that it was Chou. Between Chou and the butterfly there must be some distinction. This is called the

transformation of things." (The translation is from Chan Wing-tsit, *Source Book in Chinese Philosophy* (Princeton, 1963), 190. (3) *Ch'ü* could also refer to Ch'ü Po-yü, the *locus classicus* of which sense is in the *Analects*, 15:7, where Confucius says, "How gentlemanly Ch'ü Po-yü is! When the Way prevails in the state, he takes office, but when the Way falls into disuse in the state, he allows himself to be furled and put away safely." (The translation is D. C. Lau's [Penguin, 1979].) All these meanings of the word could have been indicative of Yeh's self-image when he wrote his autobiographical annals.

16. Yeh, *Ch'ü pien*, chuan 1 and 2; chuan 10, 6b.

17. Ibid., chuan 10, 4a–5b; chuan 19, 1a–2b.

18. Dunne, *Generation of Giants*, 113.

19. The essay is found in Yeh, *Ts'ang-hsia yü ts'ao*, chuan 2, 1a–3b. For background, see Hsieh Kuo-chen, *Ming-Ch'ing chih chi tang-she yün-tung k'ao* (A study of the factions and cliques in the late Ming, early Ch'ing periods) (Shanghai, 1934), chapters 2 and 3, esp. p. 58.

20. Yeh's narration of the events and of his own reactions to them can be found in his *Ch'ü pien*, chuan 11–18.

21. Wang, *Ming shih kao*, lieh-chuan 95, 19a–19b.

22. Yeh, *Ch'ü pien*, chuan 10, 12a; chuan 17, 9a.

23. Ibid., chuan 18, 1b–2a, 3a, 5a–5b.

24. Ibid., chuan 9; chuan 10, 7b–8a; chuan 18, 1a–1b.

25. Ibid., chuan 19, 3a–3b.

26. Ibid., chuan 20, 3a.

27. Yeh Hsiang-kao, *Lun-fei hsü ts'ao* (More grand secretariat papers), reprinted in *Lun-fei tsou ts'ao* (Grand secretariat papers) (reprint of late Ming woodblock edition, Taipei, 1977), 6:2697–2703.

28. See preface to Yeh, *Ts-ang-hsia yü ts'ao*, chuan 2, 1a–3b.

29. Yeh, *Ch'ü pien*, chuan 20, 1a.

30. Giulio Aleni, *San-shan lun hsüeh chi* (Learned conversations at San-shan [Foochow]) (Hangchow, 1627?; reprint edition, Taipei, 1965), 425–39.

31. Ibid., 439–40.

32. Ibid., 440–42.

33. Yü T'ung, *Chung-kuo che-hsueh wen-t'i shih* (A thematic history of Chinese philosophy) (Hong Kong, 1968), 37–86. Chan Wing-tsit, "The Evolution of the Neo-Confucian Concept of *Li* as Principle," in his *Neo-Confucianism, etc.: Essays by Wing-tsit Chan*, comp., Charles K. H. Chen (Hong Kong, 1969), 45–87. T'ang Chun-i, "Lun Chung-kuo che-hsüeh ssu-hsiang shih chung li chih liu-i" (The six different interpretations of *li* in the history of Chinese philosophy), *Hsing-Ya Hsüeh-pao* (New Asia Journal) 1 (1955):45–98. Feng Yu-lan, *Chung-kuo che-hsüeh shih* (A history of Chinese philosophy) (reprint edition, Hong Kong, n.d.). 896–903.

34. Aleni has explained this at some length in his *Hsing-hsüeh ts'u shu*, chuan 1, 1a−4a.

35. Aleni, *San-shan lun*, 442.

36. Ibid., 442−43.

37. Ibid., 444.

38. Ibid., 444−45.

39. Ibid., 445−48.

40. Ibid., 448.

41. Ibid., 449−52.

42. Ibid., 452−54.

43. Ibid., 445.

44. Meng Sen, *Ming-tai shih* (History of the Ming period) (reprint edition, Hong Kong, n.d.), 335−36.

45. Aleni, *San-shan lun*, 455−58.

46. Ibid., 458−62.

47. See Aleni's notices on Europe in his *Chih-fang wai-chi*, in Li, *T'ien-hsüeh ch'u-han*, 3: 1355−1412. See also Dunne, *Generation of Giants*, 64−65; and Bernard Hung-kay Luk, "A Study of Giulio Aleni's *Chih-fang wai chi*," *Bulletin of the School of Oriental and African Studies*, University of London 40.1 (1977):58−84.

48. Aleni, *San-shan lun*, 462−63.

49. Ibid., 463−69.

50. Ibid., 469.

51. Ibid., 469−71.

52. Ibid., 472−77.

53. Ibid., 477−81.

54. Ibid., 482−92.

55. Yeh, *Ch'ü pien*, chuan 20, 1b−2b. Dunne, *Generation of Giants*, 205.

56. *Ming shih*, chuan 240, 24:7400.

57. Fang Hao, *T'ien-chu-chiao shih*, 1:85−97.

58. Dunne, *Generation of Giants*, 113.

59. Yeh, *Ts'ang-hsia yü ts'ao*, chuan 5, 24a.

60. Yeh, *Hsi-ch'ao ch'ung cheng chi* (Poems to honor the orthodox gentlemen), in Wu, *Tien-chu-chiao tung ch'uan*, 1:633.

61. Yeh, *Ts'ang-hsia yü ts'ao*, chuan 5, 22a−23b.

PART THREE

Jesuit Interpretation of China to the West

8

A Western Interpretation of China: Jesuit Cartography

THEODORE N. FOSS

Since the earliest days of their mission there, the Jesuits in China took as a major goal the geographical delineation of the empire. The cartographic materials they accumulated served to instruct and satisfy the curious among the Chinese about the relationships of the world's continents. The missionary maps positioned China in its place in modern cartography and also answered the question of the Chinese: Where had these "wise men from the West" originated? Jesuit cartographers in China also published works for the instruction of Europeans interested in the East and were fully aware of the benefits that derived from the pictorial quality and visual accessibility of maps, all of which transcended language. The cartographic labors of the Jesuits also served a more direct missionary need of aiding the task of evangelization throughout the vast empire of China.

From the first days of the China Jesuit mission until the suppression of the Society in the final third of the eighteenth century, mapping was seen as a cooperative project among the Jesuit fathers and brothers and their Chinese colleagues, Christian and non-Christian. The Jesuits produced cartographic works in the service of the Chinese imperial court for the furthering of the Catholic mission and for the unsated European scholarly appetite for information on China.

This tradition of Jesuit cartography of China is a story with a climax. The high point of the Jesuit mapping of China was the production of an atlas based upon actual surveying of the whole of the Chinese empire, a project sponsored by the K'ang-hsi emperor (r. 1661–1722) in the first quarter of the eighteenth century. The results were published both in China and in Europe and provided both those worlds with the most accurate image of the Chinese empire yet seen; this atlas served well until the mid-nineteenth century.

A strong tradition of geographical description and cartography in China had developed apart from and prior to the Western intrusion. Grand atlases and more specific provincial maps had been produced. The positioning of points on Chinese maps had not been done by astronomical observation but rather by measuring distances from point to point. However, by these means, surprisingly accurate maps were produced.[1] While there was a tradition in China, as in Europe, of religious cosmography, most Chinese cartography was created for administrative purposes. Recently, for instance, maps have been discovered dating from ca. 150 B.C. which seem to have had military and bureaucratic functions. The study of traditional mapping in China is now a topic of vibrant scholarship. A map of the empire, depicting with some great accuracy its eastern coast and its river courses, was carved on stone in A.D. 1137.

Chinese cartography reached its height in the Yüan dynasty (1271–1368) when Chu Ssu-pen (ca. 1273–1337) compiled his *Geographical Map* (*Yü ti t'u*), printed 1311–12. This atlas does not survive in its original form, "but other maps produced at about the same time . . . make it clear that Chinese cartography during the Yüan completely overshadows anything that was being produced in the West at the same time."[2] Lo Hung-hsien (1504–1564), relying upon the work of Chu Ssu-pen as a primary source, produced a grand synthesis of all previous geographical work in his masterpiece, the *Comprehensive Map* (*Kuang-yü t'u*), composed about 1540. This atlas was first printed in 1555 — just twenty-eight years before the arrival of Matteo Ricci (1552–1610) into the Chinese empire.

With the coming of the Jesuits, European geographical practices were introduced to China. Since the first days of the mission in the final quarter of the sixteenth century, the Jesuit scientist-missionaries had been interested in comprehending the geography of the lands in which they were laboring. They studied Chinese cartography, made their own maps of the regions, and interpreted European mapping knowledge for the interested and sceptical Chinese.

A major first step in the European process of mapping China was the map by the Portuguese cartographer, Luís Jorge de Barbuda (fl. 1580), published in the *Theatrum Orbis Terrarum* of Abraham Ortelius (1527–1598) in 1584 (fig. 8.1). Cited as "the first separate map of China to appear in Europe,"[3] it answered the question for Europe: What does China look like? It also set the European stage for the Jesuit cartography of China, for in that same year, 1584, Ricci, who had arrived in China the year before, produced a Chinese version of a European map of the world, which he had brought with him. While no copy of Ricci's first Chinese map is known to exist[4], we do know from his writings that he was familiar with an edition of Lo's *Comprehensive Map* and another Chinese map, *Map of the Configurations Ancient and Modern (Ku-chin hsing sheng chih t'u)*, which had been reprinted in 1555.[5] He also writes of possessing the works of Ortelius and Gerard Mercator (1512–1594).[6]

Ricci continued to improve his world map. The extant version of his 1602 world map has become one of the most celebrated maps in the history of cartography (fig. 8.2). Ricci translated all terms and place names into Chinese, and positioned China toward the center of the map, thus giving the Chinese their traditional pride of place as the "middle kingdom" *(chung kuo)*.[7] He produced this map to answer the questions put to him by the Chinese: Where do you come from? How do you describe the world?[8] The map proved to be an important device for interesting the Chinese in his work, for its information and the various prefaces and descriptions on it served as a major propaganda tool. He himself tells us that many thousands of copies of his map were made, some under his supervision, while others were pirated. Indeed, his world map was quite influential in Asia decades after his death. Copies continued to be made, but often these versions were but travesties of the originals.

The Jesuits continued to produce world maps for the Chinese — translations and refinements of European maps combined with information derived from Chinese sources. Giulio Aleni, S.J. (1582–1649) produced in 1623 a geographical work,

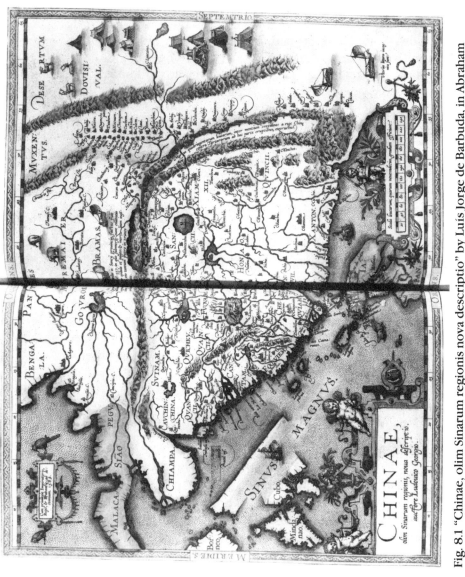

Fig. 8.1 "Chinae, olim Sinarum regionis nova descriptio" by Luís Jorge de Barbuda, in Abraham Ortelius, *Theatrum Orbis Terrarum* (Antwerp, 1584). Photograph courtesy of The Newberry

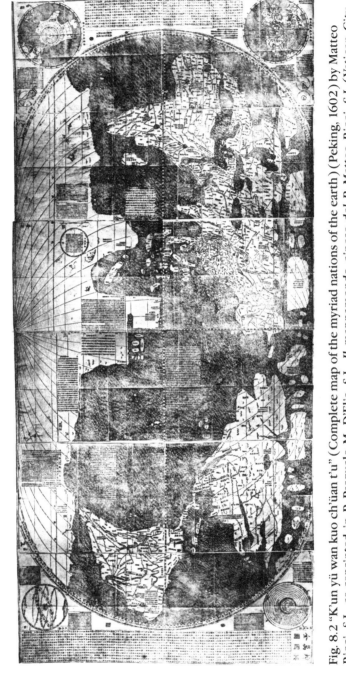

Fig. 8.2 "K'un yü wan kuo ch'üan t'u" (Complete map of the myriad nations of the earth) (Peking, 1602) by Matteo Ricci, S.J., as reprinted in P. Pasquale M. D'Elia, S.J., *Il mappamondo cinese del P. Matteo Ricci, S.I.* (Vatican City, 1938). Photograph courtesy of The Newberry Library, Chicago.

Account of Countries Not Listed in the Records Office (*Chih-fang wai-chi*)[9] (fig. 8.3). This is not only a map but also a geographical treatise describing the various parts of the world. Bernard Hung-kay Luk states that this geography may have been produced as "an inducement to the converted literati"[10] — knowledge in the service of the faith.

Refinements were also made of Ricci's map, such as a 1648 world map made by the Jesuit missionary Francesco Sambiasi (1582–1649). A much simplified work, with many fewer place names than on the Ricci map, the Sambiasi map does reflect some new knowledge gleaned since Ricci's map, for example, New Guinea correctly depicted as an island. In deference to the new Chinese dynasty, China is not named "The Great Ming" (*Ta Ming*) as on the Ricci map but is given a traditional name for China, physically denoting the Chinese middle kingdom (*chung hua*).

Ferdinand Verbiest, S.J. (1628–1707) produced an expanded edition of Aleni's geographical work to accompany a Chinese version of a contemporary European world map divided into two hemispheres. Verbiest's map, the *Complete Map of the Terrestrial Globe* (*K'un yü ch'üan t'u*) (1674) took as its substantive source the 1661 map of Nicolaus à Wassenaer.[11] Verbiest switched the hemispheres in deference to the Chinese custom of having their country near the middle.

From the Ricci world map and its descendants and from the Aleni geography, the Chinese, the Japanese, and the Koreans derived much of their knowledge of the outside world. At the same time, traditional depictions of the world persisted.

In the seventeenth century, the emphasis of the China Jesuits switched gradually from the interpretation of Europe and the world for the Chinese to the geographical exploration and mapping of East Asia for the Europeans. The Far East had appeared on European maps since classical times, but only slowly did it begin to bear much resemblance to reality.[12]

Not only did the Jesuits provide geographical information that was new to the Chinese, but conversely they sent back fresh and more accurate depictions of China to Europe. In fact, it can be safely said that the geographic and cartographic

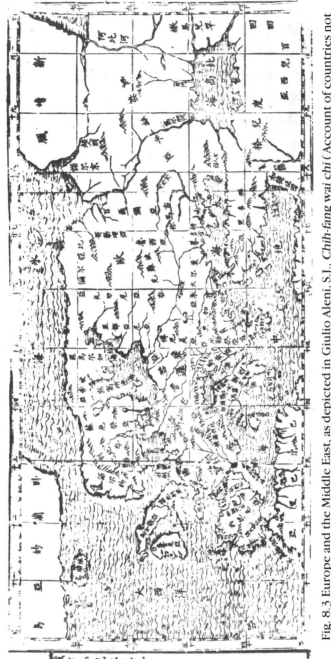

Fig. 8.3 Europe and the Middle East, as depicted in Giulio Aleni, S.J., *Chih-fang wai chi* (Account of countries not listed in the Records Office) (Hangchow, 1623).

image of China held by Europeans of the seventeenth and eighteenth centuries was drawn almost entirely from Jesuit information. The Jesuits, in turn, relied much upon the Chinese cartographic tradition. Most scholars have been too quick to ascribe single Chinese sources to many of the Jesuit maps of China. However, Kenneth Ch'en has identified some of the many sources drawn upon by Ricci.[13]

The Chinese scholar Ma Yong argues that the long-held belief that the maps of Martino Martini, S.J. (1614–1661) were primarily translations from the *Comprehensive Map* is too simple. He makes his point in a recent study of Martini's *Novus Atlas Sinensis,* the major Jesuit cartographic work on China in seventeenth-century Europe.[14] Martini relied upon many late Ming dynasty local gazetteers, critically comparing texts and drawing reasoned conclusions, and defined the Chinese empire for Europe in a volume that included not only accurate provincial maps but also detailed written descriptions of the various areas of China. He gave statistical, physical, economic, and political geographic information on each of the provinces; and by means of cartographic symbols, he designated administrative centers, ore-bearing mines, Jesuit residences, and geographical details such as mountains and lakes. He freely admitted that he had not created his geographical work single-handedly but had relied upon the work of Jesuit colleagues who had preceded him. He was also assisted by Chinese friends who led him to the best sources and sometimes even made abstracts of longer Chinese materials.[15] Upon the publication of Martini's *Atlas* in Europe in 1655 (fig. 8.4), a fellow Jesuit missionary remarked: "Father Martini in his *Atlas* has made a Geographical Description of the Chinese Empire so complete and full, that there hardly remains anything more for us to desire."[16]

At the same time that Martini's *Atlas* was being compiled, another China Jesuit, the Polish-born Michel Boym (1612–1659), was creating an atlas that consisted of provincial maps and of a description of China. While Martini was working with the newly established Ch'ing royal family (1644–1911), Boym arrived in Europe to represent the Ming pretender, the Yung-li emperor (Chu Yu-lang) (1623–1662), in a vain hope of securing Western aid in reestablishing Ming dynasty control of the Chinese empire. While en route to Europe in 1651–52, Boym

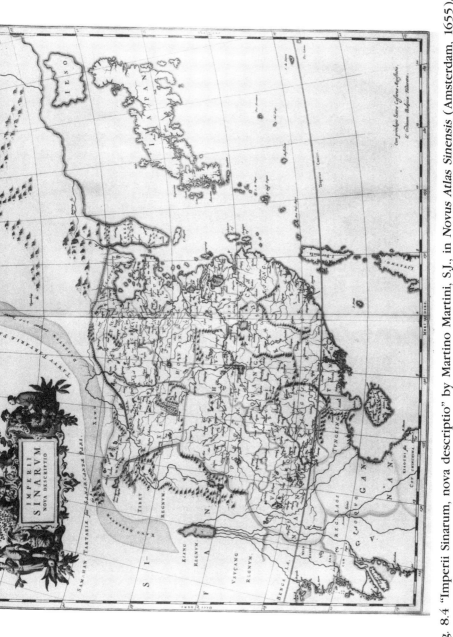

Fig. 8.4 "Imperii Sinarum, nova descriptio" by Martino Martini, S.J., in *Novus Atlas Sinensis* (Amsterdam, 1655), published as part 6 of Joan Blaeu, *Theatrum Orbis Terrarum sive Novus Atlas*. Photograph courtesy of The Newberry Library, Chicago.

Fig. 8.5 "Paradigma XV provinciarum et CLV urbium capitalium sinensis imperii cum templis quae cruce signantur et domiciliis Societatis Jesu" by Philippe Couplet, S.J., in his *Tabula chronologica Monarchiae Sinicae* (Paris, 1686). Photograph courtesy of The Newberry Library, Chicago.

worked on the maps and geography of China, but his atlas was never published, probably because of the appearance of Martini's work. Manuscripts of Boym's maps are scattered, some are lost.[17] One of his maps, however, was published, thanks to the French cartographer Nicolas Sanson d'Abbeville (1600–1667).[18] Because Martini and Boym were working on atlases of the Chinese empire at the same time, Walter Fuch's question whether any relationship exists between the two works is quite relevant.[19]

Philippe Couplet, S.J. (1624–1693) provided a map to accompany his *Tabula Chronologica Monarchiae Sinicae* (fig. 8.5). Like Martini and Boym before him, he returned to Europe on a propaganda tour and, like them, brought with him a young Chinese Christian. The map in Couplet's *Tabula* is drawn after Martini's, and while Couplet had freely taken information from other of his Jesuit confreres, he still kept to the Ming division of China into fifteen provinces years after the creation of three more provinces in the Ch'ing.[20] This reliance of one Jesuit upon the work of his predecessors in China was, as Boleslaw Szczesniak points out, very common.[21] Many of the scholarly projects carried on by the China missionaries can be seen as ongoing refinements of earlier efforts transcending the work of any one man and all "for the greater glory of God."

Martini and his confreres had been encouraged to make a consistent effort to fix positions around their mission stations whenever they could. Martini himself took many readings to determine the accuracy of his maps. However, it was not until the arrival of the first official French Jesuit mission in China in 1687 that a conscientious effort was made to create a cartography of the empire based upon Western methods of survey.[22]

From the outset of the French mission to China, geography was envisioned as playing a large role, reflecting the significant French interest in Chinese geography. Of the first French contingent of Jesuits, several were chosen because, among other reasons, of their geographical training. During the voyage East, they divided their scholarly pursuits, since upon their arrival in China, each man was to specialize, and a new and more organized corporate scientific effort was to be inaugurated.

In Europe, Paris had become the center of cartographic progress in the late seventeenth century. The Italian-born astronomer and topographer Jean-Dominique Cassini (1625–1712) was summoned to Paris in 1669 to direct the observatory there. In 1679, he constructed a great planisphere which was to be corrected constantly as new discoveries, measurements, and observations were made.[23] It was his plan to remap the world. Louis XIV's minister, Jean-Baptiste Colbert, raised money for scientific expeditions and encouraged various types of scientific activity. Louis XIV himself visited the Paris observatory on 1 May 1682, and was quite impressed with the progress being made in cartography and with the precision of the geographical discoveries. Little wonder then that when Couplet arrived in Paris the same year fresh from the Chinese mission, the request he carried from the emperor of China for French Jesuits was welcome and timely.

Scholars from all over the world contributed data to assist Cassini in his mapping efforts. Among them was Jean de Fontaney, S.J. (1643–1710), professor of mathematics at the Collège Louis-le-Grand. While preparing to head the first French Jesuit mission to China, he conferred with Cassini about the possibility of obtaining astronomical data for the Paris observatory and of making geographical observations. Before he left Paris in 1685, Fontaney had been trained in geographical technique and had promised to contribute data on Asia.[24]

A further connection exists among France, the missionaries, and the geographical description of China. The study of geography in France during the seventeenth and the first half of the eighteenth centuries is tied intimately to Jesuit education.[25] Geography was taught within the framework of the curriculum of rhetoric and belles-lettres. History, literature, chronology, and geography all were in the realm of the liberal arts. Jesuits such as Philippe Labbé (1607–1667) and Philippe Briet (1601–1668) taught geography as part of the curriculum at Collège Louis-le-Grand in Paris, where all of the missionary envoys sent by Louis XIV in 1685 to China had studied.[26] Instruction was taken from manuals and geographical dictionaries.[27]

Many of the prominent cartographers of the day were products of Jesuit education. How they came to be trained scientists, despite the unbending and superficial course of geography outlined above, can be explained only if the double function of the

Jesuit college is understood. The colleges existed as training places for the pious elite of France; the years of rhetoric and belles-lettres were designed to give a cultural "finish" to the laity. However, they were also centers of Jesuit learning and inquiry, institutions for higher learning and research of the Jesuit scholar-philosophers. It is within this latter function, lying beyond the manuals and pedagogy of high school geography, that we must look to find the training ground for the scientific methods and activities of France's gifted map makers.

Cartography in the late seventeenth and early eighteenth centuries was a family enterprise dominated by two French clans, the Sansons and the Delisles, all educated by the Jesuits. In addition to formal schooling, father taught son and nephew, and maps flowed for over a century from these two families. Like the Sansons, Guillaume Delisle (1675–1726) along with his father Claude (1644–1720) and brother Joseph-Nicolas (1688–1768) analyzed great amounts of material gleaned from reported voyages, observations, and surveys.[28] Geography and astronomical observations were given a prominent place in the journals of the day, such as the *Journal de Trévoux*[29] and *Mémoires de l'Académie des Inscriptions et Belles-Lettres*. The reports of voyages of circumnavigation, nautical records, and astronomical findings sent from the missionaries to their correspondents and confreres in Europe all proved to the scientific cartographers of the day the inaccuracy of former maps and demonstrated the need for cartographic reform.

A bond of union, strengthened by a common membership in learned societies, grew up between the cartographers of Europe and the Jesuit missionaries so deeply involved in geographical inquiry. Jean-Baptiste Riccioli, S.J. (1598–1671) worked out longitude and latitude bearings from mission posts outside Europe; and by the turn of the eighteenth century, the missionaries had fixed the positions of most of China's major cities. Unfortunately, measurements for the longitude and the circumference of the earth were not yet accurate.[30] It was not until modern geographical methods were employed by Guillaume Delisle that China would be placed more or less correctly. He abandoned the Ptolemaic measures used in Nicolas Sanson's classic maps of Asia (Sanson's map of 1669 has the longitude of

China too far to the east by some twenty degrees) in favor of the direct observational calculations of the missionary Martini in his *Atlas*.[31] Delisle's world map of 1700 puts the Far East in proper position for the new calculations of the circumference of the earth. In addition to his use of the Jesuit China missionary material, Delisle had availed himself of Russian accounts of Muscovy's eastern regions.[32] His was a map of contemporary sources. This, then, is the background from which the Jesuit cartographers in China emerged and the milieu out of which the European cartographic editor of the grand Jesuit survey of the Chinese empire of 1708–18 would emerge.

After the arrival of the French Jesuits in China in 1687, there was much activity on their part: proselytizing for the Christian faith, strengthening the Jesuit position in the K'ang-hsi court, pursuing the scientific and cultural studies they had planned. One of the greatest projects the Jesuits undertook was the overseeing of the imperial survey of the Chinese empire. By the first decade of the eighteenth century, a genuine need for an accurate geographical representation of China was quite apparent to the K'ang-hsi emperor because of the rapidly expanding Ch'ing empire. The Jesuits had proved their interest and had given ample evidence of their expertise and capabilities in survey and map making. Support from the emperor, combined with a sufficient number of Jesuits trained in cartographic technique and with enough background information on the areas to be covered, allowed the fathers to contemplate the production of a complete, scientifically produced atlas based on a survey of the empire. The work on this project fulfilled the Jesuits' desire to map China and provided them with an opportunity once again to prove their worth at the imperial court. The resulting atlas was the first truly accurate portrayal of the whole expanded Chinese empire on either a Chinese or a European map. The maps produced by this scientific expedition and study not only provided the Chinese imperial government with an atlas, but they were also sent to Europe and became a European atlas of China as well.

According to Joseph Needham,[33] it was Jean-François Gerbillon, S.J. (1654–1707) who gave the K'ang-hsi emperor the idea of producing an imperially sponsored atlas of the expanded

Chinese empire, using the Jesuit missionary talents of survey and cartographic technique. However, Antoine Gaubil, S.J. (1689–1759) credits his confrere Dominique Parrenin, S.J. (1665–1741) with encouraging the emperor. He writes: "It is Father Parrenin who found the means by which to nurture in the K'ang-hsi emperor a desire to see a map of the Great Wall."[34] This map of the Great Wall was one of the first produced by the surveyors; Gerbillon then further encouraged the emperor to continue the project.[35] The Great Wall map and smaller surveys were, in part, the impetus for (and became part of) the grand project; in addition, inspiration for the project came from the close contact between the emperor and his Jesuit companions at court.

The periodic flooding of the Pei River and the Wen yu River, for instance, convinced the K'ang-hsi emperor of the need for a detailed survey of the environs of the capital city of Peking. In 1700, the Jesuits Antoine Thomas (1644–1709), Joachim Bouvet (1656–1730), Jean-Baptiste Régis (1663–1738), and Parrenin were called upon to map the region.[36] As Jean-Baptiste Du Halde, S.J. (1674–1743) says in his *Description de la Chine*: "This grand prince had given the command to the missionaries to make up a map of the environs of Peking, in order to judge for himself how many of the European methods were exact."[37] Within seventy days, the map was complete and in the hands of the emperor.

The monarch, quite satisfied with the map, called upon Régis, Bouvet, and Pierre Jartoux (1669–1720) to map the area surrounding the northern Great Wall from Yung-p'ing to Hsi-ning Kansu.[38] This ancient barrier to alien invasion from the north had been expanded, strengthened, and repaired under the previous Ming dynasty. That the wall had deterred the Manchu Tartars from overthrowing the exhausted Ming and that it stood as a symbol of Chinese resistance to northern barbarians may have inspired the K'ang-hsi emperor's interest in the wall's situation.

In any case, Régis, a trained geographer, took charge of the project and set out on 4 June 1708 (K'ang-hsi 47, 4th month, 16th day) with his small band of Jesuit surveyors. Joseph Anne Marie de Moyriac de Mailla, S.J. (1669–1748), though not involved

personally in this project, left a chronicle of the trip,[39] supple-
menting the accounts given by Régis and Gaubil. The three
Jesuits, Bouvet, Régis, and Jartoux, journeyed to Shan-hai-kuan,
the pass at which the Great Wall meets the sea,[40] and followed
the wall to near Suchou, then continued on to the northern
extremity of Shenhsi province. From there they descended to
Hsinan and returned to Peking on 10 January 1709.[41] Although
Bouvet had fallen ill after two months of working on the project,
Jartoux and Régis continued the work, plotting exact positions,
and returned with a map some fifteen feet in length. Very detailed, it included rivers and forts and some three hundred gate
entrances in the wall as well as each gorge and hill upon which
the wall wound its route.[42]

The emperor was well pleased with the resulting map, and
with the exemplary surveys of the environs of Peking and the
Great Wall in hand, judged the projects a success and saw the
value in having the Jesuits map the entire empire. Such mapping
was viewed as a necessary contribution to the successful polic-
ing of scattered local governments, to the maintenance of imperial control, and, above all, to the understanding of the geographical situation and extent of the empire.

Charged by imperial request to provide an accurate and
specific atlas of the Chinese empire, the Jesuits set out to survey
all of the Chinese provinces and to gather information on the
outlying regions of Tibet, Tartary, and Korea. Within a decade,
this immense work was finished, and a remarkable and precise
masterpiece could thus be presented to a satisfied K'ang-hsi
emperor.

By 8 May 1709,[43] Jartoux and Régis, together with the Aus-
trian Jesuit Ehrenberg Xaver Fridelli (1673–1743), began the difficult project of mapping eastern Tartary, the homeland of the
Manchu — Mukden, Jehol, the Ussuri River (*Wu-su-li Chiang*),
and the mouth of the Amur River (*Hei-lung Chiang*).[44] As Du
Halde wrote:

> This was a difficult Task, because that Country having been as
> it were abandoned for many Years, it seem'd scarce possible to
> find the necessary Supplies of Men, Horses and Provisions, for
> a Work that was to continue for several Months. But as nothing
> escaped the Emperor's foresight, he gave so good Orders to the
> Manchew Mandarins who govern the Cities, whereon those

uninhabited Countries depend, and those Orders were so punc-
tually executed, that the Work was never retarded.[45]

To undertake such a vast project as mapping the empire required the emperor's sponsorship, and one sees here the importance of imperial aid in facilitating the arduous work.

As a starting place, the Jesuits were able to use the earlier
survey of the Great Wall as the southern boundary of their new
project. The map of eastern Tartary was finished by the end of
the year. Like the earlier maps, this one was well received, again
with a personal sense of satisfaction on the part of the Manchu
emperor: "This Work was very agreeable to the Emperor, as well
as to the Manchews born at Pe-king, who there beheld their
ancient Country, and were able to learn more from it in a
quarter of an Hour than by discoursing with ever so many Travel-
lers."[46]

The three fathers were then ordered to proceed to the mapping of the Peichihli, or the imperial province wherein lies the
capital of Peking, and worked there from 10 December 1709
to 29 June 1710. This map was significant because of the area's
importance as the seat of government of the empire.

> This Map was the more acceptable, as the Province it described
> was well known. The Emperor took the Pains to examine it
> himself, and seeing the Places justly exhibited which he had
> often passed thro', and caused to be measured by the Manchews,
> (whose Business it is to survey the Roads when he goes into
> the Country) he signify'd to the Missionaries that he wou'd ans-
> wer for the Accuracy of it; and that if the rest proved as good,
> their Performance wou'd satisfy him, and be out of the reach
> of Criticism.[47]

Thus it appears that until this time the Jesuit cartographers
were still on trial. There were those in the Chinese intellectual
community who were opposed to the European influence in
map making, men who had positions that were threatened by
the Jesuit scientific and cartographic intrusion. The K'ang-hsi
emperor in ordering a mapping of the capital province, an area
well documented, could study the new maps and see their
superiority.

With the success of the map of Peichihli, the missionaries,
Régis, Jartoux, and Fridelli, were sent to the middle course of

the Amur River,[48] to the area of the Selenga River *(Seh-leng-eh)*,[49] and north of Ulaanbaator in Mongolia; they worked on the survey of those plans from 22 July 1710 to 14 December of the same year. Regarding this map, "tho' it was empty enough, ... the emperor was pleased with it"[50] as he was desirous to see the position of the cities he had founded for the purpose of establishing strategic bases in this vast area of nomadic Mongol tribes.[51] The area around the Amur River had also acquired importance with the conclusion of the Treaty of Nerchinsk between Czar Peter the Great (1672–1725) and the K'ang-hsi emperor in 1689. Vast areas of sparsely settled land had been in dispute; the Manchu side had won a diplomatic victory and wished to keep its winnings.[52]

By 1711, with the emperor now strongly behind the Jesuit mapping project, it became apparent that in order for the survey to be completed speedily, the Jesuits should divide into several surveying companies. Thus, the mapping of the provinces of China proper as well as remaining outlying areas would be completed by groups working simultaneously.[53] Régis, together with a Portuguese Jesuit mathematician,[54] João Cardoso (1671–1723), went to Peking's neighboring province of Shantung. Jartoux, Fridelli, and Guillaume Fabre-Bonjour (1669–1714), an Augustinian friar,[55] mapped the Ordos, and then the upper course of the Amur and Selenga rivers and the region around Hami (Kumul, in the present-day Uighur Autonomous Region).[56] The year 1711 drew to a close, and the emperor asked if more Jesuits could not be found who were skilled in geography and pressed into service. Three were recruited: the aforementioned de Mailla, Pierre-Vincent de Tartre (1669–1724), and Romain Hinderer (1669–1744). All were accepted by the K'ang-hsi emperor. After this, three separate groups worked to complete the project of surveying the provinces.[57]

Maps of Shanhsi and Shenhsi were completed in 1712 and early in 1713 by de Tartre and Cardoso. These maps are described by Du Halde as being "each ten feet square."[58]

The Mandarin who presented these Maps to the Emperor, having informed his Majesty, that if he required any Thing to be explain'd, Père de Tartre was in waiting to obey his Commands, the Emperor sent for him in, to point out some Places he had himself observ'd in these Provinces: Which done, that Prince said several times *I-tyen-pu-tso* [I tien pu tso], "He is right in every Thing."

There happened one Thing pretty remarkable in this Audience: The Emperor alledged that the Course of a River was wrong in another Map, which had relation to the Maps of Shan-si and Shen-si: Père De Tartre, sensible to his Majesty's Mistake, maintained the Truth (with all due Respect,) in so clear a Manner, that the Monarch came into his Opinion; *Tso Iyau* [Tso liao], says he, "I am mistaken." A great Concession in an Emperor of China![59]

By the end of 1715, the remaining eleven provinces had been mapped:[60] Chianghsi, Kuangtung, and Kuanghsi (1713–14, by de Tartre and Cardoso); Honan (1713, by Régis, de Mailla, and Hinderer); Chiangnan (1713–14, by Régis, de Mailla, and Hinderer); Chechiang and Fuchien (1714, by Régis, de Mailla, and Hinderer); Ssuchuan (ca. 1713–14, by Fabre-Bonjour and Fridelli); Yünnan (ca. 1714–15, by Fabre-Bonjour [died during the survey, 1714],[61] Régis, and Fridelli); Hukuang and Kueichou (1715, by Régis and Fridelli). Régis, who had directed the survey, returned with Fridelli to Peking in January 1717. There, under the direction of Jartoux, who had been forced to stay in Peking because of illness, they worked on the compilation of a general map of all the provinces; it was presented to the emperor in 1718.

The methods and devices used by the Jesuit cartographers in their China survey are recorded in several documents. Antoine Gaubil wrote of the cartographic techniques in a letter from Peking(?) in 1728 to Étienne Souciet, S.J. (1671–1744), a correspondent in Paris:

> These fathers requested a quadrant of two inches in radius; they often checked it carefully and they constantly found that it constantly represented the altitudes as too great. They had a great compass, several other instruments, a pendulum and other things needed for the fulfillment of the emperor's orders. With cords divided exactly, they accurately measured the way from Peking. On this road, they often took observations of the meridian of the sun. At every moment they observed the rhumb and took great care in observing the variation and declination of the peak.
>
> In all these vast regions, the fathers Régis, Jartoux, Fridelli, [Dominique] Parrenin, have observed the height of the pole,

measured the distances, observed the rhumb lines, and familiarized themselves in detail with the country of which Father Verbiest had already made his acquaintance.[62]

Earlier, Bouvet in his *Voiage de Siam* outlined the scientific preparations and described the instruments the French Jesuits took from Paris to Peking.[63] Régis in his manuscript work, "Nouvelle géographie de la Chine et de la Tartarie orientale," also included a detailed outline of the methods used in collecting the data.[64] He praised the method of triangulation and pointed to the care with which the Jesuits proceeded, namely, their observing longitude for verification, noting eclipses, and carefully making measurements for all areas. He stated that the present work of the Jesuit cartographers in China was even more accurate than contemporary maps of Europe and singled out defects in Ptolemy's geographical system and the uncertainty of ancient measures. Finally, he observed that inequality in degrees of latitude were discovered and that longitudinal recording could not be taken by variation of the compass.

Other sources mention the procedures, but none documents them so well as Régis. Basically, points were plotted by triangulation, the resulting work being the first major atlas derived from measurements obtained by this method.[65] John F. Baddeley estimates that the Jesuits took a total of 641 points of both longitude and latitude fixed by astronomical or geographical measurements and reminds us that they collected whatever material could be obtained in the provincial administrative institutions.[66] The twentieth-century historian of the mission, Henri Bernard-Maitre, S.J., describes the method succinctly:

> As one can see, the fundamental method that the cartographers used consisted of measuring distances to obtain the latitude and the longitude of different places. As for the latitude, this process was completed and verified by means of the observations of the sun's meridian and of the polar stars. As for the longitude, the missionaries were sometimes aided by eclipses of the moon and of the satellites of Jupiter, but were often prevented from carrying out their method with the precision desired.[67]

The missionaries took their longitudinal readings with Peking as meridian. They knew that their instruments were imperfect and imprecise and that to measure with Paris as a meridian would have caused even greater distortion and imposed the inaccuracy of the distance from Paris to Peking on the whole of the work.[68] By the late nineteenth century, cartographic historians, such as Julius von Klaproth and Edouard Biot, were aware that as the readings of the Jesuit survey were taken from locations farther and farther away from the Peking meridian, errors likewise became greater and greater;[69] this of course was due to the imperfection of instruments then available. Du Halde, in his author's preface, explains why the Peking meridian was used: "It is from the meridian of Peking that the longitudes are counted (and this is not exhibited at all) to fall in some error, that they did not want to reduce them on the meridian of Paris."[70] A number of critics of Du Halde's work objected to this orientation, among them Edward Cave, the cartographic editor of the *Description of China.*[71]

As Baddeley hinted, the Jesuits did not fail to rely upon native materials regarding the geographical description of the empire. Although they were at times hampered by Chinese and Manchu jealousies because of differences in method and the potential for loss of reputation and position,[72] they prevailed, thanks to imperial sponsorship. However, without the help of native functionaries trained in Western cartographic method as well as the use of Chinese explorations and the traditional Chinese cartography, the Jesuits could not have completed their survey. They collected and studied indigenous works and gathered information from local officials as they traveled. This Chinese material was, wherever possible, checked against the Jesuits' own observation in the field.

In his preface, Du Halde paraphrases Régis and plays down the importance of the work of non-Jesuits:

> The case is otherwise [than those earlier geographical works which appeared in Europe based on Ptolemaic systems and Chinese sources] in the Work we offer the Publick; for vast as it is, we judged we ought not to confine ourselves either to the Maps of the Chinese Governers, or to the Distances measured almost throughout the whole Empire, and particularly in Tartary, with great Labour and Exactness, by the Manchews; nor yet to the printed Memoirs, whereof we had divers: But we resolved to begin the whole anew, employing those Materials no farther than as Guides, in the Roads we were to take, and in the Choice of Places for Observation; it being our Intention to reduce all that we had, to the same Measure, as well as design.[73]

In fact, the Jesuits relied more heavily on native help than on their own decision as to which "Roads [they] were to take."[74] Their dependence on Chinese work for the maps of Tibet was almost total. They used Chinese assistants and Manchu material extensively in other maps. Earlier in his preface, Du Halde himself had outlined the emperor's insistence that several mandarins take charge of making measurements for the Jesuit survey.

> [The Kang-hsi emperor] commanded to great Tribunals to nominate Mandarins to superintend the Measurements, to the end that they might give the exact Names of the most remarkable Places they were to pass thro'; and cause the Magistrates of Towns to attend on the Bounds of their respective Districts with their People, and afford such other Assistance as shou'd be deem'd requisite. All this was performed with surprizing Punctuality; which is a manifest Proof of the admirable Order and Policy observ'd thro' that vast Empire.[75]

Many other functions were performed for the Jesuits by the Chinese and Manchu under order of the emperor.

Du Halde, although inaccurate in his acknowledgment, does allude to the debt of the Jesuits to the continued Chinese awareness of the importance of geography and cartography. As Needham, perhaps in a typical sinophilic overstatement, writes: "It was owing to the solid work of generations of Chinese mapmakers that knowledge of this part of the world became incorporated in modern geography."[76] That the Jesuits could produce an atlas of the vast Chinese Ch'ing empire in one decade was due as much to the tradition of Chinese cartography, upon which they could draw, as it was to the cartographic expertise of the Jesuit scientists. The imperial backing of the interested K'ang-hsi emperor was, of course, of enormous importance also.

Certainly one of the most obvious parts played by the Chinese was in the gathering of material for the making of the maps of Tibet; for, although the maps of that region were contained in the Jesuit atlas, Tibet was not part of the Jesuit cartographic survey project. In order to produce maps of this region, as well as of a few other inaccessible areas (Japan, Korea, and the extremities of Manchuria, for instance), the Jesuits used local information provided by Chinese and Manchu officials.[77] For example, the K'ang-hsi emperor had ordered Ho-shou (d. 1715), a Manchu official and his newly appointed imperial representative to Lhasa, to have a map of Tibet drawn up.[78] Du Halde records: "During the two Years that this Ambassador continued in Tibet, he employed some of his Attendants, who he had carry'd with him for that Purpose, in making a Map of all the Territories immediately subject to the Great Lama."[79] In 1711, upon Ho-shou's return to Peking, his cartographic sketches were given to Régis. These became the basis for the four maps of Tibet in an early version in twenty-eight sheets of the Chinese edition of the Jesuit atlas of China.[80] Thus, Ho-shou has been called the founder of modern cartography in Tibet.[81] One must remember that the Chinese had explored the mountain areas of Tibet long before the Europeans ever arrived.[82]

The maps of Tibet given to Régis in 1711 were not totally satisfactory, and at intervals over a two-year period (1715–17), he so informed the emperor. As a result, since the conflict in Tibet had been subdued and a puppet of the Ch'ing installed as Dalai Lama, another imperial geographical survey group was sent out. It included three imperial envoys and two lamas whom the Jesuits had instructed in Western science. This scientific mission, which seems to have had no diplomatic purpose, was under the command of the secretary of the Mongolian superintendency, Sengju (Seng-chu). The mission had orders to procure more detailed geographical information on Tibet (fig. 8.6), the determination of coordinates, and the measurement of the altitude of the chief mountains.[83]

This cartographic material was employed to draw new maps of Tibet for the second woodblock edition of the Jesuit atlas (in thirty-two sheets) published in China in 1721.[84] The information was also used in the first draft of the description of Tibet in the Chinese work *General Geography of the Ch'ing Empire (Ta Ch'ing i t'ung chih)*.

The cartographic material for Korea also was derived from Chinese sources, as the Jesuits were not able to make survey expeditions into that kingdom. Régis, who once again was responsible in major part for the compilation of the Korean map, analyzed the Chinese findings, comparing them with Korean border sightings made by his Jesuit colleagues. In this way, he was able to judge, although somewhat unsuccessfully, the accuracy of the material provided him.

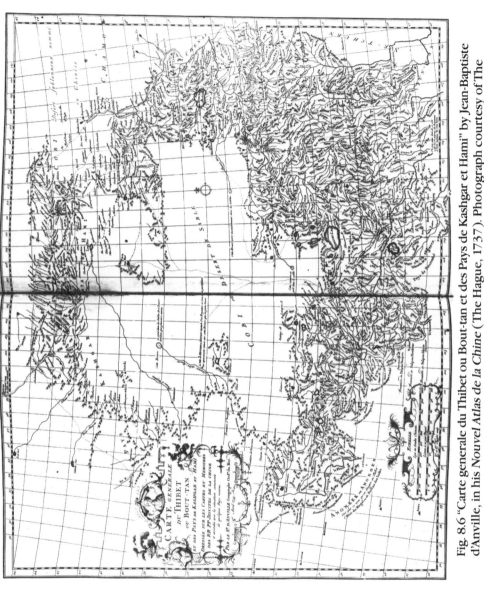

Fig. 8.6 "Carte generale du Thibet ou Bout-tan et des Pays de Kashgar et Hami" by Jean-Baptiste d'Anville, in his *Nouvel Atlas de la Chine* (The Hague, 1737). Photograph courtesy of The Newberry Library, Chicago.

In addition to their reliance on Chinese materials for places inaccessible to them, the fathers availed themselves of Chinese and Manchu scholars, helpmates, and assistants who labored with them on the survey project. Among them was Ho Kuo-tung (18th C.).[85] Régis, Hinderer, and de Mailla were also aided by Chinese co-workers in the mapping of Formosa.[86]

The great geographical and cartographic activity that took place in the K'ang-hsi period certainly aided the Jesuits in their work. The personal interest of the emperor and his knowledge of the vastness of his dominions acted as a catalyst not only to the Jesuit survey but also to the expeditions of Chinese, Manchu, and Mongol explorers.[87] To know the extent of the empire, to aid in communication, and to stem revolt were of paramount importance to the effective control of this vast territory.

One might well ask who was tending the Chinese Christian flock while these Jesuit scientists were so deeply engaged in their geographical work. In 1717, about 120 Jesuits were at work in China; of these, twenty-eight belonged to the French mission.[88] Louis Pfister, in his biographies of the China Jesuits, is quick to remark that, even when on scientific expeditions, they never missed a chance to preach the Gospel in the hinterlands they passed through on survey; for example, he says of Fridelli that "in his long voyages from the north to the middle of the empire [Fridelli] was still more apostolic than geometric [scientific] and [he] never missed the occasion to announce the Gospel and to preach to the pagans."[89] Hinderer, Régis, and de Mailla also made it clear that they availed themselves of the opportunity for extensive travel to proselytize where the Christian message had yet to be heard.[90] The present-day Jesuit historian of the missions, Joseph Dehergne, gives the figure of 300,000 Catholic Chinese in 1700.[91]

The maps prepared by the Jesuits for the K'ang-hsi emperor were presented in Peking as a completed survey, and plans were made to print a Chinese edition. Four different editions appeared during the period 1717–26. The first, that of 1717, was a xylographic printing of twenty-eight maps. Entitled a *Comprehensive Imperial Geographic Atlas* (*Huang yü ch'uan lan t'u*), this edition, although important to the history of cartography because it was the first printing of the assembled data, was soon superseded by corrected and revised editions. In 1719, a manuscript version including thirty-two maps was drawn up, the additional three maps being of the Tibetan and upper Yellow River regions. The nomenclature had been standardized, and no Manchu words appeared on the maps. This copy, in turn, was divided into forty-four plates engraved on copper by the secular priest in Peking, Matteo Ripa (1682–1745), who had participated in the Jesuit survey and would later found the Collegio de' Cinesi della santa famiglia di Napoli upon his return to Europe. A skilled engraver, he had earlier done a set of thirty-six copper plates — views of the imperial villa at Jehol.[92] He had begun his work on the plates for the maps in 1718,[93] and produced an atlas of forty-four plates entitled *Modern Complete Geographical Atlas of the Great Ch'ing Empire (Yü chin ta Ch'ing i t'ung chüan t'u)*[94] on a scale of 1:1,400,000.[95] The Ch'ien-lung emperor (r. 1736–1796) in his poetic introduction to the Jesuit atlas produced for him in the 1750s spoke of this edition of the K'ang-hsi atlas, "Engrave copper plates in order to print [that the atlas might be] handed down for all eternally."[96] The copper plate edition was sent to Louis XV of France in appreciation for his support of the mission,[97] and copies are preserved in the topographical collection of George II of England[98] and in the Istituto Universitario Orientale di Napoli (successor to Ripa's Collegio de' Cinesi.).[99]

In 1721, a second xylographic edition was printed in thirty-two plates identical in format to the manuscript version of 1719 upon which Ripa had relied, the only emendations to this edition being that many details on the maps of Tibet and the upper Yellow River were further corrected and the Manchu nomenclature was standardized to Chinese.[100] This definitive revised woodblock edition was sent by the Jesuits to Europe and would provide Du Halde with the material for the projected maps to be added to his *Description de la Chine*. The scale of this Chinese woodblock version and that of the separate provincial maps and the detailed maps of Tibet and Tartary in Du Halde's work is identical: 1:2,000,000.[101] This allows one to compare the European version with its Chinese original by merely placing one on top of the other. The historian of cartography Marcel

Destombes, who has traced the very copy of the 1721 xylograph which was used to draw the maps of the *Description de la Chine*, states that it was housed in the Archives des Affaires Étrangères in Paris until 1943[102] when it was taken to Germany, where it has yet to surface.[103] Henri Cordier reported on this copy before it disappeared:

> The original maps of the fathers in the Society of Jesus are registered today at the Archives of Foreign Affairs. They were bought from d'Anville by M[r] Vergennes, in exchange for a lifetime annuity of 3000 francs. These maps form a Great Atlas (No. 1648a); they are on paper from China, mounted on stronger paper and surrounded by a border of blue Chinese silk. The names of the cities are marked in Chinese characters.[104]

In 1726, individual dissected sheets of China proper and of Manchuria, but none of Tibet or Mongolia, were included without coordinates in the great Ch'ing encyclopedic collection *Synthesis of Books and Illustrations of Ancient and Modern Times (Ku chin t'u shu chi cheng)*.[105] In addition, there have been re-editions of the woodblock edition of 1721. In 1832, a map to the same scale as the edition of 1721 was reprinted, the only difference being that this new edition was done in a long strip rather than as separate maps. It is entitled *Comprehensive Geographical Atlas of the Present [Ch'ing] Dynasty (Huang Ch'ao i t'ung yü ti ch'uan t'u)* and was in turn reprinted as late as 1894.[106]

Later in the eighteenth century, the Ch'ien-lung emperor authorized a second Jesuit survey. The Portuguese Jesuits Felix da Rocha (1713–1781) and João de Espinha (1722–1788) were sent out to survey and make maps of Sungaria, Turkestan, and the land of the Eleuths, territories that had been recently annexed to the Chinese empire. Working from 1756 to 1759 on the project,[107] they turned over their information and maps of these outlying regions to the emperor. In 1769, Michel Benoist, S.J. (1715–1774), who had recently completed a world map in Chinese for the Ch'ien-lung emperor, was ordered by that monarch to draw up a new map of the empire; it was to include the unpublished data, on the lands surrounding the empire, that had been provided by the Rocha-Espinha expedition of 1756–59. Within the same year (1769), and assisted by others,

Benoist produced a xylographic edition, and, despite his protests that he was not adept at the art of copper engraving, he
brought out a copper-printed edition of the same map in
1775.[108] His maps drew heavily on the K'ang-hsi/Jesuit survey
endeavors of 1708–18 but differed principally from those maps
by their inclusion for the first time of the new cartographic
data that had been gathered by the Rocha-Espinha expedition
on Sungaria, Turkestan, and the land of the Eleuths. Benoist's
atlas, however, was not so influential as that of the earlier Jesuits
in China, for it lacked a European editor who could interpret
the data for the West.

From the correspondence of Antoine Gaubil, we find that
Jean-Baptiste Régis sent a copy (copies?) of the K'ang-hsi/Jesuit
atlas, in the woodblock edition of 1721, to France,[109] whereupon
"The Jesuit map was offered in 1725 to the king of France by
Father de Linière, a Jesuit, confessor to His Majesty, and Father
Du Halde had this map in Paris."[110] Du Halde, in turn, employed
a rising star of cartography in France, Jean-Baptiste Bourgiunon
d'Anville (1697–1782), as cartographic editor of a European
version of the China Jesuit atlas, and the maps he created for
Du Halde's *Description de la Chine* were truly impressive (figs.
8.7 and 8.8).

The excellent maps in Du Halde's *Description de la Chine*
were the result of a complex set of fortuitous circumstances.
As noted earlier, many of the French Jesuits who went to China
in the late seventeenth century were skilled in mathematics
and geography, and of special importance was their knowledge
of trigonometric survey. Their arrival coincided with the rapid
expansion of Ch'ing control, which occasioned imperial authorities to give thought to the drawing up of a comprehensive
atlas of a greatly expanded empire. The Jesuits, building on
their corporate tradition of cartography in China, demonstrated
their scientific expertise and received willing imperial sponsorship for this mammoth cartographic project.

The Jesuits' motives for pursuing such a project were many.
Certainly scientific inquiry was an important factor. The drawing of earlier maps of China, those of Martini, for instance, had
not employed triangulation methods of survey and often had
been grounded only in the tradition of Chinese cartography

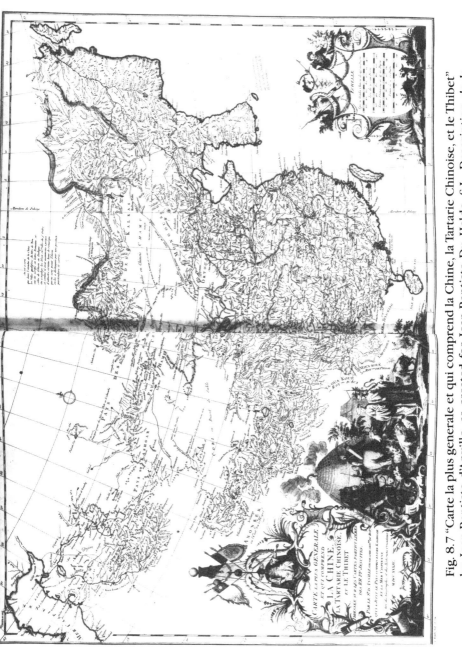

Fig. 8.7 "Carte la plus generale et qui comprend la Chine, la Tartarie Chinoise, et le Thibet" by Jean-Baptiste d'Anville, as created for Jean-Baptiste Du Halde, S.J., *Description de la Chine* (Paris, 1735). Photograph courtesy of The Newberry Library, Chicago.

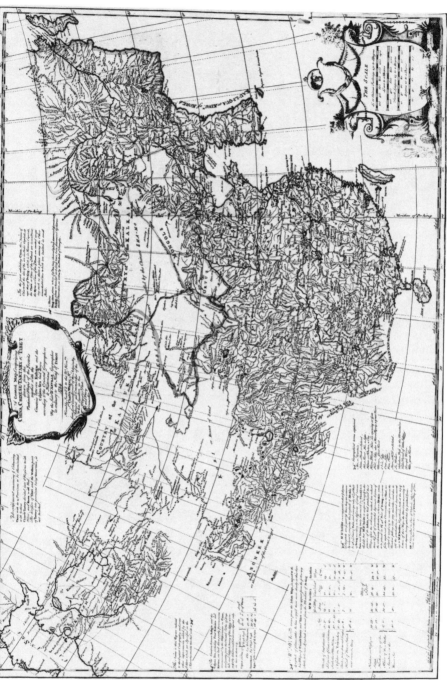

Fig. 8.8 "A General Map comprizing China, Chinese-Tartary & Tibet" by Jean-Baptiste d'Anville, in Jean-Baptiste Du Halde, S.J., *A Description of the Empire of China* (London, 1738–41). Photograph courtesy of The Newberry Library, Chicago.

rather than in new expeditionary research. Martini's maps also reflected the smaller empire of the Ming dynasty. The compilation of new maps using up-to-date methods was needed; and the French Jesuits seized the opportunity to demonstrate to the Chinese, and to the K'ang-hsi emperor in particular, that the knowledge and methods brought from Europe could prove useful.

The ten-year survey of 1708–18 also provided an opportunity for the Jesuits to travel widely on official business as recognized representatives of the court. Not only did the missionary scientists ingratiate themselves with the emperor by working on this important project, but they were also able to break new ground in their apostolic work. When visiting out-of-the-way places, when working with native talent on the survey, or when meeting with local officials, they never forgot that their primary charge was to spread the Christian message.

During this ten-year map making project, the Jesuits found that they could not carry on cartographic research in all parts of the Ch'ing realm. They were too few in number, and the region was too vast. Therefore, the scientist-missionaries were forced often to rely on the efforts of trained native researchers, a good example being the compilation of the maps of Tibet. For some regions, notably Korea, native maps of the area were employed after having been studied to determine their relative accuracy.

National rivalry among the European Jesuits in China also played a part in the making of the maps. From the very first, the French fathers separated themselves from the Portuguese, who until 1700 were nominally in direct control over all the Jesuits in China. With the creation of the Mission française in 1685, the French Jesuits occupied an independent position unique in the Jesuit administrative system. They were answerable only to Rome and to the French provincial. Relations were strained between French and Portuguese Jesuits from the very arrival of the first contingent of the Paris fathers in 1688, a strained relationship that continued in the eighteenth century.[111] Gaubil and the other French missionaries were particularly concerned that the Portuguese fathers would arrange to publish the Jesuit atlas of China in Portugal, even though the maps had been produced almost exclusively by French Jesuits. Therefore, those in China were eager to see the maps appear in an edition printed at Paris as quickly as possible. After they had dispatched the maps to France around 1725, they could not understand Du Halde's delay in printing them. Frequent inquiries were made by the China Jesuits to their correspondents in France as to why the maps had not appeared. Du Halde's motive, of course, was to hold the maps until he could compile a commentary to accompany them. That project, which began as a complement to the atlas, grew to become the four-volume *Description de la Chine,* a work made much more desirable with the addition of the spectacular atlas.

The China survey represented a mapping of a vast region of interest to European scholars, merchants, and missionaries and to the public. The maps that Du Halde and d'Anville created were so well produced and the material of the Jesuit survey so comprehensive that China was depicted more accurately than many regions of Europe in the maps available in mid-eighteenth century Europe. The Jesuit *Atlas* of 1708–18 and its various editions remained a basis for the maps of China, Tartary, and Tibet until the late nineteenth century.

In this *Atlas,* the threads of Jesuit cartographic enterprise came together. The earlier efforts of 125 years of missionary activity, together with the study of indigenous Chinese cartography, provided a foundation on which later Jesuits could build. The China-Jesuit *Atlas* was a corporate effort of the French Jesuits that had the evangelization of the empire as its ultimate objective, although its great scientific value was also readily acknowledged. It was looked upon as a means to an end. The result was a work that won the Jesuits the favor of the emperor of China, gave them a better view of their mission territory, and allowed them to travel to remote places in the empire.

NOTES

1. On native Chinese cartography, see Joseph Needham, *Science and Civilisation in China,* 7 vols. to date (Cambridge, England, 1954–), 3:497–590.

2. Yolande Jones and others, *Chinese and Japanese Maps. An Exhibition Organised by the British Library at the British Museum, 1 February–31 December 1974* (London, 1974), no page number.

3. Donald F. Lach, *Asia in the Making of Europe*, 2 vols to date (Chicago, 1965–), 1, bk. 2:818.

4. See, however, Theodore N. Foss, "La cartografia di Matteo Ricci," in *Atti del convengo internazionale di studi ricciani*, Macerata-Roma, 22–25 ottobre 1982, ed. Maria Cigliano (Macerata, 1984), 177–95.

5. P. Pasquale M. D'Elia, S.J., *Il mappamondo cinese del P. Matteo Ricci, S.I. (terza editione Pechino 1602) conservato presso la Biblioteca Vaticana, commentato tradotto e annotato dal . . .* (Vatican City, 1938); Kazutaka Unno, "Yōroppa ni okeru Kōyozu: Shina chizugaku seizen no shoki jokyō (The Kuang-yü t'u ["Comprehensive Map"] in Europe: Early Chinese influence upon Western cartography), in *Ōsaka daigaku kyōyō-bu kenkyū-shuroku* (Japanese Studies in the Humanities and Social Sciences) 26 (1978):3–28; Boleslaw Szczesniak, "Matteo Ricci's Maps of China," *Imago Mundi* 11 (1954):129.

6. D'Elia, *Mappamondo;* see also Kenneth Ch'en, "A Possible Source for Ricci's Notices on Regions near China," *T'oung Pao* 34 (1938):179–90.

7. See Foss, "La cartografia di Matteo Ricci," 181.

8. On the 1602 world map, one of the few places in Italy Ricci names is The Marches.

9. Bernard Hung-kay Luk, "A Study of Giulio Aleni's *Chih-fang wai-chi*," *Bulletin of the School of Oriental and African Studies*, University of London 40.1 (1977):58–84.

10. Ibid., 83.

11. Gunter Schilder, *Australia Unveiled* (Amsterdam, 1976), pl. 84.

12. Lach, *Asia*, 2, bk. 3:446–89.

13. Ch'en, "Possible Source," 179–80.

14. Ma Yong, "Attività di Martino Martini in Cina e sue opere di storia e geografia della Cina," in *Martino Martini, geografo, cartografo, storico, teologo. Trento 1614-Hangzhou 1661. Atti del convengo internazionale 9–11 ottobre 1981*, Edizione bilingue italiana-inglese, a cura di Giorgio Melis (Trent, Italy, 1983), 229–47. (This is an Italian translation of a paper read in Chinese. The Chinese text has been published in *Li shih yen chiu* [Historical research] [Peking] 6 [1980]:153–68.)

15. See Giorgio Melis, "Presentazione," in Martino Martini, S.J., *Novus Atlas Sinensis. Ad Lectorem Praefatio. Versioni* (Trent, Italy, 1981), 19–21.

16. Gabriel de Magalhães (Magaillans), S.J., *A New History of China*, trans. John Ogilby (London, 1688), preface.

17. Robert Chabrié, *Michel Boym, Jésuite polonais et la fin des Ming en Chine (1646–1662)* (Paris, 1933), 228–34, 256; Walter Fuchs, "A Note on Father M. Boym's Atlas of China," *Imago Mundi* 9 (1952):71–72; Boleslaw Szczesniak, "The Mappa Imperii Sinarum of Michael Boym," *Imago Mundi* 19 (1965):113–15.

18. "Abbregé de la Chine du R. P. Bouyn" (1658). See Boleslaw Szczesniak, "The Seventeenth Century Maps of China. An Inquiry into

the Compilations of European Cartographers," *Imago Mundi* 13 (1956):116–36.

19. Fuchs, "Note on Boym," 72.

20. Szczesniak, "Seventeenth-Century Maps," 128–31. A word about the number and names of the provinces in the Ch'ing dynasty: China encompassed Outer Mongolia, Alashan, Inner Mongolia, Ch'inghai, and Tibet, as well as China proper. Within that China, the Ch'ing government under K'ang-hsi designated eighteen provinces; moving from west to east and north to south, they were: Kansu, Shanhsi, Shenhsi, Suchuan (or Suchou), Kueichou, Yünnan, (Pei-)Chihli (capital, Peking), Honan, Hupei, Hunan, Kuanghsi, Anhui, Chianghsi, Shantung, Chiangsu, Chechiang, Fuchien, Kuangtung. During the Ming, China was grouped into fifteen provinces. In 1645, the new Ch'ing Manchu government created a sixteenth province, the Mukden province of Manchuria, as the second metropolitan province. Then in 1676, the K'ang-hsi emperor divided China into eighteen provinces. Shenhsi and Kansu in the Ming dynasty had been known as Shenhsi; Hunan and Hupei had been called Hukuang; and Chiangsu and Anhui were formerly known collectively under the names Nanchihli, Nanchang, or Chiangnan. Peichihli included Hopei and part of Chahar and Jehol. The name *Chih-li* means "direct rule" or "metropolitan province." Before 1421 (when the capital of the empire was moved from Nanking to Peking), the province of Nanchang or Chiangnan had been known as Chihli. After that move, that province was sometimes referred to as Nanchihli or "southern metropolitan province," and the province of the new capital was called Peichihli or "northern metropolitan province." The People's Republic of China is divided into twenty-two provinces. To the Ch'ing list add the names Liaoning, Chilin, Heilungchiang, Taiwan, Chinghai, and delete the name Kuanghsi.

21. Ibid.

22. See the contribution of John W. Witek, S.J. to the present volume (chapter 3).

23. Lloyd A. Brown, *Jean Dominique Cassini and His World Map of 1696* (Ann Arbor, 1941), 40–41.

24. Ibid., 42.

25. See C. Daniel, "La Géographie dans les collèges des Jésuites aux XVIIe et XVIIIe siècles," *Études* 3 (1879):801–23; Henri Bernard-Maitre, S.J., "Les Étapes de la cartographie scientifique pour la Chine et les pays voisins depuis le XVIe jusqu' à la fin du XVIIIe siècle," *Monumenta Serica* 1 (1936):428–77.

26. Daniel, "La Géographie," 810.

27. Ibid., 818–23.

28. Ibid., 814–15.

29. The formal title of the journal is *Mémoires pour servir à l'histoire des sciences et des beaux-arts,* but even in the eighteenth century

it was referred to as the *Journal de Trévoux*. For more about the journal, see Alfred Desautels, S.J., *Les Mémoires de Trévoux et le mouvement des idées au XVIIIe siècle (1701–1734)* (Rome, 1956).

30. Abbé Joseph Brucker, "Communication sur l'exécution des cartes de la Chine par les missionaries du XVIIIe siècle d'après documents inédits," in *IVe Congrès international des sciences géographiques tenu à Paris en 1889*, 2 vols. (Paris, 1889), 1:384–86.

The problem of longitude reckoning would not be solved until the use of the chronometer was adopted. See Norman J. W. Thrower, "The Discovery of the Longitude. Observations of Carrying Timekeepers for Determining Longitude at Sea, 1530–1770," *Navigation* 5 (1957–1958): 375–81.

31. See Sven Hedin, *Southern Tibet: Discoveries in Former Times Compared with My Own Observations in 1906–1908*, 9 vols. (Stockholm, 1917–1922), 1:216–22; Bernard-Maitre, "Les Étapes," 463; Brucker, "Communication," 1:381.

32. John F. Baddeley, ed., *Russia, Mongolia, China: being some record of the relations between them from the beginning of the XVIIth century to the death of Tsar Alexei Mikhailovich, A.D. 1602–1676*, 2 vols. (London, 1919), 1:vi–vii.

33. Needham, *Science and Civilisation*, 3:585.

34. Antoine Gaubil, S.J., *Correspondance de Péking, 1722–1759* (Geneva, 1970), 214. The original French is: "c'est le P. Parrenin qui trova le moyen de faire naître à l'empereur Kang-Hi le désir de voir une carte de la grande muraille."

35. Ting Tchao-ts'ing (Ting Ch'ao-ch'ing), *Les Descriptions de la Chine par les Français (1650–1750)* (Paris, 1928), 47.

36. This mapping project is mentioned in a letter to Gottfried Wilhelm von Leibniz, 4 November 1701, printed in *Journal de Trévoux* 11 (1704):155. See above, note 29.

37. Jean-Baptiste Du Halde, S.J., *Description géographique, historique, chronologique, politique, et physique de l'empire de la Chine et de la Tartarie chinoise*, 4 vols. (The Hague, 1735), 1:xxxvi. The original French is: "Ce grand Prince ayant ordonné aux Missionaires de dresser une Carte des environs de Peking, jugea parlui-même combien les méthodes Européanes sont exactes."

38. On this mapping project, see Henri Cordier's note to manuscripts of Antoine Gaubil: "Mélanges géographiques et historiques. Manuscrit inédit du Père A. Gaubil, S.J. publié avec notes par H. Cordier," *T'oung Pao* 16 (1915):529–44. A fascinating comparison of Western and contemporaneous Chinese mapping practices can be made between the Régis map and a Ch'ing dynasty military map; the latter dates from ca. 1680–1700, depicts about three-quarters of the length of the 10,000 *li* wall (one *li* = ca. ½ kilometer), and shows garrisons, etc. For an illustration of the Chinese map, see M. J. Meijer, "A Map of the Great Wall of China," *Imago Mundi* 13 (1956); 110–15.

39. See his *Histoire générale de la Chine, ou Annales de cet Empire; traduites du Tong-Kien-Kang-mou* (. . . translation of the essential points of the "Universal Mirror"). Pub[liées] par l'abbe Grosier. 13 vols. (Paris, 1777–1785), 11:314–17.

40. In the Ming dynasty, the Shantung province included both the Liao-tung and the Shan-tung peninsulas. The Shan-hai-kuan, literally "mountain sea pass," was of strategic importance because it was level ground, between the sea and the mountains, at which the Liao-tung peninsula could be cut off.

41. Baddeley, *Russia, Mongolia, China*, 1:clxxxi, citing de Mailla, *Histoire générale de la Chine*, 11:314. Baddeley points out that the wall had been carefully examined previously by a Father Alexander some time before 1694. See Evert Ysbrandszoon Ides, *Driejaarige reize naar China, te lande gedaan door den Moskovischen afgezant, E. Ysbrants Ides van Moskou af* (Amsterdam, 1704), 138.

42. Du Halde, *Description de la Chine*, 1:xxxviii.

43. Ibid.

44. Walter Fuchs, *Der Jesuiten-Atlas der K'anghsi-zeit. Seine Entstehungsgeschichte nebst Namensindices für die Karten der Mandjurei, Mongolei, Ostturkestan und Tibet* (Peking, 1943), 9–10.

45. Jean-Baptiste Du Halde, S.J., *A Description of the Empire of China and Chinese Tartary*, 2 vols. (London, 1738–1741), 1:vii. Unless otherwise indicated, all references in Roman numerals to this English edition are to Du Halde's preface.

46. Ibid., 1:viii.

47. Ibid.

48. Louis Pfister, S.J., *Notices biographiques et bibliographiques sur les Jésuites de l'ancienne mission de Chine 1552–1773*, 2 vols. Variétés sinologiques nos. 59 and 60 (Shanghai, 1932–1934), 1:531.

49. Du Halde, throughout his *Description de la Chine*, calls the area "Saghalian."

50. Du Halde, *Description of China*, 1:viii.

51. On the Mongols in this area at that time, see René Grousset, *The Empire of the Steppes: A History of Central Asia*, trans. Naomi Walford (New Brunswick, 1970), 529–33.

52. On the treaty of Nerchinsk and the Jesuit part in the Manchu victory, see Joseph Sebes, S.J., *The Jesuits and the Sino-Russian Treaty of Nerchinsk (1689): The Diary of Thomas Pereira, S.J.* (Rome, 1961); Praskovia Tikhovleva, *Pervy Russo-Kitaysky dogovor 1689 goda* [The first Russian-Chinese treaty, 1689] (Moscow, 1958); and Mark Mancall, *Russia and China: Their Diplomatic Relations to 1728* (Cambridge, 1971).

53. Antoine Gaubil, S.J. gives details of the expedition of 1711 in his "Histoire des Thang," in *Mémoires concernant l'histoire, les sciences, les arts, les moeurs, les usages, etc. des Chinois: par les missionaries*

de Pékin, ed. C. Batteux and others, 16 vols. (Paris, 1776–1814), 15:402.

54. This is the appellation that de Mailla gives to most of these Jesuit cartographers.

55. Fabre-Bonjour carried the "red hat" from Europe to Macao to the beleagured Cardinal Maillard De Tournon. He was being held in detention (since 1707) in that city by order of the K'ang-hsi emperor, and in 1707 had been made a cardinal in Rome without his knowledge. Fabre-Bonjour arrived on 4 January 1710. Two days later, the ceremony of investiture took place very privately, but within six months the "detained" prelate was dead. See Francis A. Rouleau, S.J., "Maillard de Tournon, Papal Legate at the Court of Peking," *Archivum Historicum Societatis Iesu* 31 (1962):264–323.

56. See Fuchs's translation into modern geographical terms, *Jesuiten-Atlas,* 10. For Gaubil's description of this expedition, see Cordier, "Mélanges géographiques et historiques," 526, 536–37.

57. De Mailla, *Histoire générale de la Chine,* 11:316.

58. "dix pieds en quarré."

59. Du Halde, *Description of China,* 1:viii–ix, author's preface.

60. Fuchs, *Jesuiten-Atlas,* 9–11.

61. Régis was sent to replace Fabre-Bonjour after the latter's death in Yünnan.

62. Gaubil, *Correspondance,* 214. The original French is:

> Ces Péres prirent un quart de cercle de deux pieds deux pouces de rayon; on eut souvent soin de le vérifier, et on trouva constamment qu'il représentoit les hauteurs trops grandes d'une minute. Ils avoient de grandes boussoles, plusieurs autres instruments, une pendule et autres choses propres à l'exécution des ordres de l'empereur. Avec des cordes divisées exactement ils mesurèrent exactement le chemin depuis Péking.... Dans ce chemin ils prirent souvent par observation la hauteur méridienne du soleil; ils observaient à tout moment le rhumb et eurent grand soin d'observer la variation et déclinaison de l'aiguille....
>
> Dans tous ces vastes pays, Les P. P. Régis, Jartoux, Fridelli, [Dominique] Parrenin ont observé la hauteur du pôle, mesuré les distances, observé les rhumbs et ont fait connaître en détail un pays dont le P. Verbiest avait déjà donné plusieurs connaissances.

Verbiest's biography can be found in a work by R. A. Blondeau, *Mandarijn en astronoom: Ferdinand Verbiest, S.J. (1623–1688) aan het hof van de Chinese Keizer* (Bruges, 1970). Verbiest's work was *Astronomia Europaea sub Imperatore tartare-sinico Cam-hy appelato* (Dillingen, 1687).

63. Joachim Bouvet, S.J., *Voiage de Siam du Père Bouvet,* ed. Janette C. Gatty (Leiden, 1963), 15–16.

64. Du Halde took much of his geographical information from this work. The Régis manuscript is housed in the Bibliothèque Nationale, Paris, MS. fr. 17242, fols. 5v–11v.

65. Brucker, "Communication," 1:388.

66. Baddeley, *Russia, Mongolia, China,* 1:clxxxvii.

67. Henri Bernard-Maitre, S.J., "Note complémentaire sur l'atlas de Kang-hsi," *Monumenta Serica* 11 (1946):198–99. The original French is:

> Comme on le voit, la méthode fondamentale qu'employèrent les cartographes consistait à mesurer les distances pour obtenir la latitude et la longitude des différénts endroits. Ce procédé était complété et contrôlé au moyen de l'observation méridienne du soleil et des étoiles polaires pour la latitude. Quant à la longitude, les missionaires s'aidèrent parfois des éclipses de la lune et des satellites de Jupiter, mais ils furent souvent empêchés d'effectuer cette opération avec la précision désirable.

68. Du Halde, *Description de la Chine,* 1:xxxvi. However, d'Anville made such a conversion to the Paris meridian on his version of the general map in *Description de la Chine.* Note that, by keeping the error which increases as one gets farther and farther from the Chinese capital, the survey methods are better understood than if the meridian were changed to Paris. However, the cartographic editor of the English edition did not think so. See Du Halde, *Description of China,* 1:translator's preface.

69. This from Pfister, *Notices,* 1:534.

70. Du Halde, *Description de la Chine,* 1:xxxvi. The original French is: "C'est sur le méridien de Péking que sont comptées ces longitudes; & c'est pour ne point s'exposer à tomber dans quelque erreur, qu'on n'a pas voulu les réduire au méridien de Paris."

71. The problem of longitude is one that perplexed cartographers until the end of the eighteenth century. See Thrower, "Discovery of the Longitude," 376–77; Numa Broc, *La Géographie des philosophes, géographes, et voyageurs français au XVIIIe siècle* (Paris, 1972), 16. See also Du Halde, *Description of China,* 1:translator's preface.

72. This was a constant problem for the Jesuit missionaries in China from the beginning. The problem was particularly acute when the missionaries assumed leadership in the Bureau of Astronomy.

73. Du Halde, *Description of China,* 1:xi, author's preface.

74. It is interesting to compare how closely Du Halde holds to Régis's manuscript original. Du Halde, in the original French (passage quoted above in English, cited note 73), states:

Il n'en est pas de même dans l'Ouvrage qu'on donne au Public; tout vaste qu'il est, on n'a pas cru devoir s'en tenir, ni aux Cartes des Gouverneurs Chinois, ni aux dimensions faites presque partout, principalement dans la Tartarie, par les Mantcheous également laborieux & exacts, ni à divers Mémoires imprimez. Mais on s'est déterminé à recommencer tout de nouveau, n'usant de ces connoissances que pour se régler dans les routes qu'on avoit à prendre, & dans le choix des lieux dignes de remarque, rapportant tout ce qu'on faisoit, non seulent à un même dessein, mais encore à une même mesure employée sans interruption [Du Halde, *Description de la Chine*, 1:lii].

And the original from Régis's manuscript:

Aulieu que dans l'ouvrage qu'on donne au public, tout vaste qu'il soit en effet, on na pas cru devoir sen tenir ni aux Cartes des Gouverneurs Chinois ni aux dimensions faites presque partout, surtout dans la Tartarie quelques années — au paravant par des mantcheoux [word scratched out] également laborieux et diligents ni à divers mémoires imprimés mais on sest déterminé à recommencer tout de nouveau ne se scrivant de ces connoissences que pour se régler dans les routes qu'on avoit à prendre et dans le choix des lieux dignes de remarque et rapportant tout ce quon faisoit non seulement à un mesme dessein mais enchore à une mesme mesure employée sans interruption [Régis manuscript, Bibliothèque Nationale, Paris, MS. fr. 17242, fol. 9r].

75. Du Halde, *Description of China*, 1:vii, author's preface.

76. Needham, *Science and Civilisation*, 3:590.

77. Shannon McCune, "Geographical Observations of Korea: Those of Father Régis Published in 1735," *Journal of Social Science and Humanities* (Seoul) 44 (1976):7–8.

78. Luciano Petech, *China and Tibet in the Early Eighteenth Century* (Leiden, 1972), 18–20. Ho-Shou's was not the first geographical expedition by a Chinese to Tibet; Needham notes an earlier one: "Lasi and Sulan conducted a five-month expedition in Tibet in 1704, which led, after further investigation of Amida in 1782, to the official publication of the *Ch'ing ting ho yuan chi lüeh* [Imperially ordered record of river sources]" (*Science and Civilisation*, 3:585).

79. Du Halde, *Description of China*, 2:384. In the beginning of the eighteenth century, a split had formed among the lamas of Tibet dividing those (the "red hats") whose allegiance remained with the Dalai Lama and those (the "yellow hats") whose sentiments fell to the Ch'ing conquerors. Ibid., 4:570.

80. Fuchs, *Jesuiten-Atlas*, 14–18, and nos. 16–19.

81. Ibid.

82. Hedin, *Southern Tibet*, 3:29. At this period, there were Europeans, both lay and religious, in Tibet; among them were Ippolito Desideri, S.J. (1648–1733) and J. G. Renat, a Swedish gun maker and cannon founder. On Desideri, see Carlo Puini, "Il Tibet (geografia, storia, religione, costumi) secondo la relazione del viaggio del P. Ippolito Desideri (1715–1721)," *Memorie della Società geografica italiana* 10 (1904): lxiv–402. On Renat, see Hedin, *Southern Tibet*, 1:253–61.

83. See Du Halde, *Description de la Chine*, 4:571. This information Du Halde had also taken from the Régis manuscript, "Nouvelle géographie."

84. Petech, *China and Tibet*, 20; see Fuchs, *Jesuiten-Atlas*, 12–18.

85. Ho Kuo-tung was the brother of Ho Kuo-tsung (d. 1766), who would later help in the survey of Sungaria (Chun-ko-erh) in 1755, a project also conducted by Jesuits as part of the second Jesuit survey of China for the Ch'ien-lung emperor. See Arthur W. Hummel, ed., *Eminent Chinese of the Ch'ing Period (1644–1912)*, 2 vols. (Washington, D.C., 1943–1944), 1:285–86; Fuchs, *Jesuiten-Atlas*, 35–36.

86. See de Mailla's letter of August 1715 from Kieou-kian (Chiu-chiang), in *Lettres édifiantes et curieuses, d'écrits des missions étrangères, par quelques missionaries de la Compagnie de Jésus*, 4 vols. ed. L. Aimé-Martin (Paris, 1838–1843), 3:253–67. Keeping track of the editions of the separate volumes of the *Lettres* is a bibliographic nightmare. For a sorting through of the editions, see Victor Hugo Paltsits, "Data concerning the 'Lettres édifiantes,'" in *The Jesuit Relations and Allied Documents*, 73 vols., ed. Reuben Gold Thwaites, (Cleveland 1896–1901), 66:298–334.

87. Needham, *Science and Civilisation*, 3:585.

88. Joseph Dehergne, S.J., *Répertoire des Jésuites de Chine de 1552 à 1800* (Rome, 1973), 338. These Jesuits were grouped under three separate juridical bodies: under the province of Japan, 52 men, of whom 34 were priests, and with about 10 residences in Kuangtung and Kueilin; under the vice-province of China, 40, of whom 36 were priests, with 4 colleges and 37 residences; under the Mission française, 28 priests and brothers with "several" houses (ibid.). Edwin O. Reischauer and John K. Fairbank give these figures for 1701: China had 59 Jesuits, 29 Franciscans, 18 Dominicans, 6 Augustinians, and 15 secular priests, most of the latter from the French Society for Foreign Missions (Société des Missions Étrangères). The Jesuits in 1701 had 70 mission residences and 208 churches and chapels. *East Asia: The Great Tradition* (Boston, 1960), 249. See Dehergne, *Répertoire*, 352–53, for a map of the mission stations in China in 1701; a text (357–59) accompanies the map.

89. Pfister, *Notices,* 2:608, quoting Augustin von Hallerstein, S.J., *Epistolae anecdotae,* letter 1a. The original French is: "dans ses immenses voyages du nord au midi de l'empire, il fut encore plus apôtre que géomètre et ne manqua jamais l'occasion d'annocer l'Évangile et de prêcher aux païens.

90. Pfister, *Notices,* 2:612, 597, 532. Pfister's work is, of course, an invaluable source, but at times it is written in a kind of nineteenth-century hagiographic Catholic orthodox style.

91. Dehergne, *Répertoire,* 336.

92. On these, see Paul Pelliot. "Les 'Conquêtes de l'Empereur de la Chine,'" *T'oung Pao* 20 (1920–1921):273. For more on Ripa, see Christophe Comentale, *Matteo Ripa, peintre-graveur-missionarie à la Cour de Chine. Mémoires traduits, présentés et annotés par . . .* (Taipei, 1983).

93. Evidently Ripa had begun his work using the material from the first edition as an early guide.

94. The edition has either forty-one or forty-four plates. Walter Fuchs writes: "Ob diese indessen mit den Mukdener Platten identisch sind [a modern edition printed in Mukden in 1929 and entitled *Man han ho pi Ch'ing nei-fu i-t'ung yü-ti pi-t'u*] erscheint wegen der Differenz in der Anzahl der Platten — dort sind es nur 41 — fraglich." "Materialien zur Kartographie der Mandju-Zeit," *Monumenta Serica* 1 (1935–1936):426–27.

95. Marcel Destombes, "Les Originaux chinois des plans de ville publiés par J. B. Du Halde, S.J., en 1735," in *Actes du colloque international de sinologie, 20–22 septembre 1974, Chantilly. La Mission française de Pékin aux XVII*^e^ *et XVIII*^e^ *siècles* (Paris, 1976), 86.

96. Quoted in Fuchs, "Materialien," 398.

97. Hedin, *Southern Tibet,* 3:29.

98. This copy has the separate maps pasted together to form a large mural, 3.17 x 2.95 meters. The George II collection came to the British Museum in 1828. See Helen Wallis, "Missionary Cartographers to China," *Geographical Magazine* 47 (1975):752.

99. Fuchs, *Jesuiten-Atlas,* 7. In addition, Fuchs reports that as of 1943 a copy was housed in the imperial palace at Mukden.

100. Petech, *China and Tibet,* 186.

101. This atlas of 1721 is the one reproduced by Fuchs as the companion volume (box of maps) to his *Jesuiten-Atlas* study. Ibid., 44–48.

102. Destombes, "Les Originaux chinois des plans de ville," 86. Henri Cordier, *Bibliotheca Sinica,* 5 vols. (Paris, 1904–1924), 1:col. 184: "Ces cartes forment un Grand Atlas (No. 1648^a^)" in the Archives des Affaires Étrangères.

103. Destombes, "Les Originaux chinois des plans de ville," 86.

104. Cordier, *Bibliotheca Sinica,* 1:col. 184. The original French is:

Les Cartes originales des Pères de la Compagnie de Jésus sont déposées aujourd'hui aux Archives des Affaires Étrangères. Elles furent achetées de d'Anville, par M. Vergennes, moyennant une rente viagère de 3000 francs. Ces cartes forment un Grant Atlas (No. 1648^a): elles sont sur papier de Chine, montées sur du papier fort et entourées d'une bordure de soie bleue chinoise. Les noms des villes sont marqués en caractères chinois.

Cordier seems to have been unaware that several editions of the Jesuit atlas were printed in China. For a more complete description of the manuscript, see Fuchs, both his "Materialien," 398, and his *Jesuiten-Atlas*, 43–48. Joseph-Nicolas Delisle also had a copy of the Chinese atlas in St. Petersburg.

105. The above information is digested for the most part from Fuchs, *Jesuiten-Atlas*. On the maps in *T'u shu chi cheng* (Imperial encyclopedia [of matters] ancient and modern), see Needham, *Science and Civilisation*, 3:585; Bernard-Maitre, "Note complémentaire," 192. Fuchs also mentions that the maps may have been engraved on sheets of white jade. See his "Materialien," 397 n. 45, where he quotes Cordier, *Bibliotheca Sinica*, 1:col. 184. Baddeley also speaks of "Chinese versions in jade, copper and wood." *Russia, Mongolia, China,* clxxxix. The passage in Cordier tells us that the information was gathered from the survey and then transferred "sur de minces lames de jades blanc, larges de deux pieds et demi environ. Les contours et les noms de villes étaient marqués par des traits dorés. On conservait ces planches au palais du Youen ming youen [Yüan-ming Yuan, the Manchu summer palace]; elles existaient encore à l'époque du pillage [during the reprisals by the Europeans against the Boxer Rebellion], mais on ignore ce qu'elle sont devenues depuis." Gaston Cahen likewise follows Cordier. See his *Les Cartes de la Sibérie au XVIIIe siècle. Essai de bibliographie critique* (Paris, 1911), 55–56, 59, 101–29, 139, 199–200, 280, 339. A common practice was the carving of maps onto stone, put there for posterity. Ink squeezes could be made from these; some of the early extant maps of China have been preserved this way. See Needham, *Science and Civilisation*, 3:548; Howard Nelson, "Maps from Old Cathay," *Geographical Magazine* 47 (1975):704.

106. Pfister, *Notices*, 1:533.

107. On this project, see ibid., 2:774–77, 865; Wallis, "Missionary Cartographers, 752.

108. In a letter from Michel Benoist to "M ———," ca. 1773, in *Lettres édifiantes*, 4:231–32.

109. Gaubil, *Correspondance*, 216, 735.

110. Ibid., 302. The original French is: "La Carte des Jésuites fut offerte en 1725 au Roy de France par le R. P. de Linière, Jésuite, confesseur de Sa Majesté, et le P. Jean Baptiste Du Halde a cette carte à Paris."

Louis XV was probably given the Ripa copperplate edition, although he may have received the woodblock issue as well. The king's copy of the atlas remained in the private royal library until the time of the French Revolution, according to Hedin, *Southern Tibet*, 3:29.

111. See Sebes, *Jesuits and Sino-Russian Treaty*, 137–41.

9

The Seventeenth-Century Jesuit Translation Project of the Confucian Four Books

DAVID E. MUNGELLO

INTRODUCTION

BETWEEN 1662 AND 1711, five editions of the Confucian *Four Books (Ssu-shu)* were published in European-language translations. It is widely known that Jesuit missionaries were responsible for these first European-language translations of the Chinese Classics. But two other points must be made: First, these works were part of a continuous translation project traceable to the founder of Jesuit accommodation in China, Matteo Ricci (1552–1610); second, these works were a reflection of Ricci's accommodative approach. There are no documents this writer has found containing concise formulation of such a plan, mainly because the project evolved gradually out of practical linguistic as well as strategic needs of the China mission. However, the more one works with seventeenth-century materials and the more familiar one becomes with the collective and cohesive manner in which the Jesuits in China worked, the more compelling the evidence for these claims becomes.

RICCI'S POLICY OF ACCOMMODATION AND THE *FOUR BOOKS*

As is well known, Matteo Ricci (Li Ma-tou, *tzu* Hsi-t'ai) was not the first Jesuit missionary to begin working in China, but he was the chief architect of the Jesuit mission strategy there. His program was grounded on a policy of accommodation between Chinese and European cultures. This accommodation was to allow for the creation of a Chinese-Christian synthesis that consisted of blending social and moral elements from Chinese culture with Christian teachings. After an unsuccessful experiment with Buddhism, the Jesuits found that Confucianism had preceded Ricci to Macao and after his return to Europe published a fragmentary translation of the first part of the *Great Learning* in 1593. It appeared in the *Bibliotheca selecta* of the Jesuit Antonio Possevino (1559–1611).[2]

It was fundamental to Ricci's policy of accommodation that the Jesuits become highly versed not only in the spoken language of China but also in its literature. Therefore, the practical need of language instruction for the newly arrived Jesuits contributed to the initiation of the Jesuit translation project of the *Four Books*. It was in the context of teaching Chinese to the newly arrived Jesuit Francesco de Petris (Shih Chen-yu, 1562–1593) from December 1591 until November 1593 at Shaochou that Ricci began to translate the *Four Books* into Latin.[3] According-ing to Pasquale D'Elia, Ricci's translation of three of the *Four Books* — the *Great Learning*, the *Doctrine of the Mean*, and the *Analects* — was finished by 10 December 1593. It is said that Ricci finished the *Mencius* by 15 November of the following year and hoped to send a copy, sometime in 1595, to Claudio Aquaviva, the Jesuit General in Rome, but it is not known if this manuscript was ever sent. Certainly there is no record of its being preserved there today, and some scholars have concluded that it is lost.[4] Though Ricci's manuscript is said to have had many annotations, this writer believes that this is more a reflection of its working, in-progress nature than of its finished character. Such a characteristic would reinforce the conclusion that Ricci's translation was not lost but was used by later Jesuits as a Chinese language primer. As such, it was handed down from one student generation of Jesuits to the next, was probably improved, and was eventually incorporated into the published translations of the *Four Books*.[5]

THE JESUIT CHOICE OF A COMMENTARY ON THE *FOUR BOOKS*

The archaic language and antiquity of the allusions in the Confucian Classics made it necessary for the Chinese to use commentaries in order to comprehend these works fully. In the two millennia since the composition of the Classics, commentarial traditions had developed, each of which emphasized a particular philosophical outlook and interpretation. As the Jesuits from Ricci onward continued to work with and refine their translation of the *Four Books*, they faced a decision over which of these commentarial traditions to use.

The most orthodox commentary of the time was that of the Sung period Neo-Confucian Chu Hsi (1130–1200).[6] Since the early Ming, the commentarial interpretations of Chu Hsi and his school had officially dominated the examination system. It would perhaps have simplified their accommodative endeavor had the Jesuits been able to accept this commentarial tradition, but few could do so. Most, though not all, Jesuits in China, beginning with Ricci, found the interpretations of Sung Neo-Confucians to be filled with philosophic materialism, polytheism, or even atheism, which were irreconcilable with the proposed Confucian-Christian synthesis. Consequently, the Jesuits had to look elsewhere for a commentary. Happily for them, the late Ming period was marked by an eclectic cultural atmosphere in which the options for non-orthodox philosophies were more easily made than at other times in Chinese history.

In their search for a commentary appropriate for the Confucian-Christian synthesis, one may assume that the Jesuits experimented with several commentaries. They finally settled on one by Chang Chü-cheng (1525–1582).[7] The circumstances that had originally produced Chang's commentary were a near ideal Confucian blend of philosophy with the practical affairs of government. At the ascent of the Wan-li boy emperor in 1572 (r. 1573–1620), Chang successfully cultivated court forces to achieve the supreme scholar-official position of chief grand secretary. Out of his responsibility for the education of the young emperor, Chang composed his commentary on the *Four Books*. He wrote in a simplified or colloquial style *(chih-chieh)* that would be comprehensible to the ten-year-old emperor; hence, the title of his commentary became *Colloquial Commentary on the Four Books (Ssu-shu chih-chieh)*. This work was presented to the Wan-li emperor in 1573.[8]

The appeal of Chang's commentary for the Jesuits lay, in part, in this blending of philosophy and practical affairs. Though Chang fell temporarily into disgrace after his death in 1582, his name had been fully rehabilitated by the mid-seventeenth century. This rehabilitation was reflected in the republication of Chang's *Colloquial Commentary on the Four Books* in 1651 under the editorship of Wu Wei-yeh (1609–1672). The Jesuits' awareness of Chang's commentary was shown as early as 1668 in *Nouvelle relation de la Chine* by Jesuit Gabriel de Magalhães (Magaillans) (An Wen-ssu, 1610–1677). He drew from the commentaries of both Chu Hsi and Chang in making a translation-paraphrase of the opening passage of the *Great Learning* which included the Chinese text.[9] The date at which the Jesuits began using Chang's commentary can only be approximated. The first printed edition of his commentary (ca. 1574–84) is very rare, and it is unlikely the Jesuits had access to it. The next edition that can be dated is that of 1651, although Wu complains in his preface to it of the poor quality of earlier editions. Since the later known editions of 1672, 1677, and 1683 were too late to have been used by Magalhães writing in 1668, a tentative conclusion is that he was using the edition of 1651 and that the Jesuits became aware of Chang's commentary sometime between 1651 and 1668. This date would coincide with the Jesuit publication of the *Four Books*, which began in 1662.

As a former chief grand secretary whose name had been fully rehabilitated, Chang offered an authority and a status the Jesuits needed in order to support their Confucian-Christian synthesis. In addition, Chang was sometimes critical of the Sung Neo-Confucians, though his attitude as a whole is mixed and his criticisms are muted in the text of the commentary on the *Four Books*.[10] His commentary offered to the Jesuits an alternative interpretation to that of Chu Hsi, though in their need to discredit Chu Hsi's philosophy, the Jesuits exaggerated the differences between the two commentarial interpretations. A second feature of Chang's commentary that made it attractive to the Jesuits was a practical one: its simple colloquial style (for the boy emperor), as noted above. In their struggle with the difficult literary language of the Chinese, the Jesuits welcomed Chang's relative simplicity of language. One must stress the relative factor because Chu Hsi's commentary is also composed in a relatively simple literary style.

THE EARLY JESUIT TRANSLATIONS OF THE *FOUR BOOKS*

Ruggieri had been the first (in 1593) to publish a translation of a Confucian Classic into a European language, but this had been a very fragmentary treatment of the shortest Classic (*Great*

Learning). In 1662, the Jesuits published in *Sapientia Sinica* (Wisdom from China) a full Latin translation of the *Great Learning*. This woodblock edition was printed by the Jesuit mission house at Chiench'ang in Kiangsi province and dated 13 April 1662. It was a folio edition of ninety-three pages with the following contents: (1) a preface of one page, (2) a two-page life of Confucius, (3) a fourteen-page translation of the *Great Learning*, and (4) a translation of the first five parts of the *Analects* in seventy-six pages.[11] The translation of the segments of the latter two works is attributed to Inácio da Costa (Kuo Na-chüeh, 1603–1666), a Portuguese Jesuit who had been in China since 1634. However, this writer is convinced that any such attributions must not be regarded as individual but rather as the latest in a series of collaborative efforts involving a number of Jesuit predecessors. This conclusion is based upon the manner in which the Jesuit translations of the *Four Books* which appeared between 1593 and 1711 fit together as consecutive fragments of a whole as well as upon certain similarities of rendering among the various translations and upon the collective manner in which Jesuits labored in China. This can be seen in other Jesuit works on China where the authorship is frequently very fuzzy. For example, in a study of a parallel endeavor of seventeenth-century Jesuits composing maps of China, the scholar Boleslaw Szczesniak concludes that since Jesuits shared the same missionary goal in China, their efforts were marked by a teamwork in which individual authorship was subsumed to the greater cause of the mission.[12]

One link of continuity between the various Jesuit translations of the *Four Books* is provided by the editor of *Sapientia Sinica*, Prospero Intorcetta (Yin Tuo-tso, 1625–1696). A Sicilian who arrived in China in 1659, he proceeded to the Jesuit mission house at Chiench'ang.[13] A highly talented priest, he applied himself not only to the serious study of Chinese and the translation of the *Four Books* but also to administrative tasks, including the crucial role of Jesuit procurator to Europe. His work with the Confucian Classics resulted in a bilingual manuscript entitled "Lucubratio de tetrabiblio Confucii Sinice *Su Xu* dicto," which was a paraphrase translation into Latin of the Chinese text of the *Four Books*.[14] In 1686, the Jesuit Philippe Couplet

(Po Ying-li, 1622–1693) published a list of European-authored works in Chinese which included what seems to be a similar work by Intorcetta but with a different Latin title, "Confucii Philosophi sententiae in latinam linguam traductae."[15] What is especially significant about this bilingual manuscript of the *Four Books* is its Chinese title: *Hsi-wen ssu-shu chih-chieh* (A Western language colloquial commentary on the *Four Books*). Intorcetta's incorporation of the title of Chang's commentary on the *Four Books* is unlikely to be mere coincidence and indicates that the Jesuits probably were using Chang's commentary in the composition of *Sinarum scientia politico-moralis*, if not *Sapientia Sinica* as well, during the 1660s.

At the time of the publication of *Sapientia Sinica* in 1662, Intorcetta had been in China for only three years and would have been unable to have played a leading role in any translation effort involving the *Four Books*. However, the fact that he is designated as editor of *Sapientia Sinica* indicates he was actively assisting in the translation project and possibly being groomed by da Costa as a future translator. The strategic importance of the assignment given to Intorcetta is reinforced by the fact that from 1658 to 1661 da Costa occupied the authoritative position of vice-provincial of China.[16] Five years after the publication of *Sapientia Sinica*, the fruits of Intorcetta's work with the Classics were revealed in the publication of a Latin translation of the *Doctrine of the Mean*. Nevertheless, even allowing for a superior linguistic talent on Intorcetta's part, it is unlikely that eight years after arriving in China he would have been able single-handedly to produce the first European-language translation of this work. To write a paraphrase in manuscript for private circulation among the missioners, as Ricci had done, was one thing, but to publish and subject a literary work to the scrutiny of outsiders demands a great deal of confidence in the result. A poor translation not only would have reflected poorly upon Intorcetta but would have damaged the entire accommodative effort for the meeting of Chinese and European cultures that Ricci had first formulated. Therefore, it is likely that when Intorcetta's superiors selected him as Jesuit procurator, they felt the sort of confidence in this translation product that would have been engendered by a team effort.

The publication of the Jesuit translation of the *Doctrine of the Mean* was entitled *Sinarum scientia politico-moralis* (1667–69) and included a short preface by Intorcetta, a fifty-four-page bilingual (Latin-Chinese) text of the *Doctrine of the Mean*, and an eight-page biography of Confucius, which differed from the brief biography found in *Sapientia Sinica*.[17] On the opening pages of *Sinarum scientia politico-moralis*, one finds confirmation of the collective nature of this work's production. The names of seventeen Jesuits are listed as contributors, whether as author, moderators, or reviewers.[18] The author is listed as Intorcetta. Four Jesuit moderators are cited as giving formal approval: Inácio da Costa, Jacques le Faure (le Favre) (Liu Ti-wo, 1613–1675) of France, Matias da Maia (Maya) (Li Ma-ti, 1616–1677) of Portugal, and Feliciano Pacheco (Ch'eng Chi-li, 1622–1687) of Portugal. Twelve Jesuits are listed as having reviewed the work: António de Gouvea (Ho Ta-hua, 1592–1677) of Portugal, Pietro Canevari (Canevare) (Nieh Shih-tsung, 1596–1675) of Genoa, Francesco Brancati (Brancato) (P'an Kuo-kuang, 1607–1671) of Sicily, Giovanni Francesco de Ferrariis (Ferrari) (Li Fang-hsi, 1609–1671) of Piedmont, Humbert Augery (Hung Tu-Chen, 1618–1673) of France, Adrien Grelon (Greslon) (Nieh Chung-ch'ien, 1618–1696) of France, Jacques Motel (Mu Ti-wo, 1619–1692) of France, Giandomenico Gabiani (Pi Chia, 1623–1694) of Piedmont, Manuel Jorge (George) (Chang Ma-no, 1621–1677) of Portugal, Philippe Couplet of Belgium, François de Rougemont (Lu Erh-man, 1624–1676) of Belgium, and Christian Herdtrich (Herdtricht) (En Li-ko, 1625–1684) of Austria.

This list of participants in the compilation of *Sinarum scientia politico-moralis* coincides with the Jesuits who were expelled to Canton in September of 1665 as part of the anti-Christian movement led by Yang Kuang-hsien.[19] However, since da Costa died on 11 May 1666, and since it appears that not all the Jesuits on this list arrived in Canton by that time — de Ferrariis and le Faure may have arrived as late as 1668 [20] — it seems likely that the participation of these Jesuits consisted of long-term study and discussion of the translations and commentary of the *Four Books* rather than any concentrated period of consideration. This approach would have been consistent not only with the gradual evolution of the translation of the *Four Books*, which had been underway since the days of Ruggieri and Ricci, but also with the importance the Jesuits attached to the translation of the *Four Books* as part of their program of accommodation. At any rate, this Canton phase of the Jesuit translation project would have ended by 1671 when most of the exiled missionaries were able to leave Canton for a return to inland China or elsewhere.

The list of seventeen contributors in *Sinarum scientia politico-moralis* not only confirms the collective nature of the work's production but also supports the contention that *Sapientia Sinica*, *Sinarum scientia politico-moralis*, and *Confucius Sinarum philosophus* of 1687 all represent part of an interlinked and evolving translation project. The linkage is shown by the presence of certain names such as da Costa, who was listed as the primary author of *Sapientia Sinica*. When *Confucius Sinarum philosophus* was published at Paris two decades later, four names were listed on the title page as authors: Intorcetta, Herdtrich, Rougemont, and Couplet. All four of these names were among the *Sinarum scientia politico-moralis* contributors. In the same way that Intorcetta took a minor role in preparing *Sapientia Sinica* and a major role in preparing *Sinarum scientia politico-moralis* for production, Couplet took a minor role in the preparation of *Sinarum scientia politico-moralis* and a major role in producing *Confucius Sinarum philosophus*.

Sinarum scientia politico-moralis had a two-stage printing history. The first half of the *Doctrine of the Mean* was printed at Canton in 1667; the remainder was printed at Goa and dated 1 October 1669.[21] C. R. Boxer believes that the printer of both *Sapientia Sinica* and *Sinarum scientia politico-moralis* was a Chinese convert named Paul who traveled with Intorcetta from China to Goa and, after completing the printing of *Sinarum scientia politico-moralis* there, returned to China.[22] The dual publication sites are probably explained by Intorcetta's appointment as Jesuit procurator of the China mission and his trip to Rome in this capacity which occupied the years 1669–74. The procurator was charged with producing favorable publicity for the China mission in Europe and thereby eliciting monetary and material support from Europeans of substance as well as inspiring new recruits from Jesuit ranks to enlist in the mission. This campaign was to be conducted within the context of Ricci's accommodation policy, the Confucian-Christian synthesis of which represented a two-way formula for the intellectual assimilation of China by Europeans as well as for the assimilation of information about Europe by the Chinese. A European-language translation of the canonical *Four Books*, with their supreme importance to Chinese culture and society, admirably facilitated this sort of mission strategy. Like Couplet, who followed twelve years later as Jesuit procurator to Europe, Intorcetta was charged with the editorial task of seeing a partial translation of the *Four Books* through publication. His publicity effort received a boost at Paris when Melchisédec Thévenot chose to publish (1672) a French translation of *Sinarum scientia politico-moralis* in his famous collection of travel literature, *Relations de divers voyages curieux.*[23]

CULMINATION OF THE *FOUR BOOKS* TRANSLATION PROJECT IN *CONFUCIUS SINARUM PHILOSOPHUS*

The Jesuits continued to study the *Four Books* and to improve their translations. They arrived in China and began their study of Chinese using the more elementary segments of the *Four Books* as language primers. Later, the more difficult parts of these Classics served as advanced texts and provided scenarios for accommodative tactics. Consequently, the Jesuits of one student generation would successively become the teachers of the next. Through this practical application in language training, a text of translations of the *Four Books* was improved and passed down. The continual process of modification of the translation is apparent in a comparison of the opening line of the *Great Learning* in *Sapientia Sinica* with its counterpart in *Confucius Sinarum philosophus*. In *Sapientia Sinica*, "ta hsüeh chih tao tsai ming ming-te" is rendered: "The great men's principle of knowing consists in illuminating by virtues the spiritual power given by Heaven, namely, the soul, so that it [the soul] can return to its original clarity which the appetites had beclouded." (*Magnorum* virorum *sciendi institutum consistit in illuminando* virtutibus *spiritualem potentiam* a coelo inditam, nempe, Animam, ut haec redire possit ad originalē[m] claritatem, quam appetitus animales obnubilaverant.)[24]By contrast, the translation of the same sentence published twenty-five years later by the Jesuits shows the effects of reworking the refinement: "And so indeed, the leading men's great principle of knowing consists in polishing or cultivating the rational nature given by heaven, so that this nature, to be sure, can return to its original clarity as if to a very clear mirror, with the stains of debased appetites wiped away." ([1]Magnum adeoque virorum Principum [2]sciendi [3]institutum [4]consistit in [5]expoliendo, seu excolendo [6]rationalem [7]naturam a coelo inditam; ut scilicet haec, ceu limpidissimum speculum, abstersis pravorum appetituum maculis, ad pristinam claritatem suam redire possit).[25]

An important difference between the two Jesuit renderings was the change from "illuminating by virtues the spiritual power" to "polishing or cultivating the rational nature." Though the *Confucius Sinarum philosophus* rendering is more precise than the earlier *Sapientia Sinica* translation, it is not necessarily an improvement in the translation of *ming-te,* which most modern translators render as "illuminated virtue." Motives for emending the translation were not entirely due to an improved understanding of the Chinese text. A more likely reason for this particular change stemmed from the Jesuit program of accommodation and the attempt to make the Confucian Classics meld harmoniously with the role they had been assigned in the Confucian-Christian synthesis. The rendering of *ming-te* as "polishing or cultivating the rational nature" fits more aptly with an attempt to see China as possessing a natural religion whose morality complements Christianity, but which lacks the more spiritual component of revelation. The *Sapientia Sinica* rendering of "illuminating by virtues the spiritual power," while not directly contradicting the role ascribed to Confucianism in its accommodative synthesis with Christianity, does raise difficult questions by transcending the limits of natural religion through the reference to "spiritual power." Though the Jesuits in China may have been able to resolve such apparent discrepancies, a European audience less familiar with Chinese culture and without access to the Chinese text would not. In short, the refinements of the Latin translation of the *Four Books* found in *Confucius Sinarum philosophus* were important to the promotion of the Jesuit program of accommodation in Europe.

Confucius Sinarum philosophus was an impressive folio of 412 pages, published at Paris in 1687 under the editorial direction of Couplet. It was bound together with his *Tabula chronologica Monarchiae Sinicae* in 126 pages, which had been printed in the previous year by the same printer, Daniel Horthemels. *Confucius Sinarum philosophus* contained a long "Proemialis Declaratio" (Introductory Exposition) and complete translations of the *Great Learning*, the *Doctrine of the Mean*, and the *Analects*, though not of the *Mencius* which was promised by Couplet for a later date. It is not known whether Couplet personally carried the manuscript of *Confucius Sinarum philosophus* with him to Europe or whether it was already there when he arrived with the task of publication before him. Of the four names that appear on the title page, Intorcetta had been involved with both *Sapientia Sinica* and *Sinarum scientia politico-moralis*, while Herdtrich, Rougemont, and Couplet had formally reviewed *Sinarum scientia politico-moralis* in Canton prior to its publication; Herdtrich remained in Canton and died there in 1684. These four names constitute merely the *primary* contributors. It is this writer's contention that a complete list of contributors would begin chronologically with Ruggieri and Ricci and include most of the one-hundred-plus Jesuits who participated in the China mission in the intervening century between the time of Ricci and the publication of *Confucius Sinarum philosophus*.

Couplet's visit to Europe in the years 1682–92 stirred a great deal of interest. He was received by both Pope Alexander VII in Rome and Louis XIV at Versailles. With his Chinese companion, clothing, and accouterments, Couplet appears to have launched a rage for *chinoiserie* in France. He corresponded with European savants and helped launch the important French Jesuit mission to China of 1685 sponsored by the French king and the Académie des Sciences. (See Witek's essay, chapter 3 this volume.) While in Paris, Couplet arranged for the publication of *Confucius Sinarum philosophus*. Consequently, this work was published amid the publicity Couplet's European visit had engendered, and its publication was eagerly awaited by European scholars. Although it would not be the last fruit of the seventeenth-century Jesuit translation project of the *Four Books*, it was in an important sense a culmination of Ricci's policy of accommodation, which promoted Confucius and his philosophy as the synthesizing medium.

The elevation of Confucius's name to the main title of the work, while reducing "scientia Sinensis" (learning of China) to the subtitle, reflects the Jesuits' continuing evolution and refinement of Ricci's policy of accommodation to its logical conclusion. Confucius's morality, obvious rationality, and vague spirituality made his philosophy eminently blendable with the explicit spirituality of Christianity. When Ricci began formulating his synthesis in the late 1500s, China's cultural climate was in a remarkably creative and tolerant phase. With the intervening chaos of dynastic decline and transition from the Ming to Ch'ing, the situation one century later had changed, and the Jesuits were driven to seek new allies. While Ricci had cultivated the friendship and support of the literati class, Jesuits in the late 1600s began focusing more and more on the Chinese throne. The emperor's political power provided the Jesuits with protection not only in China but also in Europe where Jesuit opponents were being increasingly fomented by the Rites and Term Controversy. When the Jesuit Joachim Bouvet (Po Chin, 1656–1730) traveled to Europe in 1697–98, he acted unlike previous Jesuit procurators in several ways. He was traveling at the command of a Chinese emperor and was no longer interested in expanding and elaborating the Jesuit translations of the *Four Books* but instead published a famous panegyric on the K'ang-hsi emperor (r. 1662–1722).[26]

It is noteworthy that the seventeenth-century Jesuit translation project of the *Four Books* was almost entirely associated with south China mission centers. Unlike Jesuits such as Johann Adam Schall von Bell (T'ang Jo-wang, 1592–1666) and Bouvet, whose survival depended upon cultivating the imperial court in Peking, those Jesuits who translated the *Four Books* were almost exclusively located in the provinces, where cultivation of intellectual and social ties with the literati was fundamental. Although Ricci spent the last nine years of his life at the court in Peking, the recluse nature of the Wan-li emperor made Ricci's ties with scholar-officials far more important than they were to be for Schall and Bouvet who were in close and intimate contact with the early Ch'ing emperors. The increasing orientation of the Jesuits in the late seventeenth century toward the imperial court and away from the provinces, probably contributed to the shift in accommodative tactics and to the de-emphasis of the *Four Books* translation project.

THE LAST FRUIT OF THE SEVENTEENTH-CENTURY
JESUIT TRANSLATION PROJECT

The collaborative Jesuit effort of translating the *Four Books* did not end with Couplet and *Confucius Sinarum philosophus*. The translation of the *Mencius*, which Couplet had promised to European readers in 1687, was finally realized in 1711 with its publication by the Jesuit François Noël (Wei Fang-chi, 1651–1729). Noël arrived in Macao in 1685 and worked at mission centers primarily in the Kiangsi province — Nanchang, Chien-ch'ang, and Nanfeng.[27] We can conclude from certain of Noël's dated manuscripts that he probably finished his translations of the Chinese Classics by 1700.[28] During the years 1702–7, he traveled to Europe as Jesuit procurator and possibly attempted to have his translations of the Confucian Classics published. After a brief return to China, he was back in Rome in 1708. He is said to have lived some time in Prague in order to see his translations through publication in 1711.[29] Unsuccessful in his attempt to return to China, he returned eventually to his home province where he died at Lille in 1729.

It is probable that Noël used the previous Jesuit translations as the basis for his *Sinensis Imperii libri classici sex*.[30] This work includes the Classics published in *Confucius Sinarum philosophus*, as well as the *Mencius* and two short works of near-classical status: the *Book of Filial Piety (Hsiao ching)* and the *Learning for Minors (Hsiao hsüeh)*. Nevertheless, a comparison of *Confucius Sinarum philosophus* with Noël's translations of the *Four Books* reveals some substantial differences deriving from uses of different commentaries.

Whereas the earlier Jesuits had spurned Chu Hsi's commentary on the *Four Books* because of the polytheistic and materialistic elements in Chu's philosophy, Noël followed Chu Hsi's commentary closely in making his translation, in addition to using Chang's commentary. The differences are apparent from the outset. For example, *Confucius Sinarum philosophus* translators rendered *"ta hsüeh"* as *"Magna Scientia"* (Great Knowledge) or "magnum virorum Principum sciendi institutum" (the leading men's great principle of knowing). By contrast, Noël rendered *"ta hsüeh"* as *"adultorum doctrina"* (the learning of adults).[31] These differences of interpretation reflect careful reflection as well as a familiarity with the Chinese commentarial tradition. In the case of *ta hsüeh,* more ancient commentators interpreted *ta* as *"t'ai"* (great) in the sense of excellence of government and highest principles. This view is recorded in the oldest extant commentary on this Classic by the well-known scholar Cheng Hsüan (*tzu* K'ang-ch'eng, d. ca. A.D. 200) of the late Han and was elaborated and expanded upon by K'ung Ying-ta (A.D. 574–648) early in the seventh century.[32] Later, Chu Hsi reinterpreted *ta hsüeh* to mean "the learning of adults," as opposed to *hsiao hsüeh* (the learning of children), which is the name of another work of near-classical status that was included by Noël in his work of translations.

Not only did the *Confucius Sinarum philosophus* translators oppose using Chu Hsi's commentary on the *Four Books* because of his philosophy, but it is quite possible to argue that they preferred rendering *ta hsüeh* as "the learning of great men" because it complemented their accommodative approach better than "the learning of adults." The Jesuits admired the learning of Chinese antiquity, which they noted contained a possibly monotheistic equivalent in Lord on High (*Shang-ti*). However, they echoed a common criticism of orthodox Chinese literati, namely, that intellectual and moral degeneration had set in since antiquity and had corrupted the ancient tradition. The preference for antiquity would reinforce the Jesuits' rejection of the moderns' (i.e., the school of Chu Hsi) reinterpretation of *ta hsüeh.* The reference to "great men" was clearly associated in China with antiquity, whereas the term "adults" had a more contemporary connotation.

How then does one explain Noël's rejection of this line of earlier Jesuit reasoning and his use of Chu Hsi's commentary?

It must be viewed, it would seem, in the context of late seven-teenth-century changes in Jesuit accommodation discussed above. Changes in the intellectual climate in China had made the literati less open to the sort of persuasion Ricci had built into his accommodation formula. With the death of literati con-verts of the stature of Li Chih-tsao (1565–1630) and Hsü Kuang-ch'i (1562–1633) and with the failure to convert new literati of like stature after the ascent of the Manchus in 1644, the Jesuits were increasingly dependent upon imperial support. This was forthcoming under the Shun-chih (r. 1644–1661) and K'ang-hsi emperors. In their search for new forms of persuasion, a new group of Jesuits emerged who worked at the Peking court close to the emperor rather than in the south China prov-inces in intimate association with the literati, and this new group began to make significant changes in the content of Ricci's accommodation formula.

For the literati class, the *Four Books* were works of pervasive pedagogical, moral, ideological, and social significance; and a deep involvement with them was prerequisite for an aspiring scholar-official. For the Chinese emperors, the *Four Books* com-manded an important but far less consuming significance. As the Jesuits gradually shifted the primary focus of their accom-modation strategy in China from the literati to the imperial court, this produced a shift in the content of their Chinese-Christian synthesis. The *Four Books* were displaced by other Classics and by works extolling the person of the emperor and the excellence of the Chinese imperial system of government, both of which became highly prominent themes in the eighteenth-century Sinophilia of the European Enlightenment.

Preeminent as a creative thinker among this new group of Jesuits was Bouvet, who, instead of exalting Confucius, elevated the K'ang-hsi emperor in his *Portrait historique* (1697). Instead of emphasizing the translation of the Confucian *Four Books*, he focused his scholarly research on the Classic *Book of Changes (I Ching)* as the supreme embodiment of Chinese antiquity. Appealing to the K'ang-hsi emperor's interest in mathematics, he stressed the numerical qualities of the diagrams of the *Book of Changes*. He believed that Chinese was a hieroglyphic script whose symbols contained all the secrets of Christianity.

Consequently, he was more interested in interpreting the Chinese Classics symbolically than historically.[33] A few highly talented Jesuits were enthusiastic about his approach, but most Jesuits found these *"ykingnistes"* (*I-ching*-ists, in the sense of followers of the *Book of Changes*) or "Figurist" interpretations extreme.

In addition, most Jesuits found the elevation of Chinese antiquity at odds with the Biblical priority assigned to the Israelites. Nevertheless, as the most creative proponents of accommodation in the late seventeenth century, the Figurists became pacesetters who provoked reactions among their confreres. This author believes that Noël's shift from the Jesuits' prior use of Chang's commentary on the *Four Books* to that of Chu Hsi is an example of one reaction. It is interesting, though perplexing, to note that the Jesuit historian Louis Pfister calls Noël "one of the most zealous defenders of the system adopted by certain missionaries which consisted of finding in the ancient Chinese books the principal truths of Christianity."[34] This is a reference to Figurism, though Noël's association with Figurism appears to have been only peripheral. Even so, this association would help explain his differences with the approach of earlier Jesuit translators of the *Four Books*, though it does not explain why he adopted the most orthodox and officially sanctioned commentary on the *Four Books* then available, namely, that of Chu Hsi.

The fact that Jesuit accommodation was no longer focused on the *Four Books* is confirmed by the unenthusiastic response that greeted the publication of Noël's remarkable translation effort.[35] Unlike the publicity generated by Couplet's visit to Europe and the heightened sense of expectation that greeted the publication of *Confucius Sinarum philosophus*, the appearance of Noël's work was little noted by the powerful forces of Jesuit publicists in Europe. Also, unlike *Confucius Sinarum philosophus*, which is today widely available in even the smaller collections of seventeenth-century books, Noël's work is more difficult to locate. So ended the seventeenth-century Jesuit translation project of the *Four Books* — not by the loud and controversial debates associated with the peaking Rites and Term Controversy, but by a scholarly fading into obscurity.

SUMMARY

In summary, then, this writer believes that the seventeenth-century Jesuit translation project of the *Four Books* emerged both out of Ricci's accommodative mission strategy for forging a Confucian-Christian synthesis and out of the associated practical need for newly arrived Jesuits in China to learn the difficult Chinese written language with a suitably simple body of literary texts. This comprehensive strategy helps to explain the continuity of effort that seventeenth-century Jesuits in China expended in translating the *Four Books*. This continuity can be documented by the interlinkage of names of certain translators and editors among the various published editions of The *Four Books*. Ricci's accommodation formula involved a two-way transfer of knowledge — from China to Europe as well as from Europe to China — and the fulfillment of this strategy involved the publication of the *Four Books* in Latin editions and sometimes French translation in Europe. Because of a shift in mission tactics, the Jesuit translation project of the *Four Books* began to end prematurely and prior to its full realization in the publication of all the *Four Books*. As the Jesuit mission shifted its focus from the south China provinces with a cultivation of the literati toward the Peking court with a cultivation of the emperor, the Jesuits began to give less attention to literati concerns, such as the *Four Books,* and more attention to the concerns of the emperor, such as the *Book of Changes* and imperial politics.

NOTES

1. See Evelyn Sakakida Rawski, *Education and Popular Literacy in Ch'ing China* (Ann Arbor, 1979) 47–48.

2. See his *Bibliotheca selecta qua agitur de ratione studiorum in historia, in disciplinis, in salute omnium procuranda* (Rome, 1593), liber ix, p. 583. This work is treated in an article by Knud Lundbaek, "The First Translation from a Confucian Classic in Europe," *China Mission Studies (1550–1800) Bulletin* 1 (1979):1–11.

3. Pasquale M. D'Elia, S.J., ed., *Fonti Ricciane: documenti originali concernenti Matteo Ricci e la storia delle prime relazioni tra l'Europa e la Cina 1579–1615,* 3 vols. (Rome, 1942–1949), 2:33.

4. For one example, see the German sinologist Otto Franke, "Das chinesische Geistesleben im 16. Jahrhundert und die Anfänge der Jesuiten-Mission," *Orientalistische Literaturzeitung* 41 (1938):480.

5. Several years after arriving independently at this conclusion on the Ricci manuscript, the present writer found his view confirmed by Father D'Elia, who several decades before had written on the great probability that Ricci's manuscript-translation of the *Four Books* was the primary basis and nucleus of the work *Confucius Sinarum philosophus*, which was published by the Jesuits at Paris in 1687. See D'Elia, *Fonti Ricciane*, 2:33. This mutual arrival at the same conclusion is due not so much to any remarkable coincidence as to the logical obviousness of such a conclusion to one familiar with the material. This conclusion is treated in its broader seventeenth-century context in the present writer's *Curious Land: Jesuit Accommodation and the Origins of Sinology* (Stuttgart, 1985).

6. See Chu Hsi, *Ssu-shu chi-chu* (Collected commentary on the *Four Books*) (reprint edition, Taipei, 1969).

7. The Jesuits' use of Chang's commentary on the *Four Books* has been treated in complementary articles: Knud Lundbaek, "Chief Grand Secretary Chang Chü-cheng and the Early China Jesuits" and David E. Mungello, "The Jesuits' Use of Chang Chü-cheng's Commentary in Their Translation of the Confucian *Four Books* (1687)," *China Mission Studies (1550–1800) Bulletin* 3 (1981):2–11, 12–22, respectively.

8. Although *A Descriptive Catalogue of Rare Chinese Books in the Library of Congress*, compiled by Wang Chung-min and edited by T. L. Yuan, 2 vols. (Washington, D.C., 1957), 1:46, refers to this edition of *Ssu-shu chih-chieh* as a 1573 edition, an unsigned letter of 19 November 1981 to Mr. Lundbaek from the Chung-kuo kuo-chia t'u-shu-kuan (National Library of China) of Peking stated that although this work was presented to the Wan-li emperor in 1573, it is difficult to state exactly when it was printed. The author of the unsigned letter estimated that, for reasons of style of woodblock characters and honorary titles used in referring to Chang, the date of printing must have been between 1574 and 1584.

9. Gabriel de Magalhães (Magaillans), *Nouvelle relation de la Chine* (Paris, 1690). This work was composed in 1668 and published in France twenty-two years later.

10. For a brief discussion of Chang's criticism of Sung Neo-Confucianism, see Robert B. Crawford, "Chang Chü-cheng's Confucian Legalism," in *Self and Society in Ming Thought*, ed. Wm. Theodore de Bary (New York, 1970), 399.

11. See Henri Cordier, *Bibliotheca Sinica*, 5 vols. (Paris, 1905–1906), 2:col. 1386, or the same material in his *L'Imprimerie sino-européenne en Chine* (Paris, 1891), 16–17. See also Robert Streit, O.M.I. and others,

Bibliotheca Missionum, 28 vols. (Rome, 1916–1971), 5:850, 965;
Carlos Sommervogel, S.J., *Bibliothèque de la Compagnie de Jésus,* 12
vols. (Brussels, 1890–1932), 4:641–42; C. R. Boxer, "Some Sino-European Xylographic Works, 1662–1718." *Journal of the Royal Asiatic Society of Great Britain and Ireland* (April 1947):199, 202. According to
Cordier, there is a copy of the *Sapientia Sinica* in the British Library,
London, and a partial copy in the Bibliothèque Nationale, Paris.

12. See his "The Seventeenth-Century Maps of China: An Inquiry
into the Compilations of European Cartographers," *Imago Mundi* 13
(1956):130–31. Szczesniak notes that the influential book *De Christiana expeditione apud Sinas* (1615) was for many years regarded as
the work of the Jesuit Nicolas Trigault (Chin Ssu-piao, 1577–1628)
until twentieth-century research of the Jesuits D'Elia and Pietro Tacchi
Venturi revealed the primary contribution of Ricci. Szczesniak also
cites other examples of the collaborative nature of Jesuit scholarship,
such as the contribution of twenty-seven missionary scholars to the
four-volume *Description de la Chine* (1735) by the Jesuit Jean-Baptiste
Du Halde (1674–1743). Szczesniak believes that the *Novus Atlas Sinensis* (1655) of Martino Martini (1614–1661) was based upon the research of other missionaries. The Jesuit scholar Henri Bernard-Maitre
also believed that Martini's *Atlas* represented the completion of the
earlier work of Trigault and Ricci. See Bernard-Maitre, "Les Étapes de
la cartographie scientifique pour la Chine et les pays voisins depuis
le XVIe jusqu' à la fin du XVIIIe siècle," *Monumenta Serica* 1
(1936):446. In this same vein, Szczesniak concludes that the Jesuit
translation of the *Four Books* in *Confucius Sinarum philosophus*
(1687) was the result of teamwork. For more on these cumulative
and collaborative efforts of the Jesuits, see Theodore N. Foss's essay
(chapter 8) in this present volume.

13. Joseph Dehergne, S.J., *Répertoire des Jésuites de Chine de 1552
à 1800* (Rome, 1973), 129.

14. Carlos Sommervogel says this manuscript was deposited at
Rome; he cites as his source of information a manuscript ("MS. R.")
by the Jesuit (Giandomenico?) Gabiani. See Sommervogel, *Bibliothèque,* 4:643. See also Louis Pfister, S.J., *Notices biographiques et
bibliographiques sur les Jésuites de l'ancienne mission de Chine,
1552–1773,* 2 vols. Variétés sinologiques, nos. 59 and 60 (Shanghai,
1932–1934), 1:328.

15. Henri Bernard-Maitre, S.J., "Les Adaptations chinoises d'ouvrages
européens. Bibliographie chronologique depuis la venue des Portugais
à Canton jusqu' à la mission française de Pékin 1514–1688," *Monumenta
Serica* 10 (1945):55.

16. Dehergne, *Répertoire,* 65.

17. Original copies of *Sinarum scientia politico-moralis* are almost
as rare as *Sapienta Sinica.* Cordier claims that copies are preserved

in the Bibliothèque Nationale, Paris; Österreichische Nationalsbib-
liothek, Vienna; Biblioteca Nazionale, Palermo; a damaged copy in
the Staatsbibliothek, Munich; and a partial copy in the former Jesuit
college library at Siccawei [Zikawei] in Shanghai. See his *Bibliotheca
Sinica*, 2:col. 1387–88. Paul Pelliot located copies of *Sinarum scientia
politico-moralis* in the collections of the School of Oriental and African Studies, London, and in the Biblioteca Vaticana (fonds Rossi, Ros-
siani stampati XV, 422). See his "La *Brevis Relatio*," *T'oung Pao* 23
(1924):356. Boxer found a copy in the National Library of China,
Peking. See his "Sino-European Xylographic Works," 202.

18. See Cordier, *L'Imprimerie*, 17–18 or *Bibliotheca Sinica*, 2:col.
1387.

19. Dehergne, *Répertoire*, 347.

20. Ibid., 71, 147.

21. Cordier, *L'Imprimerie*, 17–29 or *Bibliotheca Sinica*, 2:col. 1387–
93; Sommervogel, *Bibliothèque*, 4:641–42; Streit, *Bibliotheca Missionum*, 5:850; Boxer, "Sino-European Xylographic Works." 202. Both
Cordier and Boxer reproduce the title page of *Sinarum scientia
politico-moralis*, and Cordier reproduces in addition a second page
from the work.

22. Boxer, "Sino-European Xylographic Works," 199.

23. See his *Relations*, 4 vols. in 2 (Paris 1663–1672), 4:1–24; 2
vols. (reprint edition, Paris, 1696), 2:349–74.

24. da Costa-Intorcetta, *Sapientia Sinica*, 1. Italics were used by the
Jesuit editors to indicate original text as opposed to the translators'
commentary/explication. With respect to "originalē," the macron over
the ē makes it the equivalent of *em* (originalem), a common method
of spelling in the seventeenth century.

25. Philippe Couplet and others, eds. *Confucius Sinarum
philosophus sive scientia Sinensis latine exposita* (Paris, 1687), book
1, p. 1. For assistance in translating certain Latin passages, the present
writer would like to express a debt of gratitude to John P. Murphy,
S.J., associate professor of Classical Studies at Loyola University of
Chicago.

26. See his *Portrait historique de l'empereur de la Chine* (Paris,
1697), 264 pp., 12°.

27. Dehergne, *Répertoire*, 186; Pfister, *Notices*, 1:415.

28. According to Pfister, ibid., 1:417, the manuscripts of Noël's trans-
lations of the *Meng-tzu* and *Chung yung* are preserved at the National
Library in Brussels, MSS. 1930, 1931. The manuscripts contain Chinese
characters and Latin translation and are dated 1700 at Nanan in China.
According to Cordier, a manuscript of Noël's "Exercises de traduction
de la langue chinoise en langue latine par le Jésuite Noël, ou . . . Liber
Sententiarum," Nanchang, 1700, 3 in-4, is preserved at the St.
Petersburg (Leningrad) Library. Cordier, *Bibliotheca Sinica*, 2:col. 1395.

29. Pfister, *Notices,* 1:416.

30. François Noël, S.J., *Sinensis Imperii libri classici sex* (Prague, 1711). This magnum opus was published by the Charles-Ferdinand University ("typis Universitatis Carolo-Ferdinandeae"). See David E. Mungello, "The First Complete Translation of the Confucian *Four Books* in the West," in *Chi-nien Li Ma-tou lai hua ssu-pai chou-nien Chung-Hsi wen-hua chiao-liu kuo-chi hsüeh-shu hui-i lun wen-chi* (Collected essays of the international symposium [Fu Jen University] on Chinese-Western cultural interchange in commemoration of the 400th anniversary of the arrival of Matteo Ricci, S.J. in China), ed. Lo Kuang (Taipei, 1983), 515–39.

31. Couplet and others, *Confucius Sinarum philosophus, Ta hsüeh,* 1; and Noël, *Libri classici sex,* 10.

32. James Legge, ed. and trans., *The Chinese Classics,* 5 vols. (Oxford, 1893–1895), 1:14, 355.

33. Claudia von Collani, *Die Figuristen in der Chinamission* (Frankfurt am Main, 1981), 20, 41–42.

34. Pfister, *Notices,* 1:516.

35. Ibid., 417. Pfister gives high praise to the quality of Noël's translations, with the exception that, following Jean-Pierre Abel Rémusat, he criticizes Noël's excessive explanatory elaborations which are inserted into the text and which destroy the originally concise character of the Classics. See the two works by Rémusat, *Mélanges asiatiques* in-8°, 2 vols. (Paris, 1825–1826), 2:300 and *Noveaux mélanges asiatiques* in-8°, 2 vols. (Paris 1829), 2:128.

Glossary of Chinese Terms

Ai Ju-lüeh	艾儒略 (T. Ssu-chi 思及)
An-hui	安徽
An Wen-ssu	安文思
Canton (Kuang-chou)	廣州
Chahar	察哈爾
Chala	柵欄 (Cha-la-erh 柵欄兒)
Ch'an	禪
Chang Chü-cheng	張居正
Chang Huang	章潢
Chang Hung	張宏
Chang Ma-no	張瑪諾
Chang P'eng-ko	張鵬翮
Chang T'ing-yü	張廷玉
Ch'ang-ning	常寧
Chao Ch'ang	趙昌
Chao-ch'ing	肇慶
Chao Chiung	趙璚
Chao I	趙翼
Chao Nan-hsing	趙南星
Chao Tso	趙左
Chechiang	浙江
Chekiang (see Chechiang)	
Chen-shih she	眞實社
Ch'en Yüan	陳垣
cheng-chiao	正教
Cheng Ho	鄭和
Cheng Hsüan	鄭玄 (T. K'ang-ch'eng 康成)
Cheng Ta-yü	奠大郁
Cheng-te	正德
ch'eng	誠
Ch'eng Chi-li	成際理
Ch'eng-Chu	程朱
Ch'eng-shih Mo-yüan	程氏墨苑
Ch'eng Ta-yüeh	程大約
Chi-jen shih-p'ien	畸人十篇
Chi-lin	吉林
ch'i	氣

Chia-ching	嘉靖
Chiang-nan	江南
Chiang Shao-shu	姜紹書
Chianghsi	江西
Chiangsi (see Chiang-hsi)	
Chiang-su	江蘇
Chiao Hung	焦竑
Chiao Ping-chen	焦秉貞
Chiao-yu lun	交友論
Chien-an	建安
Chiench'ang	建昌
Ch'ien Ku	錢穀
Ch'ien-lung	乾隆
chih	楨
"*chih-chieh*"	直解
Chih-fang wai-chi	職方外紀
chih-hsien	知縣
"*chih-jen*"	至人
"*chih-jen wu chi*"	至人無己
chih-li	直隸
Chin Hung	金鉉
chin-shih	進士
ching-ch'i	精氣
Ching-hai	青海
Ching-kuo hsiung-lüeh	經國雄略
"*Ching-shih*"	經世
Ching-shih shih-yung pien	經世實用編
Ching-te chen	景德鎮
Ch'ing	清
Ch'ing-ting ho-yüan chi-lüeh	欽定河源記
Chou Tzu-yü	周子愚
chu	主
Chu Ch'ang-lo	朱常洛
Chu Hsi	朱熹
Chu-hung	袾宏
Chu Shih-lu	祝世祿
Chu Ssu-pen	朱思本
Chu To-chieh	朱多㸅
Chu Yu-lang	朱由榔
Ch'ü-pien	蘧編
chüan	卷
Ch'üan-chou	泉州

Chuang-tzu	莊子
Chun-ko-erh	准格爾
Chün-ch'i t'u-shuo	軍器圖說
"*Chung-hsüeh wei ti, hsi-hsüeh wei yung*"	中學爲體，西學爲用
Chung-hua	中華
Chung-kuo	中國
Chung Ming-jen	鐘銘 (or 鳴)仁 (T. Nien-chiang 念江)
Chung-yung	中庸
Ch'ung-chen	崇禎
En Li-ko	恩理格
Erh-shih wu-yen	二十五言
Fan Chung-yen	范仲淹
Fang I-chih	方以智
Fang-sheng hui	放生會
Fang-shih mo-p'u	方氏墨譜
Feng Tsung-wu	馮從吾
Feng Ying-ching	馮應京
Fo-lan-chi	佛郎機
Foochow (see Fu-chou)	
Fuchien	福建
Fu-ch'ing	福清
Fu-chou	福州
Fukien (see Fuchien)	
Hai-nan	海南
Han	漢
Han-lin	翰林
Hang-chou	杭州
Hangchow (see Hang-chou)	
Hei-lung chiang	黑龍江
Ho Kuo-tsung	何國宗
Ho Kuo-tung	何國棟
Honan	河南
Ho-pei	河北
Ho-shou	赫壽
Ho Ta-hua	何大化
hsi-chiao	西教
hsi-hsüeh	西學
Hsi-hsüeh shih-chieh chu-chieh	西學十誡註解
Hsi-kuo chi-fa	西國記法
Hsinan	西南
Hsi-ning	西寧
Hsi-wen ssu-shu chih-chieh	西文四書直解

Hsiao-ching	孝經
Hsiao-hsüeh	小學
Hsieh Shih-ch'en	謝時臣
hsieh-shuo	邪說
Hsien-ch'ü yüan	閑閑園
Hsing-li hsüeh	性理學
Hsiung T'ing-pi	熊廷弼
Hsü Kuang-ch'i	徐光啟
Hu-kuang	湖廣
Hu-nan	湖南
Hu-pei	湖北
Hua-ta	畫答
Huang Ching-fang	黃景昉
Huang-ch'ao i-t'ung yü-ti ch'üan-t'u	皇朝壹統輿地全圖
Huang Hui	黃輝
Huang Hung-en	黃洪恩 (see San-huai)
Huang Kung-wang	黃公望
Huang Lin	黃鏻
Huang-yü ch'üan lan-t'u	皇輿全覽圖
hun	魂
hung-mao i	紅毛夷
Hung Tu-chen	洪度貞
Hung-wu	洪武
i	異
I-ching	易經
i-jen	異人
"*I-tien pu-tso*"	一點不錯
Jehol	熱河
jen	仁
Jen Jen-fa	任仁發
ju	儒
Kan-su	甘肅
Kao P'an-lung	高攀龍
K'ang-hsi	康熙
Keng chih-t'u	耕織圖
Kiangsi (see Chianghsi)	
Ku Ch'i-yüan	顧起元
Ku-chin hsing-sheng chih t'u	古今形勝之圖
Ku-chin t'u-shu chi-ch'eng	古今圖書集成
Ku Hsien-ch'eng	顧憲成
Kuan-yin	觀音
Kuanghsi	廣西

Kuangsi (see Kuanghsi)	
Kuangtung	廣東
Kuang-yang tsa-chi	廣陽雜記
Kuang-yü t'u	廣輿圖
kuei	鬼
Kuei-chou	貴州
Kuei-p'ing	桂平
K'un-yü ch'üan-t'u	坤輿全圖
K'un-yü wan-kuo ch'üan-t'u	坤輿萬國全圖
kung-an	公案
K'ung Ying-ta	孔穎達
Kuo Na-chüeh	郭納爵
Kuo Ying-p'ing	郭應聘
Lan-ch'i	蘭谿
Lang-po-kao	浪白滘
Lang Shih-ning	郎世寧
Lao-tzu	老子
Lei-pien ku-chin shih-chien ku-shih ta-fang	類編古今史鑑故事大方
"*leng-jan-te shen-chih*"	冷然得深旨
li	里
li	理
Li Chih	李贄
Li Chih-tsao	李之藻 (T. Wo-ts'un 我存)
Li Fang-hsi	李方西
Li Ma-ti	利馬弟
Li Ma-tou	利馬竇 (T. Hsi-t'ai 西泰)
Li-pu	禮部
Liao-ning	遼寧
Liao-tung	遼東
Liu Chi-wen	劉繼文
Liu Hsien-t'ing	劉獻廷
Liu Ti-wo	劉迪我
Lo-ch'a	羅刹
Lo Hung-hsien	羅洪先
Lo-ma	羅馬
Lo Ming-chien	羅明堅 (T. Fu-ch'u 復初)
Lu Erh-man	魯日滿
Lun-fei tsou-ts'ao	綸扉奏草
Lun-yü	論語
Lung-ch'ing	隆慶
Man Han ho-pi Ch'ing nei-fu i-t'ung yü-ti pi-t'u	滿漢合璧清內府一統輿地秘圖
Meng-tzu	孟子

Ming	明
Ming-shih	明史
ming-te	明德
Mo-tzu	墨子
Mu Ti-wo	穆廸我
Nanchang	南昌
Nanchihli	南直隸
Nan-ching	南京
Nanfeng	南豐
Nanking (see Nan-ching)	
Nan-t'ang	南堂
Nei-wu fu	內務府
Nieh Chung-ch'ien	聶仲遷
Nieh Shih-tsung	聶石宗
Ningpo	寧波
Nung-cheng ch'üan-shu	農政全書
O-lo-ssu	俄羅斯
P'an Kuo-kuang	潘國光
Peichihli	北直隸
Pei-ching	北京
Pei-ho	北河
Peking (see Pei-ching)	
Pei-t'ang	北堂
Pi Chia	畢嘉
Pi Mao-k'ang	畢懋康
p'i-hsieh yün-tung	闢邪運動
Po Chin	白晉
"po-wen yu tao-shu chih jen"	愽文有道術之人
Po Ying-li	柏應理
Pu-ju i-fo	補儒易佛
"Pu-li yü chen, wei chih chih-jen"	不離於眞，謂之至人
san-chiao	三敎
San-huai	三淮 (see Huang Hung-en)
San-shan lun-hsüeh chi	三山論學記
San-ts'ai t'u-hui	三才圖會
Seh-leh-eh	色楞厄
Seng-chu (Sengju)	勝主
Shan-hai-kuan	山海關
Shan-hsi	山西
Shansi (see Shan-hsi)	
Shantung	山東
Shang-chu	上主

Shang-ch'uan	上川
Shanghai	上海
Shang-ti	上帝
Shao-chou	邵州
Shen Ch'üeh	沈潅
Shenhsi	郟西
Shensi (see Shenhsi)	
sheng-chiao	聖教
Shih Chen-yü	石鎮宇
Shih Hsing	石星
shih-lang	侍郎
Shou-shan	首善
shu-yüan	書院
Shun-chih	順治
Sian-fu	西安府
Songgatu	索額圖
Soochow (see Suchou)	
Ssu-chuan	四川
Ssu-i k'ao	四夷考
Ssu-shu	四書
Ssu-shu chi-chu	四書集註
Ssu-shu chih-chieh	四書直解
Suchou	蘇州
Su Mou-hsiang	蘇茂相
Sung	宋
Sung Ying-hsing	宋應星
Szechuan (see Ssu-chuan)	
Ta Ch'ing i-t'ung chih	大清一統志
ta-chu	大主
Ta-hsüeh	大學
"*ta-hsüeh chih tao tsai ming ming te*"	大學之道在明明德
Ta Ming	大明
Tai-i p'ien	代疑篇
t'ai	太
T'ai-chi	太極
T'ai-pei	台北
T'ai-wan	台灣
T'ang	唐
T'ang Jo-wang	湯若望
T'ang Yin	唐寅
tao	道
Tao-hsüeh	道學

tao-wen hsüeh	道問學
te	德
t'ien	天
T'ien-ch'i	天啟
T'ien-chu	天主
T'ien-chu chiao	天主教
T'ien-chu chih tao	天主之道
T'ien-chu shih-i	天主實義
T'ien-chu shih-lu	天主實錄
T'ien-hsüeh	天學
T'ien-hsüeh ch'u-han	天學初函
T'ien-hsüeh shih-i	天學實義
T'ien-kung k'ai-wu	天工開物
Ting Chih-lin	丁志麟
Ting Yün-p'eng	丁雲鵬
Tsang-hsia yü ts'ao	蒼霞餘草
Ts'ao Hsüeh-ch'üan	曹學佺 (T. Neng-shih 能始)
Tseng Ching	曾鯨
"Tseng Ssu-chi Ai hsien-sheng shih"	贈思及艾先生詩
Tsinan (Chi-nan)	濟南
Tso-fang ssu	作坊司
"Tso liao"	錯了
Tsou Yüan-piao	鄒元標
"Tsun te-hsing"	尊德性
Tu-hsing jen	獨行人
T'u-shu pien	圖書編
Tung Ch'i-ch'ang	董其昌
Tung-lin	東林
Tzu-kuang ko	紫光閣
wako (wou-k'ou)	倭寇
wan-hua	萬化
Wan-li	萬曆
"wan-shih pu-k'o i-chih fa"	萬世不可易之法
Wang Hua-chen	王化貞
Wang Hung-hui	王弘誨
Wang P'an	王潘
Wang Yang-ming	王陽明
Wei Chung-hsien	魏忠賢
Wei Fang-chi	衛方濟
Wen Cheng-ming	文徵明
Wen-yü Ho	溫榆河
Wu-hsi	無錫

Wu-li hsiao-chih	物理小識
Wu Pin	吳彬
Wu-su-li chiang	烏蘇里江
Wu Wei-yeh	吳偉業
Ya-hsi-ya	亞細亞
Yang	陽
Yang Ch'i-yüan hsien-sheng ch'ao-hsing shih-chi	楊淇園先生超性事蹟
Yang Chu	楊朱
Yang-hsin tien	養心殿
Yang Kuang-hsien	楊光先
Yang Lien	楊漣
Yang Shih	楊時
Yang T'ing-yün	楊廷筠 (T. Ch'i-yüan 淇園)
Yangtze (Ch'ang-chiang)	長江
Yeh Hsiang-kao	葉向高
Yen-lo	閻羅
Yin	陰
Yin-jeng	胤礽
Yin-t'i	胤禔
Yin Tuo-tso	殷鐸澤
Yung-cheng	雍正
Yung-li	永曆
Yung-lo	永樂
Yung-p'ing	永平
Yü chih ta Ch'ing i-t'ung ch'üan-t'u	御製大清一統全圖
yü-shih	御史
Yü-ti shan-hai ch'üan-t'u	輿地山海全圖
Yü-ti t'u	輿地圖
Yüan	元
yüan-chih	元質
Yüan-ming yüan	圓明園
Yüeh	越
Yün-ch'i	雲棲
Yünnan	雲南

Select Bibliography

WITH FEW EXCEPTIONS, only the writings used by the authors in the making of this book are listed in the Select Bibliography. A Supplementary Bibliography of pertinent post-1981 publications follows this Select Bibliography.

BOOKS

Actes du Colloque international, 1974, Chantilly. See Destombes.

Aleni, Giulio, S.J.艾儒略 *Chih-fang wai-chi* 職方外紀 (Account of countries not listed in the Records Office). Hangchow, 1623. Reprint. Taipei, 1965. (For reprint, see Wu Hsiang-hsiang, *Collectanea.*)

————. *Hsing-hsüeh ts'u shu* 性學觕述 (An outline of human nature). Hangchow, 1623. Woodblock edition. Shanghai, 1873.

————. *Hsi-hsüeh fan* 西學凡 (A summary of Western learning). Hangchow, 1623. Reprint. Taiwan, 1965. (For reprint, see Wu Hsiang-hsiang, *Collectanea.*)

————. *San-shan lun hsüeh chi* 三山論學記 (Learned conversations at San-shan [Foochow]). Hangchow, 1627? Reprint. Taipei, 1965. (For reprint, see Wu Hsiang-hsiang, *Collectanea.*)

————. *Ta-hsi Hsi-t'ai Li hsien-sheng hsing-chi* 大西西泰利先生行蹟 (The career of Ricci from the Far West). Peking, ca. 1630. Reprint. Edited by Hsiang Ta. Peking, 1947.

————. *T'ien chu chiang-sheng Ch'u-hsiang ching-chieh* 天主降生出像經解 (The life of Our Lord, Jesus Christ, Savior of men, drawn from the four evangelists). Foochow, 1635–37.

Aleni, Giulio, S.J., and Andrius Rudamina, S.J. *K'ou-to jih-chao* 口鐸日抄 (Daily records taken from the dialogues between the Jesuit missionaries and some Chinese scholars in Fukien). Foochow, 1630. Reprints. T'ou-sè-wè, 1872, 1922.

Alonso, Martín. *Enciclopedia del Idioma.* 3 vols. Madrid, 1958.

Ars Hispaniae: historia universal del arte hispánico. 14 vols. Madrid, 1946–57.

Atti del convego internazionale di studi ricciani, 1982. See Foss.

Augustine, Saint. *Confessions.* Translated by R. S. Pine-Coffin. Baltimore, 1961.

Baddeley, John F., ed. *Russia, Mongolia, China: being some record of the relations between them from the beginning of the XVIIth century to the death of Tsar Alexei Mikhailovich, A.D. 1602-1676.* 2 vols. London, 1919. Reprints. New York, 1964, 1976.

Bartoli, Daniello, S.J. *Dell'istoria della compagnia de Giesù. La Cina. Terza parte dell'Asia.* Rome, 1663.

Beazley, Charles R. *Prince Henry the Navigator: the hero of Portugal and of modern discovery, 1394–1460 A.D.* New York, 1895.

————. *The Dawn of Modern Geography.* 3 vols. London, 1897–1906.

Bensaude, Joaquim. *Les Légendes allemandes sur l'histoire des découvertes maritimes portugaises: réponse a M. Hermann Wagner.* 2 vols. Geneva, 1917–20.

————. *Lacunes et surprises de l'histoire des découvertes maritimes, I^e partie.* Coimbra, 1930.

————. *A cruzada do infante d. Henrique.* Lisbon, 1942.

Bernard-Maitre, Henri, S.J. *Aux Portes de la Chine. Les Missionaires du Seizième Siècle, 1514–1588.* Tientsin, 1933.

————. *Le Père Matthieu Ricci et la Société Chinoise de son temps, 1552–1610.* 2 vols. Tientsin, 1937.

————. *Matteo Ricci's Scientific Contribution to China.* Translated by E. C. Werner. Peking, 1935. Reprint. Westport, Conn., 1973.

Bettray, Johannes, S.V.D. *Die Akkomodationsmethode des P. Matteo Ricci S.J. in China.* Rome, 1955.

Beurdeley, Cécile and Michel. *Giuseppe Castiglione: A Jesuit Painter at the Court of the Chinese Emperors.* Translated by Michael Bullock. Rutland, Vt., 1971.

Blondeau, R. A. *Mandarijn en astronoom: Ferdinand Verbiest, S.J. (1623–1688) aan het hof van de Chinese Keizer.* Bruges, 1970.

Bouvet, Joachim, S.J. *Portrait historique de l'empereur de la Chine.* Paris, 1697.

————. *Histoire de l'empereur de la Chine.* The Hague, 1699. Reprint. Tientsin, 1948.

————. *Voiage de Siam du Père Bouvet.* Edited by Janette C. Gatty. Leiden, 1963.

Boxer, C. R. *Fidalgos in the Far East 1550–1770: Fact and Fancy in the History of Macao.* The Hague, 1948. 2d ed., rev. with corrections. Oxford, 1968.

————, trans. and ed. *South China in the Sixteenth Century. Being the Narratives of Galeote Pereira, Fr. Gaspar da Cruz, O.P., Fr. Martín* de Rada, O.E.S.A., 1550–1575. Hakluyt Society Publications, 2d ser., vol. 106. London, 1953.

———. *The Great Ship from Amacan. Annals of Macao and the Old Japan Trade, 1555–1640.* Lisbon, 1959. Reprint. Lisbon, 1963.

Braga, José Maria. *O primeiro accordo Luso-Chinês realizado por Leonel de Sousa em 1554.* Macao, 1939.

———. *The Western Pioneers and Their Discovery of Macao.* Macao, 1949.

Brancati (Brancato), Francesco, S.J. *De Sinensium ritibus politicis acta seu responsio apologetica ad R. P. Dominicum Navarette Ordinis Predicatorum.* 2 vols. Paris, 1700.

Broc, Numa. *La Géographie des philosophes, géographes, et voyageurs français au XVIIIe siècle.* Paris, 1972.

Brown, Lloyd A. *Jean Dominique Cassini and His World Map of 1696.* Ann Arbor, 1941.

Brucker, Abbé Joseph. "Communication sur l'exécution des cartes de la Chine par les missionaires du XVIIIe siècle d'après documents inédits." In *IVe Congrès international des sciences géographiques tenu à Paris en 1889.* 2 vols. Paris, 1889.

Cahen, Gaston. *Les Cartes de la Sibérie au XVIIIe siècle. Essai de bibliographie critique.* Paris, 1911.

Cahill, James. "Wu Pin and His Landscape Painting." In *Proceedings of the International Symposium on Chinese Painting.* Taipei, 1970.

———. *The Compelling Image: Nature and Style in Seventeenth-Century Chinese Painting.* Cambridge, Mass. 1982.

Cassirer, Ernst, Paul Oskar Kristeller, and John Herman Randall, Jr., eds. *The Renaissance Philosophy of Man.* Phoenix Books. Chicago, 1948.

Catálogo de los documentos relativos a las Islas Filipinas existentes en el Archivo de Indias de Sevilla por D. Pedro Torres y Lanzas y Francisco Navas del Valle, y precedido de una erudita historia general de Filipinas por el P. Pedro Pastells, S.J. 8 vols. Barcelona, 1925–33.

Ch'a Chi-tso 查繼佐. *Tsui Wei-lu* 罪惟錄 (A complete history of the Ming dynasty). 2 vols. Reprint. Shanghai, 1928.

Chabrié, Robert. *Michel Boym, Jésuite polonais et la fin des Ming en Chine (1646–1662).* Paris, 1933.

Chan, Albert [S.J.]. *The Glory and Fall of the Ming Dynasty.* Norman, Okla., 1982.

Chan, Wing-tsit, trans. and comp. *A Source Book in Chinese Philosophy.* Princeton, 1963.

————. "The Evolution of the Neo-Confucian Concept of *Li* as Principle." In Wing-tsit Chan, *Neo-Confucianism, etc.: Essays by. . . .* Compiled by Charles K. H. Chen. Hong Kong, 1969.

Chang Chü-cheng張居正*Ssu-shu chih-chieh*四書直解(Colloquial commentary on the *Four Books*). In *A Descriptive Catalogue of Rare Chinese Books in the Library of Congress.* Compiled by Wang Chungmin. Edited by T. L. Yuan. 2 vols. Washington, D.C., 1957.

Chang Hsieh. 張燮 *Tung-Hsi-yang k'ao* 東西洋考 (A maritime geography of South Asia). Shanghai, 1937.

Chang P'u. 張溥 "Wu-jen mu-pei chi." 五人墓碑記 (The tombstone inscription of five [martyrs]). In *Ming-wen-hui*明文彙(Ming literature collection) edition. Taipei, 1958.

Chang T'ing-yü.張廷玉 See *Ming shih.* 明史

Chang Wei-hua. 張維華*Ming-shih Fo-lang-chi, Lu-sung, Ho-lan, I-ta-li-ya ssu-chüan chu-shih* 明史佛郎機呂宋和蘭意大里 亞四傳注釋 (A commentary on the four chapters on Portugal, Spain, Holland, and Italy in the history of the Ming dynasty). *Yenching Journal of Chinese Studies.* Monograph Series, no. 7. Peking, 1934.

Chao I 趙翼*Erh-shih-erh-shih cha-chi* 二十二史箚記 (Miscellaneous notes on the twenty-two dynastic histories). 2 vols. Shanghai, 1963.

————. *Yen-pao Tsa-Chi* 簷曝雜記 (Miscellaneous notes from under the exposed eave). In *The Translation of Art: Essays on Chinese Painting and Poetry.* Renditions No. 6. Special Art Issue. Hong Kong, 1976.

Chao Nan-hsing.趙南星 *Wei-po-chai wen-chi* 味檗齊文集 (Essays by Chao Nan-hsing). In *Ts'ung-shu chi-ch'eng ch'u-pien*叢書集成初編 (First series of the collection of collectanea). Edited by the Commercial Press. 5 vols. Shanghai, 1935.

Chaoying Fang. See Goodrich.

Ch'en Hou-kuang.陳侯光 *Pien-hsüeh ch'u-yen* 辨學芻言 (Philosophical writings of Ch'en Hou-kuang). N.p., n.d.

Ch'en Jen-hsi.陳仁錫 *Huang-Ming shih-fa lu*皇明世法錄 (Collection of government documents of the Ming period). 4 vols. Reprinted after a late Ming edition. Taipei, 1965.

Ch'en Lung-cheng.陳龍正 *Chi-ting wai-shu* 幾亭外書 (Miscellaneous writings of Ch'en Lung-cheng). 6 vols. Late Ming edition.

Ch'en Shou-yiu. 陳受頤 "Ming-mo Yeh-su-hui-shih ti Ju-chiao kuan chi ch'i-t'a." 明末耶穌會士的儒教觀及其他 (The late Ming Jesuits' view of Confucianism, etc.). In *Ming-tai tsung-chiao* 明代宗教 (Studies on Ming religion). Edited by Pao Ts'ung-p'ang. 包遵彭 Taipei, 1968.

Ch'en Tien. 陳田 *Ming-shih chi-shih* 明詩紀事 (Miscellaneous annotations to the poems of the Ming period). 10 vols. *Kuo-hsüeh chi-pen ts'ung-shu* 國學基本叢書 (Essential works for Chinese Studies Series) edition. Shanghai, 1936.

Ch'eng Shu-te. 程樹德 *Lun-yü chi-shih* 論語集釋 (A collection of commentaries on the *Analects* of Confucius). 2 vols. Taipei, 1965.

Chou K'ang-hsieh, ed. 周康燮 *Li Ma-tou yen-chiu lun-chi* 利瑪竇研究論集 (Collected essays on Matteo Ricci). Hong Kong, 1971.

Chou Shun-ch'ang. 周順昌 *Chou-chung chieh-kung chin-yü lu* 周忠介公燼餘錄 (Some incomplete writings of Chou chun-ch'ang). In *Ts'ung-shu chi-ch'eng ch'u-pien* 叢書集成初編 (First series of the collection of collectanea). Edited by the Commercial Press. 5 vols. Shanghai, 1935.

Chronicon Societatis Jesu. In *Vita Ignatii Loiolae et Rerum Societatis Jesu Historia*. Edited by Johannes Alphonsus de Polanco, S.J. 6 vols. (Vols. 1, 3, 5, 7, 9, 11 of *Monumenta Historica Societatis Iesu*) Rome, 1894–98.

Chu Ch'ien-chih. 朱謙之 "Yeh-su-hui tui-yü Sung Ju li-hsüeh chih fan hsiang" 耶穌會對於宋儒理學之反響 (The Jesuit response to Sung Neo-Confucianism). In *Ming-tai tsung chiao* 明代宗教 (Studies on Ming religion). Edited by Pao Ts'un-p'ang. Taipei, 1968.

Chu Huai-wu. 朱懷吾 *Chao-tai chi-lüeh* 昭代紀略 (A brief history of the contemporary Ming period). 6 vols. Late Ming edition.

Chu Hsi. 朱熹 *Ssu-shu chi-chu* 四書集註 (Collected commentary on the *Four Books*). Reprint. Taipei, 1969.

Chuang-tzu 莊子 Harvard-Yenching Sinological Index Series. Peking, 1947.

Chuang T'ing-lung. 莊廷鑨 *Ming-shih ch'ao-lüeh* 明史鈔略 (A glimpse of the history of the Ming dynasty). 2 vols. Reprint. Shanghai, 1935.

Chün-fang Yü. *The Renewal of Buddhism in China: Chu-hung and the Late Ming Synthesis*. New York, 1981.

Coleridge, Henry, S.J. *The Life and Letters of St. Francis Xavier*. 2 vols. London, 1912.

Collani, Claudia von. *Die Figuristen in der Chinamission*. Frankfurt am Main, 1981.

Collected Essays of the International Symposium (Fu Jen University). See Hwang.

Comentale, Christophe. *Matteo Ripa, peintre-graveur-missionaire à la*

Cour de Chine. Mémoires traduits, présentés et annotés par.... Taipei, 1983.

Confucius. *Analects.* Translated by D. C. Lau. Harmondsworth, Middlesex, England, 1979.

Cooper, Michael, S.J. *Rodrigues the Interpreter: An Early Jesuit in Japan and China.* New York, 1974.

Cordier, Henri. *Bibliotheca Sinica.* 2d ed. 5 vols. Paris, 1904–24. 3d ed. 5 vols. Paris, 1905–6. Reprints. Peking, 1938–1939; Taipei, 1966; New York, 1968; San Francisco, 1979.

————. *L'Imprimerie sino-européenne en Chine.* Paris, 1891, 1901. Reprint. San Francisco, 1979.

Cortesão, Armando, trans. and ed. *The Suma Oriental of Tomé Pires and the Book of Francisco Rodrigues.* 2 vols. Hakluyt Society Publications, 2d ser., vols. 89–90. London, 1944. Reprint. Nendeln/ Liechtenstein, 1967.

Costa, Emmanuel (a Costa) da, S.J. *Rerum a Societate Jesu in Oriente gestarum ad annum usque a Deipara Virgine MDLXVIII, commentarius.* Translated by Giovanni Maffei, S.J. Dillingen, 1571.

Costa, Inácio da, S.J., and Prospero Intorcetta, S.J. *Sapientia Sinica.* Ch'ienchang, 1662.

Couplet, Philippe, S.J., Prospero Intorcetta, S.J., Christian Herdtrich, S.J., and François de Rougemont, S.J., eds. *Confucius Sinarum philosophus sive scientia Sinensis latine exposita.* Paris, 1687.

Crawford, Robert B. "Chang Chü-cheng's Confucian Legalism." In *Self and Society in Ming Thought.* Edited by Wm. Theodore de Bary. New York, 1970.

Cummins, J. S., trans. and ed. *The Travels and Controversies of Friar Domingo [Fernández de] Navarette, 1618–1686.* Hakluyt Society Publications, 2d ser., vols. 118–19. Cambridge, England, 1962.

de Bary, Wm. Theodore, ed. *Self and Society in Ming Thought.* New York, 1970.

————, ed. *The Unfolding of Neo-Confucianism.* New York, 1975.

Dehergne, Joseph, S.J. *Répertoire des Jésuites de Chine de 1552 à 1800.* Rome, 1973.

D'Elia, Pasquale M., S.J., ed. *Fonti Ricciane.* See Ricci.

————. *Il mappamondo cinese del P. Matteo Ricci, S.I. (terza edizione, Pechino, 1602) conservato presso la Biblioteca Vaticana, commentato tradotto e annotato dal....* Vatican City, 1938. Also see Ricci.

Dernières nouvelles de la chrétienté de la Chine. Paris, 1668.

Desautels, Alfred, S.J. *Les Mémoires de Trévoux et le mouvement des* *idées au XVIIIe siècle (1701–1734).* (Vol. 8 of Bibliotheca Instituti Historici Societatis Iesu) Rome, 1956.

A *Descriptive Catalog.* See Chang Chü-cheng.

Destombes, Marcel. "Les Originaux chinois des plans de ville publiés par J. B. Du Halde, S.J. en 1735." In *Actes du Colloque international de sinologie. 20–22 septembre, 1974, Chantilly. La Mission française de Pékin aux XVIIe et XVIIIe siècles.* Paris, 1976.

Diversi avvisi particolari dall'Indie di Portogallo ricevuti dall'anno 1551 fino al 1558. Venice, 1558.

Du Halde, Jean-Baptiste, S.J. *Description géographique, historique, chronologique, politique, et physique de l'empire de la Chine et de la Tartarie chinoise.* 4 vols. The Hague, 1735.

———. *A Description of the Empire of China and Chinese Tartary.* 2 vols. London, 1738–41.

Dunne, George H., S.J. *Generation of Giants: The Story of the Jesuits in China in the Last Decades of the Ming Dynasty.* Notre Dame, Ind., 1962.

Duyvendak, Jan J. L. *China's Discovery of Africa.* London, 1949.

Fairbanks, John K. See Reischauer.

Fang Hao. 方豪 *Li Chih-tsao yen-chiu* 李之藻研究 (Research on Li Chih-tsao). Taipei, 1966.

———. *Chung-kuo T'ien-chu-chiao shih jen-wu chuan* 中國天主教史人物傳 (Biographies of eminent persons in the history of the Catholic Church in China). 3 vols. Hong Kong, 1967–73.

———. *Fang Hao liu-shih tzu ting kao* 方豪六十自定稿 (The collected works of Maurus Fang Hao revised and edited by the author on his sixtieth birthday). 2 vols. with Supplement. Taipei, 1969.

———. "Li Ma-tou Chiao-yu lun hsin-yen" 利瑪竇交友論新研 (A new study on Matteo Ricci's *Chiao-yu lun*). In Fang Hao, *Collected Works,* as cited above.

———. "Ming-mo Ch'ing-ch'u T'ien-chu-chiao shih-ying Ju-chia hsüeh-shuo chih yen-chiu" 明末清初天主教適應儒家學說之研究 (A study of Catholic accommodation with Confucianism during the late Ming, early Ching periods). In Fang Hao, *Collected Works,* as cited above.

Feng, Yu-lan. 馮友蘭 *Chung-kuo che-hsüeh shih* 中國哲學史 (A history of Chinese philosophy). Reprint. Hong Kong, n.d.

Fernández de Navarette, Domingo, O.P. *Tratados históricos, políticos, éthicos y religiosos de la monarchía de China.* Madrid, 1676. Also see Cummins.

Foss, Theodore N. "La cartografia di Matteo Ricci." In *Atti del convengo internazionale di studi ricciani*. Macerata-Roma, 22–25 ottobre 1982. Edited by Maria Cigliano. Macerata, 1984.

Fu, Lo-shu. *A Documentary Chronicle of Sino-Western Relations, 1644–1820*. Tucson, Ariz., 1966.

Fuchs, Walter. *Der Jesuiten-Atlas der Kanghsi-Zeit. Seine Entstehungsgeschichte nebst Namensindices für die Karten der Mandjurei, Mongolei, Ostturkestan und Tibet.* (One volume and one box of maps) Monumenta Serica Monograph Series, no. 4. Peking, 1943.

Gallagher, Louis J., S.J. See Trigault, *China in the Sixteenth Century.*

Gaubil, Antoine, S.J. "Histoire des Thang." In *Mémoires concernant l'histoire, les sciences, les arts, les moeurs, les usages etc. des Chinois: par les missionaires de Pékin*. Edited by C. Batteux, L. G. Oudart, Fendrix de Brequigny, J. de Guigness, and A. J. Silvestre de Sacy. 15:399–516. 16 vols. Paris, 1776–1814.

————. *Correspondance de Pékin, 1722–1759*. Publiée par Renée Simon; préface par Paul Demiéville; appendices par le P. Joseph Dehergne, S.J. Geneva, 1970.

Gernet, Jacques. "Sur les différentes versions du premier catéchisme en chinois de 1584." In *Studia Sino-Mongolica. Festschrift für Herbert Franke*. Edited by Wolfgang Bauer. Wiesbaden, 1979.

————. *A History of Chinese Civilization*. Translated by J. R. Foster. Cambridge, England, 1982. Reprint. Cambridge, England, 1985.

————. *Chine et Christianisme. Action et réaction*. Paris, 1982.

————. *China and the Christian Impact: A Conflict of Cultures*. Translated by Janet Lloyd. (Translation of Gernet, *Chine et Christianisme*) Cambridge, England, 1985.

González de Mendoza, Juan. *Historia de las cosas más notables, ritos y costumbres de gran reyno dela China*. Rome, 1585. Reprint. Madrid, 1944.

Goodfellow, Sally W., ed. *Eight Dynasties of Chinese Painting*. Essays by Wai-kam Ho, Sherman E. Lee, Laurence Sickman, and Marc F. Wilson. Cleveland, 1980.

Goodrich, L. Carrington. *A Short History of the Chinese People*. 3d ed. New York, 1959.

Goodrich, L. Carrington, and Chaoying Fang, eds. *Dictionary of Ming Biography 1368–1644*. 2 vols. New York, 1976.

Goto Motomi. 後藤基己 *Min-Shin shisō to Kirisuto-kyō* 明清思想と キリスト教 (Ming Ch'ing thought and Christian religion). Tokyo, 1979.

Greenblatt, Kirsten Yü. "Chu-hung and Lay Buddhism in the Late Ming." In *The Unfolding of Neo-Confucianism*. Edited by Wm. Theodore de Bary. New York, 1975.

Greene, Thomas M. *The Light in Troy: Imitation and Discovery in Renaissance Poetry*. New Haven, 1982.

Grousset, René. *The Empire of the Steppes: A History of Central Asia*. Translated by Naomi Walford. New Brunswick, 1970.

Hedin, Sven. *Southern Tibet: Discoveries in Former Times Compared with My Own Observations in 1906–1908*. 9 vols. Stockholm, 1917–22.

Herrmann, Albert. *Historical and Commercial Atlas of China*. Cambridge, Mass., 1935.

Hou Wai-lu, 候外廬 chief comp. *Chung-kuo ssu-hsiang t'ung-shih* 中國思想通史 (A general history of Chinese thought). 7 vols. Peking, 1949–60. (multiple editions)

Hsia Hsieh. 夏燮 *Ming t'ung-chien* 明通鑑 (A chronological history of the Ming dynasty). 3 vols. Shanghai, 1959.

Hsiang Ta. 向達 "European Influences on Chinese Art in the Later Ming and Early Ch'ing Period." Translated by Wang Teh-chao. In *The Translation of Art: Essays on Chinese Painting and Poetry*. Renditions No. 6. Special Art Issue. Hong Kong, 1976. (Article originally published in Chinese in *Tung-fang Tsa Chih* 東方雜誌 [Studies of the East] 27 [1930] and later collected into *T'ang-tai Ch'ang-an yü Hsi-yü Wen-ming* 唐代長安與西域文明 [Ch'ang-an and West areas culture in the period of T'ang]. [Peking, 1933].)

Hsieh Chao-che. 謝肇淛 *Wu tsa-tsu* 五雜組 (Encyclopedic notes). 2 vols. Shanghai, 1959.

Hsieh Kuo-chen. 謝國楨 *Ming-Ch'ing chih chi tang-she yün-tung k'ao* 明清之際黨社運動考 (A study of factions and cliques in the late Ming, early Ch'ing period). Taipei, 1967.

————. *Ming-tai she-hui ching-chi shih-liao hsüan-pien* 明代社會經濟史料選編 (Selected materials for the socioeconomic history of the Ming dynasty). 3 vols. Fukien, 1980.

Hsü Kuang-ch'i. 徐光啟 "Pa Erh-shih-wu yen" 跋二十五言 (Postscript to the twenty-five discourses). In Hsü Kuang-ch'i, *Hsü Kuang-ch'i chi* 徐光啟集 (Collection of writings of Hsü Kuang-ch'i). Peking, 1963.

————. "K'o Chi-ho yüan pen hsü" 刻幾何原本序 (Preface for the printing of the elements of geometry). In *Collection of Writings*, as cited above.

————. "T'ai-hsi shui fa hsü" 泰西水法述 (Preface for the Western methods of water control). In *Collection of Writings*, as cited above.

Hsü Tsung-tse. 徐宗澤 *Ming-Ch'ing-chien Yeh-su-hui-shih i-chu t'i-yao* 明清間耶穌會士譯著提要 (An annotated bibliography of Jesuit translations and writings during the late Ming, early Ch'ing periods). Shanghai, 1949. Reprint. Taipei, 1958.

Huang Po-lu, S.J. 黃伯祿 *Cheng-chiao feng-pao* 正教奉褒 (Public praise of the true religion). 3d ed. Shanghai, 1904.

Huang Tsung-hsi. 黃宗羲 *Ming-ju hsüeh-an* 明儒學案 (A systematic historical survey of all the important schools of thought throughout the Ming period). Shanghai, 1933.

Huard, Pierre, and Ming Wong. *Chinese Medicine*. New York, 1972.

Hummel, Arthur W., ed. *Eminent Chinese of the Ch'ing Period (1644–1912)*. 2 vols. Washington, D.C., 1943–44. Reprint. Taipei, 1967.

Hung Wei-lien. 洪煨蓮 "K'ao Li Ma-tou te shih-chieh ti-t'u" 考利瑪竇的世界地圖 (A study of Matteo Ricci's world map). In *Li Ma-tou yen-chiu lun chi* 利瑪竇研究論集 (Collected essays on Matteo Ricci). Edited by Chou K'ang-hsieh. 周康燮 Hong Kong, 1971.

Hwang, Jane. "The early Jesuits-Printings [sic] in China in the Bavarian State Library and the University Library of Munich." In *Chi-nien Li Ma-tou lai hua ssu-pai chou-nien Chung-Hsi wen-hua chiao-liu kuo-chi hsüeh-shu hui-i lun wen-chi* 紀念利瑪竇來華四佰週年史西文化交流國際學術會議論文集 (Collected essays of the international symposium [Fu Jen University] on Chinese-Western cultural interchange in commemoration of the 400th anniversary of the arrival of Matteo Ricci, S.J. in China). Edited by Lo Kuang. 羅光 Taipei, 1983.

I Ching. 易經 (Book of changes). Translated by James Legge. Edited with introduction and study guide by Ch'u Chai and Winberg Chai. New York, 1969.

Ides, Evert Ysbrandszoon. *Driejaarige reize naar China, te lande gedaan door den Moskovischen afgezant, E. Ysbrants Ides van Moskou af.* Amsterdam, 1704.

Intorcetta, Prospero, S.J. *Sinarum scientia politico-moralis.* Quam Cheu-Goa, 1667–69. Also see da Costa and Couplet.

Jann, Adelhelm, O. Min. Cap. *Die katholischen Missionen in Indien, China und Japan. Ihre Organisation und das portugiesische Patronat vom 15. bis ins 18. Jahrhundert.* Paderborn, 1915.

The Jesuit Relations. See Paltsits.

Jones, Yolande, and others. *Chinese and Japanese Maps. An Exhibition Organised by the British Library at the British Museum, 1 February–31 December 1974.* London, 1974.

Journal de Trévoux. See *Mémoires pour servir à l'histoire des sciences et des beaux arts.*

Kao I-han. 高一涵 *Chung-kuo yü shih chi-tu te yen-ke* 中國御史制度的沿革 (Development of the censorial system in China). Shanghai, 1933.

Kao P'an-lung. 高攀龍 *Kao-tzu i-shu* 高子遺書 (Posthumous works of Kao P'an-lung). Late Ming edition.

Ku Ying-t'ai. 谷應泰 *Ming-shih chi-shih pen-mo* 明史紀事本末 (History of the Ming dynasty in topical form). 2 vols. Shanghai, 1935.

Kuo Shang-pin. 郭尚賓 *Kuo chi-chien shu-kao* 郭給諫疏稿 (Draft of the memorials to the throne by the censor Kuo Shang-pin). In *Ts'ung-shu chi-ch'eng ch'u-pien* (First series of the collection of collectanea). Edited by the Commercial Press. 5 vols. Shanghai, 1935.

Lach, Donald F. *Asia in the Making of Europe.* 2 vols. to date. Chicago 1965–.

Lau, D. C. See Confucius.

Le Comte, Louis, S.J. *Nouveaux Mémoires sur l'état présent de la Chine.* 3d ed. 2 vols. Paris, 1701.

————. *Memoirs and Remarks Geographical, Historical, Topographical . . . Made . . . in Travels through the Empire of China.* London, 1737.

Le Gobien, Charles, S.J. *Histoire de l'édit de l'empereur de la Chine, en faveur de la religion chrestienne.* Paris, 1698.

Legge, James. *The Religions of China. Confucianism and Taoism described and compared with Christianity.* New York, 1881.

————, trans. and ed. *The Chinese Classics.* 2d ed. rev. 5 vols. Oxford, 1893–95. Reprint. Hong Kong, 1960. Vol. 1 contains the Confucian *Analects, Doctrine of the Mean,* and *Great Learning.* Vol. 2 contains *Works of Mencius.*

Lettres édifiantes et curieuses, d'écrits des missions étrangères, par quelques missionaires de la Compagnie de Jésus. 4 vols. Edited by L. Aimé-Martin. Paris, 1838–43.

Li Chih. 李贄 *Hsü Fen-shu* 續焚書 (Second series of Li Chih's collected works). Shanghai, 1959.

Li Chih-tsao, 李之藻 ed. *T'ien-hsüeh ch'u-han* 天學初函 (First collection of writings on Learning from Heaven). Reprint. Taipei, 1965. (For 1965 reprint, see Wu Hsiang-hsiang, *Collectanea.*)

Liang Chia-mien. 梁家勉 *Hsü Kuang-ch'i nien-p'u* 徐光啟年譜 (Chronological account of the life of Hsü Kuang-ch'i). Shanghai, 1981.

Lo Kuang.羅光 *Hsü Kuang-ch'i chuan* 徐光啟傳 (Biography of Hsü Kuang-ch'i). Hong Kong, 1953.

Loehr, George. *Giuseppe Castiglione (1688–1766) pittore di Corte di Ch'ien lung, Imperatore della Cina*. Rome, 1940.

Longobardi (Longobardo), Niccolò, S.J. *Traité sur quelques points de la religion des Chinois*. Paris, 1701.

Luk, Bernard Hung-kay. "And Thus the Twain Did Meet? — the Two Worlds of Giulio Aleni." Ph.D. diss. Indiana University, 1977.

Luzbetak, Louis J. See *New Catholic Encyclopedia*.

Ma Yong, "Attività di Martino Martini in Cina e sue opere di storia e geografia della Cina." In *Martino Martini, geografo, cartografo, storico, teologo. Trento 1614-Hangzhou 1661. Atti del convengo internazionale 9–11 ottobre 1981*. Edizione bilingue italiana-inglese. A cura di Giorgio Melis. Trent, 1983. (Chinese text published in *Li shih yen chiu* 歷史研究 [Historical research] [Peking] 6 [1980]: 153–68.)

Maas, Otto, O.F.M. *Die Wiedereröffnung der Franziskanermission in China in der Neuzeit*. Münster, 1926.

Magalhães (Magaillans), Gabriel de, S.J. *A New History of China*. Translated by John Ogibly. London, 1688.

———. *Nouvelle relation de la Chine*. Translated by Sr. B[ernou]. Paris, 1690.

Mailla, Joseph-Anne-Marie de Moyriac de, S.J., trans. *Histoire générale de la Chine, ou Annales de cet Empire;* traduites du Tong-Kien-Kang-mou. 通鑑綱目 Pub[liées] par l'abbé Grosier. 13 vols. Paris, 1777–85.

Mancall, Mark. *Russia and China: Their Diplomatic Relations to 1728*. Cambridge, Mass., 1971.

Martini, Martino, S.J. *Novus Atlas Sinensis*. Munich, 1655. Reprint. Trent, 1981.

———. *Sinicae Historiae Decas Prima*. Munich, 1658.

———. *Chiu-yu pien* 逑友編(A treatise on making friends). Hangchow, 1661. Also see Ma Yong.

Melis, Giorgio. "Presentazione." In Martino Martini, S.J. *Novus Atlas Sinensis. Ad Lectorem Praefatio. Versioni*. Trent, 1981.

Mémoires pour servir à l'histoire des sciences et des beaux arts. (Commonly known as *Journal de Trévoux*.) 265 vols. Trévoux, 1701–31; Lyons, 1731–33; Paris, 1734–62. Reprint. Geneva, 1968–69.

Meng Sen. 孟森 *Ming-tai shih* 明代史 (History of the Ming Period) Taipei, 1957. Reprint. Hong Kong, n.d.

Merkel, R. F. *Die Anfänge der protestantischen Missionsbewegung. G. W. Leibniz und die China-Mission.* Leipzig, 1920.

Ming shih 明史 (Ming history). Compiled by Chang T'ing-yü 張廷玉 and others. 28 vols. *Chung-hua shu-chu* 中華書局 punctuated edition. Peking, 1974.

Ming Wong. See Huard.

Minshin no Kaiga 明清の繪畫 (Paintings of the Ming Ch'ing dynasties). Exhibition Catalogue with text by Kawakami Kei. Tokyo, 1964. Plate 122.

Moidrey, Joseph de, S.J. La *Hiérarchie catholique en Chine, en Corée et au Japon 1307–1914.* Variétés sinologiques, no. 38. Zi-Ka-Wei, 1914.

Mungello, David E. *Leibniz and Confucianism: The Search for Accord.* Honolulu, 1977.

————. "The First Complete Translation of the Confucian *Four Books* in the West." In *Chi-nien Li Ma-tou lai hua ssu-pai chou-nien Chung-Hsi wen-hua chiao-liu kuo-chi hsüeh-shu hui-i lun wen-chi* (Collected essays of the international symposium [Fu Jen University] on Chinese-Western cultural interchange in commemoration of the 400th anniversary of the arrival of Matteo Ricci, S.J. in China). Edited by Lo Kuang. Taipei. 1983.

————. *Curious Land: Jesuit Accommodation and the Origins of Sinology.* Stuttgart, 1985.

Navas del Valle, Francisco. See *Catálogo de los documentos relativos a Filipinas.*

Needham, Joseph. *Science and Civilisation in China.* 7 vols. to date. Cambridge, England, 1954–.

New Catholic Encyclopedia. s.v. "Missionary Adaptation," by Louis J. Luzbetak.

————. s.v. "Chinese Rites Controversy," by Francis A. Rouleau, S.J.

Noël, François, S.J. *Sinensis Imperii libri classici sex.* Translated. Prague, 1711.

Paltsits, Victor Hugo. "Data concerning the 'Lettres édifiantes.'" In *The Jesuit Relations and Allied Documents.* Edited by Reuben Gold Thwaites. 66:298–334. 73 vols. Cleveland, 1896–1901.

Pao Ts'ung-p'ang. See Ch'en Shou-yi and Chu Ch'ien-chih.

Pastells, Pedro, S.J. See *Catálogo de los documentos relativos a Filipinas.*

Pastor, Ludwig von. *Geschichte der Päpste seit dem Ausgang des Mittelalters.* 16 vols. Freiburg im Breisgau, 1891–1933.

Petech, Luciano. *China and Tibet in the Early Eighteenth Century.* 2d rev. ed. Leiden, 1972.

Peterson, Willard J. "Western Natural Philosophy Published in Late Ming China." In *Proceedings of the American Philosophical Society* 117, no. 4. August 1973.

———. "Fang I-chih: Western Learning and the 'Investigation of Things.'" In *The Unfolding of Neo-Confucianism.* Edited by Wm. Theodore de Bary. New York, 1975.

Pfister, Louis, S.J. *Notices biographiques et bibliographiques sur les Jésuites de l'ancienne mission de Chine 1552–1773.* 2 vols. Variétés sinologiques, nos. 59 and 60. Shanghai, 1932–34. Reprint. Nendeln/ Liechtenstein, 1971. (The reprint does not carry the list of corrigenda of the original.)

Pliny. *Natural History.* Loeb Classical Library. Cambridge, 1942.

Polanco, Johannes Alphonsus de, S.J. See *Chronicon.*

Possevino, Antonio, S.J. *Bibliotheca selecta qua agitur de ratione studiorum in historia, in disciplinis, in salute omnium procuranda.* Rome, 1593.

Proceedings of the International Symposium on Chinese Painting. See Cahill.

Pullapilly, Cyriac K. See Van Kley.

Rawski, Evelyn Sakakida. *Education and Popular Literacy in Ch'ing China.* Ann Arbor, 1979.

Reischauer, Edwin O., and John K. Fairbank. *East Asia: The Great Tradition.* Boston, 1960.

Rémusat, Jean-Pierre Abel. *Mélanges asiatiques.* 2 vols. Paris, 1825–26.

———. *Nouveaux mélanges asiatiques.* 2 vols. Paris, 1829.

Ricci, Matteo, S.J. *Hsi-kuo chi fa* 西國記法 (Western memory techniques). Nanchang, 1595.

———. *Chiao-yu lun* 交友論 (Treatise on friendship). Nanchang, 1595.

Li Ma-tou k'un-yü wan-kuo ch'üan-t'u 利瑪竇坤輿萬國全圖 (Ricci's complete map of the myriad nations of the earth). Nanking, 1598. Reprint. 1936.

———. *T'ien-chu shih-i* 天主實義 (True Meaning of the Lord of Heaven). Peking, 1603. Reprints. Taipei, 1965; Taichung, Taiwan, 1966; St. Louis, 1985. (For the 1965 reprint, see Wu Hsiang-hsiang, *Collectanea.*)

———. *Erh-shih-wu yen* 二十五言 (Twenty-five discourses). Peking, 1604.

———. *Chi-jen shih p'ien* 畸人十篇 (Ten essays on the extraordinary man). Peking, 1608. Reprints. Peking, 1965; Taichung, Taiwan, 1966; Taipei, 1967. (For the 1965 reprint, see Wu Hsiang-hsiang, *Collectanea*.)

————. *Opere storiche del P. Matteo Ricci, S.J.* Edited by Pietro Tacchi Venturi, S.J. 2 vols. Macerata, Italy, 1911–13. The first volume of this work contains Ricci's *Della entrata nella Cina de' padri della Compagnia del Giesù* (commonly known as his *Journals* or *Historia*) in its original form, but it has been superseded by Pasquale D'Elia's superbly critical edition found in his *Fonti Ricciane*. The second volume of Tacchi Venturi contains Ricci's letters; the revised edition of these, begun by D'Elia, remains to be completed.

————. *Fonti Ricciane: documenti originali concernenti Matteo Ricci e la storia delle prime relazioni tra l'Europa e la Cina 1579–1615.* Edited by Pasquale D'Elia, S.J. 3 vols. Rome, 1942–49. D'Elia gives a title different from Tacchi Venturi's to Ricci's original manuscript, namely, *Storia dell'Introduzione del Cristianesimo in Cina*. The manuscript is known under both titles.

Rosso, Antonio Sisto, O.F.M. *Apostolic Legations to China of the Eighteenth Century.* South Pasadena, Calif., 1948.

Rouleau, Francis A., S.J. See *New Catholic Encyclopedia*.

Rudamina (Rudomina), Andrius, S.J. See Aleni.

Saeki, P. Y. *The Nestorian Documents and Relics of China.* Tokyo, 1951.

Schilder, Gunter. *Australia Unveiled.* Amsterdam, 1976.

Schurhammer, Georg, S.J. *Franz Xavier. Sein Leben und seine Zeit.* 2 vols. in 4. Freiburg, 1955–73.

————. "Die Jesuitenmissionare des 16. und 17. Jahrhunderts und ihr Einfluss auf die japanische Malerei." In *Gesammelte Studien.* 4 vols. 2:769–79. (Vol. 21 of Bibliotheca Instituti Historici Societatis Iesu) Rome, 1963. (Article first published in *Jubiläumsband herausgegeben von der Deutschen Gesellschaft für Natur-und Völkerkunde Ostasiens anlässlich ihres 60 jährigen Bestehens 1873–1933*. Teil I. Tokyo, 1933.)

————. *Francis Xavier, His Life, His Times.* Translated by M. Joseph Costelloe, S.J. 4 vols. Rome, 1973–82.

Schurhammer, Georg, S.J., and Josef Wicki, S.J., eds. *Epistolae S. Francisci Xaverii Aliaque Ejus Scripta.* Nova Editio. 2 vols. Rome, 1944–45. (Vols. 67 and 68 of Monumenta Historica Societatis Iesu).

Schütte, Josef Franz, S.J. *Valignanos Missionsgrundsätze für Japan.* I. Band *Von der Ernennung zum Visitator bis zum ersten Abschied von Japan (1573–1582)*; I. Teil: *Das Problem (1573–1580)*. Rome,

1951; II. Teil: *Die Losung (1580–1582)*. Rome, 1958. Both these parts have been translated into English by John J. Coyne, S.J. under the title *Valignano's Mission Principles for Japan: From His Appointment as Visitor until His First Departure from Japan (1573–1582)*. Part I: *The Problem (1573–1580)*. St. Louis, 1980. Part II: *The Solution (1580–1582)*. St. Louis, 1985.

————. *Die Wirksamkeit der Päpste für Japan im ersten Jahrhundert der japanischen Kirchengeschichte (1549–1650). Versuch einer Zusammenfassung.* Rome, 1967.

————. *Introductio ad historiam Societatis Jesu in Japonia 1549–1650.* Rome, 1968. Also see Valignano.

Sebes, Joseph, S.J. *The Jesuits and the Sino-Russian Treaty of Nerchinsk (1689): The Diary of Thomas Pereira, S.J.* (Vol. 18 of Bibliotheca Instituti Historici Societatis Jesu) Rome, 1961.

Severin, T. *The Oriental Adventure: Explorers of the East.* Boston, 1976.

Shen Te-fu. 沈德符 *Wan-li yeh-huo pien* 萬曆野獲編 (Miscellaneous notes written on the late Wan-li period). Shanghai, 1959.

Silva Rego, António da. *O Padroado Português do Oriente; esboço histórico.* Lisbon, 1940.

————. *Curso de missiologia.* Lisbon, 1956.

Sinica Franciscana. Relationes et Epistolas Fratrum Minorum saeculi XVI et XVII. Edited by Anastasius Van den Wyngaert, O.F.M. 7 vols. Quaracchi-Florence and Rome, 1929–65.

Sommervogel, Carlos, S.J. *Bibliothèque de la Compagnie de Jésus.* 12 vols. Brussels, 1890–1932. Reprint. Louvain, 1960.

Spence, Jonathan. *Emperor of China: Self-Portrait of K'ang-hsi.* New York, 1975.

————. *The Memory Palace of Matteo Ricci.* New York, 1984.

Ssu-k'u ch'üan-shu tsung-mu t'i-yao 四庫全書總目提要 (Summary reviews of the general bibliography of the great encyclopedia of the four treasuries). N.p., n.d.

Ssu-shu 四書 (Four Books). See Legge.

Streit, Robert, O.M.I., and others. *Bibliotheca Missionum.* 28 vols. Rome, 1916–71.

Sullivan, Michael. "Some Possible Sources of European Influence on Late Ming and Early Ch'ing Painting." In *Proceedings of the International Symposium on Chinese Painting.* Taipei, 1970.

Ta Ch'ing Sheng-tsu jen (K'ang-hsi) Huang-ti shih-lu 大清聖祖仁（康熙）皇帝實錄 (Veritable records of the K'ang-hsi reign). 6 vols. Taipei, 1964.

Tacchi Venturi, Pietro, S.J. See Ricci.

Ta-hsüeh 大學 (Great Learning). See Legge.

Teng Chih-ch'eng. 鄧之誠 *Chung-hua erh-ch'ien-nien shih* 中華二仟年史 (Two thousand years of Chinese history). 5 vols. Hong Kong, 1964.

Teilhard de Chardin, Pierre, S.J. *L'Énergie humaine.* Vol. 6 of *Oeuvres de Pierre Teilhard de Chardin.* Paris, 1962.

Thévenot, Melchisédec. *Relations de divers voyages curieux.* 4 vols. in 2. Paris, 1663–72. Reprint. 2 vols. Paris, 1696.

Thomaz de Bossièrre, Mme. Yves de. *Un Belge mandarin à la cour de Chine aux XVIIe et XVIIIe siècles. Antoine Thomas, 1644–1709. Ngan to P'ing-che.* Paris, 1977.

Thwaites, Reuben Gold. See Paltsits.

T'ien-hsüeh ch'u-han. See Li Chih-tsao.

Tikhovleva, Praskovia. *Pervy Russo-Kitaysky dogovor 1689 goda* [The first Russian-Chinese treaty, 1689]. Moscow, 1958.

Ting Chih-lin. 丁志麟 *Yang Ch'i-yüan hsien-sheng ch'ao-hsing shih-chi* 楊淇園先生超性事蹟 (Manifestations of the surpassing character of Yang Ch'i-yüan). N.p., n.d.

Ting Tchao-ts'ing (Ting Ch'ao-ch'ing). *Les Descriptions de la Chine par les Français (1650–1750).* Paris, 1928.

Torres y Lanzas, Pedro. See *Catálogo de los documentos relativos a Filipinas.*

Treadgold, Donald. *The West in Russia and China: Secular and Religious Thought in Modern Times.* Cambridge, England, 1973.

Trigault, Nicolas, S.J., ed. *De Christiana Expeditione apud Sinas.* Rome, 1615. This Trigault translation into Latin of Ricci's *Della entrata nella Cina de' padri della Compagnia del Giesù* (commonly known as his *Journals or Historia*) is an untrustworthy account of Ricci's views. See Tacchi Venturi.

———, ed. *China in the Sixteenth Century: The Journals of Matthew Ricci, 1583–1610.* Translated by Louis J. Gallagher, S.J. Foreword by Richard J. Cushing, Archbishop of Boston. New York, 1953.

———. *Histoire de l'expédition chrétienne au royaume de la Chine, 1582–1610.* Introduction par Joseph Shih. Établissement du texte et annotations par Georges Bessière. Tables et index par Joseph Dehergne, S.J. Paris, 1978.

Tsao Shu-ming. 曹叔明 *Hsin-an Hsiu-ning ming-tsu chih* 新安休寧名族志 (Records of the eminent families of Hsin-an and Hsiu-ning). In Hsieh Kuo-chen, ed. 謝國楨 *Ming-tai she-hui ching-chi shih-liao hsüan-*

pien 明代社會經濟史料選編 (Selected materials from the socioeconomic history of the Ming dynasty). Fukien, 1980.

Valignano, Alexandro, S.J. *Il cerimoniale per i missionari del Giappone.* Edited by Josef Franz Schütte, S.J. Rome, 1946.

Verbiest, Ferdinand, S.J. *Astronomia Europaea sub Imperatore tartaresinico Cam-hy appelato.* Dillingen, 1687.

Vergil. *Aeneid.* Translated by William Francis Jackson Knight. Penguin Classics. New York, 1970.

Wang Cheng. 王徵 *Ch'ung-i-t'ang hsü-pi* 崇一堂隨筆 (Miscellaneous writings of Wang Cheng). N.p., n.d.

Wang Chung-min. 王重民 *Hsü Kuang-ch'i.* 徐光啓 Shanghai, 1981. See Chang Chü-cheng.

Wang Hung-hsu. 王鴻緒 *Ming shih kao* 明史稿 (Draft history of the Ming dynasty). Reprint. Taipei, 1962.

Wicki, Josef, S.J., ed. *Documenta Indica,* 17 vols. to date. (Vols. 70, 72, 74, 78, 83, 86, 89, 91, 94, 98, 103, 105, 113, 118, 123, 126, 132 of *Monumenta Historica Societatis Iesu*) Rome, 1948-.

William Rockhill Nelson Gallery of Art and Mary Atkins Museum of Fine Arts exhibition catalogue. *Eight Dynasties of Chinese Painting.* See Goodfellow.

Witek, John W., S.J. *Controversial Ideas in China and in Europe: A Biography of Jean-François Foucquet, S.J. (1665–1741).* (Vol. 43 of Bibliotheca Instituti Historici Societatis Iesu) Rome, 1982.

————. "Transmission of a Comparison: Father Joachim Bouvet's View of the K'ang-hsi Emperor and Louis XIV." In *Chi-nien Li Ma-tou lai hua ssu-pai chou-nien Chung-Hsi wen-hua chiao-liu kuo-chi hsueh-shu hui-i lun-wen chi* (Collected essays of the international symposium [Fu Jen University] on Chinese-Western cultural interchange in commemoration of the 400th anniversary of the arrival of Matteo Ricci, S.J. in China). Edited by Lo Kuang. Taipei, 1983. (Article appeared in revised form in *Tonga Yon'gu* 東亞研究 [East Asian Studies], no. 3 [December 1983].)

Wu Hsiang-hsiang 吳相湘 [ed]. *Chung-kuo shih-hsüeh ts'ung-shu* 中國史學叢書 (Collectanea of Chinese historical studies). Reprints. Taipei, 1965, 1966, 1972.

————, [ed.] *T'ien-chu-chiao tung ch'uan wen-hsien hsü-pien* 天主教東傳文獻續編 (Documents on the Catholic Church in China: second collection). 3 vols. Taipei, 1965. Reprints. Taipei, 1966, 1972.

Wu Li. 吳歷 *Hsü k'ou-to jih-chao* 續口鐸日抄 (A second series of the *K'ou-to jih-chao*). N.p., n.d.

Yang Chen-o. 楊振鍔 *Yang Ch'i-yüan hsien-sheng nien-p'u* 楊淇園先生年譜 (Chronological account of the life of Yang Ch'i-yüan). Shanghai, 1944.

Yang T'ing-yün. 楊廷筠 *Hsi hsüeh shih-chieh ch'u-chieh* 西學十戒註解 (A first explanation of the Ten Commandments of Western learning). N.p., n.d.

Yazawa Toshihiko, 矢澤利彦 ed. *Gonsāresu de Mendōsa Shina daiō kokushi* ゴンサーレス・デメンドーサシナ大王國誌 ([Juan] González de Mendoza's account of the great kingdom [China]). Tokyo, 1965.

Yeh Hsiang-kao. 葉向高 *Tseng Ssu-chi Ai hsien-sheng shih* 贈思及艾先生詩 (Ode to Mr. Ai Ssu-chi [Giulio Aleni]). N.d., n.p.

———. *Ch'ü pien* 蓬編 (Ch'ü annals). Photo reprint of late Ming woodblock edition. Taipei, 1977.

———. *Hsi-ch'ao ch'ung cheng chi* 熙朝崇正集 (Poems to honor the orthodox gentlemen). In Wu Hsiang-hsiang. *T'ien-chu-chiao tung ch'uan wen-hsien hsü-pien* 天主教東傳文獻續編 (Documents on the Catholic Church in China: second collection). See Wu Hsiang-hsiang, *Documents*, as cited above.

———. *Lun-fei hsü ts'ao* 綸扉續草 (More grand secretariat papers). In *Lun-fei tsou ts'ao* 綸扉奏草 (Grand secretariat papers). Photo reprint of late Ming woodblock edition. Taipei, 1977.

———. *Lei-pien ku-chin shih-chien ku-shih ta-fang* 類編古今史鑑故事大方 (Categorized collection of anecdotes from ancient and modern history). Late Ming woodblock edition. Library of The Chinese University of Hong Kong.

———. *Ts'ang-hsia yü ts'ao* 蒼霞餘草 (More azure sky verses). Microfilm copy of late Ming edition. Library of The Chinese University of Hong Kong.

Young, John D. *East-West Synthesis: Matteo Ricci and Confucianism*. Hong Kong, 1980.

Yü Chün-fang. *The Renewal of Buddhism in China. Chu-hung and the Late Ming Synthesis*. New York, 1981.

Yü T'ung. 宇同 *Chung-kuo che-hsüeh weh-t'i shih* 中國哲學問題史 (A thematic history of Chinese philosophy). Hong Kong, 1968.

Yuan, T. L. See Chang Chü-cheng.

Zürcher, Erik. "The First Anti-Christian Movement in China (Nanking 1616–1621)." In *Acta Orientalia Neerlandica*. Proceedings of the Congress of the Dutch Oriental Society held in Leiden on the occasion of its 50th anniversary, 8th–9th May 1970. Edited by P. W. Pestman. Leiden, 1971.

ARTICLES

Ayuzawa, Shintarō. 鮎澤信太郎 "Matteo Ricci no sekaizu ni kansuru shiteki kenkyū マテオリツチの世界圖に関する史的研究 (A historical study of Matteo Ricci's world map). *Yokohama shiritsu daigaku kiyō* 横濱市立大學紀要 (Journal of Yokohama Municipal University) 18 (August 1953):1–239.

Bernard-Maitre, Henri, S.J. "Whence the Philosophic Movement at the Close of the Ming?" *Bulletin of the Catholic University of Peking* 8 (1931):67–73.

———. "Les Étapes de la cartographie scientifique pour la Chine et les pays voisins depuis le XVIe jusqu' à la fin du XVIIIe siècle." *Monumenta Serica* 1 (1936):428–77.

———. "Les Adaptations chinoises d'ouvrages européens. Bibliographie chronologique depuis la venue des Portugais à Canton jusqu' à la mission française de Pékin 1514–1688." *Monumenta Serica* 10 (1945):1–57, 309–88.

———. "Note complémentaire sur l'Atlas de Kang-hsi." *Monumenta Serica* 11 (1946):191–200.

Boxer, C. R. "Portuguese and Spanish Rivalry in the Far East during the 17th Century." *Journal of the Royal Asiatic Society of Great Britain and Ireland* part 3 (December 1946):150–64; part 4 (April 1947):91–105.

———. "Some Sino-European Xylographic Works, 1662–1718." *Journal of the Royal Asiatic Society of Great Britain and Ireland.* (1947):199–215.

Chang Lin-sheng. "The Enamel Snuff Bottles in the Palace Museum Collection." *National Palace Museum Bulletin* (Taipei) 15 (1980):5–29.

Ch'en, Kenneth. "A Possible Source for Ricci's Notices on Regions near China." *T'oung Pao* 34 (1938):179–90.

———. "Matteo Ricci's Contribution to and Influence on Geographical Knowledge in China." *Journal of the American Oriental Society* 59 (1939):325–59.

Cordier, Henri. "Cinq lettres inédites du Père Gerbillon, S.J." *T'oung Pao* 7 (1906):437–68.

———. "Mélanges géographiques et historiques. Manuscrit inédit du Père A. Gaubil, S.J. publié avec notes par H. Cordier." *T'oung Pao* 16 (1915):515–61.

Daniel, C. "La Géographie dans les collèges des Jésuites aux XVIIe et XVIIIe siècles." *Études* 3 (1879): 801–23.

Dehergne, Joseph, S.J. "Le Premier voyage missionaire d'est en ouest dans la Chine des Ming." *Bulletin de l'Université l'Aurore* (Shanghai) (1942):618–42.

————. "Les Lettres annuelles des missions jésuites de Chine au temps des Ming (1581–1644)." *Archivum Historicum Societatis Iesu* 49 (1980):379–92.

D'Elia, Pasquale M., S.J. "Contributo alla storia delle relazioni tra l'Europa e la Cina, prima dell'arrivo di P. Matteo Ricci, S.J. (1582)." *Rivista degli studi orientali* 16 (1936):223–26.

————. "Il Trattato sull'Amicizia. Primo Libro scritto in Cinese da Matteo Ricci, S.J. (1595). Testo Cinese. Traduzione antica (Ricci) e moderna (D'Elia). Fonti, Introduzione e Note." *Studia Missionalia* 7 (1952):425–515.

————. "Musica e canti Italiani a Pechino (marzo–aprile 1601)." *Rivista degli studi orientali* 30 (1955):131–45.

————. "Further Notes on Matteo Ricci's *De Amicitia*." *Monumenta Serica* 15 (1956):356–77.

————. "Il metodo di adattamento del P. Matteo Ricci, S.J. in Cina." *Civiltà Cattolica* 3 (anno 107) (July 1956):174–75.

Demiéville, Paul. "The First Philosophic Contacts between Europe and China." *Diogenes* 58 (Summer 1967):75–103.

Fang Hao, Maurus. "Notes on Matteo Ricci's *De Amicitia*." *Monumenta Serica* 14 (1949–50):574–83.

Franke, Otto. "Zur Geschichte des *Keng Tschi T'u*." *Ostasiatische Zeitschrift* 2 (1914):169–208.

————. "Das chinesische Geistesleben im 16. Jahrhundert und die Anfänge der Jesuiten-Mission." *Orientalistische Literaturzeitung* 41 (8–9) (August–September 1938):473–84.

Fuchs, Walter. "Materialien zur Kartographie der Mandju-Zeit." *Monumenta Serica* 1 (1935–36):386–427; 3 (1937–38):189–231.

————. "A Note on Father M. Boym's Atlas of China." *Imago Mundi* 9 (1952):71–72.

Gernet, Jacques. "A Propos des contacts entre la Chine et l'Europe aux XVIIᵉ et XVIIIᵉ siècles." *Acta Asiatica* 23 (1972):78–92.

————. "La Politique de conversion de Matteo Ricci et l'évolution de la vie politique et intellectuelle en Chine aux environs de 1600." *Archives des sciences sociales de religions* 36 (1973):71–89.

Harris, George. "The Mission of Matteo Ricci, S.J.: A Case Study of an Effort at Guided Culture Change in China in the Sixteenth Century." *Monumenta Serica* 25 (1966):1–168.

Holzman, Donald. "Conversational Tradition in Chinese Philosophy." *Philosophy East and West* 6 (October 1956):223–30.

Laufer, Berthold. "Christian Art in China." Peking, 1939. Reprinted from *Mitteilungen des Seminars für Orientalische Sprachen an der k. Friedrich-Wilhelm-Universität zu Berlin* 13 (1910):100–18, XX plates.

Laures, Johannes, S.J. "Die Bücherei der älteren Jesuitenmission im Pei-t'ang zu Peking Erinnerungen an P. Adam Schall, S.J." *Katholische Missionen* 65 (1937):76–77, 100–102, 129–30.

———. "Die alte Missionsbibliothek im Pei-t'ang zu Peking." *Monumenta Nipponica* 2 (1939):124–39.

Loehr, George. "Missionary-Artists at the Manchu Court." *Transactions of the Oriental Ceramic Society* (London) 34 (1962–63):51–67.

Luk, Bernard Hung-kay. "A Study of Giulio Aleni's *Chih-fang wai chi.*" *Bulletin of the School of Oriental and African Studies* (University of London) 40.1 (1977):58–84.

Lundbaek, Knud. "The First Translation from a Confucian Classic in Europe." *China Mission Studies (1550–1800) Bulletin* 1 (1979):1–11.

———. "Chief Grand Secretary Chang Chü-cheng and the Early China Jesuits." *China Mission Studies (1550–1800) Bulletin* 3 (1981): 2–11.

McCune, Shannon. "Geographical Observations of Korea: Those of Father Régis Published in 1735." *Journal of Social Science and Humanities* (Seoul) 44 (1976):1–19.

Meijer, M. J. "A Map of the Great Wall of China." *Imago Mundi* 13 (1956):110–15.

Mungello, David E. "The Jesuits' Use of Chang Chü-cheng's Commentary in Their Translation of the Confucian Four Books (1687)." *China Mission Studies (1550–1800) Bulletin* 3 (1981):12–22.

Nelson, Howard. "Maps from Old Cathay." *Geographical Magazine* 47 (August 1975):702–11.

Pelliot, Paul. "A Propos du *Keng Tche T'ou.*" *Mémoires concernant l'Asie orientale (Inde, Asie centrale, Extrême-Orient)* 1 (1913):65–122.

———. "La Peinture et la gravure européennes en Chine au temps de Mathieu Ricci." *T'oung Pao* 20 (1920–21):1–18.

———. "Les 'Conquétes de l'Empereur de la Chine.'" *T'oung Pao* 20 (1920–21):183–274.

———. "La *Brevis Relatio.*" *T'oung Pao* 23 (1924):355–72.

————. "Un Ouvrage sur les premiers temps de Macao.." *T'oung Pao* 31 (1934–35):58–94.

Puini, Carlo. "Il Tibet (geografia, storia, religione, costumi) secondo la relazione del viaggio del P. Ippolito Desideri (1715–1721)." *Memorie della Società geografica italiana* 10 (1904):lxiv-402.

Reinhard, Wolfgang. "Gegenreformation als Modernisierung? Prologomena zu einer Theorie des Konfessionellen Zeitalters." *Archiv für Reformationgeschichte* 68 (1977):241.

Rouleau, Francis A., S.J. "Maillard de Tournon, Papal Legate at the Court of Peking." *Archivum Historicum Societatis Iesu* 31 (1962):264–323.

Santambrogio, M. "Il Confucio dell'Occidente: P. Giulio Alenis [sic], gesuita bresciano, missionario e scienziato in Cina, 1582–1649." *Memorie storiche della diocesi di Brescia* 17 (1950):21–54.

Sebes, Joseph, S.J. "China's Jesuit Century." *The Wilson Quarterly* (Winter 1978):170–83.

————. "Matteo Ricci Chinois avec les Chinois." *Études* 357 (October 1982):361–74.

————. "The Summary Review of Matteo Ricci's *T'ien-chu shih-i* in the *Ssu-ku ch'üan-shu tsung-mu t'i-yao.*" *Archivum Historicum Societatis Iesu* 53 (1984):386–91.

Spalatin, Christopher, S.J. "Matteo Ricci's Use of Epictetus' *Encheiridion.*" *Gregorianum* 56/3 (1975):551–57.

Szczesniak, Boleslaw. "Matteo Ricci's Maps of China." *Imago Mundi* 11 (1954):126–36.

————. "The Seventeenth Century Maps of China. An Inquiry into the Compilations of European Cartographers." *Imago Mundi* 13 (1956):116–36.

————. "The Mappa Imperii Sinarum of Michael Boym." *Imago Mundi* 19 (1965):113–15.

T'ang Chun-i. 唐君毅 "Lun Chung-kuo che-hsüeh ssu-hsiang shih chung li chih liu-i." 論中國哲學思想史中理之六理 (The six different interpretations of *li* in the history of Chinese philosophy). *Hsin-Ya Hsüeh-pao* 新亞學報 (New Asian Journal) 1 (1955):45–98.

Thrower, Norman J. W. "The Discovery of the Longitude. Observations of Carrying Timekeepers for Determining Longitude at Sea, 1530–1770." *Navigation* 5 (1957–58):375–81.

Unno Kazutaka. 海野一隆 "Yōroppa ni okeru Koyozu: Shina chizugaku seizen no shoki jokyō ヨロパにおける廣輿圖シナ地圖學西漸の初期状況 (The Kuang-yu-t'u 廣輿圖 ["Comprehensive Map"] in Europe:

Early Chinese influence upon Western cartography) in *Osaka dai-gaku kyōyō-bu kenkyū-shuroku* 大坂大學教養部研究集錄 (Japanese Studies in the Humanities and Social Sciences) 26 (1978):3–28.

Verhaeren, Hubert, C.M. "L' Ancienne bibliothèque du Pei-t'ang." *Bulletin Catholique de Pékin* 27 (1940):82–96.

Wallis, Helen. "Missionary Cartographers to China." *Geographical Magazine* 47 (September 1975):751–59.

Young, T. Kue-hing. "French Jesuits and the 'Manchu Anatomy'— How China Missed the Vesalian Revolution." *Canadian Medical Association Journal* 111 (21 September 1974):565–68.

Zhu Jiajin. "A Study of the Manufacture of Painted Enamelware of the Qing Dynasty." *Gugong Bowuyuan Yuankan* 故宮博物院院刊 (Peking Palace Museum Records) 3 (1982):67–96.

Supplementary Bibliography

BOOKS

Cronin, Vincent. *The Wise Man from the West*. London, 1955. Reprint. London, 1985.

Dehergne, Joseph, S.J., and Donald D. Leslie. *Juifs de Chine à travers la correspondance inédite des Jésuites du dix-huitième siècle*. 2d. ed. Rome, 1984.

Foss, Theodore N. "Nicholas Trigault, S.J. — Amanuensis or Propagandist? The Role of the Editor of *Della entrata della Compagnia di Giesù e Christianità nella Cina*." Published as Supplement to *Chinien Li Ma-tou lai hua ssu-pai chou-nien Chung-Hei wen-hua chiaoliu kuo-chi hsüeh-shu hui-i lun-wen chi* (Collected essays of the international symposium [Fu Jen University] on Chinese-Western cultural interchange in commemoration of the 400th anniversary of the arrival of Matteo Ricci, S.J. in China). Edited by Lo Kuang. Taipei, 1983.

Hucker, Charles O. *A Dictionary of Official Titles in Imperial China*. Stanford, 1985.

Kircher, Athanasius, S.J. *China Illustrata*. Translated by Dr. Charles D. Van Tuyl from the 1677 original Latin edition. Muskogee, Okla., 1987.

Libbrecht, Ulrich, Willy vande Walde, and others. *Belgae in China*. Ferdinand Verbiest Research Project. Louvain, 1985.

Minamiki, George, S.J. *The Chinese Rites Controversy from the Beginning to Modern Times*. Chicago, 1985.

Ricci, Matteo/Trigault, Nicolas. *Entrata nella China de' Padri della Compagnia del Gesù (1582–1610)*. Volgarizzazione di Antonio Sozzini (1622). Introduzione di Joseph Shih e Carlo Laurenti. Rome, 1983.

———. *Li Ma-tou* 利瑪竇 [Matteo Ricci] *Chung-kuo cha-chi* 中國札記 (Reading notes of Matteo Ricci in China). Li Ma-tou, Chin Ni-ko 金尼閣 (Matteo Ricci, Nicolas Trigault) authors. Ho Kao-chi, et al., 何高濟 translators. Ho Chao-wu, 何兆武 proofreader. In *Chung-wai kuan-hsi shih ming-chu yi ts'ung* 中外關系史名著譯叢 (Collection of translations of famous works on the history of Sino-Western relations). 2 vols. Peking, 1983.

————. *Lettere del manoscritto maceratese.* Introduzione di Piero Corradini. A cura di Chiara Zueli. Macerata, 1985.

————. *True Meaning of the Lord of Heaven* (T'ien-chu shih-i) 天主實義 . Translated, with an introduction and notes, by Douglas Lancashire and Peter Hu Kuo-chen, S.J. A Chinese-English edition edited by Edward Malatesta, S.J. St. Louis, 1985. This edition was published by The Institute of Jesuit Sources in St. Louis in cooperation with the Ricci Institute for Chinese Studies in Taipei, Taiwan. The Institut Ricci (Taipei-Paris-Hong Kong) also published a 1985 edition in English of this same work (Variétés sinologiques, nouvelle série, no. 72) in cooperation with The Institute of Jesuit Sources, St. Louis University, St. Louis, Missouri; the Faculty of Theology of Fujen Catholic University, Taiwan, Republic of China; and The Institute for Chinese-Western Cultural History, University of San Francisco, San Francisco, California.

Ritchi, Mateo. (Japanese spelling of name). *Chugoku kirisutokyō fukyō shi* 中國キリスト教布教史 (History of the propagation of Christianity in China). I. In *Dai kōkai jidai sōsho* 大航海時代叢書 (Collectanea of the great era of ocean voyages) no. 1, vol. 8. Tokyo, 1982. (This volume contains a Japanese translation of books one through four of Ricci's five-volume *Della entrata nella Cina de' padri della Compagnia del Giesù* (commonly known as his *Journals* or *Historia*).

Ritchi, Mateo, and Álvaro Semedo. *Chugoku kirisutokyō fukyō shi* (History of the propagation of Christianity in China) II. In *Dai kōkai jidai sōsho* (Collectanea of the great era of ocean voyages) no. 2, vol. 9. Tokyo, 1983. (This volume contains a Japanese translation of Ricci's *Della entrata nella Cina*, pp. 1–258. The rest of the volume is devoted to Álvaro Semedo's *Imperio de la China* [Madrid, 1642], a translation of the Portuguese original.)

Rienstra, M. Howard., ed. and trans. *Jesuit Letters from China, 1583–84.* Minneapolis, 1986. A publication from the James Ford Bell Library at the University of Minnesota.

Standaert, Nicholas. *Confucian and Christian in Late Ming China: The Life and Thought of Yang Tingyun.* (Sinica Leidensia 19) Leiden, 1987.

Thomaz de Bossière, Mme. Yves de. *François-Xavier Dentrecolles (Yin Hong-Siu Ki-tsong)* 殷弘緒繼宗 *et l'apport de la Chine à l'Europe du XVIIIe siècle.* Paris, 1982.

Van Kley, Edwin J., and Cyriac K. Pullapilly, eds. *Asia and the West. Encounters and Exchanges from the Age of Explorations. Essays in Honor of Donald F. Lach.* Notre Dame, 1986.

Wills, John E., Jr. *Embassies and Illusions. Dutch and Portuguese Envoys to K'ang-shi, 1662–1687.* Cambridge, Mass., 1984.

Young, John D. *Confucianism and Christianity: The First Encounter.* Hong Kong, 1983.

ARTICLES

Chan, Albert, S.J. "A European Document on the Fall of the Ming Dynasty (1644–1649)." *Monumenta Serica* 35 (1981– 83):75–109.

Foss, Theodore N. "Current Research on the History of the Jesuits and China." *International Bulletin* 9 (April 1985):62.

Lundbaek, Knud. "The Image of Neo-Confucianism in *Confucius Sinarum philosophus.*" *Journal of the History of Ideas* 44 (1983):19–30.

Mungello, David E. "China Mission Studies (1550–1800) Bulletin." *International Bulletin* 9 (July 1985):109.

Polgar, Laszlo, S.J. "Bibliographie sur l'histoire de la Compagnie de Jésus." *Archivum Historicum Societatis Iesu* 52 (1983):375, 416; 53 (1984):passim, 589–96, 601, 607, 617–28; 54 (1985):passim, 413–33, 447–52; 55 (1986):377–78, 387, 397, 402, 411–12.

————. *Bibliographie sur l'histoire de la Compagnie de Jésus, 1901–1980.* II. 330–76. Rome, 1986. (These valuable Polgar bibliographies, apart from listing books and articles pertaining to the Jesuits in China written between 1901 and 1986, also give detailed information on the various Ricci and Martini symposia and their participants held in Europe and Asia in 1982 and 1983. Lack of space prevents this information being entered here in specific form.)

Standaert, Nicolas. "Matteo Ricci en het probleem van de inculturatie." *Streven* (Antwerp) 51 (1984):915–27.

Wills, John E., Jr. "Some Dutch Sources on the Jesuit China Mission, 1662–1687." *Archivum Historicum Societatis Iesu* 54 (1985):267–94.

Editors

Bonnie B. C. Oh, formerly associate professor of history at Loyola University of Chicago, is presently assistant dean for academic services at St. Mary's College of Maryland.

Charles E. Ronan, S.J. is professor emeritus of history at Loyola University of Chicago.

Contributors

Albert Chan, S.J. is a member of The Institute for Chinese-Western Cultural History at the University of San Francisco. Among his publications are *The Glory and Fall of the Ming Dynasty* and a number of articles on related topics.

Theodore N. Foss is associate director of The Institute for Chinese-Western Cultural History at the University of San Francisco. His fields of interest are the Jesuits and Chinese cartography and the impact of China on eighteenth-century Europe. He has published a number of articles on these and related topics.

Bernard Hung-kay Luk is a lecturer in the School of Education, The Chinese University of Hong Kong. His main scholarly interests are in Sino-Western cultural relations and Ming-Ch'ing social and legal history. He has published a number of articles in these areas.

David E. Mungello is associate professor of history at Coe College in Cedar Rapids, Iowa. Among his publications are *Leibniz and Confucianism: The Search for Accord* and *Curious Land: Jesuit Accommodation and the Origins of Sinology.* He is also editor of *China Mission Studies 1550–1800 Bulletin.*

Willard J. Peterson is professor of East Asian Studies at Princeton University. His publications include *Bitter Gourd: Fang I-chih and the Impetus for Intellectual Change* and a number of articles.

Joseph Sebes, S.J. is professor emeritus of history at Georgetown University and editor of the *Monumenta Sinica,* which the Jesuit Historical Institute in Rome is preparing for publication. Among his publications are *The Jesuits and the Sino-Russian Treaty of Nerchinsk (1689): The Diary of Thomas Pereira, S.J.* and a number of articles.

Jonathan D. Spence is George Burton Adams Professor of History at
Yale University. Among his publications are *Emperor of China: Self-
Portrait of K'ang-hsi* and *The Memory Palace of Matteo Ricci.*
Harrie Vanderstappen, S.V.D. is professor of art history at the University
of Chicago and editor of *The T. L. Yuan Bibliography of Western
Writings on Chinese Art and Archeology.* He has also authored a
number of articles.
John W. Witek, S.J. is associate professor of history at Georgetown
University. Among his publications are *Controversial Ideas in China
and Europe: A Biography of Jean-François Foucquet* and a number
of articles.

The China-Jesuit Symposium Committee wishes to thank the commen-
tators and panelists who participated in the symposium proceedings
and expresses regret that, for lack of space, their contributions were
unable to be included in this volume.
Commentators: Yu-ming Shaw (director, The Institute of International
Relations, National Chengchi University, Taipei, Taiwan); Edwin Van
Kley (professor of history, Calvin College, Grand Rapids, Michigan);
Donald F. Lach (Bernadotte E. Schmitt Professor of Modern History,
Department of History, University of Chicago).
Panelists: Julia Ching (professor of religion, University of Toronto);
Piero Corradini (professor of history and institutions of Afroasiatic
countries, Macerata University, Macerata, Italy); Wm. Theodore de
Bary (John Mitchell Mason Professor of the University, Oriental
Studies Program and Department of East Asian Languages and Cul-
tures, Columbia University); Joseph Dehergne, S.J. (director, Paris
Province Archives of the Society of Jesus); Peter Hu Kuo-chen, S.J.
(doctoral graduate student at Fu Jen University, Taipei, Taiwan);
Donald F. Lach (Bernadotte E. Schmitt Professor of Modern History,
Department of History, University of Chicago).

Index